Michael Caulfield has been a composer, musician, and TV and film producer and director. He was producer of the ABC TV series 'Australians at War', and together with producer Liz Butler, conceived and produced the Australians at War Film Archive. He is also the editor of *Voices of War*.

THE VIETNAM YEARS

FROM THE JUNGLE TO THE AUSTRALIAN SUBURBS

MICHAEL CAULFIELD

HACHETTE AUSTRALIA

HACHETTE AUSTRALIA

Published in Australia and New Zealand in 2007
by Hachette Australia
(An imprint of Hachette Livre Australia Pty Limited)
Level 17, 207 Kent Street, Sydney NSW 2000
Website: www.hachette.com.au

National Library of Australia
Cataloguing-in-Publication data

Caulfield, Michael.
The Vietnam years : from the jungle to the Australian suburbs.

ISBN 978 0 7336 1985 4 (pbk.).

1. Vietnam War, 1961–1975 - Participation, Australian. 2. Veterans - Mental health - Australia. 3. Veterans - Australia - Family relationships. I. Title.

959.7043394

Cover design by Luke Causby
Front cover images Australian War Memorial (top)
and Fairfaxphotos (bottom)
Map concept by Lizzie Butler
Map design by Kinart
Text design by Bookhouse, Sydney
Typeset in 11/15.6 pt Sabon
Printed in Australia by Griffin Press, Adelaide

Hachette Livre Australia's policy is to use papers that are natural, renewable and recyclable products and made from wood grown in sustainable forests. The logging and manufacturing processes are expected to conform to the environmental regulations of the country of origin.

This book is dedicated, with love, to Lizzie.

CONTENTS

INTRODUCTION

Q: How many Vietnam vets does it take to change a light bulb?

A: How would you know – you weren't fucking there.

I was told that joke by a man named Charlie. Several times. He loved it so much that his telling of it always ended with the same gut-busting laugh that rapidly deteriorated into a rattling cough, threatening to shake him apart. Only another beer would return his breathing to normal. He was in his early sixties then and so thin and wiry he called himself a 'pull-through'. A roll-your-own cigarette was permanently attached to his bottom lip and it waved like a signal flag as he told me his story all through a long, hot, Queensland day.

Charlie had been what I had not – a soldier, an infantryman and a veteran of the Vietnam War. He was one of many I was to spend time with for this book and I speak of him in the past tense because Charlie's not around anymore, his death hurried on him by the booze and the fags and a tired heart that could no longer heal itself. But I remember him.

The joke was a challenge of course, a calculated piss-take aimed at anyone who presumed to understand him or his history. But it was also a deliberate and bitter isolation, a curious payback of sorts for what he considered to be betrayal by his own country. He wasn't the only one to feel that way; I encountered it often among the veterans of that war. And even though it wasn't a typical response because there is no typical vet, the feeling smouldered in many of the men I spoke with and they struggled with it; a residue of unease, of anger, a nagging presence that never went away.

Vietnam was Australia's longest war and the one we've tried hardest to forget. But it hasn't worked. It's our symbol for political and military disaster and every new conflict that sucks us in breathes life into the old ghost. The question inevitably arises – is Somalia another Vietnam? Or Rwanda? Or Iraq? The divisions and unhappiness the Vietnam War visited on Australia continue to surface.

How the hell did that happen? It wasn't just that good men died in a foolish war for no good reason, because God knows we'd been through that before and managed to turn sacrifice and defeat into a national religion. And it can't have been because we sent troops to a country that had never threatened us – that had never stopped us in the past. This war was different. This one cut deeply into the national soul while it raged but was then discarded, isolated from the warm glow that shines on Gallipoli and Tobruk, Kokoda and East Timor.

Maybe it was because the Vietnam War brought hundreds of thousands of Australians into city streets in protest. Or maybe it was because families and friends tore into each other in hard arguments about the war and conscription. Or that politics was revealed to be the shoddy craft of convenience and deceit we'd always suspected it was.

At the end of it there was one harsh, unpalatable fact that separated this war from all the others: for the first and only time in our history Australian soldiers were sullied and defamed by their own people for carrying our name into battle.

Whatever the reasons, Vietnam as a term, as a memory, still carries a volatile charge and careless handling can cause instantaneous detonation.

When the World War II generation speak of *the war*, there is no doubt as to what they mean. The entire six years of that war were contained for them inside that one phrase whether they were talking about the battlefront or the home front. All the diverse experiences, all the tragedy and hurt, the bad and the good memories, had been compressed into one understanding.

But we had two Vietnam Wars – the one men like Charlie fought in, and the war watched in rising discord and discontent at home. And we still do. War, it's been said, has no end for those who fought it, and I've listened to too many veterans' dark dreams to disagree. When Charlie looked through the prism of memory back to Vietnam, that was what he saw – bad dreams and persistent heartache. But turn the prism a little and the light from those years, from 1962 to 1972, falls differently, away from the front line and onto the suburbs.

That decade did not just encompass the war. It was also a time of youthful disobedience, street protests, hippies, freaks and potheads. Of 'Friday on My Mind' and *Easy Rider*, Sir Robert Menzies and Gough Whitlam, Holden Monaros and the Datsun Bluebird, assassinations and moon landings, moratoriums . . . and, God help us, paisley shirts and flared pants.

Revisiting the past is never easy, no matter who you were. Most folks don't want to be reminded of exactly what happened or what they did or didn't do. Very few of us are comfortable with the unvarnished truth. So the memories of the men and women whose voices speak out in this book sometimes coincide, but more often they conflict, banging up against each other and challenging the right of any one person to tell the history or own the myth.

And the survivors have developed some serious myths over the years. The '60s have been drowned in a wave of saccharine nostalgia, a merchandised hell of baby boomer TV shows and feel-good films along with radio stations that play the same 'golden oldies' so relentlessly you want to reach inside the box and rip out the memories. A generation that held such promise is inevitably growing old, but maybe not growing up.

And the mythology about the war is even more intense.

Soldiers returning from Vietnam were attacked by organised anti-war protesters who spat at them, threw blood on them and called them 'baby-killers'.

No, they weren't.

Vietnam veterans are social misfits, loners, prone to alcoholism and violence.

No, they're not.

Australians did not support the war.

Yes we did, by a large majority until the last couple of years.

Australian soldiers were never welcomed home.

Yes, they were.

And on and on.

The gap between veterans' memories and popular belief about what Australia did in Vietnam, why we did it and even whether we succeeded, remains deep and wide and leaves most people either ignorant or confused. Even now, 40 years later, those two Vietnam Wars have never really come to terms with each other, never really been at peace. Which memory, which version you believe in, depends on who you were and what you saw. And while there has been tacit agreement of late that it was all a bit sad really, there's still not much understanding either way.

But it is important to try. A country that ignores its past or unconsciously conspires to forget the hard stuff is not a country at all but a loose collection of people held together by money and fear and the occasional sporting triumph. There is always the danger that, in looking back, one can be overcome by sentiment, by regret, perhaps even take guilty pleasure in melancholy. But until we know how we came to be the way we are now – until we can, with clear eyes, understand what we lost along the way, we cannot possibly look forwards. The men and women who served in Vietnam, those Australians who were made to feel personally and morally responsible for a war their country banished, deserve no less.

MICHAEL CAULFIELD, 2007

A NOTE TO THE READER

I am not an historian, so I did not wish to write a traditional, historical narrative which followed the chronology of the war from beginning to end. There are other books about the Vietnam War which do that, and they provide a significant store of existing knowledge. This is a book that moves at a faster pace through those 10 years, stopping to examine events both great and small wherever there is a chance for a different kind of understanding. It is not the definitive history of Australia's role in the Vietnam War; it is the story *behind* the history, the one that lies outside the box of dates and statistics, revealing those places where passion and human spirit are found.

Every voice you read in here tells things as they happened to the people who were actually there – mud, blood, rock 'n' roll and all. I did not want any pretenders in this book and, thanks to the generosity of hundreds of men and women, there are none.

For the last eight years I have been immersed in nothing else but war. And not just a particular war, but every conflict, battle, campaign and peacekeeping mission in which this country has been involved. As the producer of the eight-hour television series *Australians at War* in 2001, and the project director responsible for the filming of the 12 000 hours of interviews that constitute The Australians at War Film Archive, I have had the privilege of a unique and remarkable education. On those productions I learned much about our wars from Australia's most distinguished military historians . . . and even more from the men and women who fought in them.

I've had the good fortune to sit and talk at great length with hundreds of veterans – from a 104-year-old stretcher bearer in World War I to an ace fighter pilot who was shot down over the north African desert in World War II; from a prisoner of war captured by the Chinese in Korea to an SAS trooper just back from a tour in Iraq. I am intrigued and uplifted by all of them, but it is the Vietnam veterans to whom I have always been drawn. Their war was of my time and, but for a wooden ball falling to the left instead of the right, I may well have joined them.

I interviewed over 100 Vietnam veterans and plunged into the interview transcripts of hundreds more in the Archive. I walked on the battlefields around Nui Dat and through the Vietnamese streets that had seemed so alien to those young Australians over 40 years ago. And I interviewed the forgotten veterans, Vietnamese–Australians, men who had fought in the South Vietnamese Army and who were then forced to make desperate escapes from their beloved country to find refuge in the place they call 'the Southern Land'. Without exception, everyone I interviewed gave of their time and their lives unselfishly, and I remain permanently in their debt. Their only concern was truth, as elusive as that can sometimes seem.

Over 60 000 Australians were in Vietnam during the war. They saw service in the air, on and under the water, in armoured vehicles, in hospitals and offices, in interrogation rooms and with indigenous tribes in the hills. They drove trucks, entertained troops, repaired broken bodies, fed and clothed the lost and forgotten, and served their country well. I hope all those people will pardon me when I say however, that it is mostly with the infantry that this book is concerned, for it is among those men that this story lies, along with the musicians, the uni students, the protestors and the grown-ups of my Vietnam years.

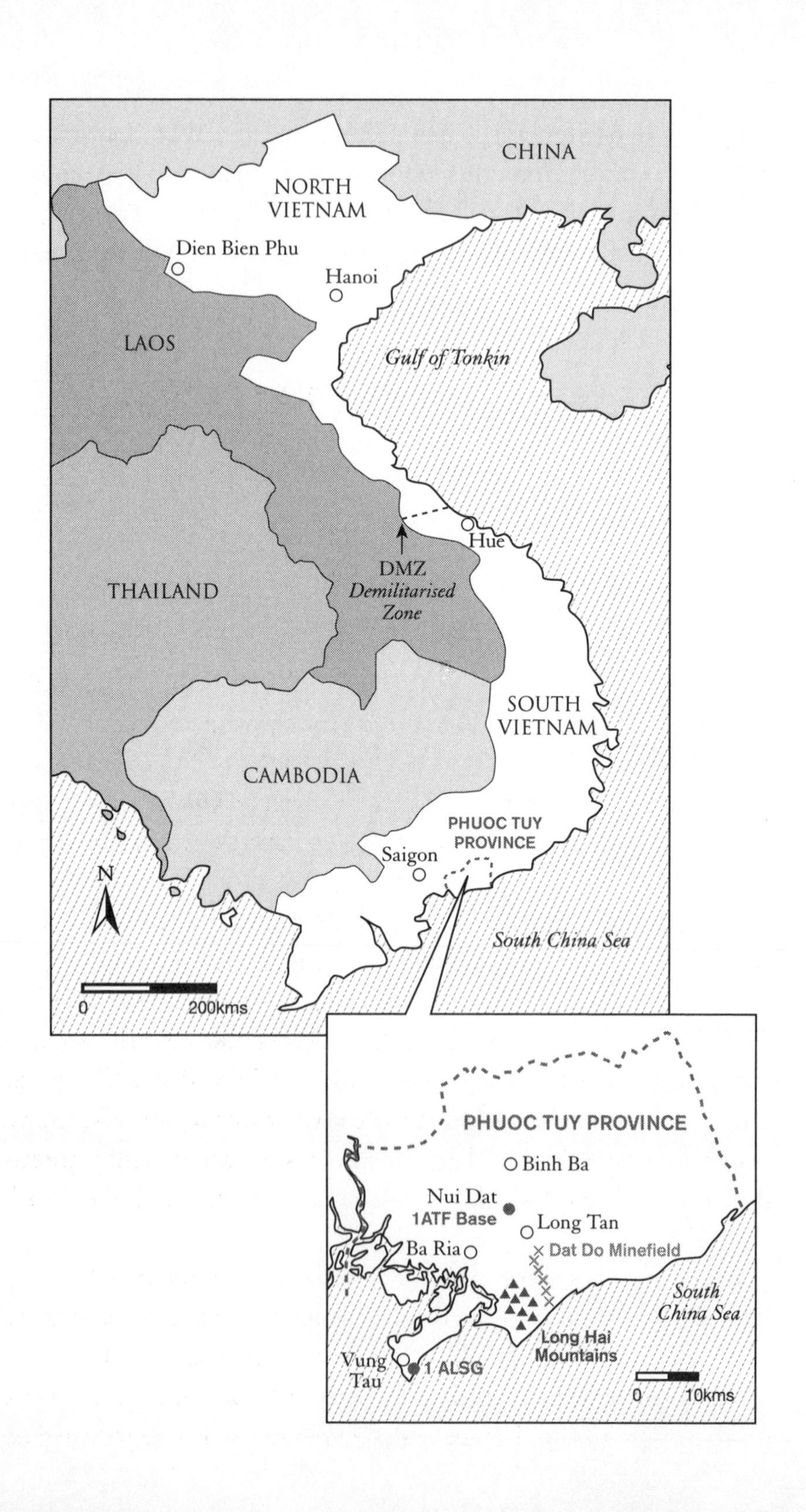

CHINA
NORTH VIETNAM
Dien Bien Phu
Hanoi
LAOS
Gulf of Tonkin
Hue
DMZ
Demilitarised Zone
THAILAND
SOUTH VIETNAM
CAMBODIA
PHUOC TUY PROVINCE
Saigon
N
South China Sea
0
200kms
PHUOC TUY PROVINCE
Binh Ba
Nui Dat
1ATF Base
Long Tan
Ba Ria
Dat Do Minefield
South China Sea
Long Hai Mountains
Vung Tau
1 ALSG
0
10kms

I

FAITH IN OUR FATHERS

PHUOC TUY PROVINCE, SOUTH VIETNAM
SOMETIME IN THE LATE 1960S

It's morning in the Australian base camp on a small hill called Nui Dat. Reveille cuts through the still air, the flag is raised and another cycle of routine begins. More patrols will go out through the perimeter wire into the surrounding countryside this morning. It's always 'more patrols' in this war.

The base is an island in the middle of the bush, the size of a small town, with its own post office, canteens, boozers, doctors' offices, garbage disposal, streets, roads, water, and power supplies. The soldiers live in separate, tented villages scattered throughout the base and the tents are old – really old; World War II vintage and looking every day of it. If the canvas walls could talk, they'd probably swear. Inside them, the men who are on duty quietly prepare for 'a walk in the weeds' while others thank Christ it's not them today.

It's completely male, this town. The only women to walk in its red dirt are the occasional visiting entertainers or nurses, and they're always carefully shepherded around by officers. No women means lots of blokes dressed in boots and nothing else on their way to the showers or the lavatories. Big, boofy blokes and nuggety, small fellas, tattooed or hairy, pink-pale or with truck-driver tans round their necks and arms.

Delta Company, a total of about 120 men, will be the first to go on patrol today and the platoons gather together. Already there is an air of isolation about them, a separation from the men remaining behind in camp. They walk in a loose group through the acrid, chemical mist floating down from the aerial mosquito spraying and the drifting cordite smoke of the occasional artillery fire.

Every man walking towards the wire is closing down now, narrowing his focus to the job. Running his checklist through his head – ammo, rations, weapons, water. Transistor radios blare out from tents as they walk by but they don't hear them.

In sports news, Australia has defeated the West Indies in the Third Test at the Sydney Cricket Ground. Doug Walters featured with a smashing 118.

They pass some 'pogos', otherwise known as 'Saigon Commandos', 'base bludgers' and 'blanket folders'. They're the clerks, cooks, supply jockeys and drivers who provide critical support to the infantry and, for once, there's no exchange of insults. Legend has it that the name 'pogo' comes from 'pogo stick', rhyming slang for 'prick', and if it isn't true it should be. The pogos live and work in Nui Dat and the nearby coastal town of Vung Tau, and while they might pull sentry duty now and then, they rarely go outside the wire. The riflemen take the piss out of them because of their starched uniforms, comfortable beds, proper tables and chairs, movies, good food and plenty of sleep. All the things they don't have. The dislike can be mutual, but it would be unwise to stir up a man about to go out on patrol.

The company divides, some board choppers at the airfield, the less fortunate will walk past the long rolls of barbed wire and gun pits out into the surrounding forest. Now the packs are shouldered and they help one another to load up. Each of these men is carrying a weight on his back that would leave the rest of us keeled over and crushed – 45 kilos of water, weapons, food, equipment, maps, blanket, a green plastic shelter called a 'hootchie', cigarettes, toilet paper, a slab of C4 plastic explosive, Claymore antipersonnel mines and spare ammunition, including belts of ammunition for the M60 machine gun. On top of that they share amongst them the radio, spare batteries, an M66 rocket-launcher and an M79 grenade launcher plus ammo, medical kits and helicopter marking panels. Just one bottle of water weighs a kilo and they're carrying eight bottles each. The ration packs, enough for five days, contain food such as date rolls, tinned omelette, compressed meats, Irish stew, cereal blocks, dry biscuits, cheese, rice and tinned fruit. Their stomachs often shrink on patrol and they eat less and less as the days and weeks pass. Complaints about the rations are legendary, but some remember them with a curious kind of fondness.

> We had a mixture of Australian and American C [combat] rations. We preferred the American for the greater variety . . . the advantage of the Australian over the American, of course, was they were much lighter. With the American ration packs, Jesus Christ, carry five days of them and you are like a bloody pack horse.
>
> . . . In the Australian packs we would keep the tins. There were two tins. One for morning, one for evening and 'dog biscuits' for lunch. A tin of margarine, a roll of toilet paper, which was like greaseproof paper and no bloody good anyway. Box of matches, sachets of sugar, a tube of condensed milk, tea bags . . . sachets of coffee, a packet of rice and that was it, but we'd keep the two tins, condensed milk, tube of jam. Oh, a bar of chocolate. Yeah, keep that. A packet of lollies as well, we'd keep them. Jam, rice, and that was about right. The cereal box and the dog biscuits. Stuff them. Throw that

> away. Get rid of all the extraneous crap and just keep what you need.
>
> ... Really, when you look back at our Australian rations, diggers will bitch like shit about anything anyway. There was nothing bloody wrong with them. As a matter of fact, I know this may sound funny, but I still keep tins of corned beef in the pantry cupboard, would you believe? I still love the crap. And so do most diggers.
>
> 'Do you want a tin of corned "dog", mate? Stick that up your bloody gibber, you mongrel.'
>
> It is bloody beautiful. My missus reckons I'm bloody mentally defective but that's her problem, eh?
>
> ANTHONY HUGHES, 7RAR

It was a hell of a load. Forty-five kilos on every back. For weeks without end.

Finally they get their packs on and everyone's ready. Ready for a world of silence and signals, expectation and oppressive heat. They will suffer long hours of intense concentration and a bleeding of energy through tension, fear and anticipation, until they collapse in exhaustion. The choppers take off in a haze of dust and grit and the foot patrols disappear silently into the vegetation.

It is combat these soldiers are aimed at and the object of the exercise is to wound, maim or kill the enemy. What they must not forget is that their opponent wants to do the same to them. Right now they cannot afford to contemplate what led them to this war, to this moment. They have neither the time nor the inclination to consider politics, people or the past. So we will do it for them, and go back; back to 1962, when it all began.

I honour my God, I serve my Queen, I salute my flag.

SCHOOL ASSEMBLY PLEDGE, 1960

At the start of the 1960s my family had been living for a while in an old army camp at the edge of a suburb called Merrylands, in Sydney's west. Like Nui Dat, it had been as big as a small town, but the soldiers who occupied it had long gone by the time we arrived. World War II had been won and they were intent on a new and better world, on peace and the relief of forgetting.

The camp had become a kind of halfway house for working-class families, all of them with young children, living in row after row of tin Quonset huts that looked like huge half-pipes buried in the ground. The huts were made from corrugated iron and mercilessly hot, so as soon as we could after a dinner that was always called 'tea', all the children escaped outside into the dusty patches of miserable grass to play games until dark. We were all waiting for change; waiting for better times, for the Housing Commission to allocate us 'our house' somewhere in Sydney, waiting for that fibro or brick-veneer castle with the backyard we knew was our birthright – and we were confident it would come.

There were giant waiting rooms like our camp in every city then. Some held people like us and we were called 'Australians'. Other camps held different kinds of people who sadly had not had the advantage of being born here, so they were called 'New Australians', or migrants. A lot of them were Poms and the ones who weren't, who couldn't speak English, the government called 'Displaced Persons'. We called them reffos, or wogs, or dagoes. Over a million of them arrived here between the end of the war and the beginning of the '60s and they added their numbers to the thousands of us being born in the flush of hope that came with peace. Australia's population grew by half its size again in just 20 years as our parents got down to the business of creating families, and the dispossessed and dislocated found their way to the new world.

Some were children, like Urmas 'Audie' Moldre. Audie was born as an Estonian refugee in a displaced persons' camp in occupied Germany in 1948. When he was 18 months old, the camp authorities said to his father, 'There is a ship leaving for Australia tomorrow and you, your wife and two sons can be on it. Choose.'

Audie's father, who hated the Communists, asked for an atlas, opened it to the page that showed the world, found Australia, traced a line with his finger all the way back to Europe and said, 'It's the furthest place from Moscow in the world. We go.'

As simple and as momentous as that.

> They had no idea of what the future held and the past was in ruins. What happens with refugees, with my mother and father, is that that generation is lost; lost in a world where they can't speak the language so their children become their interpreters ... that doesn't make life easy for those parents who have good minds, they're educated but they don't have the words ... their life essentially ends the day that they leave their country.
>
> AUDIE MOLDRE, SAS, AATTV

But for Audie and the thousands of other postwar babies who arrived here then, life was just beginning. Australians were keen to settle down, earn a good living and have a good life. And it was happening. Each year seemed to be getting a little rosier, a little more successful. New houses were popping up like mushrooms as new suburbs were created with new cars on their streets and new washing machines humming away in the laundries promising whiter washes in half the time. Everywhere you looked Australia was clearly a vibrant part of the all-new 20th century. We had our own nuclear reactor ... we had TV! And you could see exactly the same programs in Melbourne and Sydney *at exactly the same time*! There could be no doubt that things were looking up. It was a good time to be Australian, to be confident in 'the Australian way of life'.

But we were also complacent, perhaps even smug. It certainly seemed to be all rosy in the garden but only if you agreed that it was all rosy in the garden. Anyone who expressed unease about the way we were or what we might become was turned on and ridiculed. It was even worse for those who occupied that time-honoured place in Australia's Hall of Hate – 'the others', the migrants who were different to us.

Audie's father took a job in a factory and his mother cleaned up after the races at Randwick. As soon as he was able to, his father took the entire family down to Sydney Town Hall to be naturalised, his way of saying thank you to the country that had accepted them. But we are a nation of heartbreakers sometimes.

> A lot of people did not enjoy the idea that there were now people amongst them who spoke foreign languages. Mum and Dad were regularly told, 'Shut up and speak English!' in public places, on trams or on buses or trains. They're the sorts of things that kind of stick in the craw a bit. But as you reflect on it, you think, well, it's understandable.
>
> AUDIE MOLDRE

Everyone was on the move. My family, along with thousands of others, moved into the brand-new Housing Commission settlement of Dundas Valley, in Sydney's northwest. We were just a small part of a remarkable upsurge Australia-wide, a tectonic-plate-like shift of people into newly created suburbs where once there had been farms or scrub. By the time of the 1961 census, half of Australia's population lived in the state and federal capitals and most of the rest in the other major towns.

Dundas was desolate – treeless and grassless with ugly scars from the impossibly fast construction still gouged into the landscape. But the moment my father put the key in the door of our new house for the first time and we ran from room to room, astonished at the space (real doors!), they could have put that house on the moon and we would have said thank you and moved in. It even *smelled* new . . . and it was ours. We didn't have to share it with anyone. Everywhere we looked, up and down every street in the Valley, families were moving in, and as my brothers and I helped manhandle the symbol of every good Catholic family (bunk beds) across the red dirt lawn, I saw my father hug my mother, and I saw her tears, and I knew we were where we were supposed to be.

In working-class suburbs across Australia everyone was aiming upwards; everyone was trying to 'make things better for the kids'. Our fathers were mechanics and carpenters, cleaners and factory workers, and we all shared in the eagerly awaited routine of the weekly pay packet – Thursday was always a good day in our street. Hire purchase agreements (or being 'on the never-never') meant that every family could now have a car, or a TV, or one of those amazing new lounge suites that folded out into a bed for when Auntie Peg and Uncle Clarrie came to stay. But you had to time and budget your outgoings with the skill of a chartered accountant.

It was always crisis time when the HP man came to the house to collect his weekly payment and the family didn't have it. Many a child learned to keep absolutely still and quiet when he knocked on the door, all the while furtively peeking through the venetian blinds until he'd gone, taking his unwelcome receipt book to some other poor bugger.

Somehow, most of us managed and the bailiffs never came. Across Australia, in Broadmeadows, Elizabeth and Dundas Valley, our parents (and therefore we) began to rise up the ladder. It's been said that during this time the average Australian became wealthier more quickly than in any other period of our history. I don't know about wealth but with our fathers *and* our mothers working, life did improve. The old bogeymen of our parents' nightmares – unemployment and the Depression – were beaten back and jobs became so plentiful you could leave one today and get another tomorrow.

It was the same in the bush. Farmers were seen as kings then, lords of the economy – wool made up a third of our exports, followed by wheat, meat and sugar. In the city we knew about farming of course, because we laboured over elaborate 'projects' in Social Studies and Geography; big sheets of cardboard covered with pictures of sheepshearing and wheat harvesting, but we knew little of the lives being led 'beyond the black stump'.

> We never had power to the farm the whole time I was there. We had an old 12-volt battery radio . . . and we used to listen to the news at five o'clock. I used to listen if I could, at six o'clock to *Tarzan*.
>
> We had a Silent Knight kerosene fridge, a wooden fire in the kitchen, two water tanks and we had a woodchip heater for the tank for the bathroom, so we were self-sufficient. But power would have been nice; we had a telephone, which was a modern contrivance, I guess. It was one of those big box things with a little speaker in the middle and you lift up the side bit and listen there and wind the side and talk into the central speaker, real old thing but it worked. Yeah.
>
> BERNIE MCGURGAN, AATTV

That's the voice of Bernie McGurgan. Born in 1944, Bernie is a big man with a bluff, no-nonsense manner. He lives in the north of Australia and drives the most ornately equipped four-wheel drive I've ever seen. If we're ever attacked, I'm heading for Bernie and his truck. In the hallway of his house a framed poster of the ex-Queensland Premier Joh Bjelke-Petersen glares at you as you enter the bathroom. Bernie's kind of old school.

> The nuns were very strict, you only had to muck up there once and they used to get a peppercorn twig, quite thick, about as thick as your little finger, peel the bark off it and whack you on the muscle on the leg, on the same spot. It really hurts you know, you've got to stand, you aren't allowed to move, and they go whack, whack, whack and it really hurts. Or they'd box you on the ears, hit you on the head with a ruler; they don't muck around and that was the discipline in schools in those days. And it worked; if you got caught mucking up you accepted the strap or whatever you got.
>
> The Marist Brothers were worse because they used to use the big rulers and hit you on the knuckles, your knuckles would be up here, swollen, or they'd belt you in the head with a fist, no problems. Throw keys at you, in the face, you know. In this day and age it wouldn't be allowed but I think we're sadly lacking it these days in some regards, yeah, it worked.
>
> BERNIE MCGURGAN

We were an accepting people then, compliant in fact. Faith in our fathers might have been a little hard to find all the time, but as a nation we did have faith in our institutions, even our politicians. It is difficult to understand and accept now, but in 1962 we believed that generally the government knew what was best for us. Vietnam changed all that.

Phuoc Tuy Province, South Vietnam
Sometime in the late 1960s
Delta Company – anywhere in the scrub

On patrol, three men form a team at the front – the forward scout, the section commander and the machine gunner. The scout is a gardener with a deadly touch – secateurs in one hand, weapon in the other. He cuts a path through vines, bamboo and undergrowth . . . silently. One eye on the blade, the other searching for trip-wires and booby traps, or the small signs of disturbance that might mean mines in his path or an enemy ambush. And all the while he waits for the bullet that will come unseen and catch him in the gut. It's a bugger of a job.

A few feet behind him, the section commander has a weapon in one hand and a compass in the other, and following close after him is the machine gunner, safety catch off, finger ever so gently resting on the trigger. If they contact the enemy, he has one task – to lay down a curtain of fire that will allow the scout and the commander to pull back. The rest of the section stretch out in their wake, each man able to see only the man in front.

They do not speak. Sound must be controlled because sound will betray you. In close country they use only field signals, hand movements that indicate the actions they will take. No vocal orders, not even a whisper, will be spoken until the first shot rings out, and then bedlam will reign. In single-file patrols a soldier maintains contact using these signals with only two other men – the one immediately in front of him and the one behind. Sometimes all they see all day is the arse of the bloke in the front and the whites of the eyes of the bloke behind. Everything else is camouflage cream and jungle greens. They become so attuned to each other that they know instinctively when another rifleman is trying to get their attention. ESP for mates.

They walk in a three-dimensional battlefield, 360 degrees of potential danger. Each man has an arc of observation and responsibility, like sections on the face of a clock, from twelve to three say, and he is expected to respond to any action in his area. Their rifles constantly pan, left to right and back again, and their eyes follow the barrel with the intense focus of a kelpie mustering cattle. They search all the corners of this hot, enclosed world – the ground immediately in front where booby traps can lie, then eye level where you can see a man standing, then further away in the distance, looking for movement in the trees, a disturbance of shadows and light. They are processing information at warp speed, questions and answers that can mean survival or death.

What is out of place? What doesn't fit?

Where does the threat lie?

What can I hear, smell, see?

Where would I hide if I were the enemy?

The base of that tree? Left side? Right?

That rock gives a better view of our approach . . . is he there?

Where is my cover? From where could I fire?

They will do this from first light to dusk, for weeks at a time. At the end of a day, they cannot tell you much about the country they have passed through, yet they can retrace their trail with unerring accuracy. The little things do not escape their attention, but the weight of interminable concentration empties their minds and fills them instead with hazy memory and soft shadows, a feeling of pessimism and dullness.

They endure time that has no edges to grasp, no unit to measure its passing. Like a clockwork train they will simply go on, one part of them alert, one part dazed, till the spring winds down and the key stands still in its slot. Then they will go on again.

> You patrol for a while, you stop, have breakfast, patrol, patrol, patrol, have lunch. Patrol, patrol, walk, walk, walk, ah evening meal. Beautiful. Then you all head towards a night defensive position . . . the next morning up we get again, stand-to, pack

up 'the house', patrol, patrol, patrol, simple. And we do the same shit all over again.

Unless of course the shit hits the fan somewhere in between. Then things get a little bit different. Priorities are somewhat different then. You are in the shit and you already know it anyway because the poofters are shooting at you and then the boredom has ceased and you don't actually worry when you are in a shit-fight. You don't actually think much. You do think but you react at the same time. You do the worrying when it is all over. You think, 'Holy snapping ducks, that was close!' And then when that shit's all over, saddle up, move out, patrol, patrol, patrol. All over again and that's the way it was, mate. It was just never-ending.

ANTHONY HUGHES

In the thickest jungle of Vietnam, the one they called the 'J', a patrol might travel 100 metres in just two hours. Then the ground can suddenly change from dense vegetation to rice paddies, or dry forest with undergrowth that crackles so loudly underfoot you may as well announce your presence with a megaphone. Or you might enter the eerie, linear structure of a rubber plantation. Row after row of trees, planted in straight lines that bewilder the eye as you walk till parallel lines become curved and the trees seem to move. Every change of environment means a change in patrol formation, single file becomes a staggered front, or groups of two, or a straight line of walking men. They adjust automatically, orders are not needed.

In the wet season, they're permanently drenched, so dank and waterlogged that their skin peels off like an orange's when they make it back to Nui Dat. In the dry it's heatstroke, dehydration and the tension that arises when one man foolishly drinks his water ration too early and hits on his mates to share. They're vulnerable to dysentery, malaria, parasites that eat away at their intestines and exotic skin diseases that leave them with disgusting, suppurating infections. And as for the animal life...

> Scorpions were really bad over there. Really bad...so you always shake your boots. Before you put anything on, shake your clothes, check your pockets, smack your pockets first before you put your hand in them and all this sort of stuff because you just didn't know where they were. In your packs, in your locker, stand back when you open a locker, you just didn't know.
>
> Leeches, yeah, we had a problem. See our uniform, our jungle greens, you had this tick and leech spray, you had to spray all your seams, your buttons, your pockets, the rims of your pants, you had to spray everywhere. The leeches were so small in the wet season you'd walk past bushes and if you didn't spray yourself, which happened to a few blokes, the leech would get on you and crawl into the fly in your pants, no lie, and they'd get into the eye of your penis. True, true. They were that small and a couple of blokes I do know had to have it surgically removed...and they were pretty savage. I mean, how savage can a leech get, it hasn't got sabre-toothed tiger teeth or anything but they were a bit of a worry... If you felt anything move beside you or onto you, don't touch it, just let it go at night because you couldn't see it. Let it go.
>
> BRIAN WOODS, 9RAR

The larger animals make for a different kind of problem. In a hair-trigger world where any movement could mean the enemy, more than one mammal would meet a premature death.

> We were on an ambush. It was only a couple of nights after I was in country. Me and a mate were in a graveyard and we are laying on this mound and Bert said to me, 'Hey,' he said. 'You notice what we are on?'
>
> I said, 'Yeah. What about it?'

'It's some bastard's grave!'

I said, 'But we're off the deck.'

He said, 'What does that mean?'

I said, 'Well if it rains, we are not in the water, we are above it.'

He said, 'Yeah, but it's someone's grave!'

'Shut up. We are not here to worry about the bloody ethics of the business.'

And all of a sudden there was noise from my right coming along this track. Well, all hell let loose. In the finish, when we did a sweep, we found we'd got a water buffalo, but there were definitely incoming rounds at one stage. We didn't find any bodies or blood trails, but there was just this poor, innocent buffalo. So someone had a feed of buffalo in the local district. It was our first time and it was negligible, or bloody humorous in fact, I suppose. As far as money we expended through barrels, we got a goddamn buffalo. Ridiculous.

ANTHONY HUGHES

Occasionally, the local wildlife and the patrolling Australians interact in a more human way.

We were down near a stream, and because you're down near a watercourse, the trees are naturally bigger. Roots are deeper and so on, well, we got picked up in the morning by a friendly ape, an orang-utan or a gibbon or some such, and this thing's just adopted us. And the silliness of the situation, if you're down below moving at, sort of a hundred yards in half an hour sometimes, and above you, you've got 'whoo, whoo, whoo' . . . swinging from tree to tree, you're thinking, 'You bloody idiot, for Godsake leave us alone!'

Anyway, he adopted us, he loved us for some reason, and it didn't bother us because it's just jungle noises anyway so there's no harm done.

But we stopped for lunch, and he stopped too and he was sitting in the tree and he's looking down at us, and we're doing something boring like eating a cold can of whatever. So he decides to show off and he's leaping around us from tree to tree, these great big swings, beautiful, arcing away from tree to tree. All of a sudden he's let go of this tree and as soon as he did he realised, 'I'm not going to make that branch!' and for about 30 feet there was this horrendous 'Ahhhhhhh!'... Scream, thump, and these five guys with their cans and their weapons across their laps all stand up, all looking for their little monkey mate.

The monkey, he got up, I swear he walked over to the tree that he'd missed, grabbed it with both arms and started banging his head against the tree, gibbering to himself all the while. You could almost see, you know, 'You stupid, stupid monkey, how old are ya? You made it to this age and you still can't grab the...!' and he wandered off. He was too embarrassed ever to look at us again.

AUDIE MOLDRE

If no enemy are encountered, the days on patrol slip by without connection to each other, each one marked only by small events – yesterday it pissed down, the day before we crossed a creek. Tomorrow? Tomorrow was in limbo.

But the nights are different. They go into what they call 'harbour', a place to rest, though never completely. Just before dusk, the men break off from patrolling and circle back over their own track, partly to cover it and partly to ensure that they are not being followed. A piece of ground is nominated as camp and they automatically begin their routine – search patrols go out to ensure the area is clear, gun pits are dug, the machine gun set up and Claymore mines are placed in protective positions, facing away from the camp. Again, arcs of responsibility and fire are allotted to each man by the commander. That way, if they're attacked in the night, they will not accidentally shoot one another.

They quickly set to, heat and eat their evening meal. No fires after dark. At dusk, they insert detonators into the Claymores and run wire back to the 'clackers', the plungers that will send an electric current to the mine and detonate the slab of plastic explosive, sending lead ball bearings blasting away from them at ankle height.

'Stand-to' is called and each man faces outwards, weapon cocked, waiting. This is the most likely time for an enemy ambush. Darkness arrives, 'Stand-down' is whispered and they settle. From now until morning, they will rotate sentry duty every two hours.

Each man constructs his own sleeping place by clearing a small patch of sticks and rocks, making sure not to disturb ants or other biting bastards who could make their night a misery. A plastic sheet on the ground, then the silk sleeping-bag liner on top. A small comfort in a hard place. They lay out their oil bottle, cleaning rag, pull-through cord and brush, and begin the nightly ritual of the infantryman – cleaning the rifle that keeps them safe and gives them strength.

When they're done, their weapon and webbing are placed beside their sleeping patch. Some men put it near their head, others by their side. Wherever it lies, it is always in the same place for each soldier. When the night explodes with gunfire, they do not want to be searching in the dark. When it rains, and it often will, they either erect their plastic poncho over their head, or simply endure it. Cold will come later, along with the mosquitoes who roughly resemble small aeroplanes.

They communicate in soft whispers, curled up in their silk like some kind of exotic jungle creature, exchanging stories and memories. They speak of cars . . . and women, and sport . . . and women, and bloody officers and pogos . . . and women. These moments bond them together as much as combat does. Australian life and culture does not allow or encourage men to share much more than the shallowest of dips into each other's internal life, so these small confessions and truths in the dark have about them a genuine intimacy. In the face of isolation and threat, they at least have each other.

Sleep comes easily to some, but not many. Men living at the end of their nerves or cursed with imagination do not do well at night on patrol. Too many sounds, too many sinister possibilities. Then there are the snorers, the dreamers and the sleepwalkers, all a liability to patrol security. The blokes could understand how it happened, but they didn't like it at all.

We used to call him 'Nightmare' 'cos he was a prick – he'd have nightmares every night. You know, you'd be just getting off to sleep in the bush and he'd scream and oh, fuck! We used to give him a piece of tape to put over his mouth of a night, 'Breathe through your nose!' And it was terrifying, everything's perfectly quiet and you're just relaxing and then he screams and it was a fucking terrifying scream.

We got him to put his head down, stick the old neck cloth in his mouth, 'We don't give a shit what you do, Nightmare, for Christ's sake!' And you'd shit yourself every time you went into an ambush with him.

'He's on 100 per cent wake up all night. Do not give him 50–50. Keep him awake all night. Keep your hand near his mouth and if he looks like he's even gonna breathe the wrong way just shove it in there.'

And that probably went on for about three months before he went back to his natural self. I don't know why he was having them but that name stuck with him. When he rings up these days, 'Is that you, Nightmare?' My wife calls him 'Nightmare'. I explained it to her and she thought it was rather funny. I said, 'Well, I didn't see the funny point at the time.'

He's a top bloke. He got a Military Medal for what he done as a medic when we got blown up.

Barry Fitton, 5RAR

In truth, they don't really sleep, not as we understand that word. They drift in an in-between state, waiting for the sound that will snap them awake, reaching for their weapons. The SAS on patrol sleep in a circle with their feet touching so that any movement will wake them all. Some infantrymen tie string to each other for the same reason.

It's a state of mind called hyper-vigilance and it will leave its mark so deeply on many of them that their lives back in Australia will be cursed by the habit. Curiously, when they return to Nui Dat after a patrol, these same men fall on their beds and sleep through artillery crashes that shake the ground underneath their tents. Volleys of small arms and machine-gun fire from the testing range obliterate the peace, but it doesn't matter to them. They sleep through anything when they know it's safe.

After 10 days of patrol, regulations stated that they had to have some fresh food. Resup it's called, for resupply, and they're red-letter days. A smoke grenade to mark the spot and a heavily laden Iroquois chopper descends like Santa Claus. The entire company comes together and the platoons can catch up and exchange news and bullshit. The choppers deliver water, more C-rations, cigarettes, cold cans of drink (called 'goffas'), chocolate-flavoured milk and the salad rolls and oranges that allegedly equal fresh food. They carry new jungle greens for those whose uniforms are destroyed, spare weapons parts and the mixed blessing of mail.

News from home is critical for morale and optimism, the belief that this will end one day and another life will be waiting. It was ever thus for the infantryman. Letters bring softness and affection into a grim place; connecting them back to a world they can visualise only dimly. The men share their news, sometimes even the letters themselves, particularly with those who don't receive mail. One person's good news is everyone's. Unfortunately, so is the bad.

The section commanders wait with trepidation to see whether anyone has received that traditional soldier's kick in the guts, the Dear John letter. Sorry Kevin, or Jack, or Geoff, or Martin... we're through. I've found somebody else, I don't love you anymore, I can't wait for you... sad little justifications, some real, others a lie. In a section of just 10 men, one of these missives can be like a rock in a pond, the ripples of anger and worry overwhelming the others. If it can happen to him, why not me? What's my missus up to? Hope, always a weak flame on patrol, can be extinguished in a moment. It's all too easy to believe that you're forgotten.

The NCOs get them moving, stowing away rations and burying all the rubbish. Time to walk the weeds again. Silence returns as Delta Company divides and each man is left with his own thoughts, whether they were of home or what might be waiting down the track. They all say the same thing about this moment when you faced up to the task again – that the last thing you wanted and the only thing you wanted were one and the same – to see some bloody action.

I knew only one prime minister from birth to adolescence – Robert Gordon Menzies, or, as he was often referred to: 'Ming the Merciless' (the name of the evil emperor in the comic strip *Flash Gordon*). Menzies was a one-off amongst Australia's prime ministers. He was a tall, big-framed man, with a not unappealing face, an enviable head of white hair and twin, black, caterpillar eyebrows of such size and ferocity that in newspaper photographs and on television they seemed to live life independently of the rest of him. He had a superb, caressing voice, and though it was often said that he sounded a little too 'posh' for an Australian, his wit and vocabulary could play that instrument to wondrous effect. He was charismatic and commanding – the prime minister from Central Casting . . . and the man who took us into Vietnam.

Menzies had been prime minister before, in 1939, when his sorrowful voice, tolling like a bell, had informed the nation that England was at war and that 'as a result, Australia is also at war'. But his autocratic ways led to his downfall and for the rest of World War II, he remained a minor figure. He fought his way back, founded the Liberal Party, regained government, and by 1962 dominated Australian political life to such a degree that his authority seemed unshakeable and his right to office unquestionable.

No one could have called Menzies a visionary; he was too practical for that – tough, cunning and politically astute. He had only one blind spot – an obsession with the British monarchy that bordered on the strange and there is a wonderful moment contained in Australia's film archives when his adoration overflowed. It's 1963 and the Queen is visiting Canberra. Prime Minister Menzies, resplendent in regalia and medals, is officially welcoming Her Majesty and then, in an unscripted moment, he breaks into an Elizabethan love lyric and delivers these lines to her with such naked devotion that even after all these years it can still make most Australians cringe with embarrassment:

> There is a lady sweet and kind,
> Was never face so pleased my mind;
> I did but see her passing by,
> And yet I love her till I die.

Even though it's black-and-white footage, you can see the young Elizabeth II blush profusely. She hides her face with a giggle and Menzies, like your slightly drunk Uncle Alf after Christmas lunch, smiles benignly at everyone. Magic, utter magic.

But he was no fool. Menzies' hold on power was rarely threatened, least of all by his opposite number. Elected by the Labor Party as opposition leader in 1960, when he was 63, Arthur Calwell was one of those unfortunate politicians whose thankless task it is to lead their party after disaster and chaos have brought it to the brink of ruin.

Briefly, what happened is that the Labor Party had split in two in the middle '50s. A large part of its right wing, mostly Catholics, decided that the party was too soft on Communism (and other matters) and left in high dudgeon. They set up their own organisation – the Democratic Labor Party – and then proceeded to stick it to their old mates by winning Senate seats and allocating their preferences to Menzies and the conservatives. It was a mess.

It feels like, and is, somewhat dry history now, but I saw grown men punch each other's lights out over the DLP split at gatherings in Catholic Church halls and homes. We kids never knew much about it apart from overhearing dark mutterings about 'Commo bastards' and 'bloody traitors' but it was terrifically exciting to see the grown-ups square-off.

The upshot of it all was that the Labor Party was a lonely voice in the wilderness. It didn't help that Calwell was never going to have Menzies' charm and appeal. It would be kind to describe his face as craggy, and his voice was a harsh, nasal whine, reminiscent of a rusty tin lid being forcibly dragged across concrete. He had an unfortunate look for television and where Menzies presented a vision of well-tailored urbanity, Calwell, in his ill-fitting suits and Coke-bottle glasses seemed out of place and old-fashioned, particularly to young Australians.

Yet he was an honest man, Arthur, a true believer and hater in the way that only the Irish and their descendants can manage; implacably hostile towards the British and their imperialist ways.

He was suspicious of the gentry and all those who would lord it over the working man. He was a racist and a bigot, convinced of the rightness of the White Australia Policy, but over the next 10 years he would prove to be a consistent and fierce opponent of conscription and the Vietnam War, often in defiance of his party and most of Australia.

But neither Menzies nor Calwell occupied much of our thinking time then. One of the more attractive qualities of politics in 1962 was its lack of presence in our lives. Mr Menzies was the Prime Minister; Mr Calwell led the Opposition and that was the way it both was and should be. Still, difference was in the air, like smoke in summer.

Australia's population was rapidly getting younger – the percentage under the age of 15 rose from 25 per cent in 1947 to almost 30 per cent by 1965. By the mid '60s, more than 38 per cent of the country was aged under 20, meaning that not one of those people had been through the two world wars or the Great Depression. That part of the population that had so innocently been called 'youths' in the 1940s had morphed into a much more difficult beast called 'teenagers' in the 1950s. They were accompanied by a burst of soundtrack that shook up the world, an irresistible cry that came from somewhere down the end of a lonely street and seemed to infect everyone under 20 with a rocking pneumonia and a boogie woogie flu.

When 'Heartbreak Hotel' came hurtling out of radios across Australia, propelled by the voice of Elvis Presley, hearts were transfixed, lives were changed. We had never heard *anything* like that before, but we knew instinctively it was ours. It was goodbye Perry Como and Pat Boone and hello '*awopbopaloobopa-wopbamboom*'. In bedrooms everywhere, acne-riddled boys practised their three chords on Maton guitars while girls watched *Six O'Clock Rock* and *Bandstand*, criticising the girl singers, all the while wishing it was them up there on the black-and-white dream machine. The true deluge was yet to come, but the door to change was being belted open and the old-time heroes were crashing and burning.

> We had the brushed-back hairstyles and the ducktails and all that sort of thing. Quite common for us to wear all black. That was the trendy thing, with the pointy-toed shoes and at the local dances and they were good times ... just young fellows who loved to ride motorbikes and make a lot of noise ... They used to cruise down the main street of Glenelg and park them all in a row outside the pub and they were all sparkling and great.
>
> TONY EY, CLEARANCE DIVING TEAM

Tony Ey had moved from a farm to the big city of Adelaide, and like many of us in 1962, he began his adolescence as a hungry innocent, looking for action in a conservative world.

> I can remember some of the guys in my class talking about the birds and the bees and I remember my first reaction was, 'That's disgusting!' and I said, 'That's bullshit because my parents wouldn't do that.' ... And of course young boys at school that's all they talk about eventually so you start to realise what it's all about and you learn by word of mouth from your mates ...
>
> My first real girlfriend ... I only ever saw her on Saturday nights at the dance and we thought it was pretty serious but her parents were so strict that I couldn't see her any other time than the dances and her father would bring her to the dances and then he was there on the spot, on the dot, when the dance finished and took her home. So we held hands between dances and things like that ... the parents were very, very strict in those days. They watched their daughters very closely ...

There were a couple of big proper dance halls in Adelaide, they were pretty big. But they were great. That was the place you had to be. Some of the blokes would pull up outside on their motorbikes and most of the time they would sit around on the motorbikes rather than go inside and dance, but real rock 'n' roll bands. You know, the real old jive of the '60s and Bill Haley and the Comets sort of music. Everybody with their ducktails, their haircuts and the girls with their short skirts and the blokes with their pointy-toed shoes. But I was never a dancer. We used to tend to sit around amongst ourselves and watch and go look at the motorbikes and sneak out the back and have a beer...

The girls would be in their groups and the boys would be in their groups and, of course, the girls would show up to the dance in a group and you couldn't split them up. They'd stay in their group and on the odd occasion you would go over and ask a girl to dance – some of them were that shy they didn't know what to do. It was really strange. We were quiet in a lot of ways; I don't know about a protected society, it was more closed in its outlook. We weren't as open-minded as they are today.

TONY EY

Not quite sex, drugs and rock 'n' roll, is it? That was to come, for some of us at least, a little later on. But even these mild, early stirrings – the motorbikes, the leathers, the music, caused an outcry from the pillars of Australian life. To our parents and grandparents we seemed to be a brand-new species – not just disobedient and disrespectful but deliberately ignorant of the hard times they had gone through so that we could be disobedient and disrespectful. 'You listen to me, sonny Jim. I fought the war for the likes of you and you should count yourself damn lucky that you're not damn well jibber-jabbering in Japanese and eating your dinner with bloody chopsticks!'

They had, after all, been robbed of their youth in many ways, and our careless freedom and irresponsibility must have seemed at the very least, unfair. We were better educated; more of us finished high school than ever before and, thanks to Menzies, many more of us were able to attend the newly created universities. Of course, we then had to show our ingratitude by using this brand-new educational experience to turn on him and his conservative cohorts.

To organisations like the Returned and Services League, the RSL, it seemed that everything they stood for was under attack during the '60s. Formed during World War I by activist veterans, principally to agitate for veterans' rights, the RSL had grown into a nationwide lobby that had a deathlike grip on the observance of Anzac Day and occasionally let rip with sensational outbursts on the failings of Australian society. Universities, and the ratbags they so obviously bred, were a favourite topic of fulmination.

The student newspaper at Sydney University, *Honi Soit*, once published an article which took a mighty swipe at Anzac Day. They called it 'an annual ritual of national narcissism-cum-Bacchanalian revel', then for good measure they also took aim at the 'blood and thunder or syrupy sentimentalism of RSL propaganda'. Predictably, the RSL responded by calling the whole thing 'complete and utter filth'.

Even more outrageous to them was Alan Seymour's play, *The One Day of the Year.* The play dealt with the generational gap between a World War II veteran and his uni student son over Anzac Day and portrayed the digger as a drunken, pathetic character who was irrelevant in a modern world. When you read it now, it feels rather clunky and unsubtle, but at the time it seemed to crystallise the divisions and the bitterness that were beginning to rise up between parents and children.

Apart from immigration, conscription and general moral decline, the subjects that always got the RSL into full frothing at the mouth mode were the Threat of Communism and the Defence of Australia. For some reason, they were always written in capital letters. Not for nothing had the RSL borrowed from an American orator their motto, 'The Price of Liberty is Eternal Vigilance'.

The men of World War I had long had a stranglehold on the RSL, not welcoming the World War II vets into the fold till they were forced by time to change, and only in the early '60s were the younger men beginning to take over. There was to be a harsh irony in this later, when the Vietnam vets came home. The World War II men had come out of their war acutely aware of Australia's vulnerability, fearful of what they saw as the Asian menace and determined that no potential enemy would ever rise up again.

Clearly, in this volatile world that featured spy planes and the Berlin Wall, satellites and the space race, Khrushchev, Castro and Mao, the greatest threat came from the Communists, who were otherwise known as 'reds', 'pinkoes', 'red-raggers' and 'Commies'. They could be found in the Soviet Union, China, most of Eastern Europe, Cuba, East Germany, Vietnam, Malaya, Indonesia and under the bed. The RSL lobbied the government fiercely over the advance of Communism and the state of our defence readiness. They were a strong, conservative force with the unique privilege of direct access to cabinet, but they were talking to the converted.

The war in the Pacific and then the Korean War had caused Australia's defence and foreign policies to swing firmly towards the United States. This was the time of 'the domino theory', an idea that proposed that if one country came under Communist control, then the countries surrounding it would also fall, one by one, to Communism.

The theory sprang from a belief in the West that Communism, fanatical, expansionist and led by the Soviet Union, was determined to gain absolute authority over the rest of the world. The situation wasn't helped by people like the Soviet Premier, Nikita Khrushchev, who cried out to the West, 'We will bury you!' To the Americans, and thus to us, it meant that existing Communist governments must be prevented from expanding and that any new ones should be killed at birth.

The great flaw in the theory was that belief in it made you blind. Blind to the fact that nations are distinct and unique, with different cultures and politics, different stories. Like life, they are complex and messy and cannot be so easily lined up and knocked over. But sometimes when you believe in something so fervently, all the evidence seems to point towards the rightness of that belief. By 1962, Australia had battled against Communism in Korea, killed Communist terrorists in Malaya, watched nervously as Communists gained influence and power in Indonesia, and in May '62, we had sent an air force squadron to Thailand in response to a Communist-led crisis in Laos. The dominoes, wavering under the hot breath of red aggression, looked like they would fall at any moment. Then there was Vietnam.

For all the iconic status that Vietnam was to ultimately occupy in Australian history, in 1962 you would have been hard put to find one Australian in ten who had actually heard of the country, let alone knew where it was. You might have done slightly better if you'd changed the name to Indochina because at least some of us remembered that from History class.

Asia was still a mystery and a worry to most Australians. It was on our list of things about which we felt vaguely uneasy – bosses, the police, homosexuality, our place in the world . . . and all those countries to our north. From time to time, when a fuss was stirred up by politicians or the RSL, then 'the Asian threat' rocketed to the top of the list. The Japanese were firmly lodged in the bad memories of our parents and as for the Chinese . . . well, many a young Australian in 1962 had grown up being warned that 'the yellow hordes' were waiting just off the coast, slavering and salivating as they looked enviously upon our riches and 'our way of life'. And if that feels a little far-fetched today, let me remind you that it was only in 1961 that *The Bulletin* had removed the slogan 'Australia for the White Man' from its masthead. The possibility that millions of Chinese neither knew of nor cared about us strangely did not seem to enter our thinking.

Vietnam hit our political radar in the late 1950s, when the conflict between the Communist North and the supposedly democratic South intensified and casualties on both sides mounted. US military involvement steadily increased under President Kennedy and, by the end of 1962, 11 000 American advisers and support personnel were stationed in the South. As ever, the Americans were sensitive to the accusation that they were being bullies and the rising protests that they had replaced the colonising French with the 'imperialist' US meant that they needed international legitimacy. They invented what they called the 'Many Flags' project (kind of like 'the Coalition of the Willing' these days, but in more innocent language) and began seeking support.

Australia received its first request for a military contribution from the American State Department in late 1961. The armies of both countries quickly poured cold water on the proposal but in the face of political expediency and need, they didn't stand a chance against the politicians. On 24 May 1962, the Minister for Defence, Athol Townley, announced that Australia would commit up to 30 military instructors to Vietnam. We were in.

It seemed so small and inoffensive really, back in 1962. Just a few blokes going over to some place called Vietnam (where?) to help the Yanks sort out some Commie guerrillas. It made only a ripple in the news and did not lodge as even a tiny blip in the collective memory of the nation. We remember it now only because of what was to follow, and there was so much else to think about after all. Rod Laver won the grand slam of tennis and Marilyn Monroe died. There were hula hoops on the streets and *The Argonauts* on the radio. Lucky Starr was singing 'I've Been Everywhere' and *The Beverly Hillbillies* and *McHale's*

Navy (not to mention *The Jetsons)* were keeping us glued to the tube. We were reaching out to the world, to whatever our future might be.

> I was a bit directionless. I got into trouble with this girl in Bendigo, got her pregnant, and I was escaping that – she was a nice girl. I ended up in Sydney, working for the PMG [Postmaster General], at one stage I was thinking of becoming a PMG technician... The army looked a bit exciting. I knew it had bases all around Australia so it was a chance to see Australia; the possibility of going to war, which I didn't think too much of at the time, and postings overseas as an officer, and I thought being an officer was the way to do it... I liked the fact that it was a nice uniform and I thought, you know, probably lots of girls like young blokes in uniform...and I thought, well, the army, I might give it a go, it's good pay.
>
> BERNIE MCGURGAN

> If you were going to go to university it was going to cost you a lot of money. Not you, but whoever was going to pay for it. I had no sense that I was ever going to get to university at that point in my life; it just wasn't going to happen...you just kind of said, 'Well, I'm 15 and I'm not going. I've got no prospects of higher education because of the cost, and it's time to think about going out there into the workforce.'
>
> AUDIE MOLDRE

> Every time a navy ship came into Adelaide I used to be onto Dad's back, 'Come on, Dad, I want to see the ships!' So every ship that came in we went down there...
>
> [HMAS] *Melbourne* came in and she was the carrier, the flagship, and we went down to Outer Harbour to see her the morning she was sailing and it was a beautiful, clear morning and the water was green and clear and there's this huge aircraft

> carrier there and the fans are humming and everything's happening and the sailors are running around and it's just a moment that is frozen in my mind. I'll never forget I was standing down near the stern of the ship down near the big quarterdeck and I noticed that the ship's divers were in the water, something to do with the propellers. They were in the water and I looked down and there's this huge warship towering above them and the divers in the water and such a beautiful day and I went, 'There's nothing else in the world for me. This is what I have to do.'
>
> TONY EY

Plans being made, dreams being dared, lives unfolding. I seriously doubt that in 1962, Tony or Audie or Bernie knew that the first members of the Australian Army Training Team Vietnam were about to go to war. Or that soon, they too would be there.

But as those first soldiers boarded their Qantas flight to Saigon, there were all kinds of echoes in the air – of the Sudan, of South Africa and Gallipoli, of Passchendaele and Tobruk, of Kokoda and Korea. We were off again, this time without fanfare or formal farewells, off to a country whose history of thousands of years of struggle, conflict and death, was about to embrace yet more, where Australians would fight, and die; off to a war which, for some, has never ended.

II

THE VIETNAMESE ARE DESCENDED FROM DRAGONS AND FAIRIES

> We depart at 8.30 AM for Tay Ninh to visit the Cao Dai Great Temple, with architecture that could easily be a Walt Disney fantasy. Then it's on to Cu Chi and the fabulous Viet Cong Tunnels. Here you will have the unique experience of guerrillas living and fighting underground during the war and gain a deep appreciation of the courage and integrity of the Vietnamese people. For those interested, there's even the opportunity to fire off rounds from an AK47 at the nearby rifle range. Allegedly, the old, wooden targets resemble U.S. Marines!
>
> Lunch and drinks included.
>
> VIETNAMESE TOURIST BROCHURE, 2006

The Cu Chi Tunnels are a must on the list of sights for visitors to modern Vietnam, along with the Mekong Delta, a temple or two, the floating market, the old city of Hoi An, cheap DVDs . . . and the wonderful world of war. The American War (as it is locally known) is very big business. A nation that recycled bombs into booby traps and drink cans into houses has no problem in making hay from history. And for many Vietnamese that's all it is now, history.

Two-thirds of Vietnam's people were born after the war and the young idolise Bill Gates far more than Ho Chi Minh, their legendary wartime leader. The comrades have gone commercial and like everyone else they want plasma screens, cell phones, Western fashions and the latest Honda Wave motorcycle. *Doi moi* it's called – 'renovation', not of a house but an entire country. Like the Chinese before them the Vietnamese have encouraged socialism to let loose its inner capitalist, but as always, only some of the people have benefited.

The average annual income in Vietnam is just US$500, mostly because about 60 per cent of the 85 million people still live and work in rural areas, and a third of them are below the poverty line. Corruption is healthy and widespread, the judicial system a bad joke and human rights either absent or ignored. Our tourist dollars may be welcome but not our freedoms. Not yet, anyway. The Socialist Republic of Vietnam remains a single party state, firmly controlled by the Communists.

Still, nothing stops the Vietnamese. You get the feeling that they'd not only survive the end of the world; they'd find a way to flourish. For the first 10 years after the war ended in 1975 this country was wracked by poverty, ripped apart by the violent suppression and jailing of thousands of its own people in prison camps, and brought to its economic knees by a bunch of old, Cold War warriors who didn't have the faintest idea how to run a country. The small problem of two additional wars, one with Cambodia in 1977 and the other with China in 1979, didn't exactly help either.

But in street and village, paddy field and warehouse, the people kept going – trading, dealing, conniving and accruing, doing what they had to do, getting by. The Vietnamese people will play the game according to whichever rules hold sway at any given time, but quietly, deeply, they are intent on one thing above all others – the survival and success of their family. Life is a long arc they believe, punctuated by inevitable injustice and tragedy and you should have no expectation that anyone else, least of all any government, will make it easier for you. You take your chances when they come. Like making money from your own war.

Vietnam has all the jewels necessary for a tourism crown – breathtaking mountains, snowy-white beaches, timeless scenery and full-tilt cities; but it's the war that has been turned into a major money-spinner. There are holy icons of the conflict around every corner, museums of memory and state rhetoric which you are enthusiastically encouraged to visit.

Some Western veterans of the war have come to Vietnam over the years with nostalgia in their hearts, looking for the 'Nam' of their youth; but most tourists arrive these days with nothing more than simple curiosity about the war. At the monuments and the museums there are thousands of them, the babble of languages echoing off the cool, concrete walls. They dutifully follow their government-appointed guides, holding their digital cameras in front of their bodies like an offering, photographing each exhibit as they trundle by – the Huey choppers, the statues of Ho, the tanks, the guns and the planes.

They don't bother to read the turgid text that accompanies each display, they just photograph it instead. They come from Australia, America, Europe, Japan and Korea and they're relentless; nothing stops or shocks them, not the horrific photographs of napalmed children, the close-ups of the disfigurement and the burns, not even the terrible, deformed foetuses preserved in jars, labelled as victims of a herbicide used during the war, Agent Orange. They move on in a kind of obedient stupor as their guides regale them with politically acceptable speeches, and all together now, it's cameras up, frame the shot, Flash! Check the shot on the LCD screen, move on. 'So, that was the war, eh?' And all the while the dollars pile up.

Most of the Vietnamese guides and attendants are far too young to have known the war and don't really believe the government line, they just parrot it. You can admire the Vietnamese for their enterprise and their adaptability, but the real fascination is their capacity to lead double lives, one outwardly, on show for the state and any other observer, and one inwardly, where they tell the truth to an empty room. Keep watching though, because every now and then the façade cracks, just a little.

At Cu Chi, before they take you down into the tunnels (which have been widened to accommodate fat Westerners), you sit through an obligatory screening of a Viet Cong propaganda film made for tourists. It's old-fashioned, pedal-to-the-metal Communist claptrap like this:

> The American devils, they shot at women, children. They shot at the poultry, they fired into pots and pans, they fired at trees and leaves, they fired into the soil! They fired at schools and even Buddha statues! . . . But who were these Cu Chi guerrillas who fought back against Washington DC? A small girl who lost her father . . . her height doesn't reach that of the trenches but her hatred lifts her much higher above the ground. With only a rifle and a grenade, in just a single day she drove back tens of well-trained Americans! She was awarded the title, Brave Exterminator of Americans . . .

You get the general drift. All the guerrillas in the film, just coincidentally of course, are good-looking young women with fresh, idealistic faces. It's clunky, amateurish sludge, probably produced by a workers' committee and my scepticism must have been showing on my face because our guide, catching my eye, winked at me and then burst into laughter. He was still chuckling 30 minutes later as he herded us into the souvenir shop where you can buy (fake) dog tags, VC flags, cleverly aged Zippo cigarette lighters inscribed with American GI mottos like, 'Yea, though I walk through the valley of death, I fear no evil because I'm the meanest motherfucker in the valley', unit patches, medals, American ID cards and VC scarves. The final touch is the gaggle of small, persistent boys selling bootlegged copies of Graham Greene's *The Quiet American.*

No possibility is overlooked, no potential sale missed. The guide, by the way, scored a sizeable tip for briefly departing from the party line.

To see the conflict transformed into tourist turns and tacky souvenirs can surprise and bemuse Australian and other visitors to Vietnam, and it nettles some veterans. They find it hard to swallow the 'war criminals' labels on some of the photographs of allied troops and the often boastful tone of the guides' spiels. And even though it's all just another way of making a buck in a hard world, it's also a symbol of the differences between us.

That's the trouble with visiting Vietnam as an Australian. You can easily find yourself thinking of it as a war rather than a country. To do so singles it out from the rest of Asia, makes it an icon of sorts. We don't look at Indonesia that way, not even Bali after the bombings. The Vietnamese, smart and entrepreneurial, feed that perception for a price and keep the war alive. But away from the monuments and the museums, the children of Vietnam reach hungrily for their future.

The true legacy of the war for the Vietnamese is memories that don't make money and are not for public consumption. They can be found commemorated and enshrined on small, wooden altars that gleam with red and gold lacquer and sit in pride of place in millions of homes and shops, restaurants, offices and businesses all over Vietnam and in faraway cities like Toronto, San Francisco, Sydney and Melbourne, wherever the refugees found shelter. They are places of worship where families honour their ancestors. There are wooden plaques resting there with names carved into their surfaces alongside photographs of people long gone. They stand on those altars in mute testament to what was really lost . . .

Count them:

- The Army of the Republic of Vietnam – 224 000 killed; 1 169 000 wounded.
- The North Vietnamese Army/ Viet Cong – 1 100 000 killed; 600 000 wounded.
- Vietnamese Civilians – the nearest estimate is 2 000 000 killed. An unknown number were wounded or maimed.

Every family in Vietnam suffered loss in the war, no one escaped untouched.

There were two soldiers, both of one family,
Both of one race – Vietnam.
There were two soldiers, both of one family,
Both of one blood – Vietnam.

There were two soldiers who were of one heart,
Neither would let Vietnam be lost.
There were two soldiers, both advancing up a road,
Determined to preserve Vietnam.

There were two soldiers, both were heroes,
Both sought out and captured the enemy troops.
There were two soldiers, both were heroes,
Both went off to 'wipe out the gang of common enemies'.

There were two soldiers who lay upon a field,
Both clasping rifles and waiting.

There were two soldiers who one rosy dawn
Killed each other for Vietnam.
Killed each other for Vietnam.

PHAM DUY

That song was composed in 1968 but it is still sung in Vietnam, still remembered. To talk with a Vietnamese veteran of war, no matter which side they were on, is to dip your hand into a deep stream. For Australian soldiers the war meant a 12-month tour, but the Vietnamese already had years of fighting behind them and years still to endure. Trace the outline of most Australian veterans' stories and you find a time capsule that begins the day they leave for Saigon and ends 365 days later. But the Vietnamese vet's story is likely to follow a winding, often tragic course for 30 years and more.

I went to Cabramatta, in New South Wales, and the suburbs around it, to speak with Vietnamese–Australian veterans, men who had served with the forces of South Vietnam during the war and now lived here. In every house I visited one symbol was always prominent – a yellow rectangle with three red stripes running in parallel across it, the flag of the long-gone Republic of [South] Vietnam.

'Red blood, yellow skin,' they told me, wanting to make a point about sacrifice. But I knew that the yellow represented the land and the three red stripes North, Central and South Vietnam. In one form or another, this flag has been the emblem of Vietnamese nationalism for 100 years and, to the veterans I spoke with, it remains the most potent and emotional symbol of a country they have lost.

Lost. There's a certain weight to that word, a lingering sadness about its very sound. It was a constant presence in the interviews I conducted with these men. There was also a fierce pride in their personal histories, a fervent hatred of contemporary, socialist Vietnam, and a deep gratitude to Australia. Without the war, it's unlikely that Australia and Vietnam would ever have been any more to each other than trading partners and so these men would have been unknown to us. But they're pieces in our jigsaw now, part of our story.

Let me tell you about three of them: Van Nhung Tran, Vo Minh Cuong and Colonel Vo Dai Ton.

They came to Australia at different times but in the same way – on the refugee road over the South China Sea in impossible boats till they hit the camps in South-East Asia. Thousands of Vietnamese, or 'boat people', were taken in by Australia in the 10 or so years after 1975.

Van Nhung Tran was a doctor, a captain in the medical corps of the South Vietnamese Army and when the war ended he was treating the wounded from both sides in a field hospital. The Communists then locked him away for three years in prison, the so-called 're-education camps'. Mr Van is slightly built, elegant and precise in his movements with impeccable, old-world manners. He now works as a medical technician in a Sydney hospital.

Vo Minh Cuong was sent to train as a helicopter pilot in America and then flew as a lieutenant with the Vietnamese Air Force on medevacs and Special Forces missions. Shot out of the sky at war's end, he spent almost six years in the camps. These days, he's a solicitor in Sydney's southwest. Mr Vo is an excitable, voluble man, with a ready laugh and a quick wit. A beautiful, wooden model of a Huey helicopter, *his* helicopter, made for him by a fellow prisoner, sat beside him during the interview.

Vo Dai Ton, always called 'Colonel' in the Vietnamese community, is the oldest of these men. His father was a mandarin, a bureaucrat in the court of the Vietnamese emperor, and he is one of 10 children, all of whom joined the South Vietnamese Army. The colonel was a member of the Special Forces and he escaped just weeks after the end of the war. Astonishingly, he returned covertly to Vietnam in 1981 in an attempt to set up a resistance network. He was caught, imprisoned and finally released 12 years later.

When you want to try to understand another human being, where do you start? With language? Emotions? Music? Perhaps with shared experiences? Some of the Vietnamese–Australian veterans I interviewed are my age and so I looked for some commonality with them – books, music, world events; all the usual trappings of a life lived that cling to us over the years. But there was no common ground down those paths.

Then one of them gently scolded me, pointing out that my childhood was totally different to his. 'You could dream,' he said. 'You could imagine what your life might become, what *you* could become. In Vietnam, there were no dreams.' For his generation there was no sense of the future, just the hard facts of living every day. There was no optimism, just a fragile hope of survival.

Ask either nationality, 'Why did you fight?' and the comparisons are just as stark. We had choices in Australia – to go or not to go, to support the war, protest against it, or just ignore it. For the Vietnamese the only choice was which path to choose through the chaos and the blood. Should they be on the side of the 'liberation war' or 'the fight for freedom and democracy'? The Communists or the Americans? Whichever way they went, death would haunt their steps and the only constants were fear, sacrifice and loss.

It wasn't simply a question of right or wrong. The moral compass of the Vietnamese swung wildly for every man, woman and child. Many changed sides, often more than once, but most . . . well, most were just picked up by the anonymous and cruel wave of war and unceremoniously dumped – bruised, bloodied or lifeless, wherever it chose to drop them. War was not just a way of life in Vietnam, it *was* life. It made the Vietnamese into fatalists, knowing there was nothing they could do against the great forces grinding away all around them. If those forces wanted to take you, they would. They *owned* you.

Yet these men love the country of their birth. I do not mean they indulge in empty flag-waving or even aggressive patriotism. I mean they love the land itself, their history and their people. With loyalty and honest faith they gave what they had to defend that love and they lost. That is, of course, the nature of war, but there are no memorials to their sacrifice, no recording of their valour. There is nothing that would bring them at least some small measure of comfort that they too are remembered.

Every public trace of their existence in Vietnam has been obliterated by the victors – cemeteries desecrated, monuments bulldozed. Australian Vietnam veterans, themselves no strangers to dispossession, have encouraged these men to march on Anzac Day, and in that spirit, I want to try to widen the lens a little. In the telling of our Vietnam years, I must also attempt to tell something of theirs. It is important to at least try to understand the land they left behind, the world into which we stumbled.

> The coat of arms of the Republic of Vietnam has, as its central theme, the flexible bamboo, symbolising consistency, faithfulness and vitality... An ancient proverb says, 'the taller the bamboo grows, the lower it bends', meaning that a great man is humble, modest and tolerant. A fierce storm may uproot proud, stately and seemingly indestructible trees, but after the storm subsides, the flexible bamboo emerges as straight and verdant as before. This may reflect an approach to life.
>
> AMERICAN MILITARY COUNTRY STUDY AND STATION BRIEFING REPORT, 1961

The Vietnamese are descended from dragons and fairies, or at least that's how the ancient myth goes. The Dragon Lord of the Seas and a fairy princess from the mountains had 100 children together. Not surprisingly the marriage failed, so the Dragon Lord returned to the sea with half the children and the fairy took the others and settled near the Red River, beginning the nation of Vietnam.

A more pedestrian explanation is that the Vietnamese are descendants of Mongols from China and migrating Indonesians. About 3000 years ago, a culture emerged in the north of Vietnam that can be traced to the modern Vietnamese and little by little these people moved slowly south, occupying more and more arable land as they went, forcibly removing the original inhabitants until they had it all.

There was good reason for them to covet this land. Vietnam is the shape of an 'S', long and thin, and just 1600 kilometres from north to south. In the middle, where it looks like it's been squeezed by a giant hand, it's a mere 50 kilometres wide. It's mostly tropical, on the same climatic belt as Nicaragua and the Republic of Congo and, as Australian soldiers were to uncomfortably discover, the monsoon season can make life sodden and miserable. But those rains encourage the cultivation of rice and, in a country that has always been heavily populated, rice can mean life itself.

Vietnamese history has one, repetitive plotline – struggle. That narrow stretch of land has seen centuries-long battles; first to establish a nation and then to defend it against enemies within and without. It may be the reason that the Vietnamese are unafraid of a fight and don't seem to care that they consistently take on opponents well above their size.

Their first bout was with a heavyweight; the country that looms directly above them on the map – China. A hundred or so years before the birth of Christ, the legendary Han dynasty did the impossible and unified China, then turned their gaze south. They overwhelmed Vietnam and ruled it as a colonial province for the next 1000 years.

But the Vietnamese are nothing if not patient and eventually regained their independence. The Chinese, who rather fancied this fertile land, tried to reconquer them again and again and again, but the Vietnamese would not accept China's heavy hand for long. Seemingly, whenever they were needed, new heroes would rise up out of the countryside and lead the revolt. All Vietnamese know and revere the names and deeds of these warrior ancestors who defended their motherland against the invader, and there are monuments and temples in their honour still scattered across the country. Perhaps the unwelcome guests who arrived later in the 20th century should have kept that in mind.

To live in Vietnam was to survive as best you could in an uncertain and dangerous world – wars, social upheaval and hunger were constants and the best way to stay alive lay in combined strength. The family was stronger than the individual, the village stronger than the family, the nation stronger than the village, and each in their turn bowed to the discipline and needs of the greater group. Family was the basis of everything and only through membership of the family could you have worth in this life. It's a belief that's still at the very core of Vietnamese society.

> We were bound up in a very strict understanding of the family and everything in life we learned from our parents. We had to obey every instruction given to us by our father. The father was the 'big boss' in the family, like a king. Everybody had to obey his instructions. All the people who lived in the village were like a big family. We were surrounded by bamboo fences and lived under our own rules, our own instructions. It was a good time for everybody to live in peace and everybody knew each other. No stranger could enter without being noticed

> and we lived in peace and order and strictly followed Vietnamese traditions and customs.
>
> COLONEL VO DAI TON, SPECIAL FORCES

Discipline, patience and endurance are the birth gifts given to every Vietnamese. They just hate to give up and, even when they are apparently defeated, they will regroup and come at you again from another angle and then another, until it ends in either death or victory. As they would do later with other would-be conquerors, they outlasted the Chinese, driving them away for good in the 15th century.

But the Vietnamese are also enterprising (some might even say cunning), and before removing them, they took from the Chinese everything they considered valuable. For the next 900 years Vietnam mirrored much of Chinese political, social and administrative life. Just as the Chinese did, they had an emperor who was all things to all people, even acting as the intermediary between his subjects and heaven. They followed the Confucian doctrine, just as China did, and education was valued above all other achievements. The scholars, the mandarins, ran the country, and learning was the main path to power, status and money.

> From the Chinese, thousands of years ago, we were taught to respect three things, it came from Confucianism. The first one is the king, the second one is the teacher and the third one is your parents. When your father wished to discipline you, you would lie down on the floor and he would whip you. As a young child, when I would do something wrong, he would say, 'Lie down. I am going to teach you the right thing.' And it would be how to write properly, or not to disturb the neighbours, not to go and steal fruit, not to go and do something wrong with the other children. And after he said that, he would give you some whip.
>
> VAN NHUNG TRAN, MEDICAL CORPS

But it was a decaying society. By the 18th century, the great European empires of Spain, Portugal, France and England were pushing each other out of the way in their greed to grab as much of the southern world as they could. Vietnamese society had begun to fragment (as had China) between warring factions and opposing rulers. The country was again in turmoil and vulnerable to conquest, only this time the pathway in was through the cross of Jesus Christ.

French Catholic priests arrived in Vietnam to set up permanent missions and begin recruitment and conversion. Unfortunately they also instructed their newly baptised Vietnamese followers to give their first loyalty to God rather than the emperor. The inevitable happened – hostility from the ruling class, and imprisonment and murder of the missionaries. Retribution by the West was inescapable.

In one of those curious coincidences that prove history has all the best stories, the American naval ship, USS *Constitution*, landed in Da Nang in 1845 and a company of United States marines was sent to rescue a French bishop who had been captured by the Vietnamese. The marines would land at Da Nang again 120 years later, only then they would wade through the surf to join the Vietnam War. At least the first time they arrived, the death toll was low. The church continued to send pioneer priests to Vietnam and, for a while, an uneasy truce existed.

But behind the missionaries came the merchants and the moneymakers and they convinced the French government that unless they wanted to be considered a second-rate power they should grab Vietnam while they could. In 1858, using the excuse of aggression against French clergy, Napoleon III sent in his navy and by the 1880s France had captured the lot – all of Vietnam and Cambodia under the newly coined title, French Indochina. Laos was added in 1893.

There's a theory of history that suggests all colonisation took one of two forms. One led to permanent settlement, where the land was taken from its traditional owners by the colonists, cultivated, and a new country began to form. Australia and America were like that. The other kind was even more exploitative – take out all the money and resources you can, build nothing of substance and bugger the consequences. Vietnam under the French was closer to that.

Pursuing wealth at speed, the French upended Vietnamese traditions, agriculture and society. They built rail and road links and a system of canals and dikes, but they also took control of rice cultivation, introducing landlords and tenants, manipulating the market and, in the process, destroyed 1000 years of village ownership and harmony.

They turned village culture into a Western-style class system with the French at the top and the Vietnamese at the bottom. The old Confucian way, where education determined your social position, was replaced by class differences based on economics and race. The Vietnamese, the French believed, were to be pitied as a poor, backward and beaten people, while they on the other hand, were rightfully masters of all they surveyed. But they could not extinguish the passion the Vietnamese held for the land nor their desire to regain it. Nor did they count on the skill and power of just one man.

> Nothing is more precious than independence and liberty.
>
> Ho Chi Minh

When you visit Hanoi, the capital city of the Socialist Republic of Vietnam, there are several things you are expected to do:

take a boat around the fabulous Ha Long Bay, risk your life dodging motorcycles in the narrow streets of the Old Quarter, take in a performance of the Water Puppets – and visit the body of Ho Chi Minh. Ho was the first President of the Republic and after death his body was preserved, against his will, for the edification of his people. You can visit him almost any day, except for two months of the year when he's removed for maintenance.

His final resting place is in possibly the ugliest building in Vietnam, in the middle of the city, in a place called the Ho Chi Minh Mausoleum Complex. To enter, you follow a red line on the ground ('Only one person on the red line at a time, not two!') and are relieved of your bag and camera. After the electronic security control you move on inexorably towards the tall, grey, monolithic building standing on its own in the middle of the square.

Visitors are kept moving at a steady clip, up marble stairs, into the entrance, more stairs, then into *the room*. You move around three sides of a rectangle looking down at Ho where he lies in a glass sarcophagus, an army guard in a white dress uniform at each corner. He looks rather unreal, like a tall doll. Simple, black clothes, a wisp of a beard still grazing his chest.

Then it's over. You're ushered outside, wondering. Thousands of people do this daily and though it's probably just another tourist stop for the backpackers and tour groups, the many Vietnamese who come each day are visibly affected by their pilgrimage. Ho is their Winston Churchill, their George Washington, their Mao Zedong. He is father and mother to the land and dangerously close to a state religion.

His story is a curious mix of myth, guesswork and known fact. He was born around 1890 as Nguyen Van Thanh ('Nguyen who will be victorious') and his father was a minor official at the Imperial Court in Hue who was dismissed by the French for dissent. His mother, so the legend goes, died in jail after being caught stealing weapons from the French and Ho got his subversive training wheels as a nine-year-old, carrying messages for the revolutionaries in his district. He left Vietnam at the age of 20 on a merchant ship, with the lowly job of galley boy.

Travelling the world, he spent time in North America, Europe, Africa, Australia and London, where, during World War I, he worked for a few years as a pastry chef under the tutelage of the French master chef, Escoffier. Finally, he ended up in Paris.

In one of those twisted ironies that abound in Vietnam's story, Ho became one of the founders of the French Communist Party. Mostly self-educated, he was a rising star in the radical-Communist world and the talent spotters in Moscow encouraged him to come to Russia. He was formally trained at the gloriously named 'University of the Toilers of the East' as a covert agent for Communist International and sent into China. Now at last, he could begin his long and patient road towards the liberation of Vietnam.

From southern China, he coordinated the peasants and workers in Vietnam to take mass actions, just as he had been trained to do. By 1930, his influence was strong enough to unite all the smaller dissident groups into the Indochinese Communist Party and the trouble really began. North Vietnam was enduring a famine and Ho and the Communists took advantage of a wide-ranging peasant uprising in May 1930. In a small taste of the ruthless killing that was to come, they executed Vietnamese officials in the pay of the French, as well as local landholders, trying to encourage a full-scale revolt. It didn't succeed.

Retaliation by the French was swift and, in the year it took them to regain control, the conservative estimate is that 10 000 Vietnamese died at their hands. Ho made his way back to Moscow, attended yet more Communist schools and then went back to China in 1938, to join Mao Zedong's army. Two years later, he slipped across the border into Vietnam for the first time in 30 years, now called Ho Chi Minh ('Ho, the bringer of light').

It wasn't too difficult for him to escape detection for the world was now consumed by World War II.

While bombs and madness destroyed much of Europe, Vietnam remained relatively unscathed. In 1940 the Japanese invaded, quickly overwhelming all of Indochina. France had by now surrendered to Germany and the new puppet government in Paris, the Vichy French, cooperated with the Japanese as the caretakers of Vietnam. Every Vietnamese nationalist organisation saw this as their chance to win the revolution against a down and out France, but only one party was fully prepared to seize control – the Communists. By 1940, they had an intricate network of support and influence across all of Vietnam and much of southern China. And there were Communist cadres in most villages, waiting for the day of revolution.

Ho and his colleagues had learned well in Moscow; they could organise, indoctrinate and lead the people. They'd adapted techniques of mass propaganda from the Russians and they had willing listeners for their new message – independence. It was clever in its simplicity and masterful in what it hid.

The bad things in your life, they said to the peasants, are due to only one thing – the French persecutors. We must get rid of them and the best way to do that is to fight. Or as Ho more poetically put it, 'It is better to sacrifice everything than to live in slavery.' Not a word about Communism or 'international solidarity with the forces of the proletariat'. Not yet. After all, you couldn't practise Communism if you didn't have a country to practise it in. The 'revolutionary transformation of the world into a Communist state' was out of favour for the moment and 'national liberation' was in.

Ho even ditched the name of the Indochinese Communist Party. He and his men disappeared into caves near the Chinese border and reappeared as the Vietnamese Independence League, otherwise known as the Viet Minh ('United for Freedom'). This was to be the guerrilla machine that would sweep the French from Vietnam. A 10 000 man force was created and battled the Japanese with modest but growing success. Cleverly, Ho invited the other nationalist groups to fight under the Viet Minh banner and regain their country from foreigners. They accepted.

Now he was leading the fight for Vietnam's independence from behind a united front, the main man in the revolutionary struggle. And other, important new friends had appeared – the Americans. Before the CIA existed there was the OSS, the Office of Strategic Services, American spooks working covertly behind Japanese lines. Ho and his men provided them with intelligence and practical assistance, even rescuing downed American pilots. In return, the OSS provided some weaponry and ammunition and, more importantly, they gave Ho the oxygen of publicity. American newspapers launched Ho into the world's view as the leading Vietnamese nationalist and an ally of the US. Ho was 'a good guy', at least while the war was on.

But the end of World War II in Vietnam brought with it a chaotic nightmare. Smelling the wind, the Vichy French administration abruptly switched sides at the last minute and attempted to fight the Japanese who had them disarmed and imprisoned within 24 hours. There was no functioning government, so Bao Dai, the last Vietnamese emperor, was declared Chief of State by the Japanese and the entire country toppled into a tragic, operatic farce.

Infrastructure failed and the telephone and transport systems collapsed. Businesses went under, banks closed, nothing worked. Everywhere people were sick, frightened and near hysteria. Starvation and disease, already widespread, turned lethal in the north when floods took much of the rice crop and the Japanese the rest. Two million people died, reduced to eating bark and leaves.

Finally, the atom bombs were dropped, Japan surrendered and Vietnam was completely leaderless. Ho was ready.

The Viet Minh rapidly seized control of much of the country. Ho Chi Minh was elected President of the grandly titled Provisional Government of the Democratic Republic of Vietnam and the guerrillas poured into Hanoi, taking it without firing a shot. On 3 September 1945, half a million people pushed their way into Hanoi's main square to watch something they had never seen, a Vietnamese government take power.

In the hush, Ho stepped forward to read his new Declaration of Independence. At a time when the life expectancy in Vietnam was just 35, Ho at 55 looked like, and was, an old man. To most of the crowd, he was also a bit of a mystery. He had only appeared in their lives two weeks before. Uniformed American officers from the OSS stood behind him, all smiles and congratulations for they knew what was coming.

'All men are created equal,' read the new president. 'They are endowed by their creator with certain inalienable rights; among these are Life, Liberty, and the pursuit of Happiness.'

In a stunning piece of plagiarism, Ho had appropriated the American Declaration. He went on to make the next step clear to everyone: 'The whole Vietnamese people, animated by a common purpose, are determined to fight to the bitter end against any attempt by the French colonialists to reconquer their country'. His mausoleum was erected on the spot from which he delivered those words.

It was a suitably grand gesture, but it was doomed to fail. If the Americans had taken their chance then to foster their relationship with Ho, it's likely that the Vietnam War would never have happened. But other agendas and bigger egos were in play elsewhere in the world and, as a result, millions of people would die. From this point on Vietnam would suffer the fate of the little bloke caught in the big blokes' fight – you get squeezed and bashed from both sides.

No one seemed to be able to get it right. The victorious Allies, nervous about the Viet Minh and their brand-new country, sent in the Chinese Nationalist Army to occupy northern Vietnam and the British arrived to accept the Japanese surrender in the south. Both decisions were disastrous. The Chinese just wanted to steal anything that wasn't tied down and the British were commanded by a certain General Gracey, who distinguished himself by refusing to deal with the 'upstart natives', otherwise known as the Vietnamese.

Gracey released and then rearmed the French troops who went on a vengeful killing rampage against the Vietnamese. The Viet Minh retaliated and Gracey set all available troops, including the still-armed Japanese, against them. While the rest of the world took a deep breath and began to emerge from the horror of the war, women and children were put to death in the streets of Saigon.

The French expected to return to Vietnam in complete control. Arrogant and deliberately ignorant of Vietnamese desires, they chose not to recognise a truth that other countries did – that the time of colonisation and Western dominance in Asia was at an end. Humiliated during World War II, they were desperate to hold on to their fading dream of being a world power and could neither believe nor accept that their time was over.

Once the Allied forces left Vietnam, de Gaulle, the French leader, sent 80 000 troops to Saigon and though Ho attempted to find a compromise, the path was set. Just as they had with the Chinese thousands of years before, the Vietnamese would never accept French control all over again. In 1947 the First Indochina War began. It was time to choose sides.

> I was in elementary school and my father was a mandarin at the royal court in Hue. In 1945, the Viet Minh issued an order for everybody to withdraw from the towns, because of the war against the French. And we moved from Da Nang back to our small village, where our father and mother had come from, about 35 kilometres away. My father resigned from the

royal court and refused to work for the French, because he did not like their domination.

My eight brothers and my sister joined the Viet Minh to fight against the French. At that time the Viet Minh was mostly composed of nationalists, not Communists. My brothers and sister were involved with propaganda; they would travel around and spread the nationalistic cause. They were too young to be fighting soldiers, so they carried propaganda leaflets, and they attended classes about the revolution.

My father and mother told me I should not stand away from the revolution because we must end French domination. They taught me the lesson of patriotism. For a while I attended *La Providence*, a lycée where I was taught by French priests. We learned about Catholicism, the French language and literature, but nothing about the history of Vietnam. My father taught me my country's history.

Under the French occupation, people were exploited. We were considered servants of the French people. Only French-speaking people could have a good job and they had to serve the French with loyalty. The French always acted like they were the big boss.

COLONEL VO DAI TON

Like Colonel Vo, virtually all Vietnamese, whether Communist or not, hated French rule and wanted freedom. For the next seven years France dithered about in Vietnam, fighting the Viet Minh on one side and on the other installing the pitiable Emperor Bao Dai as head of the newly created 'State of Vietnam' in a feeble attempt to convince the people they would one day be free. No one was fooled.

While the French held the cities, Ho and his troops went back to the mountains, the jungles and the villages. If the French followed them in they were ambushed and annihilated. Even when they won a battle, they surrendered the captured ground back to the Viet Minh within a few days, unable to hold it. With their trucks, artillery and machinery they could not react quickly nor chase the disappearing guerrillas. As a popular phrase at the time described it, the French military were 'prisoners of the roads'.

Ho wanted 'a people's war' and that's what he achieved, capturing popular support across Vietnam. It was all based on nationalist slogans – free the people, free the land, remove the imperialist oppressors . . . and it worked. Propaganda teams were in every village, exhorting the people to work harder, to fight longer in the cause of 'The Resistance War'. The rice field was renamed the battlefield and the hoe and the plough, weapons. Everything that was made, grown, thought or planned was for the revolution. Where once the village had concentrated on its own health and survival, now it was all for the nation. All together they sang:

People, rise up and exterminate the enemy!
With hearts enthusiastic and passionate to carry out
the revolution,
Struggle for a prosperous life.

It's not a particularly catchy piece but the power of belonging and a shared dream after years of suppression swept them all along.

But mankind has trouble remaining steadfast and noble, and the pure motive of freedom soon became corrupted with the possibility of power. As the French slowly bled to death, the face of the Communist leadership darkened. They did not want to split a newly independent Vietnam with their political enemies so they began to murder them, one by one. The fight for independence was their path to power, the conquest by which they would turn the country into a 'workers' paradise'. 'The nation has its roots in the people,' said Ho. But only if you agreed with him.

The Communists were thorough in everything they did, even executions and murder, and no transgression went unpunished.

> My mother was captured and killed by the Viet Minh. They were still called the Viet Minh then, even though we knew that behind them were the Communists. She was executed because she was the wife of a mandarin and her sons had left the Viet Minh.
>
> We had become very poor in the village and my brothers went back to the town, to make some money. The Viet Minh accused my brothers as traitors, but because they could not capture them, they caught and killed my mother instead, to take revenge for my brothers not obeying their instructions and staying with the revolution.
>
> The Viet Minh ambushed her on the way to Da Nang and chopped her into small pieces with machetes. Two of my uncles were also killed with her. The sentence was that she was a criminal because she had too many sons serving against them. She just disappeared. We were just waiting and waiting for her but she did not return. After a long time, we knew she must have been killed. My brothers took me back to town to stay with them and to go to school.
>
> We did not discover her fate for 12 years. One of my brothers became a major in the army and he was appointed as the chief of our province. He asked a lot of questions of the villagers and they showed him the place where my mother and my two uncles were killed. My brother called back all the brothers and we dug and found the small bones of my mother and two uncles. And we buried her, after 12 years. My father died then, of sadness.
>
> COLONEL VO DAI TON

> You can kill 10 of my men for every one I kill of yours, but even at those odds, you will lose and I will win.
>
> Ho Chi Minh

In 1949 the Communists won control of China. Communist insurgencies broke out in Burma, Malaya and Indonesia and the hammer and sickle was flying over most of Eastern Europe. The world was dividing into two and Vietnam became enmeshed in the titanic struggle of the Cold War.

The Soviets recognised Ho's alternative government in 1950 and, a week later, the Americans did the same with Bao Dai's state. The Vietnamese Communists quickly adopted the language and the brutal methods of the Red Revolution. 'Rectification' campaigns 'purified' the party and thousands of people were put through 'thought reform sessions'. Beatings, imprisonment and murder were daily events. The Korean War ended and, freed from its demands, China sent arms to Ho, so the Americans poured military aid into the south. The great powers were having a war by proxy and this small country could not sustain the pressure. Something had to give.

In the spring of 1954 the French committed their last great blunder. They stationed thousands of men at an outpost called Dien Bien Phu, trying to tempt the Viet Minh into open battle. They believed, as others would later, that when faced with the full might of a Western army, with all its technology and firepower, there was no way the Vietnamese could win. It was a fatal piece of arrogance.

The French were in a valley, completely vulnerable to artillery fire from the mountains that surrounded them but their military commanders ridiculed the notion that anyone could get the giant guns up those steep slopes. What they meant was *they* couldn't do it. But the Vietnamese could . . . and did. Quietly and secretly, mostly at night, hundreds of Viet Minh pulled, pushed and dragged their artillery a centimetre at a time till they got them in position, camouflaging their presence from French view. It was a bold, stunning achievement.

The Vietnamese bombarded the French forces from above and sent in wave after wave of suicide attacks, overwhelming French resistance. Artillery fire destroyed the airstrip, choking off the supply routes until the French were all dead, dying, or waiting helplessly for the final blow.

The Americans had been watching the French plummet towards disaster at Dien Bien Phu with increasing frustration and anxiety. In response to desperate French pleas for help, the Pentagon wanted a series of air strikes to save the besieged troops. Even nuclear weapons were considered.

While Washington agonised over what to do, thousands of men from both sides kept right on dying. Finally, the Americans refused to provide assistance. Military intervention in Vietnam under the stained flag of French colonialism was just too hard an ask for the US. They knew with certainty though that, sooner rather than later, they'd be back.

Without help from outside, the French forces were doomed. Perhaps the most symbolic death was that of the French artillery commander, Colonel Piroth, who had promised his men that the Vietnamese simply could not lift big guns onto the mountain tops. He stepped into his dugout, placed a hand grenade over his heart and pulled the pin.

The garrison at Dien Bien Phu was overwhelmed on 7 May 1954. *La sale guerre*, 'the dirty war', was over, and 100 years of French colonial rule came to an end. The methods of the Viet Minh had often been as detestable as the French, but to their own people and others they appeared to have the noblest of aims – freedom for their country. Their victory was celebrated in many places, not least because it *was* a remarkable achievement.

They had begun the war with no transport, no heavy guns, not a plane nor a tank. Their soldiers were poorly armed and their rations and equipment were barely enough. Yet they had defeated the army of one of the great Western empires and brought another Communist state into the world.

In Australia the press and the politicians reacted with passion to the French defeat. 'Indochina disaster is critical for world,' screamed the Melbourne *Age*, 'with the fall of the French fortress of Dien Bien Phu, Asia and the Western world are again brought to a point of crisis.' The Australian External Affairs Minister, Richard Casey, let rip with an oldie but a goodie, evoking the twin bogeymen of yellow hordes and reds under the bed in one sentence: 'With the black cloud of Communist China hanging to the north, we must make sure that our children do not end up pulling rickshaws with hammer and sickle signs on the side.' The Commies were clearly coming. But there was a juicy Russian spy scandal going on in Canberra and an election looming, so Australia turned its gaze away.

Others could not. The world powers gathered in Geneva for a conference that would, among other things, settle Vietnam's future. The Geneva Accords, as they became known, did at last agree that Vietnam was to become an independent country. But that was where the good news ended. Until elections were held two years on, the country would be divided into two, North and South, with the dividing line at the seventeenth parallel. All Viet Minh soldiers would go to the North, all those who fought for the French to the South. Civilians could go either way. Around one million people moved house and home, mostly Catholics travelling south, though thousands of Communist cadres and hidden caches of weapons remained behind in South Vietnam, insurance against the future.

It was a weak-kneed, ill-omened compromise. Though the Soviet Union, China, France, Britain and Ho all signed the Accords, the US and South Vietnam refused to promise they would obey them. Then, the very next day after the signing in Geneva, a new anti-Communist alliance was announced – SEATO, the South-East Asia Treaty Organization. Its members were the US, Britain, New Zealand, France, Pakistan, Thailand, the Philippines and Australia. As well as guaranteeing mutual defence, they extended their protection to Laos, Cambodia and Vietnam. Ho and the Communists were in their sights.

> As long as our country was split in half I did not believe that the Communists would ever allow us to have a peaceful reunification. My father was very fearful of them because he had witnessed the terrible things they had done. He understood that the name of the Viet Minh may have been non-Communist but their actions were not like those other nationalist parties before them. They would kill anyone who was against them or did not follow them and this was the lesson my father gave me from the time I was born.
>
> VO MINH CUONG, SOUTH VIETNAMESE AIR FORCE

The Americans immediately began to fortify the South, pouring in aid money. And they had a brand-new partner. The Emperor, Bao Dai, had been deposed by the son of a mandarin, Ngo Dinh Diem. He had been a figure on the fringes of Vietnamese politics for some time and now seized his chance. He was a pious Catholic and a patriot, committed to Vietnamese nationalism, as long as it was on his terms.

Diem was convinced of his own moral superiority and not attracted to compromise. One of his favourite sayings was 'I know what is best for my people.' He wasn't being fatherly; he believed it as only the autocratic can and he ruthlessly removed any opposition. Soon after taking power, and with the support of the US, he announced that there would be no national elections, renamed the South as another country, held his own (rigged) elections and declared himself president.

So now there were two. In the north was the Democratic Republic of Vietnam, led by Ho, with its capital in Hanoi, and in the south was the newly minted Republic of Vietnam, led by Diem from his capital, Saigon. Two austere bachelors, both unashamedly authoritarian, both ruthless, both possessed of extraordinary drive and vision and both sworn enemies. Poor, ill-starred Vietnam.

The North deteriorated into a harsh dictatorship as the Communists instigated a program of land redistribution under the insidious title of 'Land Reform Through Mass Mobilization'. For two years landlords and 'rich' peasants were accused of crimes, tried, sentenced to imprisonment or forced labour, or put to death. Any peasant who owned more than two acres of land was vulnerable.

There was no justice in any of this; it was a systematic, deliberate extermination of a social class, an eradication of known or potential enemies. Fifteen thousand people died and around 100 000 were imprisoned or deported. It ripped the heart out of North Vietnam and only Ho's intervention, when he realised it had gone too far, brought it to an end.

> In South Vietnam most people did not like the Communists. I really mean it. They knew that if the Communists were in power, nobody could have their own house, no more 'property'. One leader, one party and the same thinking. From the top to the bottom, you must all say the same words, not any other words. There was no freedom and we didn't like that... The people in the North were Communists because they were forced to be.
>
> VAN NHUNG TRAN

In the South, Diem, who already had a leaning towards authoritarian government, established what was effectively another dictatorship centred on him and his family. He hunted down those who had supported the Viet Minh and his police arrested them, beat them and killed them. Corruption and brutality were common, supported by secret police, controlled elections and state-run propaganda. It reached a point where there was as little freedom on the side of Vietnam that was supposed to be fighting for democracy as there was in the Communist North.

> All of my brothers joined the Republic of Vietnam Army at various times under President Diem and remained in it till 1975. We believed in Diem, that he was a good man, a good leader. But the regime became corrupt because of his family ties, it was a family gang. I believe he was an honest man but he was surrounded by too many corrupt officials.
>
> COLONEL VO DAI TON

For a while, Diem was successful. His harsh measures were taking their toll on the Communist organisation still in the South and the leadership in Hanoi could see that unless they intervened, their long-held ambitions would fail. They issued new orders for their operatives to come out of hiding and guerrilla resistance, supported from Hanoi, broke out in South Vietnam around 1960, taking off like a forest fire. Assassinations of government officials were a daily event and law and order in the provinces broke down.

All the while, America was stepping deeper and deeper into the morass, committing more men and money every day. By 1962, the bill was in the billions. It seemed as if the Americans were only dimly aware of the complexities, sure in their belief that the whole thing was part of 'global Communist expansionism' (it wasn't) and that if only they gave enough support to the South Vietnamese government, Diem would be able to establish a proper democracy supported enthusiastically by his people (he couldn't). After all they had endured under the French, even after finally achieving independence, the people of Vietnam were still not free, still not unified, and in danger of losing both their country and their lives.

It's like that moment as a child when you stood on the edge of the diving tower at the local pool, swaying slightly, the glittering blue water below you. You know you don't want to do it but you will, you will. It's way too embarrassing to climb back down. And as you lean forwards just a little, you pass the point of gravity; it's too late now and you're committed. It may result in a graceful swan dive or a humiliating bellyflop, but you're going down. North and South Vietnam stood teetering on the edge of all-out civil war. It wouldn't take too much of a push.

How much of this story the 30 Australian soldiers from the Training Team were aware of when they boarded the plane for Vietnam in Sydney in 1962 was not recorded. Probably very little, and it would be unfair to expect otherwise. After all, their countrymen and women knew even less, if they cared at all. Those men were simply professional soldiers, sent by their government to a country they had barely heard of, whose history and culture was far outside their own. And though they, and the others who followed them, would acquit themselves as well as their fathers and grandfathers had, the anguish and hurt of our Vietnam War was about to begin.

III

HISTORIANS WILL RECALL THIS DAY WITH TEARS

> Without any inhibitions of any kind, I make it quite clear that Australia looks to America, free of any pangs as to our traditional links or kinship with the United Kingdom.
>
> PRIME MINISTER JOHN CURTIN, 1941

On a soft, summer night in 1962, tens of thousands of people in Perth turned on all their lights – porch lights, house lights, office lights, *any* light. It was all for the benefit of one man, American astronaut John Glenn. Squashed uncomfortably inside a Mercury spacecraft, he was enduring the first American orbital mission into space. And he was about to pass over Perth. As the people in the city looked anxiously upwards, Glenn looked down. 'I can see the outline of a town,' he crackled over the radio. 'And a very bright light to the south of it.' With a talent for the obvious, Glenn dubbed Perth, 'The City of Lights'. We sighed with relief. Australia was part of what was happening. We had been recognised, and not just by anybody, but by our old friend and ally, the United States of America.

It's been a strange relationship, the one between us and the Yanks. It still is. Lopsided in power, more important to us than them, and characterised by our childish behaviour of flattering them while they're looking and muttering criticism and rebellion the moment they turn away. The 'cultural cringe' it was called in the '60s.

One thing we were not in doubt about was that the Americans had saved us in World War II. Everybody said so, every parent, every teacher and every member of the RSL who mentioned the Battle of the Coral Sea and the atom bomb in respectful tones. 'They stopped the invasion,' they all said, but then complained about the other invasion that had taken place, by stealth.

After the war, America and its products had begun to conquer the Western world and we were as vulnerable to them as anyone else. From your first Roy Rogers cowboy suit to the cool of the television series 77 *Sunset Strip*, all things American seemed exotic and desirable. It was mostly pop culture and superficial in its effects, but we loved it. Courtesy of the Americans, we now had strip clubs, drive-ins, motels, expressways, billboards, a forest of neon and our very own DJs like Ward 'Pally' Austin in Sydney, emulating his American cousins with his catchphrase sign-off, 'A rickapootie and a fandoodlie!' Blue jeans were everywhere, though if you wore them to church on Sunday, you would land yourself the inevitable lecture about respect for God and the perils of 'imitating the Yanks'.

Our leaders, however, were not troubled by insidious American influence or the uncomfortable position of clinging onto Yankee coat-tails. They welcomed it. Unnerved by the spread of Communism in South-East Asia, they subscribed to the strategic doctrine of 'forward defence' – in other words, fight the enemy anywhere but on Australian shores. The trouble was we had neither enough men nor resources to do it on our own. We needed the Americans to get involved in the neighbourhood and Vietnam provided the chance. The more men, money and matériel they poured into the war, the more committed to the region they became and the more secure Prime Minister Menzies and his cabinet felt. Of course, we had to reciprocate, to show good faith with American policy and gain credit. The 30 men of that first Australian Army Training Team Vietnam (AATTV) were the token we used.

The Americans had originally asked for navy and air force commitment as well as the army, but our defence chiefs had vetoed this. The 30 advisers of the Team were seen as a workable compromise. Tellingly, even with this first, small involvement, Australian politicians began the litany of lies and half-truths that would characterise our Vietnam years.

The Defence Minister, Athol Townley, issued a statement in which he said that the members of the Team were going at the invitation of the South Vietnamese government. It wasn't true. At the time, the press dutifully reported his words without comment. Vietnam, like Malaya, where Australian forces were also involved, was of little concern to us and Menzies did his best to keep it that way. In a televised *Talk to the Nation*, Menzies showed the viewing audience a map and pointing at it said, 'Down here in the southeast of Asia in L-A-O-S, most of us call it Laos, but I believe correctly it ought to be called "Louse", but anyhow there it is, and this country is a peaceful rural country . . . yet it is bedevilled today by civil war, by Communist pressure from the north . . . The same kind of trouble arises in relation to South Vietnam. A very gallant little country. An outpost of defence against Communism.' It was a vintage, father-figure performance. 'Trust me. I know things that you don't and it's best if you leave it to me.' We swallowed it whole.

Still, the politicians who sent the Team could have had no idea of the almost legendary status this unit would achieve. First into Vietnam it would be the last to leave, 10 years later. It was a unique group of men that would become the most highly decorated unit in Australian military history (four Victoria Crosses) and when the Vietnam War ended for Australia, so would the Team's existence.

> I was a professional soldier. I was in the army to serve; it was the only war that was on at the time. Everybody wanted to go. I would say that over 80 per cent of my contemporaries wanted to go to war, that's all we were there for... We had been training for counterinsurgency warfare for years with Malaya and Borneo or whatever, so it was the war that we were having, the one to go to.
>
> PETER JARRATT, AATTV

Professional was the right word. The larrikin image of the two-up playing, volunteer soldier from World War II had been left behind in Korea and Malaya and a disciplined, well-trained Australian Defence Force had taken its place. The Team was handpicked from the army – career soldiers, many with jungle fighting experience. They were volunteers, senior non-commissioned officers (sergeants and warrant officers) and officers – men who understood command and training.

But from the beginning, this assignment was to be like no other they had known. They were gathered together for intensive training at the School of Military Intelligence, located at Georges Heights in Sydney. It was mostly predictable classes – Communist warfare strategy, the history of Vietnam, cultural differences and so on. But then there was the small matter of the euphemistically titled, Code of Conduct Course.

> The course was... mainly run in the old military fortifications there which was handy because they could be rigged up to be cells or a prisoner of war camp compound. We were taken down in these underground ammunition storage areas, there was water on the floor and there were rats running around, you were always hooded when you were taken anywhere.
>
> ... When we were 'captured', you were stripped off and they gave you uniforms appropriate to a prisoner of war and these were normally old baggy uniforms that wouldn't fit you,

so they were trying to demoralise you and humiliate you so you had to hold your trousers together because there were no belts or anything provided. And then you were moved from these cells, from one to another with these hoods on.

All the guards were dressed in Chinese Communist kit with burp guns and red stars on their helmets, and they were all of oriental appearance... And there was a constant playing of Communist music through the cell loudspeaker... The only thing you were allowed to read was the *Tribune*, which was then the Communist newspaper circulating in Australia...

I remember one of my armoured corps mates, I walked in at one stage and he was in a cage about four foot by four foot, all bundled into this metal cage upside down on the floor. Very professionally done, to the stage when you got to the end of being a POW, you thought, 'I will get these people when I get out of here because I know they are only regular soldiers and I will really get to them and sort them out.'

PETER JARRATT

While some soldiers were being tested as POWs, others were role-playing on the opposite side.

Interrogation and indoctrination was my speciality. I was basically dressed up as a Chinese colonel and I would be the nice guy. I used to run the nightshift. I'd come on at midnight and everyone would have a file and everything you ever did or said would be recorded and down on the file. So I'd spend a couple of hours studying your background in the file...

I would specifically design specialist treatment for various officers. The idea that the military relies a lot on rank and exterior symbols such as badges or rank, we strip it all off right down to stark naked, it doesn't hold for much. Many can't stand that. Senior officers don't like it – it has a great impact on them... it was initially quite embarrassing. I got

> people to sign all sorts of dreadful confessions and oh dear. And then you'd publish these up on the wall so everyone else would see it. No, it would be turmoil.
>
> MATTHEW D'ARCY, AATTV

The slightly farcical routines continued. The Americans were very keen for Team members to be seen wearing Australian uniforms with 'Australia' flashes on the shoulders. It all helped the illusion that there were 'international' forces contributing to the war in Vietnam. But when they quietly left Australia on 29 July 1962, they were dressed in civilian clothes and each one of them was carrying a large, brown paper bag. They were on a standard Qantas flight to Singapore and Singapore refused to allow uniformed soldiers from another country on its territory or in its airport. Once their plane left Singapore for Saigon though, a line of men dressed in Hawaiian shirts and combat boots began trekking to the aircraft toilet, reappearing in uniform as Australian warriors. It was a bizarre charade that continued on all flights throughout the war. When the uniforms went on, the next stop was Saigon, an arrival they all remember.

> To fly into Tan Son Nhut Airport the aircraft would have to come at high altitude and sharp angle because of any enemy fire coming in from the surrounding areas... and you could see the reinforcements, the sandbagged areas around the strip, the aircraft hangars were protected and bagged, the fighter aircraft on line, protected with the anti-mortar shelters, that sort of thing.
>
> But I suppose the most telling thing was when I arrived, we get off the aircraft, collect our gear, walk out the front of Tan Son Nhut and here are the rows and rows of graves of the French Foreign Legion that have been killed in Vietnam. That really brought back the reality of what Vietnam was about, that was my introduction.
>
> ANTHONY THORP, AATTV

Once they arrived, the members of the Team were wined, dined and kitted out by the Americans. Vietnam was awash with weapons and equipment and the Australians were encouraged to choose whatever they wished, straight off the shelf. Australian soldiers have always been badly equipped in one way or another, and like their fathers in World War II, these men took advantage of American largesse. Each one ended up with a combination of uniforms, field gear and various rifles and pistols. The final touch was a brand-new pair of American aviator sunglasses.

Then they were off, mostly in small groups, to training establishments all over South Vietnam, from Saigon to the DMZ (the demilitarised zone that separated North and South). Their mission was to train virtually everyone who was fighting against the Communists – from the soldiers of the Army of the Republic of South Vietnam (ARVN), to the bamboo-stake wielding villagers of the local defence units. Even the CIA was given some Australians to deploy in covert missions along Vietnam's borders. All the Australians were answerable to their commander in Saigon, Colonel Ted Serong, though ultimately even he was under American command. But American methods were very different to their own, as they learned when they met the American commander, General Charles Timmes.

> The eye-opener for me was when General Timmes stood up... and he gave us a briefing. And there were Americans there as well, of course. It was chock-a-block full of Americans... And Timmes stood up the front, it was 40 years ago, but it was, 'God is on our side. The Communist pagans, we will defeat them. It is our role, our mission in the world.' And I thought, 'Oh, dear, oh, dear.' And I walked out of that and thought, 'What strange people!'...
>
> He must have harangued us for 20 minutes about how God was on our side and I didn't think God was on my side, I wasn't sure there was any God in any case, but I wasn't sure that he was sitting behind me at all... And then Ted Serong

> had his briefing. He said, 'Fellows, I know you will do your best, look after yourselves, I will see you soon.' That was his briefing. I thought, 'Thank God.'
>
> PETER JARRATT

God may not have been on anyone's side but he was certainly being claimed by a few. As the Australians fanned out across South Vietnam they got their first, hard look at the web of intrigue, corruption and just plain madness that had become the administration of President Ngo Dinh Diem.

Diem was spiralling into disaster, distrusted by the Americans and hated by his own people. No matter that his country was being shredded around him, the president, a devout Catholic, was determined that the good citizens of South Vietnam would maintain strict, moral standards. His sister-in-law, Madame Nhu (The Dragon Lady), pushed Diem to sign the Law for the Protection of Morality in 1962. Among many things, it outlawed divorce, dancing, gambling, beauty contests, cockfighting and prostitution. Later the law became even sillier, forbidding dancing in private homes, sentimental songs and the use of 'falsies' by Vietnamese women. This last was abandoned because no one could work out a way to enforce it that wasn't embarrassing to both sides.

Meanwhile insurgency grew, anyone foolish enough to oppose the government was persecuted or jailed and everywhere, in every village, death and fear were starting to feel like daily companions.

In Australia, the generational boat was beginning to rock and Madame Nhu's attempts to hold back the tide of immorality would have received sympathy in some quarters. Circumstance and history had denied our parents freedom and ease and robbed them of the power of indulged youth. Determined that our lives would be better, they provided it to us in full measure, and we would eventually seize the gift with glee and beat them about the head with it.

But it would take a while. The protest and rebellion of the '60s was never a social movement that occurred to everyone at the same time. Nor was it as widespread as some would have you believe. It was piecemeal and sporadic at first and started almost politely. There were some small protests against the decision to send the Team to Vietnam, but they were conducted mostly by older peace activists from the 1950s, not students, and confined by the restrictive police rules of the time – no placards on poles (they could be weapons) and no blocking the footpath, so everyone kept moving in a continuous circle.

The images of these protests, so serious and proper, were regarded as a bit of a laugh in working-class suburbs like Dundas Valley. Most people there had no experience of organised civil dissent and even less desire to get involved. These protesters were clearly political, faintly intellectual and obviously middle class. Despite the common myth that Australia was a classless society, genuine divisions did exist and working-class children grew up knowing that. We also knew that, unlike the World War II generation, we did not have to accept the status quo. We were headed upwards and beginning to realise our strength.

Dundas was 40 kilometres from the beach. It took all of three and a half hours to get there by public transport and, when we finally did arrive, it was six worlds away and we were not welcome. The northern beaches of Sydney were not a healthy environment for kids from the west and the tensions between us and the surfer kids would sometimes erupt into bloody encounters. Still, on most weekends there we would be, sometimes as many as 30 of us, filling up a train carriage with explosive energy as 'Wipeout' and 'Surf City' blared from the transistor radios always carried by the girls. On the beach, towels spread and bodies glistening with coconut oil, our girls had bigger hair, louder make-up and more voluptuous bodies than the lean surfer girls and, across the sand, insults and abuse would fly between the two tribes.

We went where we were not wanted to taunt the class enemy and because we were recognising the power of the group, the gang. Even though we rarely broke any serious laws or got into real trouble (our parents would have killed us), we could all see the effect we caused when 20 or 30 of us moved as one. Older people would change train carriages, shopkeepers would twitch nervously and the police would stop and interrogate us on the street. Together we were potent, a force, and inside the safety of the circle we could mock and rebel against everything and everyone.

Rebellion seemed to fit the times. The black-and-white television in the corner with the wiggly aerial on top had rapidly become the main source of news for Australian families and the world beyond was present in the lounge room every night. Fractured, troubled and sometimes bloody, the news was propelling us all into a realisation that change was everywhere and the pace was quickening. Some of the images from that time are still with me – the Cuban Missile Crisis, when we thought we were headed for nuclear war; the Great Train Robbery; Martin Luther King Jr marching in Alabama and Washington; and the glowing words and charm of John Fitzgerald Kennedy, the 35th President of the United States. Even Vietnam, that country we knew so little about, was now appearing on our screens, though its moment came with indelibly horrific images that still have the power to shock.

It was a series of photographs of a monk, an elderly Buddhist named Thich Quang Duc. Normally, like all his saffron-robed, shaven-headed brothers, he would never have drawn attention to himself but quietly pursued his faith in one of Vietnam's many temples. However, Buddhism demands of its monks that they both can and should provoke public attention when their country or their people are in danger, and South Vietnam was near collapse.

President Diem's early success in holding his country together was disintegrating into corruption, brutality and widespread civil unrest. He and his family were Catholics, and together with his brother Nhu and his sister-in-law, Madame Nhu, he unwisely began a violent suppression of Buddhists. Protesters were shot in the streets, holy places defiled and monks shot, beaten and jailed.

On 11 June 1963, Thich Quang Duc took up the lotus position in the middle of a busy intersection in Saigon. As the cyclos, the motorbikes and the little Renault taxis detoured around him, other monks poured petrol over his body and in an action called 'provoked suicide', he struck a match. The elderly monk burned alive for 10 minutes, remaining upright as the flames consumed him. Despite the intense pain, he did not move or make a sound. His body was still upright when a fire truck arrived and attempted to break through the protective cordon around him. A group of young monks lay down in front of its wheels and Thich Quang Duc died. An American journalist, pre-warned by the Buddhists, shot off a roll of film as people in the street wept and bowed low to the dead man. Within days those photos had flashed around the world.

It was incomprehensible to people in the West, an act of martyrdom that left many confused and outraged, their anger increasing when Madame Nhu was asked for a comment and said, 'I would clap hands at seeing another Buddhist barbecue show.' The end was near.

A few months later, Diem and his brother Nhu were unceremoniously shot dead in the back of an armoured personnel carrier as their generals staged a coup. The Americans had promised the military they would not interfere and the Diem regime was erased. Legend has it that only Thich Quang Duc's heart remains of the whole affair. The Vietnamese believe it did not, indeed *would* not burn and thus it became a holy relic that is kept in the custody of the Reserve Bank of Vietnam.

Then, in November 1963, we were transfixed in front of our televisions again. It's become trite now to talk about where you were when you heard that John F. Kennedy had been assassinated. Yet it *was* shocking to us at the time, shattering illusion and naiveté and ramming home a feeling that would intensify over the coming years – the uneasy sense that the old, established ways were in free fall. All the TV channels went into news overload, the first time this had happened, and we wondered what could possibly come next.

> It was a script written by Kafka and illustrated by Goya or something. It was just a nightmare of a situation and you never knew what was going on and everyone lied, misled.
>
> MATTHEW D'ARCY

News of world events reached the Australians in Vietnam but dimly, as if they had happened in a parallel universe. Out in the jungle, the soldiers of the AATTV were struggling with their mission. The Vietnamese they were training were a sergeant major's nightmare. Their marksmanship was either poor or non-existent, their weapons were not cleaned or maintained and their security would not have kept a child out. On patrol they talked, smoked and laughed, carried noisy livestock around for food and lit campfires at night. The officer system was corrupt; promotion being given on the basis of political alliances rather than merit, and the ordinary soldier was paid appallingly, if at all, and had no leave or days off. It wasn't an army; it was a cursorily organised, conscripted rabble.

Yet they were courageous and willing and if there was one thing the Australian Army was good at it was training. The men of the Team were the best military teachers we had and their readiness to try anything produced results. They had brought with them the same training devices they'd used in Australia and the Vietnamese took to them eagerly.

Their favourite was called 'the sneaker course' – an armed soldier moved through the jungle as if on patrol, following a marked path. Walking behind him, the instructor, without warning, yanked on a hidden wire and a cut-out human target suddenly popped up in front of the soldier or slid by his field of vision. He had two seconds to shoot it down before it disappeared again. The Vietnamese were delighted with this game. The advisers set up shooting galleries and demonstrations of patrolling, ambush tactics and manoeuvres, all the while giving a running commentary to the watching trainees as if it was a well-ordered footy match.

Wherever the Australians went the levels of organisation, discipline and tactical skill rose. But the sheer weight of numbers – a handful of advisers working with hundreds of thousands of soldiers, was always going to make the task impossible. And no amount of lectures or pamphlets or language classes could prepare the Australians for the clash of cultures.

> The Vietnamese soldiers, they did do some brutal things that I didn't agree with but, I mean, I'm an adviser, I can't stop what happened, you know . . . there were some wounded when we were doing this major attack, and they weren't getting any medical attention, and I said to the *dai-wi* [the Vietnamese commander], 'Look, shouldn't you . . . ?' and he said, 'No, they are criminals, don't.' And they just let them bleed to death . . .

> Asians do not understand weakness, especially in leadership... the *dai-wi* was very harsh on his own soldiers, it was nothing for him to pistol-whip somebody, if you disobeyed an order or chatted, somebody, he would just go up and hit you with his pistol and that's the way they were, you know.
>
> I think I learned more about Asians generally, in their culture. We as Europeans, and particularly the Americans, we like a conclusion to something, if we are going to do something we want to see results, 'Let's get in and do it.' Now their thinking is not that, it's like they will wear you down because they have got time, time is not of the essence, and most of Communism in South-East Asia is worked like that. It's not going to happen tomorrow, it's not going to happen next week, next year, maybe five years down the track it'll happen eventually, 'We will wear you down because you like results.'
>
> ... They didn't have much, to me, in that battalion, they had nothing those soldiers, but they were generous... I represented the Australian Army and I wanted them to see that I was a good soldier. And I did clean my weapon, I did do this and I did do that, and I did care about them as best I could, but they know if you care. See it's like the army in leadership, soldiers know if you care about it or you are just worried about your career, you know, if you really take an interest in them and you look after them, and you try to get them whatever they are entitled to. They are no fools.
>
> WALLACE THOMPSON, AATTV

It wasn't just the South Vietnamese who challenged soldiers like Wallace Thompson. The war in Vietnam was not comparable to Kokoda or Korea, or even Malaya, because the enemy was within and without, organised in ways that were more complex than anything the Australians had previously faced.

They were up against two forces. The NVA, the North Vietnamese Army, resembled a conventional military force, well-trained and organised and, for the moment, staying behind their borders. It did not suit Ho Chi Minh to be seen as an invader. Then there was the insurgency, the guerrillas in the South. They fought under the banner of an organisation called the National Front for the Liberation of South Vietnam, the NLF. Supposedly independent, it had actually been set up by North Vietnam and it was another cunning piece of propaganda.

Many in the South hated the American presence and wanted the government brought down, but they were not all Communists. Hanoi gathered them together in the NLF and promoted the line that it was an uprising of the people of South Vietnam against the 'American colonists' and the 'puppet government' to gain freedom. But it was Communist-led and supported and aimed fair and square at a unified, Communist Vietnam. Diem had derisively called these NLF fighters 'Viet Cong', literally meaning 'Vietnamese Communists', to try to combat the propaganda. But, like many a name intended to denigrate, it stuck as a badge of honour and Viet Cong or VC they proudly became.

It's intriguing to look back at how the VC were portrayed by the other side. The commonly believed theory was that they came in from the North, and overwhelmed villages with propaganda and terror, forcing them to fight. This conveniently ignored both history and the fact that hundreds of thousands of people in South Vietnam had had enough. They'd survived the French, they'd lived through the division of their country into two and now they were being told they had to fight for a government they loathed and distrusted alongside an occupying force they deeply resented. The NLF did not have trouble finding recruits. And while there can be no doubt that as the war went on the Viet Cong were responsible for brutal terror campaigns, kidnappings, executions and assassinations in villages that resisted them, this was a force of the people – the people of South Vietnam, as well as the North.

They were very, very successful and, by 1964, controlled much of the countryside. The best assessment of VC numbers at that time was 34 000 regulars and 100 000 part-time guerrillas. Ranged against them were 250 000 ARVN troops, around 215 000 local and regional forces, 21 000 American advisers and about 100 Australians. The figures don't suggest success for the VC but, unlike the ARVN, they were motivated, tightly controlled and, above all, flexible. They could choose both targets and timing and their intelligence network was astonishing, with agents in every village and military base. Using constant raids and ambushes, they kept the government forces in a defensive stance, protecting their bases. The VC had a lot of easy victories against the ARVN and local militia in those years, and it became clear that the government of South Vietnam had very short arms when it came to protecting its land and its people.

> I think my attitude was the same as everyone on the Team, that it wasn't going as well as the Americans were saying that it was going. There were far too many ambushes, there were far too many South Vietnamese units getting ambushed and getting casualties. To us it appeared the VC were gaining the upper hand, certainly in the countryside. But, despite the war, the Americans were saying everything was sweet in the garden. It wasn't.
>
> ... It was a pity really, because they lost a lot of men over there needlessly. And that's always the sad thing about it: it's bad enough when you lose people through close-contact fighting, but to lose them unnecessarily through either foolish tactics or lack of care, that's a bit galling.
>
> RONALD PERKINS, AATTV

When you talk with Australian war veterans, whether they're from World War I or Iraq, there is one constant refrain that never seems to change. 'Bloody Americans!' Our love–hate relationship in war stretches back over almost a century and Vietnam was no different. We admire their courage but are nervous of their foolhardiness. We covet their equipment but resent their extravagance and waste. And given the comparative size of our army, where we treasure every bullet and every soldier's life, we are truly uncomfortable with their 'shoot first and ask questions later' attitude. The Team had to work intimately with the Americans and the tensions sometimes broke out.

> I was posted to 11 Ranger Battalion which operated in the Da Nang area . . . So I went there as a warrant officer adviser. There were two Yanks there. There was a Yank major and a captain. The captain was hopeless. Absolutely hopeless.
>
> I was told that afternoon we're going on an ambush patrol. That's fine. So I had my gear ready, waiting for a briefing. Go to the airport, pick up the choppers and out we fly. Never once did he tell me what we were about, never had a briefing on what we were about. And this fellow's a West Point graduate! And on the way there we're fired upon and the helicopter was hit several times. But no damage sustained, just a few holes . . . And then we came across a patch of Viet Cong, so he ordered the gunships in to attack them. And I said to him, this is over the headphones, I said, 'What's your mission?'
>
> He said, 'To ambush such and such road junction.'
>
> And I said, 'You've just stirred up a hornet's nest here. You've fired on every bastard that's around the place and you're telling everybody you're arriving.'
>
> I said, 'You're a dill.'
>
> ANTHONY THORP

Despite collisions like this, the isolation of their postings helped the members of the Team to discover more than just the prejudice and insularity that can come with being part of a larger force. Generally, whether they were with Montagnard tribes in the highlands or Special Forces on the Mekong Delta, each man had only one other Australian or American alongside them in training and operations. War makes mates and these men were no different, regardless of nationality. Each would look out for the other and neither would leave the other alone on a battlefield. If necessary, they would die, as they soldiered, together.

And die they did. The Australians had finally been given official permission to enter into battle (something they had been doing unofficially anyway), and the casualties began. The first, Sergeant Billy Hacking, was killed when his own weapon snagged on some vegetation and fired into his body. Then Warrant Officer Kevin Conway was shot and killed during a Viet Cong attack on a base in Nam Dong. At dawn the next day, he was found at the bottom of the mortar pit from which he had been returning fire. Alongside him was the body of his American comrade, Master Sergeant Gabriel Alamo.

> We did have a service in Saigon for Conway. And I was part of the burial party . . . the nasty thing was they didn't know where to bury him. He was going to be buried in Singapore then he was going to be buried in Saigon. So I'm not sure, I think he ended up being buried in Singapore. But again it was a disgusting thing where government or the higher command didn't know how to react to a death and yet we were going into a war zone.
>
> ANTHONY THORP

It had long been the policy of Australian governments to bury our war dead in military cemeteries overseas. From Gallipoli to France to New Guinea, the rows of white headstones marked places of mourning and pilgrimage, and the government saw no reason to change this. Then an Australian adviser, Warrant Officer R.A. Scott, became the second member of the Team to be killed in action. His American partner, Master Sergeant Eugene Jordon, knowing that Scott wanted to be buried at home, requested leave to accompany him back. No, said the Australian Army, he'll be buried in the British War Cemetery in Malaya.

Jordon refused to accept the decision and took up a collection among the American advisers to get Scott's body home. When the other Australians heard of it, they too threw in their money. Jordon got his way and stayed with his friend till the end, on a Qantas flight home to burial in the military section of Rookwood Cemetery in Sydney.

Angered, the Team continued collecting money and then paid for two more Australian dead to be taken home. Finally, the level of embarrassment grew too great for the government and they announced that from now on, the bodies of Australian servicemen who died overseas would be flown home. At the public's expense. Mateship may be an Australian word, but in war, it knows no nationality.

> Rock and roll is the most brutal, ugly, degenerate, vicious form of expression it has been my displeasure to hear.
>
> FRANK SINATRA

In Australia, Vietnam was still on the periphery of most people's vision, though that was about to change. As for the young, we were too busy with the future, singing protest songs with complete arrogance, utterly sure of the rightness of our road and the world we were so certain we would create. Pick a topic, any topic, and you could start an argument between the generations that would reveal anger and bewilderment on one side and indifference and boredom on the other. Strange times indeed.

Music was a flashpoint. I think it was the sound of rock 'n' roll that really got up our parents' collective nose. Or maybe it was the lyrics, or the hair, or the posturing or the righteousness or . . . oh, hell it was everything. In 1964, when the Beatles toured Australia, it was like a key turning in a lock. It was primal, it was sexual and it was out of control. Ten thousand kids in Exhibition Street, Melbourne, screaming their lungs out with every wave from the band. Three hundred policemen and 100 servicemen were there to control them but they didn't stand a chance. One hundred and fifty kids falling to the ground in hysteria and ambulancemen carting them away as cameras whirred. Lennon and McCartney on the balcony of the Southern Cross Hotel in a Hitler-like pose, saluting the crowd below. As Ringo Starr said at the time, 'It was a gas, man!'

At most high schools the battlegrounds were long hair and clothes. Wear your hair over your collar at my school, Marist Brothers Eastwood, or your sideburns too long, or your fringe down to your eyebrows and you were immediately sent home with a note, for renovation and repair. Down the road at Our Lady of Mercy College, the girls were kneeling on the asphalt in front of ruler-wielding nuns at morning assembly to ensure that the length of their uniforms remained within the limits of modesty. Those who were placed above us believed they were saving our souls. But they were King Canute and we were the incoming tide.

Sex was the other field of conflict. The sexual morality demanded of teenagers had previously depended on threat – pregnancy. But once the contraceptive pill was introduced in 1961, adults made the automatic assumption that we'd be at it like rabbits. If only. Widespread use of the pill was a few years away yet and adolescent boys were still stuck in the world of father and son nights at school, boastful playground sex stories that left you feeling you were the only one not getting any, kindergarten language like 'upstairs outside' and 'downstairs inside' to describe sexual acts when all you wanted to know was *how* you did it, and desperate, surreptitious pervs at girlie magazines like *Man*, *Man Junior* and *Laughs and Lovelies* when the newsagent wasn't looking. God knows how the girls fared when a reputation could be destroyed with one casual 'Her? Oh, she's a slut!'

Still, despite the stumbling and the fumbling that characterised most of our sexual activity, like the rest of our lives then it felt charged and potent. We lived in an intoxicating haze of happenings. The charming Beatles morphed into the bad-boy Rolling Stones and the music really started to bite. Fashion got wilder, magazines raunchier and more outspoken, and while our parents complained more loudly than ever, we were living inside songs, surviving the week the best way we could, with only Friday on our minds.

Music was one way out, a path to places that promised more than the fibro and brick homes that were bursting at the seams with kids. The face of some suburbs had changed, become a little darker, a little pockmarked. Petty crime had slid in almost unseen and there were places now you wouldn't be caught in after dark. The signs were self-evident – gangs of boys with a 'don't fuck with us' attitude, single mothers with hard faces and empty purses, decaying car hulks in front yards and a sporadic vandalism that owed more to boredom than any meaning.

Rock 'n' roll was more than king now. It was tyrant, emperor and mother's milk to us all. And if you could play, if you could actually make a sound remotely approaching what came out of the radio, then you were sanctified and canonised, booted above the ruck to notoriety. Small brick halls in every suburb stopped being ordinary and became palaces of music and sex, repositories of the hopes and fantasies embedded in their walls by hundreds of teenagers. Switch on the colour wheel and the lights would change. Red. Blue. Yellow. Green. Now, turn up the music. Turn it up LOUD. Guitars and amps and a catch-every-glint-of-light drum kit. It was irresistible, and like so many before and after me, I took a step off the cliff and joined a band.

All over Australia, all over the *world*, young men were learning three chords, strapping on guitars and kicking out the jams behind rusty garage roller doors. It was always 'young *men*' because that was the Bible, the Word according to John, Paul, Mick and Keith – no chicks. Girls could be singers like Jackie DeShannon or Dusty Springfield, or even a vocal group like The Supremes or The Chiffons, but girls in a band? Please. You could lust after them, sing about them, even reveal your dreams to them, but no way could they join the band. They were left out, locked out and reduced to acolyte status. That *was* the way it was and we didn't care enough to wonder why. The future looked bright. Then Mr Menzies delivered a wake-up call.

Vietnam had entered what became known as 'the coup season'. After Diem's assassination, his generals fought like junkyard dogs over the presidency and as each new winner grabbed power, the others began plotting to bring him down. Prosecution of the war stuttered and any idea that the Vietnamese could and should fight their own war with adviser assistance had vanished. Unless combat troops were sent in, South Vietnam was lost.

This was unacceptable to the US and Australia, where political belief remained strong that, with just a bit more commitment, the VC could be beaten. An American bombing campaign had already begun – 'Rolling Thunder' it was called, a cowboy title for an operation that ultimately killed hundreds of civilians, destroyed thousands of homes and did not achieve its objective.

VC numbers kept rising and, in April 1964, North Vietnam began infiltration of NVA units into the South. It was time for boots on the ground.

Menzies obviously thought so. The new American president, Lyndon Baines Johnson (LBJ), had only asked him for more advisers to join the Team, but now Menzies went one better and offered an Australian battalion. The Americans had not even sent in their own infantry yet, but we were obviously ready to roll and wanted the Americans to be too. Of course, sending troops would mean credit for us and debt for them, so Australia could rightly expect help from the US should things get nasty with the Indonesians. In the end, we didn't need any provocation. We invited ourselves to the Vietnam War.

There had been no public debate in Australia about this potential commitment, unlike America, where vigorous argument and angst over their involvement in Vietnam were on display every day. Here, we proceeded with compliance, comfortable in the blissful certainty that the government knew best. We were kept in the dark and, if not outright lied to, then at the very least deceived by deliberate omission. Menzies wanted us in Vietnam and so did his inner cabinet. There were just a few tiny obstacles to overcome first.

One was that the Americans had to increase their commitment. That was resolved in March 1965 when the marines landed on the beaches at Da Nang. They may have had images of World War II landings in their hearts but the reality was a little different.

> I stood on the beach in Da Nang, on the day the Yanks arrived. The marines, they did a beach landing. Dinkum. They didn't have to. They all did a beach landing, got wet and everybody was on the beach. The girls were there... I think the Yanks were a bit embarrassed because they were coming to a war zone and they're greeted with garlands of flowers and seeing people clap their hands... they were greeted by dignitaries

and the girls in their *ao dais* [traditional dress], you know all very attractive women. With garlands of flowers.

ANTHONY THORP

By then Menzies had already increased the numbers in the Team and had also sent in the Royal Australian Air Force in the form of seven Caribou aircraft. Their official title was Transport Flight Vietnam but their radio call sign was the word 'Wallaby' and a picture of the marsupial was on the side of their planes. Inevitably they became and remained 'Wallaby Airlines'.

But Menzies was also receiving reports back from serving Australians and they were full of dire warnings. Colonel O.D. Jackson, the incoming commander of the Team, went on a fact-finding tour and later reflected on what the intelligence reports were saying.

I saw . . . almost every important government post. I certainly saw every place where Australians were deployed. The impression I gained, a very real impression, was the war was lost from a military point of view . . . wherever I went there were Vietnamese Army forces on hilltops, behind barbed wire. They very rarely went outside that wire. If they did go outside to relieve one post by another they were frequently ambushed in strength by the VC – and it was nothing for a whole battalion or more of South Vietnamese troops to be butchered. There was very little in the way of offensive action from anywhere in the Vietnamese Army; the Viet Cong were thoroughly on top from a military point of view. I would have said that it was just a matter of weeks or months before the war was militarily lost in Vietnam – it was as bad as that in my opinion, and a lot of people agreed with me.

COLONEL O.D. JACKSON

The intelligence assessments disappeared into the black hole that spontaneously occurs when politicians are convinced that they know best. On 29 April 1965, Prime Minister Robert Menzies stood in front of a half-full parliament and announced that Australia would be sending a battalion of regular combat troops, 1RAR (Royal Australian Regiment), to Vietnam.

It didn't seem to matter that we had no idea how our men would be deployed until the Americans told us; or that the battalion was badly equipped and ill-prepared to go thanks to the government keeping their departure secret from *everybody*. It didn't even matter that the government had had to beg for a formal invitation from the South Vietnamese that arrived only hours before Menzies' speech. We were going and that was it. We were going to help the Americans, to gain credit for our sacrifice and to free the world from the scourge of Communism.

At the very time that Menzies was speaking, Gallipoli veterans were flying home to Australia from a journey to Turkey to commemorate that campaign, another foray into war to help out our bigger brothers. It was 50 years since Gallipoli, but it seemed that the lesson had to be painfully learnt all over again.

The reactions to Menzies' announcement were rapid and varied, a true indication of the confusion and lack of knowledge in Australia. The Melbourne *Age*, Menzies' favourite newspaper, stood bravely on the front line: 'These are inescapable obligations which fall on us because of our geographical position, our treaty commitments and our friendships ... There is clearly a United States call to share, even in a small way, more of the burdens ... there was no alternative but to respond as we have.'

Most Australian newspapers were supportive, only the new kid on the block, *The Australian*, was bluntly critical.

> The Menzies Government has made a reckless decision on Vietnam which this nation may live to regret. It has decided

> to send Australian soldiers into a savage, revolutionary war in which the Americans are grievously involved – so that America may share a tiny part of her embarrassment . . . Australia has lined up her generations against the hatred and contempt of resurgent Asian peoples – without adding one iota of confidence or strength to the tragically embroiled American nation. It could be that our historians will recall this day with tears.

In parliament, Arthur Calwell opposed the decision and gave what was probably the finest speech of his career.

> And I address this message to my colleagues and that vast band of Labor men and women outside; the course we have agreed to take today is fraught with difficulty. I cannot promise you that easy popularity can be bought in times like these. Nor are we looking for it. When the drums beat and the trumpets sound, the voice of reason and right can be heard in the land only with difficulty . . . But I offer you the sure and certain knowledge we will be vindicated, that generations to come will record with gratitude that when a reckless government wilfully endangered the security of this country, the voice of the Labor Party was heard, strong and clear.

The trade unions were hopelessly divided, some going out on strike, others supporting the government. The churches were the same, all invoking God and Christian morality to either justify or condemn the decision. Not a peep was heard from the universities. The rest of us were a little bewildered but mostly blasé. Opinion polls showed that a majority supported the troops going and, for a country that was supposedly at war, there was little evidence to disturb that view.

The possibility of army boots in our future was troubling to me and my friends, but only for as long as it took to consider and then dismiss the possibility. The sun was shining, the music was loud and school was coming to an end. University, interesting (and hopefully loose) women and a freer life were beckoning and we were ready to answer that clarion call.

One month after Menzies' announcement, 1RAR sailed out on HMAS *Sydney*, bound for Vietnam. They left at 1 a.m. and there were no cheering crowds at the wharf, no breaking streamers or long-distance kisses over the water. Secrecy, high security and perhaps a smidgin of suspicion about the possibility of protest marked their departure as it had the decision to send them. But the war they were eagerly anticipating was changing, and it wasn't for the better.

> One particular operation we went on, and this was a very big operation, we had 132 helicopters in the air at once. It was called Eagle Strike. We were picked up from Da Nang, chopper after chopper... Everywhere I looked from my chopper I see choppers up to the left, down to the left, in front, behind; it was just a magnificent sight... That was the first time I'd seen napalm used and fighter aircraft in close support... Oh, it was very spectacular. I mean it was as if you were at the movies when you see across the front the napalm being dropped and then the rounds from the aircraft falling on your head, spent cartridges. They get hot. They land on top of you... Balls of fire. Balls of fire.
>
> ANTHONY THORP

IV

WHAT THE HELL AM I DOING HERE?

My father, an honourable and decent man, was like many of the men who had undergone the Depression and the war. Determined that life would be different for his children, he worked his way steadily towards heart attack so that his six sons could have the chances he'd been denied. Everyone, it seemed, wanted our generation to succeed. As we neared the end of high school and the graduation exams known as the Leaving Certificate, we heard about one goal more than any other . . . 'University . . .' breathed our teachers in heady voices. 'You should be trying for university. If you just applied yourself a little more, son . . . you could do it!' I almost believed them.

But we knew about university in Dundas – or thought we did. It belonged to those suburbs that were six train stations and a large amount of cash away. Suburbs where the mothers could stay at home and the fathers weren't beaten down by years of mindless work. People from there went to university. Not us. No one in my family had ever gone. It had never been possible. Between the endless expenses of fees, uniforms, schoolbooks, lunches and sport days, just keeping us at school stretched the family's budget till it squealed. But our parents wanted us to do it, the teachers told us we should do it and Mr Menzies opened more and more universities so we could do it. Assuming you were bright enough, there was only one obstacle for working-class families to overcome before their child could go to uni – money. And there was even an answer for that.

In that last year of school, most students nearly drowned in application forms for scholarships – commonwealth scholarships, teachers' scholarships, BHP, private foundations, even obscure offerings from rural machinery manufacturers. Without the money from a scholarship our chances of tertiary education were zero. The teachers landed on us like drill sergeants, dragging us through all kinds of extra tuition – special classes for those taking honours subjects and Saturday school for everybody. In this fever-filled world, failure was not an option.

It was worse as we neared the end. Trial exams, lunchtime cramming, short tempers and sudden panics when the teachers heard through some grapevine that the English exam would contain a trick question on *Julius Caesar* and we had two whole days of frantic revision till even death by knifing looked attractive. In my case, only Brother Elgar truly made a difference. Tall, gaunt and as articulate as an Irishman, he took us for English Honours and his incandescent words about Keats, Hopkins, Shelley and Shakespeare still light my way. He was a hell of a teacher.

And it worked. The postman delivered my (surprisingly good) results and, like so many others in those generous days, I was offered four scholarships. I had the chance to be: an accountant; join BHP; take up a commonwealth scholarship; or accept an offer from the Education Department and train to be a teacher.

No matter which box I ticked, I was going to university; not only the first in my family to do so, but the first kid in my street. This was different, this was special. For a little while, the reputation I'd developed with Valley folk as 'someone who talked like he'd swallowed a book' was forgiven and forgotten and I was slapped on the back, punched in the arm, had 15 different 'goodonya's yelled at me in one day and was embraced by teary mothers waving their Craven A cork-tipped cigarettes in the air in triumph. I'd been accepted so they'd been accepted. Bloody fantastic.

Thousands of young men and women won first prize in that scholarship bonanza. Between 1947 and 1968 the number of students enrolling at Australian universities quadrupled and the nature of society changed as a sizeable proportion of an entire generation had their adolescence extended through the privilege of free education. We went to university not necessarily to fulfil a career choice, but because we could. We were the lucky ones, allowed to procrastinate adult responsibilities, even to criticise and denigrate the very society that had made it possible for us to be at uni in the first place. We thought we were the limitless future, but the past still had power over us.

Bye Bye
(to the tune of 'Bye Bye Blackbird')

Pack up all your bags and kit,
JTC is up the shit.
Bye, Bye Canungra
Stew for breakfast, stew for tea,
No more bloody stew for me.
Bye, Bye Canungra.

No more bloody hiking over mountains.
We'll be drinking Foster's out of fountains.

No more sergeants, no more brass,
You can stick 'em up your arse.
Canungra, Bye, Bye.

ANONYMOUS

In the hinterland behind the Gold Coast the road winds relentlessly up the mountain, twisting in on itself until finally you reach the township of Canungra. There's not a lot here – a motel, a hotel, a few shops and an RSL that looks and feels like RSL clubs did when I was a teenager – more country pub than corporation. Inside were the men I had come to meet, sharing an early beer and waiting to take me on a tour. They had come to this place on a mission of war over 40 years ago, driving thousands of men to the limits of their endurance and tolerance for pain... and loving every minute of it. During the Vietnam War they were instructors at the Jungle Training Centre (JTC) in Canungra, a place that's as near as matters to being the home of soldiering in Australia. Now they lived here, enjoying the peace and their memories.

Virtually every Australian who fought in Vietnam was trained at Canungra, and a great many from World War II as well. I've heard so many horror stories about it from vets and witnessed their involuntary shudders when the name is mentioned that I'm half expecting to see some kind of hell rising up out of the forest, reeking of blood and sweat. But when we get to what was the JTC, it's actually quite an appealing place.

You walk towards a group of weathered wooden buildings, all flagpoles and manicured gardens and there's birdsong everywhere, along with that rich, mouldy aroma that rises from tropical rainforest. It's very peaceful and I could understand why many of the units that trained here have erected monuments and plaques on the grounds, particularly the surviving members of the Team. They've built a small, Asian-style building called the 'Home of the Australian Advisers'. Sent to Vietnam from all over Australia, this is the only place that's common to them all. Other Vietnam veterans have asked if they could have their ashes distributed here.

I moved along the old tent lines, trying to visualise how it would have once been, but the peace didn't last.

'C'mon. Let's show you the place where we used to bust their guts!' The ex-instructors were calling, ready with their memories, and we walked down the hill, away from the gardens and into history.

In 1942, the stunning Japanese advance made an invasion of Australia seem inevitable. Fighting in New Guinea, the AIF battalions were struggling with a different kind of war. They had no training manuals for jungle warfare and were still using British operational doctrines from Europe and the Middle East, useless in this new terrain. In November of that year the army set up the Land Headquarters Training Centre (Jungle Warfare) in the rainforests of Canungra, in southern Queensland, and began to churn out a differently trained soldier. By May 1943, Canungra had 2000 reinforcements undergoing training and 500 men graduating from the course every week to be sent straight into service in New Guinea and the Pacific. It was rough, tough and as close to combat conditions as possible.

Most of the instructors were veterans of the Middle East and the early New Guinea battles like Kokoda. They were NCOs, hard men who had no illusions about battle and no compunctions about harshness. They knew that for these young men to survive, let alone emerge victorious, their training had to be relentless and ruthless. Which is not to say that they didn't occasionally enjoy administering pain.

> We used to get a big kick out of bringing the kids off the train. We'd line them up and march 'em over the hill, but the local Canungra cemetery was on the left-hand side and as they marched up the hill with their heads bowed and struggling with their equipment, we'd say, 'Look over to the left, boys.' And they'd look over. We'd say, 'They're the blokes that didn't make it.' And they used to shiver in their boots.
>
> IAN CLARKE, 2/5TH BATTALION, WORLD WAR II

If you didn't complete the course, for whatever reason, you were sent back to the start in a khaki game of snakes and ladders. The soldiers who graduated from Canungra were fit, disciplined, combat-ready and bonded. It worked.

Then it was all closed down after the war, in 1946. The rainforest steadily reclaimed the assault courses and tent lines. The men who had sweated and cursed their way across these creeks and mountains returned to their homes and their lives, and Canungra became just another shared story on Anzac Day. They would not have imagined that some of their sons would re-enter these gates all too soon, to do it all over again.

By the 1950s, the Australian government was still committed to the Brits and the Middle East, so the army was stuck with the doctrine of desert warfare and the trench tactics of the Korean War. The result was that most of the jungle skills from World War II were lost. Then the Malayan Emergency broke out, Communism began to spread and a new kind of enemy appeared – insurgents who were part of the civilian population and guerrillas who adopted hit-and-run tactics. Jungle warfare was back on the agenda and a training centre had to be established. Canungra had done it before, they thought . . . it could do it again. They would call it the Jungle Training Centre and, this time, they'd make it a permanent fixture.

There wasn't much left from its previous incarnation, just a few concrete posts and a bit of lonely plumbing. But the freezing creeks were still there, the punishing hills and the impenetrable lantana. Colonel Ted Serong, JTC's first commandant in this new era, summed up the mission neatly when he described it as 'hard training, by hard people, for hard people'. Canungra reopened in 1954 and back came the granite-hard NCOs to train the men who went to Malaya and Borneo.

The staff combined all their knowledge into a program called the Battle Efficiency Course. Nobody escaped completing it, whether you were a private or an officer, a cook or a rifleman, a driver, a clearance diver or even a member of the AATTV. If you were going to 'the funny country' as they called it, after your initial training at camps like Kapooka and Singleton, you had to come to Canungra to graduate from the BE Course. And what a bugger of a course it was.

> There was so much of it, every day they'd put you over the assault course and you'd go over the ropes, up ladders and climbing across ropes and under barbed wire and through mud and out through a big, long tunnel and big drainpipe and into a ditch full of dirty water. When we went through it had half a dead kangaroo in it. Oh stink, and you used to come out with mud all over you and you'd go across these monkey bars, just a long piece of steel and you had to go across this and under it were a lot of rocks. One of the monkey bars was loose and used to flip over and if you were unlucky enough to hit it, especially when you were wet, what with coming out of this hole with the kangaroo in it, and there'd be mud and slush and stink all over you and you had to jump up and get this and if you missed the grip on it you went onto the rocks below, which I did one day. I had a bad fall, they picked me up, I wasn't knocked unconscious but I had the

> wind knocked out of me. I did my elbow, bruised it, they just took me up to the RAP [Regimental Aid Post] and gave me an Aspro and sent me back to training.
>
> DARCY TILBROOK, 4RAR

Officers in particular were given no quarter. On the contrary, they often received special attention.

> I wouldn't say it was hell on earth. It was tough. It had that reputation of being tough. When we went there we were the first Duntroon cadets to go . . . We were all soft. Your hands were soft. They took us into the field on the first night and we were digging in and there were mosquitoes and, of course, we had blisters on our hands and no sleep. We resented all of that and had a very bad attitude as you'd expect. The staff thought, 'These people had a bad attitude so we'll sort them out.' There was a lot of harassment of us. We were called out in the middle of the night and had to jog around the roads and those sorts of things. The jungle was difficult. Lantana is terrible. There was heaps of lantana and the only way to get through it is for someone to dive onto it, just literally run at it and dive on it, and then the next person climb onto him and dive through. It was hot and there were leeches. I can always remember being up on the border line and just sitting there this particular time and clearing away a space, and within a minute you could see all these leeches crawling towards you. There weren't a lot of pleasant experiences.
>
> MURRAY BLAKE, 5RAR

The NCOs aimed to get every individual super fit, to push each man past what he thought of as his physical and mental limits. Through drills on sneaker courses and gunnery ranges they turned them into instinctive shooters who could fire from the hip the instant they made contact with the enemy. They trained platoons in patrolling, tracking and ambushes till the men could perform without thinking, and they placed officers under extreme stress to judge their suitability for combat command.

They used a technique called 'battle inoculation', firing machine guns directly over the trainees' heads as they crawled under barbed wire, through smoke grenades and mortar explosions, and once they had them going in the direction they wanted, they introduced some refinements designed to really wake them up.

> We pulled up and we all jumped out of the trucks and they call it a 'kill group'. 'Don't stand in a group, spread out.' 'Course everyone got out and stood in a group and they had these primers with the detonator in it, just threw one amongst everybody . . . They'd kill you. I mean they'd blow a pretty big hole in the ground. They used to just lob them. 'Boom! Shit! Bang!' That was it. 'Don't stand in a kill group. If you stand together and someone lobs a grenade, you're going to cop it.'
>
> STEPHEN LAVERTY, 1 FIELD SQUADRON

> Helicopter drill. Bloody enplaning and deplaning. That's how to get off the plane quick. Bang, bang, bang. Thumbs up from the crew and away they go. Except in some cases we didn't have helicopters. We'd have a Land Rover and some dickhead standing in the back of the Land Rover with his arms out turning round going 'wokka-wokka-wokka'. Shit.
>
> ANTHONY HUGHES

> Three truckloads of a company would be going out and suddenly on this winding hill down to one of the firing areas there'd be one of our ambulances up against a big tree and fellas laying on the ground. And the trucks were driven by our drivers, they knew what to do . . . they would just stop and everyone would stand up to gawk and 'PUTT PUTT PUTT PUTT!' four or five machine guns would open up from the

> bank on the other side... And if that had of been for real they'd have suffered tremendous casualties. We'd come over and say, 'What you should have done was immediately debus and take cover and then investigate what it's all about.'
>
> KEITH HOULEY, 2RAR, JTC INSTRUCTOR

The staff didn't know these kids and they didn't really want to know them. They wanted only one thing – to send them out the gates three weeks later knowing that each one of them could do the job and not get killed. Allan Price, one of the instructors who guided me around JTC, explained the way they deliberately taught the soldiers to take over, one after the other, should death destroy their commanders.

> We used to give them more pressure than what they received over there. They were lucky if they got three to four hours sleep a night. We had them thinking the whole time. In Vietnam, you might get one contact a week; here they were getting five or six a day, plus one at night. We'd put them on their toes the whole time.
>
> Every now and then we'd kill off a commander. We'd kill off a corporal so that the lance corporal would take over the section, which meant that a digger'd have to become section commander. If he was performing okay, we'd kill off the acting section commander so a digger took over the section. We'd knock off the company commander so the CSM [company sergeant major] would have to take charge. You'd simply say, 'You're dead, you're out for 24 hours. Go to the back and be a rifleman.'
>
> ALLAN PRICE, JTC INSTRUCTOR

But no matter how difficult the course was, the instructors at JTC could depend on their students being highly motivated. They were at Canungra because they wanted to be career soldiers, proud members of the Australian Army. Then a political decision in 1964 changed all that, and along with it the potential future of every young Australian man.

—

Free Beer for All the Nashos
(to the tune of 'John Brown's Body')

The privates are the army but the buggers don't know it.
The privates are the army but the buggers don't know it.
The privates are the army but the buggers don't know it.
But they'll know it when the revolution comes.

Free beer for all the nashos.
Free beer for all the nashos.
Free beer for all the nashos.
When the revolution comes.

ANONYMOUS

Conscription and controversy have a long, paired history in Australia. In World War I, two referendums to introduce it were narrowly defeated, principally by soldiers at the front who did not want unwilling combatants alongside them in the trenches. In World War II, compulsory military service, limited to deployment in the islands to our north, had caused bitterness and division both inside the army and without.

But the RSL and the conservatives had always loved the idea, providing as it did the twin advantages of ready-made soldiers for defence and the shaping of young louts into 'men'. Others, particularly those with an Irish background like my family's, regarded it as an obsequious sacrifice to Britain and America by servile, sycophantic politicians. Now, it was back.

The government's policy of forward defence meant that more Australian troops would be needed because of Indonesia's confrontation with the new state of Malaysia, where we already had troops stationed, and the possibility of further conflict with Indonesia in New Guinea. We simply didn't have enough soldiers for the task. There was little unemployment and no sense of war to stir folks up so recruitment was struggling. Hemmed in by what he described as 'a defence emergency', Menzies abruptly announced a 'selective service scheme' in November 1964.

The voting age in Australia was 21, the conscription age, 20. 'Selective' meant that the days of the year were placed in a ballot and if your birthdate was one of the days picked out, and you passed the medical, you would serve in the army for two years, including being liable for overseas service. The plan was to conscript 4200 young men in the first year of the scheme and 6900 every year after that.

Most of the voting public believed conscription was a good idea, particularly as at first, sending conscripts to war didn't seem likely. The notion of sending combat troops to Vietnam was still not considered necessary. Only Arthur Calwell spoke out, arguing that conscription wasn't justified and that by making it selective Menzies had made it possible for the system to be rorted. In a phrase that would come to resonate like a bell, Calwell called the conscription scheme, 'a lottery of death'. Then the notices began appearing.

> Men turning 20 years of age and who are ordinarily resident in Australia are required to register with the Department of Labour and National Service. If you are temporarily absent from the country at the time of your birthday you are required to register within 14 days of returning. Failure to register is an offence.

There were two registration periods each year: one in January, the other in July. Where your twentieth birthday fell determined which one was yours. Each period lasted two weeks and the government publicised them widely – no one was getting away with claiming they hadn't heard. It was a simple act, not even as stressful as applying for a driver's licence. You just filled in the form at your local national service registration office . . . and waited. Whether you accepted conscription as your lot or struggled with your conscience, you damn well knew when your turn in the ballot was approaching. Twenty-first birthdays used to be the big one – key to the door, the right to vote and a yard of beer forced down to raucous cheers in a surburban backyard. Now turning 20 became the marker, the point of arrival of unwelcome adulthood.

The dates were inscribed on wooden marbles and placed in a barrel, and not just any everyday barrel but an old Tattslotto workhorse that had once dispensed luck and largesse to lottery winners. Australians like a gamble so why not bet your future on the fall of a wooden ball? In dubious ceremonies, 'distinguished citizens', like test cricketers or politicians, pulled the first marble out. Some ballots were even televised, the '60s version of reality TV; but after the first marble was drawn and held up to the assembled media, the shutters came down and the rest of the draw was conducted in secret. This was an honest attempt by the government to prevent fiddles, rorts and mathematical probability scams along with avoiding embarrassing questions about why this person born on 15 January was selected and this other was not. But the world loves a secret, especially when there's a government behind it and the conspiracy theories were tenacious and fantastic. The big rumour at universities was that the army only wanted science and engineering students. Poofy arts graduates were a no-no.

Another month of waiting followed for those in the ballot. Lives went on hold, and romances were derailed. Then the letters came. The brown envelopes with OHMS in bold type carried one of two messages – you were either 'balloted in', in which case you were informed of your rights to apply for exemption or deferment before they took you; or you were 'balloted out' and thus under no further obligation, indefinitely deferred.

For a short while, it appeared that conscription would be accepted by most. Then the situation in Indonesia cooled down, Vietnam heated up and it became clear that if nashos, as national servicemen were now called, *were* going to be sent overseas, it would be to a real war. Our adolescent futures had become a whole lot more complicated even if we were still bewildered by it all.

> I never heard much. I was in the very first call-up. And I don't think, if you were honest about it, there are too many 19-year-olds that buy newspapers. Even today I don't think there would be too many 19-year-olds who watch the news. We've all got our own lives, we're courting or running around, or whatever we're doing at that stage, mucking around with the car. There's not too many buying newspapers, unless it's for the races or what's on at the pictures. I didn't know anything at all myself about Vietnam. I didn't know where it was on the map. It was a place I hadn't heard of, and I didn't really know why we were fighting there.
>
> ROBERT EARL, NATIONAL SERVICEMAN, 1 FIELD SQUADRON

> I got [my notice] in Narrabri, yeah. 'What the hell's this?' And they told me. 'Oh, righto we're at war, okay.' And that was it. Didn't know a thing. Never heard.
>
> 'Where's Vietnam?'
>
> 'Oh, way overseas.'
>
> 'How the hell do we get over there?' Didn't have a clue. Strange, isn't it? Still into hotting up cars then, didn't know

a thing about it. Vietnam, Malaysia, Cambodia. 'Where the hell's all these?'

Taiwan. 'What's that? Sounds like a fish.' But that's how away from it all you were, you didn't care, you didn't know, you didn't worry. But when I did get called up, I was proud. But I was scared, really *scared.*

BRIAN WOODS, NATIONAL SERVICEMAN

War, we had been told by our fathers and grandfathers, was about mateship. Forcing someone to fight was not part of that legend and there was a growing refusal by young Australians to submit quietly to authority. Going to war in Vietnam was now a very real prospect for young men and each of us awaiting the government's pleasure had to make decisions about what we believed in, what we feared . . . what kind of person we actually were. Nowhere was this more hotly debated than at university and in the months leading up to my national service registration, I was asked the same infuriating question repeatedly, generally accompanied by a knowing look: 'So, what are *you* going to do?'

Maybe my long hair, strident student opinions and the ever-present guitar were dead giveaways as to what my views were and, generally, I knew what reaction to expect from the questioner. But people are complex, hidden creatures and it's dangerous to assume you know them. There were the usual suspects of course, relatives and other 'adults' who could loosely be described as conservative Catholics. They predictably delivered the jagged edge of fear and racism. Some of these folks were card-carrying avengers of the one, true Cross and Christ himself. They regarded it as my personal responsibility to extinguish the last breath from as many 'slant-eyed Commie bastards' as I could and only wished they could go too. At least they were consistent.

The responses that startled me though came out of the dark. Jack, our taciturn neighbour, was a widower and a New Guinea veteran, famous in the street for never engaging in small talk. He used to scare us a little when I was a kid, with his abrupt ways and his daily ration of two bottles of Reschs beer clinking gently in his Gladstone bag. It was at a neighbourhood barbecue when Jack spoke out, on a Sunday in summer. I was arguing with some of the men about Vietnam and national service and it was getting nasty when Jack intervened.

'It's not our war,' he muttered. 'He shouldn't go. No bastard should. It's just old men and politicians wanting blood. Bugger the lot of 'em.'

It was just on dusk, after too much beer and sun. Nobody spoke for a moment, then watchful wives gathered up their irascible husbands and tired kids and filled the quiet with busyness and goodbyes. I looked over at Jack nursing his beer and humming quietly, and he winked at me. Friends in strange places.

Or conversely, you encountered enemies where you least expected them. The other members of the band I was playing in then were around 10 years older than I was, way past any threat of a khaki makeover. But they were musicians so I thought we were brothers, sharing songs, booze, drugs and a healthy scorn for all authority . . . surely they'd agree that this war was not ours and that I shouldn't go. Wrong.

It was the weekly rehearsal and we had broken for coffee and a smoke. The conversation had taken a perilous turn from 12-bar blues to Communism, call-up and cowardice. The band split down the middle, the bass player and I on one side, 'patriots' on the other. The temperature rose, the language got ugly, then very ugly, and blood was splattered on the microphone. So much for the pacifism of this conscientious objector.

Then there was Matthew's story. Matthew was the only child in a middle-class family. His father, Douglas, was a bank manager and his mother, Shirley, was devoted to what we used to call 'home duties'. Matthew and I were close friends, even though much mattered in his home that didn't in mine – the right cutlery at mealtimes, cloth serviettes neatly folded inside silver rings, leather-bound copies of the classics on the bookshelves . . . and the Queen, Empire and tradition. A proud committee member of the RSL, Douglas would lecture us every Anzac Day about the values of military service and war. Matthew's grandfather Tom, a World War I man, would join in this communal hymn of praise to 'the making of a man'. Matthew was already an officer in his school cadet corps and they would both drop broad hints to him about 'Royal Military College, Duntroon' and 'family tradition'. Matthew loved both men and seemed to accept that the military lay firmly on his path, while I was equally determined that it lay nowhere on mine.

When Menzies reintroduced national service it was a free kick for Douglas and Tom. 'At last,' they said to me in particular. 'At long, bloody last and not before time. You young fellas are going to be brought into line now. You'll be shaped up and shipped out with a bit of steel up your backbone.' Their only disappointment was that some of us would escape this life-correcting makeover. We were still at school then and turning 20, the age of conscription, seemed light-years away. We nodded at them, smiled at each other and thought no more of it.

After school finished, the geography of different universities separated Matthew and me. We'd catch up now and then, fragments of conversation when he'd come to see my band play, the occasional phone call that would always leave us both helpless with shared laughter. It was never difficult to restart our conversations, the threads of lives. I knew that he'd joined his university regiment and when the time came for us to register for national service I assumed that this would keep him out of the regular army. And it would have, except that he chose otherwise.

He turned up late one night, feverish and agitated, a letter in his hand. It was addressed to his father and grandfather and he wanted me to read it before it was sent. In it, he told them that he would be registering as a conscientious objector, that he believed the war in Vietnam was morally wrong and that he could not, would not, participate in any way. It was a calm, reasoned letter and he ended it by hoping that they would understand and respect his decision. 'If the government thinks I'm old enough to fight,' he wrote, 'then I'm old enough to make the choice not to.'

We talked well into the next day, though I could not advise him. Matthew was high on ideals, as excited as I'd ever seen him. He quoted Thoreau and Gandhi and, like all new converts, could not allow for contrary views. 'They'll come round,' he said. 'I know they will.' He left to send the letter and that was the last time I saw him.

Shirley, his mother, told me the rest of the story. They cut him off, those two men whom he loved and respected; they severed him from his family as easily as you prune a diseased limb from a tree. They wrote to him, belittling his decision and calling him a coward. They told him they were ashamed of him and that he did not belong to the family anymore. They ordered him not to use the family name in any connection with them, ever again. His mother secretly contacted him, but could neither relieve his pain nor convince her husband to reconcile with their son.

Matthew ended the argument by taking his own life in the bathroom of his share house in Surry Hills. The funeral was restricted to immediate family members only. Many years later, when I was producing a television series on Australia's military history, I looked up Douglas's war record. He was a lieutenant in the Army Service Corps, transport division. He had never left Australia.

Matthew was a casualty of the Vietnam War. Over the years, we seem to have forgotten how divisive life became then, how many families and friends broke apart in bitter division, how they slashed into each other over that one word – conscription.

For others, though, the prospect of national service was a straightforward decision that did not need any agonising.

> I thought Australia should be involved. At that time, the anti-Vietnam movement really hadn't got a go on. There were only rumblings beginning... because the population at that time was in favour. I mean my attitudes changed dramatically very quickly, but at that point then, yeah, I was in favour of it.
>
> But I think, to be honest though, it was the personal things that were to the fore. I saw it as an escape from a job I didn't particularly like. I saw it as a way to see a bit more of Australia or maybe further afield... I sort of went into national service with the aim, well, I don't like teaching and I don't really want to go back to it, so let's take the opportunity to try and learn a new skill I could use back in civilian life.
>
> GEOFFREY MORGAN, NATIONAL SERVICEMAN, 104 SIGNALS SQUADRON

Indefinite deferments will be granted to registrants who are:

1. Married before the time of their call-up
2. Have a serious criminal record
3. Are a member of the Citizen Military Forces, Citizen Naval Force or Citizen Air Force

Temporary deferments will be granted to registrants on the following grounds:

1. Exceptional hardship or compassion
2. Students/apprentices/trainees engaged in training and/or studies at universities/teachers' colleges/technical colleges

Section 29A of the National Service Act provides full exemption for:

1. Persons suffering from physical or mental disability
2. Theological students, ministers of religion and members of religious orders
3. Persons whose conscientious beliefs do not allow them to engage in any form of military service.

> All claims for exemption will be considered only after the ballot has been completed.

To be considered for exemption as a CO (conscientious objector), you had to publicly declare your hand after registration and before the ballot. This could be a little tricky, as cartoonist Michael Leunig discovered.

> After my number was selected, I wanted to register as a conscientious objector. When I went to Footscray post office to get the forms, the woman at the counter said she did not know anything about them. She went out the back to ask; then all these people came out and stared at me. The guy running the post office came to the counter; he said I should go and fight for my country. He said he didn't have the forms, and to go somewhere else because he didn't want to be the one to give them to me.
>
> I was really humiliated. All these people were sniggering at me. I went back a few weeks later when they had the forms, and they resentfully gave them to me.
>
> MICHAEL LEUNIG

Like Leunig, I filled in the form that told the government I was not willing to be conscripted, but my chances of exemption were bugger-all. I was opposed to the Vietnam War but not to 'any form of military service', and neither the government nor the courts would allow this distinction. You could defend yourself all the way to the High Court if you wished (at your own expense), but every case so far had been decided in the government's favour. Jail awaited those who still refused to serve after the court's decision.

It was a long four weeks between registration and the ballot. Then, after months of soul-searching, argument, bitterness and regret, I was 'balloted out' and so did not have to face the next step. All up, over 800 000 men registered for national service during the war; 63 735 were called up and 1012 sought exemption. It was granted in full to 733. The rest were headed for the green machine.

Men who pass the final medical examination will serve for two years full-time in the Regular Army Supplement and a further three years part-time in the Regular Army Reserve. An initial 10 weeks recruit training will be followed by three months of corps training after which national servicemen will be able to apply for posting to any corps. All national servicemen are liable for special overseas service.

The night that we arrived there they were handing out gear, and anyway I got a pair of boots, and I think you have to put on the form or something what size are you and I was a ten. And when I got my boots they were tied together and I had a look and one was a ten and one was an eight. I went back and I said to this duty NCO, 'I have got a pair of boots here, one is right and one is wrong. I have got a ten and an eight.'

And he said, 'What do you want, them both the same?'

And I said, 'Well, it would help a bit, wouldn't it?'

And he said, 'You're a bit of a smart bastard, aren't you?'

And I said, 'Well, if you think I am that good, why don't you put me down for the intelligence corps?'

I got in a bit of strife for that.

JOHN ROBBINS, NATIONAL SERVICEMAN, 6RAR

A bus pulls up and 50 young men spill out into a cold, grey dawn. Some are volunteers, soon-to-be regular soldiers, others are brand-new conscripts. Stiff and restless from the long ride, they stamp their feet to force the blood down, the sound echoing slightly across a vast expanse of bitumen. Long, rectangular buildings are just visible through a swirling mist that clutches at their legs. Bags hit the ground carelessly as the bus pulls away. How quickly they establish roles. The nervous ones chatter to each other, the cool saunter about, cigarettes lit, visibly unimpressed while the cautious stand still and watchful.

'Gentlemen. Let's have some quiet please.'

Footsteps crunch on the ground. Where? Then their eyes find him. A lone man taking two steps forwards out of the fog – slouch hat, crisp khaki uniform, gleaming black boots, polished brass, three stripes on the shoulder. The chatter rises.

'QUIET!'

It's doubtful if any of them have ever heard a voice quite like it. Silence is the only possible response.

'Line up. Five ranks, ten in each. C'mon . . . get a move on!'

They obey, though not without stumbling, jostling and some surreptitious counting.

'Welcome to Kapooka, gentlemen, your home away from home for the next ten weeks. My name is Sergeant Jenkins. You will call me Sergeant . . . as in, "Yes, Sergeant . . . No, Sergeant . . . Three bags full, Sergeant." From this point on you will speak only when spoken to. Should you have a question, or in the unlikely event that you have something worthwhile to say, you will raise your right hand directly into the air and wait until such time as you are given permission to speak. Then, and only then, will you utter a sound. Are we clear?'

They mutter and mumble, one or two able to raise a firm, 'Yes, Sergeant.'

He glares, slowly moving his gaze up and down each sorry-arsed one of them, allowing them to see how comprehensively he loathes them all. Long hair, sideburns, weird-looking clothes, out of shape most of them, wouldn't know their arses from their elbows. Jesus Christ, I'm too old for this crap. He speaks again, quietly this time, but with such malicious intent that no one could mistake his meaning.

'Are we clear?'

As one, they roar back, enjoying, with a rush of recognition, the power of the group.

'Yes, Sergeant!'

Time for the spiel. The sergeant takes a breath and unleashes a torrent. The words pile up on each other, vowels chasing consonants chasing syllables into a chant that is as incomprehensible to them as an animal's mating call.

'Right. Fromthispointonwardsyouarenolongercivilians!Youare numberoneplatoonGcompanynumberfourrecruittrainingbattalion Kapooka! FirstrankisAsectionsecondrankBsectionandsoon. Doyouseethehutsbehindme?'

There is no answer. Again, slowly, he speaks as if to slightly stupid children.

'Can . . . you . . . see . . . the . . . huts . . . behind . . . me?'

'Yes, Sergeant!' The relief is tangible.

'Gooooood.'

Another breath.

'AsectionwillmoveintothenorthernmosthutBsectioninto theonenexttothatetceteraetcetera. Pickupyourbagsmovemove movestraightintothehutstakeabedanybedstowyourgearunderit andreturnhereatthedoubleyouhavesixtyseconds. Right? Move! Go! Go! Go!'

And go, they did.

All of these fellows were all detailed, 'You do this. You, go and get a haircut.'

'How do you want your hair?'

'Oh, just touched up here.'

Zzzzht, took the lot off. It was all quite an experience really. I could see that it was really daunting for some of those fellows, those that hadn't been around much, lived at home and were still at home and had never been away. Some of them were shell-shocked that this was what was going on. 'Am I going to be treated like this?' Every time they talked to you they barked at you, a bit amusing when you think about it the way they carried on. It was cold; we went there in late May or June. Bleak, all new faces, it was scary the first few days. Sleeping in those igloo huts, making your bed of a morning as neat as you could and someone coming along and saying, 'That's not good enough!' and ripping it apart. And you had a locker and all of your gear, they showed you how to fold things and everything had to be neat and facing this way and nothing out of place and you think, 'Gee, it is spot on, I have never had anything look better than that.' And then some sergeant comes in and says, 'Look at the mess in this place, you dickhead!' Throw things about, they just do it to break you.

I don't know if you could say that we were treated differently. It would be unfair of me to say that, probably they didn't at that time understand that there were fellows there that would come in as national servicemen that did have a bit upstairs. So the first few days there were quite a few negative actions, 'I am not doing that.' There was the regular soldier, the fellow that joined, he wanted to be there, but there were quite a number of national servicemen who didn't like it and didn't want to be there, it wasn't their decision. They probably had a job or a girlfriend, a life back where they came from and it had been thrown out the door and here they are at Kapooka lined up at half past five on a cold morning lined up for inspections, they thought, 'What the hell am I doing here?' And there would be some well-educated fellows there and I am not sure that they were ready for that. I am not saying that the people who joined the regular army weren't educated, I am just saying they wanted to be there and there was probably a bit of difference between them.

JOHN ROBBINS

The army was not prepared for the nashos. It wasn't just a shortage of resources, though they were caught short with that as well. It was attitude. The nashos *were* generally better educated than the usual army recruits, and many of them were already making their way in the world when they were called up. What made it confusing and frustrating for the NCOs who trained them was their refusal to accept many of the orders they were given. Men who had already established themselves as school teachers, journalists, psychologists, farmers, musicians and truck drivers were not inclined to be blindly led by other men with stripes on their arms. 'Why' was the word that triggered fury in the sergeants and corporals.

'You see this book? This is the red book. It is called the Army Manual. This is your Bible.'

'Why, Corp? It might be your Bible but it isn't mine.'

'Right. Full combat gear everyone. We go through that creek, into the trees and then up over that hill. Ready?'

'Ah, Sarge... there's a bridge a hundred yards or so downstream. Why don't we use that?'

'Yeah, Sarge. And do we have to go over the hill? Quicker to go round it, I reckon.'

One sergeant terminated the questioning with this immortal line: 'Son, I work for a democracy, I don't fucken run one. Get on with it.'

It was going to take a while, but in the end, the army would win. It had to, or these young men would not survive. Not in the lethal world of Vietnam. The same training that had succeeded with their fathers and grandfathers, those civilian soldiers who had fought so well in previous wars, would ultimately have its way with them too. In the outside world, the cult of individualism was gaining strength, but inside the perimeter fences of Kapooka, Puckapunyal and Singleton there were no individuals, only teams. There could be no rebellion, only compliance, no shades of grey, just black and white. They would learn the motto of their fathers: 'If it moves, salute it; if it doesn't move, pick it up; and if you can't pick it up, paint it.'

> Bloody hell it was cold. Every morning you'd have to race out at 'sheet call' they used to call it. You had to rip the bottom sheet off your bed and race out, whatever you had on, in the freezing cold, in the parade ground. In your pyjamas or nothing, oh, you had the sheet wrapped around you. This was to make sure that you were out of bed, one; two, that you'd make your bed, wouldn't just pull it up. You had to remake your bed... It was hard, it was very hard.
>
> It was go, go, go for three months, it was just non-stop. The food was horrible, but if you didn't eat it you didn't survive. There were inspections all the time. I mean everything was folded neatly, packed neatly, stacked neatly; your bed had to be so tight so you'd drop a coin on it and it'd bounce. Your pillow had to not have a wrinkle in it. Your socks and everything were polished, folded, ironed neatly. Your beret put on properly, your hat, oh God it was tedious work but it was there, you had to be doing it. The toilets, the showers, the hallway, all had to be cleaned every morning. Everything. I joined the army to be doing what I was doing beforehand, cleaning everything. It was a surprise to me. I thought God strife; I'll go over to Vietnam with a scrubbing brush!
>
> BRIAN WOODS

Run the bastards over!

NSW PREMIER BOB ASKIN REFERRING TO PROTESTERS, 1966

As the first nashos entered the army, public protests against conscription began. It wasn't the students, the unions or the Left that did it, though they would all eventually take up their placards and parade. It was those people on whom we all depend; those last-ditch, stand in the trenches alongside you, never-say-die women . . . the mothers. And they did it in true, no-nonsense fashion.

The group they set up in 1965 was called Save Our Sons (SOS) and its members were mostly middle-class housewives. There they stood, in their hats, gloves and sensible shoes, outside army barracks, registration offices, courts of law, houses of parliament and on city streets, brandishing their blue and white banners with slogans hand-printed on their aprons. And, by God, if you wanted them to move along, Officer, you had better learn some manners and ask nicely. They were the rightful heirs to the last, great anti-conscription warriors, the Women's Peace Army of 1916, and they were not challenging the status quo frivolously. They were 'opposed to the conscription of our sons for slaughter in Vietnam'.

SOS was a different form of protest and it brought about strong reactions, particularly from men. The Holy Mother and Wife was out of the kitchen and on the streets and many men found it not just unseemly, but downright threatening. The women were spat on, publicly abused, had their placards ripped from their hands and their pamphlets crumpled and thrown in their faces. They were called Communists, neglectful wives and, worst insult of all, 'bad mothers'. But they brought a respectability and potency to civil protest that had never been there before. What, after all, was more understandable and praiseworthy than a mother protecting her child? Even if, sometimes, the child didn't want to be protected.

> It was the time of the demonstrations. Being the first intake, there were lots of demonstrations. The main one that sticks in my mind is Central station when we were leaving for Kapooka... big, big demonstrations with mums leaning against the train and not letting it leave. It didn't go on forever but it was enough to cause a bit of a kerfuffle and, as I've often said, when you're 20 and that's going on, it's a bit embarrassing, it's a bit amusing and it's a bit of a new adventure the whole thing really... There was a lot of noise; we'd have been making enough talk anyway, just talking, laughing, people hanging out of windows and stuff, you know. I don't really remember what they were saying, the main thing I remember, how they just leant against the train and wouldn't let it leave for a while and then they got cleared away or whatever... 'Save Our Sons' or something... I mean at that stage we didn't need saving, it was day one.
>
> NOEL GRIMES, NATIONAL SERVICEMAN, 6RAR

There were two causes now, anti-conscription and anti-war. University students formed their own protest group, YCAC, the Youth Campaign Against Conscription, and stood alongside the women of SOS. Long hair, beards and peace symbols made a curious fashion statement next to twinsets and pearls, but there they were, resplendent on the front page of newspapers and leading the six o'clock news. And if the women were ever uncomfortable with their fellow travellers and their slogans, like 'Fighting for peace is like fucking for chastity', they had the good manners never to show it.

The protesters were quick to adopt new methods, especially those learnt from watching American demonstrations on television. Unfortunately, we did not have draft cards as the Americans did, so they burnt registration notices instead. And we didn't have a romantic escape route for draft dodgers into Canada either. Still, there was always New Zealand, and you didn't even need a passport.

It took a while for the forces of law to catch on to it all. Perhaps the long, dull years of conservative government and the welcome peace and prosperity after the war had lulled the establishment into complacency, but the police in particular were at a loss as to how to deal with this new breed of demonstrators. It was a big ask for them to jump from a corrective clip on the ear for the local larrikin to facing a thousand-strong, slogan-chanting, unruly mob. Not that they spent a lot of time considering the problem. It was caps off, ID badges removed, and boots, fists and a short, sharp punch to the kidneys before dragging them by the hair into the paddy wagons. Infuriated demonstrators replied in kind and the blood flowed both ways, carried along by a surge of mutual derision and loathing.

The almost daily sight of yet another protester burning his notice and flaunting the law convinced the federal government to put its legislative foot down. They added a clause to the National Service Act stating that anyone refusing to provide information concerning men who had failed to register would be fined $200. The reaction was predictable. 'Nazi Germany!' and 'Stalinist Russia!' were two of the more polite cries and, by the time university vice-chancellors refused to co-operate and the law had become known as 'the pimping provision', they'd had enough. The clause was quietly withdrawn.

They couldn't win. The wheel had begun to spin and they were left chewing dust and recalling memories of quieter times. There was no good news coming out of Vietnam. No thrilling tales of bravery; no Kokoda, Gallipoli or Pozières. The army, the newspapers and the politicians had no public heroes to stir the people's blood and warm their Aussie hearts, no pictures of a gallant fuzzy wuzzy angel leading a wounded digger to safety. Those images were all in the past. What was 'now', what was 'happening', was the photograph of a long-haired dissenter, courageously resisting a phalanx of overweight cops as they dragged him away to jail. He looked vaguely like one of Christ's apostles, definitely 'cool', a modern icon. Photos of soldiers on the other hand, even conscripts, with their identical khaki uniforms and painfully short hair, were symbols of the state, old-fashioned and irrelevant. Once they went through the gates of the camps, we forgot about them. We knew nothing about their lives and, it should be said, didn't care to know.

Not all nashos went quietly into the arms of the army. Some registered as conscientious objectors during their recruit training and, for their stand, they were bundled into military prisons and treated with disdain.

> They took me to Puckapunyal and whacked me into solitary confinement, even before my charge was heard ... it was my first experience of prison, and it was a shock. I have always hated small spaces, and the moment they shut the cell door I started going to pieces. I was not psychologically prepared for it.
>
> There were specific orders not to talk to me, not to give me any light at night, and I was to receive no news from outside. They took away my belt and shoes so I could not commit suicide, which is just a pretext for humiliating people.
>
> They only fed me once or twice in about four days and one meal was a stew I had to eat with my fingers. Although there was no violence, threats were made. You assume that if they get away with not feeding you then anything goes.
>
> After four days, I was totally terrified. I remember shouting that I wanted to go to the toilet and later heard an officer tell

the guards, 'You'll be escorting a dangerous prisoner. No one is to speak to him at all. Do not answer him if he speaks and be very careful.'

...I was escorted to the toilet by soldiers who were under the impression I was dangerous. A few of them even watched me in the toilet. I was standing there trying to have a piss and just started crying. I couldn't stand it, the whole thing unhinged me. I was taken back to the cell, still crying.

...I was in there for 10 days and then court-martialled for being absent without leave. I didn't defend myself, refused to recognise the court, and was sentenced to 48 days at Holsworthy [prison].

DENIS O'DONNELL

The nasho boys from the bush seemed to fare better than their city cousins. Maybe it was their independence, or maybe they found the blokey atmosphere of beer drinking, hard yakka and 'fuck' language in the army comfortable. The army was old Australia, and not about to change.

There was a few complainers, yeah. A few people that were not happy with the way things went. I think there was some of them just thought that you get a rifle and put on a uniform and get sent straight over, they didn't know that all this training was important. As an officer said to me, he said, 'You'll make it because you're a survivor, you've learnt, whereas the others they're not, because they've lived at home all their life, they've never had to fend for themselves.' They'd never done ironing, they'd never made their bed, they'd never done their washing. And where in the army you had to do all that, you had to learn to iron and you had to learn to starch things, you had to learn to get the creases right... some of them were not very happy about it, yeah, some of them were really, really wanting to get out every day of the week. They just wouldn't cooperate, they wouldn't and some of them tried very hard to get out... A couple of blokes I know that did get away from the army like sort of AWOL served a bit of time in lockup but come out and they served with us, they were good, there was nothing different about them. I think it was just at the time they couldn't handle the pressure or some of the films they showed you or some of the training we got scared them a bit, I don't know. Just one of those things.

BRIAN WOODS

A lot of the guys used to knock the food and I don't know why, but I used to say, 'What the frigging hell is wrong with you bastards?'

They said, 'Oh, this shit again.'

Breakfast for example now, you had toast, you had bacon, you had sausages, you had bubble-and-squeak, you had grilled tomatoes, fried eggs, poached eggs, scrambled eggs. You had milk, you had cordial, you had coffee. You had porridge. Now, how many people at home, even in this day and age, have a choice like that for breakfast? Cereals: Rice Bubbles, Cornflakes, bloody Weet-Bix. There wouldn't have been one out of a thousand who had a choice like that for breakfast at home.

'What the hell are you bitching about?'

Stupid.

ANTHONY HUGHES

In reality, rather than myth, the number of recruits who registered as conscientious objectors was very small. So too were the deserters, the disturbed and the downright mutinous. The army did what the army has always been able to and must do with its men – it built up peer pressure that efficiently removed the nonconformists and the weak. The endless drills taught instinctive obedience, and the constant physical training that pushed everyone to their limits challenged their very maleness and instilled the belief that you can't let your mates down.

By the time they were done, the nashos, city or country, were, to all intents and purposes, identical to the regular soldiers they trained with. They had responsibilities and they had support. They were family. For the next two years at least.

> There was one point when we had to do, I've forgotten how far, it might've been about 10 kilometres, 15 kilometres forced march or something like that, a fair distance, and I remember thinking beforehand, 'Can I do it? Am I capable of doing it?' And then when you find that when you do a forced march, you really are marching fairly close together and in essence you're pulling each other along, it's quite amazing the unified action that comes about. So, even if you're really puffed, just the atmosphere, the feeling between people just keeps you moving. And I can still remember at the end of that sitting in the mess, feeling absolutely elated that I'd done it.
>
> GEOFFREY MORGAN

> I must admit on the parade ground with the military band playing and you're marching, you feel pretty good. That was a thrill, you know, those days when you're not allowed to blink or do anything wrong. Particularly if you had families coming to see you . . . I can remember feeling very proud. Oh, even the day they marched us out of Kapooka actually, by then as they'd say, they'd knocked us into shape and we could all keep in step. And there were a few dignitaries there as you can imagine. You feel good. I don't know if I felt like a soldier, but I certainly felt I looked like one . . . I've always been very interested in music but musical or not you can't help but get a tingle up your spine when you're marching to a military band.
>
> NOEL GRIMES

After training, all recruits were given a choice of corps to join – infantry, signals, engineers and so on, though rarely did they get their first choice. A quarter of nashos went to Vietnam in the infantry, the 'grunts', which is not particularly surprising as it's the largest corps in the Australian Army. They received more specific training in their battalions, and then finally, Canungra was waiting.

At the bottom of the headquarters hill at Canungra is a creek that's hidden behind thick rainforest and lantana. It was along here that they ran the most hated part of the training – the Confidence Course. Imagine the world's worst obstacle course full of mud, pain and blood, where your fears are revealed and every last bit of your endurance is used up. Only it was worse than that.

The course is still there, a little rusted and decaying but still threatening. It sees little use these days. Sending men over it now would bring about howls of complaint and inevitable litigation. Warriors, it seems, need protection these days. As the instructors walked me along it their memories tumbled out and they talked over the top of each other, recreating the disasters and triumphs each new hazard could cause. In their heads the tapes were rolling and the words and phrases they used to shout at the men were called out again into the quiet day. I could see the action unfold in front of me as we stumbled along the creek.

They start you from the hill, a company of 120 men dressed in full battle gear – pack, webbing, grenades, water bottles, ammunition pouches and rifle slung over your shoulder, more than 30 kilos of extra weight on your back. If the instructors are out to get you for some reason, you also have to carry the heavy M60, the machine gun. That's another 10 and a half kilos. You go at three minute intervals, in groups of three.

> You're at 'em from the get-go. 'Don't fuck around, dickheads! Remember, it's timed and if you don't make it . . . you do the bastard again. Do not wait for your mates. I shit you not. GO!'

You hurtle forward at full pace, gear clanking against your body and the chaos begins.

> So we're throwing smoke grenades, we're throwing grenade simulators, we had machine guns firing. The smoke got that bad you couldn't breathe by the other end and they'd have to close the doors and windows in the headquarters block up the hill.

The first obstacle, three long, parallel poles set across six metres of creek. Green with slime and wet with mud. You have to balance on them and walk across. Except you can't take it at a walk. There's an instructor a few metres away and, while you're trying to stop the rifle banging into your back and the ammo pouches from slipping, this clown is bellowing at you that you're a frigging idiot who's gonna get his mates killed. The grenade explosions make your ears hurt and you slip and fall in. The water's freezing and it's hard to clamber out onto the bank. Your two mates have made it across already and you hurry after them, but the bastard instructor sends you back over the creek.

> They had to complete every obstacle. So what if you're wet? Big deal. We couldn't give a fuck. You just shouted at 'em till they went back and did it again. Yeah, they hated us. But they kept going.

There's so much coloured smoke in the air that it's hard to breathe and you're coughing up lumps of black crap. Ahead, three long pipes. Do you go into them frontwards or backwards? Backwards, I'm sure they told us backwards. Scrabble through, only just fit, and out the other end arse-first into a disgusting pond. Keep your mouth closed. Machine guns firing over your head. You know they're only blanks, but they're bloody loud. There's a hanging rope over a moat. You jump, hang on and swing, even though the rope burns on your hands will take days to heal. Off and running, shit, it's the wall. Two and a half metres high, made out of logs. You make it to the top but your mate slips and slams into it, blood streaming down his face. You reach down, can't leave him behind. The clock is ticking and the prick of an instructor has a cheesy smile on his face. Fuck him, we'll do this.

> If there was a weak man in the company, he had to be found out. And once he was, either they dragged him up to their standard or we'd get rid of him. You had to. They could all die because of that bloke and they needed to know that.

You're running close to empty and your breath is shallow and burns your throat. The weight of the pack is beyond belief. You hit the deck 'cos there's strand after strand of barbed wire entangled close to the ground. You crawl under it, machine guns and grenades going off just above your head. Your webbing catches and you rip it away from the wire in a fury. Then up a ladder, two cables stretched across the creek, a man's height apart. You grab the top one and stretch your feet out to find the bottom one but it's as slack as an alcoholic's promise and you wobble and twist in the air, four metres above the freezing water. Christ, don't let me fall.

> You just didn't let up. Always in their face, pushing 'em, pushing 'em. 'You hang round up there, dickwit, and the VC will gladly shoot you a second arsehole. Get a fucken move on!'

Back on the ground again, crawling under a cargo net through a pool that looks and tastes like shit.

> 'You're running out of time, slackarse. This is a piece of piss. A fucken girl could do it faster than you! Get the lead out!'

You don't have to take this, not from that prick. You keep running as you yell back at him, 'Get fucked!' He just grins and yells right back at you, 'That's get fucked, *Sergeant*, Private.' Another wall, shorter than the last. Ah Christ, is it the Bear Pit? You're up and over before you realise it and then you're falling down, into disgust.

> The Bear Pit was a ripper. We'd tell 'em it was full of the worst kind of shit. It wasn't *that* bad – a roo carcass or two and some blokes used to use it as a pisser or take a spew in it after a hard night. But it wasn't that bad.

You don't splash when you hit the Bear Pit; it's more like a splat, like a rock thrown into deep, black mud. You're not ready for it so it gets in your mouth and it's so foul you can't help but retch. You crawl and slide, you even try a stroke or two, anything to get out of that putrid muck. Twenty metres on there's a vertical cargo net that seems to run from the ground to the sky. Grab it and climb. You want to stop, to breathe. Anything to end this.

'Get your hands off your dick and grab that rope, man. C'mon . . . c'mon. More speed!'

Across the tarred road, dripping unmentionable liquids. Up and through the car tyres, feet struggling to find stability, water below again. Oh shit, we're here. It's The Tower. It stretches up, 10 metres above the river. Exhausted and filthy, you climb, dragging your weight to the top. There's an instructor there. He gives you a once-over check. 'Swimmer or non-swimmer?' and indicates the answer to the two divers in the water below. 'Hold your arms out . . . away from your body. That's it. Any time you like, son.' You don't really care anymore. At least it'll wash some of the crap off you. So you step off. When you hit the water, between your uniform and your gear you sink like the proverbial stone so the divers come in and grab your arms before you reach the bottom and stay there, in the mud.

> Some blokes would go straight off, others would sit there and the longer they stayed the harder it was to get 'em off. Sometimes you'd get sick of waiting and so you'd just count, 'One . . . two . . . three . . .' and then give 'em a helping hand to leave. Nobody was allowed to climb back down. I dunno what it was, but I've seen blokes reduced to panic up there . . . absolute bloody panic. With the truly petrified ones, you'd just grab their hand and jump with 'em. That worked. But, you know, once they got through that course the first time, you could see it – they'd stand taller, look you in the eye sort of thing.

That's it, you're done. You collapse on the river bank, soaked to the skin, freezing with cold and glad to be alive. You did it . . . you bloody well did it.

The NCOs I met in Canungra are typical of their kind – hard-talking and hard-drinking, with a deeply buried undercurrent of compassion and care for their men. Suggest this last fact to them and you're likely to be on the receiving end of a torrent of abuse and denial, but it's there, Sergeant, it's there. They delight in telling you tales of how they punished this bloke or knew from the start that that officer was an incompetent clown, but I cannot think of anyone I'd rather be with in the trenches. I know with utter certainty that they would save my life.

NCOs are of the men, but not *with* the men; they're not officers but that privileged class could not manage without them. God knows how many men's lives have been saved in combat by an experienced sergeant correcting the mistakes of an ignorant, gung-ho lieutenant. They prefer each other's company and express a common view that only they keep the service on the straight and narrow. They're probably right.

The men below them in the food chain have very, very mixed views about them. The disciplinary structure of the army allows the occasional sadist of an NCO to bring the object of his torture to near suicide, and if they should decide that you're a 'jackman', a soldier who doesn't contribute, a 'bludger', you'd be better off asking for an immediate transfer. Yet their men often speak about them with a perverse affection, listing their spectacular flaws and bizarre behaviour with pride – 'He may well be a bastard, but he's *our* bastard.'

In some parts of the army, they're called 'Gila Monsters', after the large lizard that likes nothing better than to sit in the sun, warming its arse. This arises from the NCO's habit of setting a platoon some puerile task, such as washing and disinfecting 100 foul-smelling garbage bins, then dozing comfortably in the sun while they struggle to complete the chore, waking only to yell at them about their various inadequacies.

They generally do this in what is known as 'Gila speak', a tormenting of the English language that is so twisted it almost forms a sub-language of its own. Drilling raw recruits can bring on an attack. 'Pregnant women and poofters stand around with their arms folded, son. Which one are you?' Or the wondrous word picture of 'If I see those hands move one more time, Private, I'll rip 'em off your shoulders, stuff 'em up your arse and ride you round the parade ground like a motorbike!' My favourites are when the word mangling approaches poetry, such as when a sergeant's charges arrived on a bivouac and, anxious to get the camp organised, he issued the order, 'Right, you lot. I want you to dismantle that tent there and re-mantle it over there!'

You've gotta love it.

At Canungra, the NCOs were lords and masters, gods of pain, and the recruits knew it.

> They were bloody good. Pack of bastards, but they were good. If they weren't good there, they got the sack, baby, real quick. Most or all were very experienced. Most certainly Vietnam. Some Malaya, Borneo, and some even Korea, so a pretty experienced pack of people. And if you weren't good, they kicked your arse until your nose bled, I'll tell you.
>
> ANTHONY HUGHES

Like old actors, they had set routines and performances that became part of the mystique that surrounded JTC. And the young men in training fell for it every time.

> 'Cranky' Jack Morrison marched us all the way up to the top of the hill . . . in the jungle and through vines and wait-a-whiles [spiky tropical vines] . . . And when we got to the top 'Cranky' Jack was standing there, and he's all dressed up and he's got all his medals on. He's got a whole chest full of medals and he said, 'If you want to come back from Vietnam looking like me, pay attention to what I'm going to teach you. You have to live in this friendly jungle. It's not a terrible thing like you

think it is because you can live off this jungle. For example, I'll show you this.' And he walks over to a puddle, puts his hand in, brings out a stubby, pulls the top off, and drinks it. He said, 'You can find anything you want in the jungle.'

That was the start of his lesson and then he showed us the food that you can eat there, the different things, the berries and the things. And when the lesson was all over, there was about 30 or 40 of us there, all huddled around in the scrub and he said, 'I'll now show you what was taking place while you were all listening to me. Stand up, Bloggs, Jones and Smith.' And all these soldiers all stood up, that were right with us. They'd been lying there for the entire lesson, camouflaged in the jungle, right near us and we could have fallen over them and we didn't see them . . . so that lesson stuck.

MICHAEL RODGER, AATTV

As the war gathered intensity more of the instructors had seen service in Vietnam and the course was changed to accommodate their experience. A mock Vietnamese village was built, complete with tunnels, booby traps and mines, and the trainees were sent through it on operations. Sometimes it worked, sometimes it didn't.

We did this search, we cordoned it, we blocked it off and then we searched it . . . and we were moving around inside the village searching everywhere and suddenly I stood on a mock mine. Boom! Up it went, smoke under my foot. 'Rodger, you're dead, stood on a mine, you're dead!' So I moved, stood on another one. Boom! Oh my God. Well I shifted again and I blew three of them up and the chief instructor yelled out, 'For Christ's sake, Rodger, stand still and leave some mines for somebody else to stand on!' . . . I'll never forget that and I learnt a lesson there, don't step on mines, especially three of them, and a funny thing was when I did get to 'the funny

> country' I never stood on one, people all around me did, all around me and I never, ever stood on one. Maybe I got my share in the training.
>
> MICHAEL RODGER

In Vietnam, as they had in other wars, the Australians earned a reputation in the field as a disciplined, deadly force that could do the hard yards. They had endurance, independence of thought and action, and a confidence in their training and each other that gave them an edge over their enemy. The instructors at Canungra, those heroes and ratbags, those clowns and crazies, were responsible for that. They were unapologetic about their methods and only at the end of each course did their guard momentarily drop.

> By the end, the sergeants were getting a little bit friendlier and talking to you like you were mates, like they knew you and they said to us, 'You understand why we do it. We have to do this. You have to be trained to this standard.' And when you go to places like Vietnam, you realise you can't just grab a rifle and run off into the bush and start shooting, so everyone's life depends on everyone else and that's what they're trying to do, to get you to work as a team. A 10-man section, or whatever it is, each man has a job to do and if you don't do your job the bloke next to you could get killed or you could get killed and that's what it's all about and it's not like just working in a bank. If you want to go and have a sit down in a corner somewhere you can have it and bludge on your mate, but in the army you can't do that, or the air force or the navy, you can't say, 'I'll fix it up tomorrow.' If you're working on an F1-11, 'I'll put that bolt back in tomorrow.' Or, 'I'll check it tomorrow.' And the bloody thing takes off and crashes,

> that's all it takes, so that's why they're very strict on it and it's good training, I reckon. There should be more of it.
>
> MAURICE FAIRHEAD, 6RAR

> I know it was extremely hard but the further you got into it, the easier it became, and I always tell people, after Canungra, you'd walk down the street and someone would bump into you. They might be twice your size and they'd just bounce off you. You were like a piece of steel; you were, you know, six foot tall and bulletproof. You could never get hurt, mate. You were in such tiptop condition that, geez oh, beautiful I was.
>
> BARRY BENSON, 3RAR

I ended my visit to Canungra back in the RSL, drinking and sharing a lunch that 'the boys' had organised. I am not, nor have I ever been a military man. I resent what I see as the mindlessness of the discipline, the petty subjugation of individuality and the ruthless confinement that comes with the 'we're all blokes in together' attitude, even while I recognise the need for it.

But I willingly admit to feeling respect and admiration for these men, both for their paradoxical devotion to saving lives and their acceptance of the unpalatable truth of war – if you have to do it, do it bloody well, do it better than the other bloke and cling to whatever honour and morality you can save from the muck. I'm better for having known these men, just as their soldier boys were.

After Canungra those same soldier boys had no worries now about ballots and medicals, or protesters and politics. No idle thoughts of the girlfriend and that last, urgent kiss that left them holding their kitbag in front of their aching body. Forget for now the Holden safely garaged at home; forget for now Mum and Dad, the bank, the farm, the office or the factory. They're driven into tomorrow by the nervous energy of the blokes around them, the bad jokes being told, the hollow-gut feeling and the slight redness round the eyes.

> It was tough and when it was finished, it was a relief. And by the time you come to the end of that you're so keyed, you're so anxious, you're so 'get me there now I'm ready' attitude that you don't care about anything, you just, 'Let me go, I want to go to war, I want to get there.' That's what it's all about, that's how the training was... I was excited, I was very excited, I was vibrating. I was anxious to get over there, I was very, very anxious. If they would've rung me up halfway through the week's leave, I would've run down to Sydney. But this is the way you're trained see, this is what happens, you get so highly trained, so anxious about everything, it's... how do I say it? You're so skilled, you want to show your skills, you want to use them, and this is what was happening. This is how we were, we were really, really trained to that perfection that we had to get over there and do something.
>
> BRIAN WOODS

We're soldiers now. Slouch hats, bright brass, black boots, determined faces. Jesus Christ, I look like my dad! That bloody picture of him on the mantelpiece! And why the fuck not? My turn now.

Board the plane. I don't believe it. Take off. I don't believe it. There's live ammo in my rifle. I don't believe it. We land in an hour. I still don't believe it.

What's that, Sarge?... I'd better believe it?

Yeah. Right.

With drums and guns, and guns and drums,
The enemy nearly slew you;
My darling dear, you look so queer,
Oh, Johnny, I hardly knew you.

V

WELCOME TO THE FUNNY COUNTRY

Nine Rules for Australian Army Forces in Vietnam

We as a military force and as individuals, are in this country to help the Vietnamese Government and People to win their long and courageous fight against the Communists. The product of victory is a democratic State with stable government and contented people. The Communists will use any weapon to discredit the Government and countries, like ours, in the eyes of the Vietnamese people. Don't let your behaviour be a propaganda weapon which helps in any way to destroy Vietnam. Here are nine simple rules for conduct whilst in Vietnam.

1. Remember we are here only to help; we make no demands and seek no special treatment.
2. Try to understand the people, their way of life; customs and laws.
3. Learn the simple greetings of the Vietnamese language and use them frequently.
4. Treat friendly people, particularly women, with respect and courtesy.
5. Don't attract attention by rude behaviour or larrickinism.
6. Avoid separating us from the Vietnamese by a display of great wealth or privilege.
7. Make friends among the soldiers and people of Vietnam.

8. Remember decency and honesty are the sign of a man and a soldier; bad manners are the sign of a fool.
9. Above all remember you are an Australian, by your actions our country is judged. Set an example of sincerity and fair play in all your dealings with Vietnamese and with other people who are assisting them.

PAMPHLET DISTRIBUTED TO THE AUSTRALIAN ARMY FORCES VIETNAM

Everyone's war is different they say. And they're right. Even men who were six feet apart in the same battle will preserve different moments, one still able to describe the way bullets dismember leaves, another the buzzing of flies round wounded bodies. The Australians who fought in Vietnam are like that, their stories presented to the listener in fragments and shards with an occasional and startling flash of light that illuminates a life. Yet there are commonalities that stand like familiar landmarks on a highway, landmarks they all seem to recognise. Like the day they arrived.

Welcome to Saigon – the Paris of the Orient.

A SIGN AT TAN SON NHUT AIRPORT

It was a hell of a way to go to war – on a Qantas jet with a courteous crew and free beer. Half the Australians who served in Vietnam caught their first glimpse of paddy fields through the windows of a Boeing 707. Sydney to Singapore to Saigon, at a time when overseas travel was still unknown to most Australians and journeys by air both adventurous and exotic.

Fourteen hours of wondering what's waiting for you at the other end when you've never been on a plane before, never really travelled *anywhere*. One hundred and twenty edgy blokes on board and only male flight attendants allowed, not the cute hosties you'd seen on telly ads. That world's been left behind. For the last half-hour of the journey, Saigon air traffic control has the Qantas pilot behaving like he's a fighter jock, pushing the plane through manoeuvres better suited to an F-18 than this lumbering jet. Then a last 90-degree dive that has everyone white-knuckled until you finally level out, heading for Tan Son Nhut Airport. All you can see below is a sparkling necklace of water, dam after dam, pond upon pond, stretching away to the mountains. Someone says that it's pretty impressive how they collect their water, and it takes a moment for the reply to register – 'They're not dams, you dill . . . they're bomb craters.'

Other Australians would go to Vietnam the traditional way, by troopship – just as their fathers and grandfathers had done. The vessel of choice was HMAS *Sydney*, an ex-Royal Navy aircraft carrier that made so many journeys back and forth to Vietnam it became known as 'The Vung Tau Ferry'. Australians are known for their adaptability, but you'd have to question the bureaucratic pen stroke that decided a ship designed for the freezing North Atlantic would make an excellent troop-carrier . . . in the tropics.

The navy did its best, but the *Sydney* was a crowded, hot and humid stinkhole for the nearly two weeks it took to get the soldiers to Vietnam. They ate and slept below decks, where the temperature was too high to do either, and after the first night many men found secret hidey-holes to sleep in among the vehicles and stores on the flight deck, out in the open air. The rest were busy being seasick. They were kept occupied during the day target-shooting coloured balloons off the stern, circuit training round the deck and attending classes in simple Vietnamese language and culture. The highlight came with the issue of one can of Foster's to each man at night, which turned into a nice little earner for the few nondrinkers.

Then quickly, what began as a bad holiday started getting real. One hundred and twenty kilometres southeast of Saigon is the old French seaside resort of Vung Tau, and that was where the *Sydney* was headed. A day or so out from docking, the mood changed. A destroyer escort slid alongside, fighter planes patrolled overhead and suddenly you were sweating your way through battle drills and action stations as the war got closer. Then it was Chinook helicopters or landing barges to the shore.

Whether you had the short, sharp trip with Qantas or languished onboard the *Sydney*, the shock on arrival struck everybody.

> I don't know how long it took for people to sail to Gallipoli, I believe the last sight of land was Albany, in Western Australia... but certainly it would have taken them weeks rather than a day... As we were flying in I could see out the side of the 707, gunships doing runs, aircraft hitting targets around the city. That kind of starts to make you think. It grabs your attention...
>
> When you get on the ground you begin to look around at all the military machinery that surrounds you. And you're watching Phantoms take off in flights of four at a time, complete with belly-lined bombs and all the other bombs that they were carrying. As four take off, four more will land, and are turned around and they're sent off again. That's just part of it, the whole business, everything around you, you suddenly realise that your path is on something pretty damn big.
>
> AUDIE MOLDRE

It was the smell that hit them first, so pervasive you got your initial blast as you stood at the top of the aircraft stairs; a putrid mix of aviation fuel, rotting vegetation, raw sewage and *nuoc mam*, the rank-smelling fish sauce beloved by every Vietnamese. That, and the heat. Two minutes in that liquid air was all it took to turn your starched, khaki uniform into a wilting green mess. At least now you looked like every other soldier in the country. Collect your rifle from the bin at the rear of the plane, down the stairs and into the confusion.

Observation 1. They told you over and over during training, 'The typical uniform of the enemy is black pyjamas.' Well, excuse me, Sir, but every bastard I can see is wearing them! Do we shoot or what?

Observation 2. As they take the garbage off the plane, Vietnamese workers are rifling through it, extricating the drink cans and squashing them. A Qantas ground crewman sees you staring. 'They make houses from 'em,' he says. What kind of place *is* this?

Observation 3. This is not a war, this is jungle green Disneyland.

Across the 25 square kilometres of airport and military base the noise from thousands of aircraft is causing the tarmac to vibrate – jet fighters vomiting flames through their afterburners, propellers flaring on antique DC-3s, the mosquito-buzzing of choppers and commercial flights arriving from all over Asia. Right now, Tan Son Nhut is the busiest airport in the world.

The uniforms of four or five different armies flash in and out of your field of vision, men carrying weapons that look more like science fiction than anything issued by your quartermaster. Huge, black Americans in white MP hats hold their eager guard dogs loosely, patrolling their little bit of country with arrogant steps. And there are wounded being shepherded out to a waiting plane – stretchers, crutches, bloodied bandaging. Behind them is a line of body bags – don't look . . . but you stare anyway.

You're being marshalled towards a bus and just before you board you catch sight of a group of soldiers waiting to go home. Their uniforms are filthy, their bodies slumped with exhaustion and, when you accidentally catch their eye, they look right through you. Clustered around them are boxes carrying duty-free tape recorders and stereos. The bus has no windows, just weldmesh where they used to be. 'To keep out grenades,' someone says knowingly. It coughs, splutters and pulls away from the terminal. Welcome to the funny country.

The buses carried their wide-eyed occupants to their next cultural shock. For some it was straight onto Hercules transports, the bare metal walls and webbing seats of that aircraft welcoming them with a miserable ride to the war. Others made their way through the madness that was Saigon traffic to HQAFV, otherwise known as Headquarters, Australian Forces Vietnam. Alan Cunningham, an army intelligence officer who served twice in Vietnam, chuckled as he remembered his first night in Saigon.

> The buses had obviously been through a bit, meaning Saigonese traffic, 'cause they were battered old things and driven by a Vietnamese bloke. Initially you think, 'Oh God, this is good, where's he going to take us?' Because you expect an army environment. You're just gobsmacked sitting in your bus seat watching all this chaos all around you as you go through these incredibly jam-packed busy streets with noises and diesel fumes, trucks belching diesel.
>
> Eventually we got to a place and they said, 'That's where you're going to sleep for the night.' And you think, 'Well okay.' The rooms were French-hotel style, high ceilings, cool, white sort of marble floors, seedy; they'd been there since the '30s, ceiling fans. The bags were dumped in the room. You were still uncomfortable in the uniform that you'd slept in all night on the Qantas flight which was now getting very sweaty, but then you were taken down to be introduced to the other occupants of the hotel and I was happy to see that there were Australians there.
>
> They brought me a drink, my first drink in Vietnam and I said, 'I'll have an orange drink.' And I remember being presented with this large tall glass, a brand-new drink called a Harvey Wallbanger, which I'd never even heard of before so I scoffed it and I think I was drunk before I'd drunk the last bit. It was mainly vodka and I thought, 'Oh God!' Then I was told to go and get a weapon because that night I was to take my turn to do guard duty on the roof of the hotel.
>
> I was amazed to be told to go down to the foyer and see a man and, 'He will give you a weapon.' The man happened to

be a Vietnamese in a black pyjama suit and he was the concierge in charge, believe it or not, of the weapons. As an intelligence officer, by this stage the hairs on the back of my neck are standing out horizontally and I thought, 'Well, this is cool. Every time I've seen someone in a black pyjama suit, they've been a VC. Here's a VC in charge of the hotel weapon store.' So he opened up this very ornate timber cabinet and said, 'Well, what do you want?' And it's all there, you know, weapons from all nations and there were Browning automatic rifles and Armalites and SLRs [self-loading rifles] and machine guns, M60s. You name it, he had it and it was like a weapons museum.

... My turn came at about two or three in the morning and I had to spend an hour walking around the roof making sure that no one did anything nasty to us, with my shotgun, and in that early morning time it gave me a pretty good look at Saigon. I was interested to see how the locals lived. We were next to a Chinese market area and they lived basically on wooden racks where the vegetables were spread out in the daytime, but they were sleeping on them and one family was going to bed late. It wasn't the rainy season but it had rained, and there was a big puddle outside where this family was living. I remember this family washing up in the puddle before they went to bed, doing their night-time ablutions and then I went for another couple of laps around the hotel roof and came back just in time to see the man from the next toast rack coming home and he was a cyclo driver, a taxi driver, and before he went to bed he urinated in the puddle. And I thought, 'Well, that's his toilet and that's their washhouse.' And I thought, 'This is going to be very interesting.'

ALAN CUNNINGHAM, INTELLIGENCE

Some new boys were given a Cook's tour of booze and brothels, as if to cram them full of the available pleasures before the truth set in.

From Saigon we landed at Da Nang... Wally, the bloke I was replacing, comes in, picks me up and away we go and Wally had decided he would take me and show me some of his local haunts. We had all day to get to the regiment.

So he took me to a place called The Pink House, which is a whorehouse in actual fact. Two or three storeys high and it's guarded by a Korean platoon, it's their financial venture, they ran the place. So you go in there and you have got all of these numbers on the wall in little boxes. And you could say, 'I would like to see number 26,' or 69, or 42, or whatever. This little chick comes down and takes you up there and away you go. And you can have a beer up there, and that was a bit of an experience.

Wally said there were a couple of numbers to be aware of, but there was no disease there because they were looked after by the Korean doctors or the American doctors. They weren't actually all Vietnamese. There were Filipina, French–Cambodian, Chinese, and Vietnamese, of course. There was quite a mixture of girls there, all young, in their twenties, very young. We stayed there about an hour and a half I guess, two hours, whatever it took.

BERNIE MCGURGAN

The diving team we were replacing was waiting for us. Put on a big BBQ. They had Victoria Bitter. Fantastic bar. The best bar in Vietnam it was. They inherited it from the Yanks in Da Nang and that first night I was sitting there. I'll never forget it, I was sitting there and I'm in a war zone and I'm eating spare ribs and drinking cold beer and nothing is going on. This is fantastic. This is going to be a good trip. But that all turned to custard pretty quick.

TONY EY

MURPHY'S LAWS OF COMBAT

- Incoming fire has the right of way.
- If the enemy is in range, so are you.
- Don't look conspicuous, it draws fire.
- If it's stupid and it works, it isn't stupid.
- When in doubt, empty your magazine.

ANONYMOUS

Consider this figure. Eight million tonnes of bombs. Too hard to imagine? It's three times more bombs than were dropped during the whole of World War II . . . and they all plummeted down on Vietnam. It wasn't so much 'shock and awe' then as it was obliterate and destroy. As a gung-ho American general said at the time, 'We will bomb them back to the Stone Age.'

Every weapon the international merchants of death could conceive of, test and produce in their factories was fired, launched, ignited or exploded somewhere on that small speck of a country. If a 500-pound bomb wasn't destructive enough . . . try a 1000-pound bomb, or a laser-guided device that provided 'surgical precision in target acquisition', or perhaps cluster bombs that exploded on impact releasing hundreds of cricket-ball-sized bomblets, each one blasting out 250 white-hot ball bearings to shred and rip the unwary. Then there was napalm, the petrol jelly inferno that stuck to any surface it touched, ate oxygen and incinerated people. It was the weapon of note in Vietnam, so much so that it even had its own, bleak, Christmas song.

Jingle bells, rocket shells, napalm's on the way,
Oh what fun it is to call an air strike in today.

While humping through the woods, my point man he did spy,
A group of NVA, trying to be sly.
Ho ho ho.
We marked them on the map, and then before they knew,
The air was filled with screaming jets and their little lives
were through.

Jingle bells, rocket shells, napalm's on the way,
Oh what fun it is to call an air strike in today.
ANONYMOUS

On the other side there were the Russian-made RPGs (rocket-propelled grenades) and SAMs (surface-to-air missiles) supplied to the NVA by the Soviets; or the landmines called 'Bouncing Bettys' and 'Jumping Jacks'. Both sides inflicted those on each other. Perhaps tanks and APCs (armoured personnel carriers) are worthy of mention, firing high explosive or splintex charges that spewed out flechettes (small, metal darts with pointed tips) or the ubiquitous ball bearings.

Then, of course, there were always the chemical weapons, Agents Orange and Blue, which defoliated and destroyed vegetation and crops; or even the incongruously named flying gunship, 'Puff the Magic Dragon'. 'Puff' was a DC-3 aeroplane that could light up the night with 200 000 candlepower flares and then let loose with its three guns, each firing 6000 rounds per minute in a vengeful rain that tore apart everything in its path.

On the surface at least, and certainly in the images that remain, this was a war of ultimate fire and awful power, but despite the array of lethal machinery, the enemy continued to survive... and fight. Small arms, not large firepower, caused over half the deaths in the Vietnam War. For all the death and destruction unleashed by the technology of a superpower, it would be on the ground, up close and personal, man against man, where this war would truly be won... or lost.

Once, over a beer or three in a sergeants' mess, an NCO recited to me a saying he maintains he read on a barracks' toilet wall: 'Academics teach and discuss history, journalists report and record history . . . soldiers make history.' It's an old soldiers' joke but it suggests an essential fact. When the bad guys are loose in the woods, it's the foot soldier, the grunt, the ordinary, everyday rifleman who has to find and kill them.

Australian infantrymen have always done this. From the gullies and ravines of Gallipoli to the flea-infested rat holes of Tobruk and the shattering horror of Kokoda, they endured and fought, and, more often than not – they won. It would be the same in Vietnam. At its core, this was an infantryman's war, and it was the North Vietnamese who made it that way. 'Asymmetric warfare' is the catchphrase for it now. What it means is a lopsided contest, a war where one side has both technological and numerical superiority and their weaker opponent tries to neutralise that by fighting in ways, and on battlefields, that cancel the advantage.

The VC and the NVA fought outside the usual game, outside the usual rules. Rarely would they fight a full-on, pitched battle. They accepted that their enemy could pretty much go where they wanted to, bombing and killing as they pleased. So they did not defend territory, but instead would hit, run, and sometimes hide among the civilian population. Their strategy was to render South Vietnam ungovernable, to prevent themselves from being crushed while the body bags piled up and the dollar cost climbed until the occupiers simply gave up. Or, to put it another way, they would win by not losing. It meant that the Australians would have to find them, chase them, and kill them on their terms.

The Australian government sent battalions to Vietnam, but it was in much smaller units that the fighting was concentrated. A battalion has four infantry companies, each one comprising about 120 men. In a company there are three platoons (33 men), and in each platoon three sections with about 10 men in each.

It was generally the sections and platoons that went hunting; small groups of men patrolling through jungle and paddy fields, forests and mountains, looking for the VC who were (sometimes) looking for them. When they found each other, battle erupted.

> Our men stand together as they have stood before, to check aggression. And I want for every boy that stands there in the rice paddy on this warm summer's day to know that every American and LBJ is with Australia, all the way.
>
> LYNDON BAINES JOHNSON, PRESIDENT OF THE UNITED STATES, 21 OCTOBER 1966, CANBERRA

Wherever Australian soldiers were stationed, they were confronted by the almost obscene might of the American war machine. Our blokes were still using World War II equipment while the US was emptying its factories and training camps and shipping the contents out in a shiny flood. While American will was there, the money was on tap; and South Vietnam, that counterfeit country, would not be allowed to fall.

> We were all overwhelmed by the sheer size of the American effort. We had an army of 35 000, we had no idea that that's the size of just one of their manoeuvre units! They would do tremendous feats of logistics, like they actually made the highway from Vung Tau to the main road of Saigon. They had flotillas of machines that just laid down asphalt on basically sand, you know, and did it well. They had squadrons of boats coming over with goods. They had whole supermarkets dotted around the country that held stationery items and hygiene equipment and stuff that units need to operate, and you

wouldn't need to sign for anything. You'd just walk through with a shopping trolley and take what you needed. Of course most Australians would sign 'E. Kelly' and the bills never, ever got back to Canberra. But it was so easy to pinch stuff that in the end you were satiated and you didn't want to do it anymore ... the effort and the logistics were just incredible and a day didn't go by that we weren't gobsmacked by yet another American excess.

ALAN CUNNINGHAM

No wonder they felt like the proverbial pimple on the backside of a bull. There were millions enmeshed in this war and the relatively small numbers of Australians were out on the edges of power ... and it showed. The first Australian battalion to arrive couldn't just set up a base of their own – they weren't big enough to be operationally viable. The 1100 men of 1RAR who arrived in Vietnam on 25 May 1965, were incorporated into the 173rd Airborne Brigade, an American unit based at a place called Bien Hoa, north of Saigon. It wasn't exactly the new Gallipoli, though that *is* what they named it, but like that 'bastard of a place', it too, would be immortalised in song.

Old Bien Hoa
(to the tune of 'Spanish Ladies')

Bien Hoa, oh Bien Hoa's a hell of a place,
Its organisation's a fucking disgrace.
Well, there's captains and majors, there's light colonels too,
With thumbs up their arseholes and fuck all to do.

Well, it's down at the 'Snakepit' they scream and they shout.
About a war they know nothing about.
For the good that they do here they might as well be,
Shovelling shit in the South China Sea.

Now when this war is over and we all go home,
Back to our round eyes, never more to roam.
We'll think of old Bien Hoa and our misery,
We'll think of old Bien Hoa, the land of VD.

And when our tour's over and we all go home,
We'll meet 'Saigon warriors' wherever we roam.
We'll know them by sight 'cos they're not in our class,
They don't have gut troubles, just a big, chairborne arse.

ANONYMOUS

The camp the Australians set up at the Bien Hoa base was unlike anything the Americans had seen and it left the Yanks baffled and bemused – intricate barbed-wire fortifications, machine-gun pits, no locals allowed inside the wire and constant patrols into the jungle around the camp to ensure no VC would catch them unawares. They even turned all the lights off at night! To the Americans it seemed ludicrously cautious but the tactics and style of the two forces were as foreign to each other as Brooklyn was to a boy from Bankstown. The only thing they agreed on was that they were both on the same side.

How could it have been otherwise? The Americans were besotted by firepower and large-scale attacks while the Australians couldn't afford to take many casualties and had little in the way of the machinery of war. On patrol, the differences were acute. The 173rd went out practically banging a drum, walking along used tracks, wearing brightly coloured insignia, smoking cigars and playing transistor radios. They were daring the enemy to take them on. Up the guts and into 'em. The Australians, remembering their lessons from Malaya, were camouflaged and secretive, quietly manoeuvring through the scrub, preferring to use time and patience, harassing the enemy and cutting him off from the civilian population till he withdrew in frustration.

> To be fair to the Americans, I think you've got to understand the situation they came from. At that stage the American Army was geared to fight the Third World War. They were geared to fight the Russians in Europe and all their training, and all their emphasis, was on that . . . and they're not particularly good at looking at history anyway, certainly not other people's history.
>
> MAJOR GENERAL ADRIAN CLUNIES-ROSS, AATTV

The Australians were rightly suspicious of the Americans out in the bush but when they first took part in a large-scale, American-led action, *they* were the naïve ones. Big, fast and furious was the American doctrine and that meant the outrageously cinematic 'air mobile operations'. Choppers lining up like cabs at a city taxi rank, ready to carry thousands of men; massed artillery pounding the jungle kilometres away to 'prepare' their landing zones; helicopter gunships strafing anything on the ground that dared to move; and, in the skies far above, fighter planes and bombers, itching for the call to descend like avenging angels. It was full-on, lock and load, take-'em-all-out war . . . unless, of course, the VC ruined the party by slipping away before it all began.

The Australians were stunned by the raw power on display, but frustrated by the inadequate and compromised intelligence that often led to waste and futility. There was no holding of territory gained. In and out of the battleground was the American way, just like a fire brigade – 'Stand back, folks, we'll take care of it. *Whoosh*! There you go, ma'am, your house has been saved. Okay, guys, let's move it on out back to the firehouse.'

In all fairness, when the 173rd did encounter the enemy they inevitably gave him a bloody nose . . . and suffered heavy casualties themselves. But the Australians were hungry for time and knowledge. They wanted to understand the enemy's patterns of behaviour, to learn his weaknesses . . . and then kill him.

Back home, their political and military masters lived in fear that the battalion would be ripped to shreds on some foolhardy American mission. How could the government possibly explain *that* to the Australian people? Or justify it? They limited the battalion's operations and tried to keep them out of harm's way. But Canberra's another world and by the end of their tour 1RAR had been on 23 major missions and experienced just about every sorrow and pain that Vietnam would offer up to Australian soldiers in the years ahead – mines, snipers, constant patrolling and the subsequent stress that brought some men to the edge of breakdown and tipped others over. They discovered the hard complexities of fighting among a civilian population and learned that every death of one of their own would cost them dearly and that no one's end was clean. It was dirt and muck and blood. This is a passage from the official history:

> On 11 January [1966] smoke and tear gas was blown down one of the [enemy] tunnels discovered by B Company . . . then Corporal R.W. Bowtell, an attached engineer, entered a little further along the system. The shaft was narrow and after proceeding five metres he became transfixed in a trapdoor leading from the first tunnel level, approximately two metres below the surface, and the second level, another metre below that. He could not go forward, turn around, or be pulled back. Soldiers on top frantically tried to dig down to widen the shaft but it took too long. After a number of unsuccessful rescue attempts, Private Jim Daly of B Company volunteered. He made four separate bids to recover Bowtell, remaining underground for long periods of time. He was eventually ordered out by his platoon commander when on the point of collapse. Bowtell's struggles had dislodged his respirator. When he was eventually recovered he was dead, overcome by tear gas, lack of oxygen, and carbon monoxide poisoning.

Movies lie. Not just by distorting the truth but insidiously, by repeating a scene so often, in so many films, that truth is replaced by its on-screen version. Hurt and anguish are leached away by repetition till a dull familiarity substitutes for honest emotion.

Scene: A comfortable, family home. A car pulls up outside and two uniformed men get out. One is an army officer, the other an army chaplain. They walk to the front door of the house, look at each other for a moment, then knock. The door opens to reveal a pretty, young wife, perhaps with a baby in her arms, or a child hanging onto her skirt. She is smiling, but only for a moment till she sees the look on the faces of the two men and realises that . . . well, you can complete it. And yes, that's what happened as the men of 1RAR began to die. Except that they were real front doors and real women and lost families and pain and grief that did not lessen or fade after the movie ended but greyed out the days like winter rain. The army contributed further by screwing up mail deliveries to and from Vietnam so badly that for months neither soldiers nor families had any contact with each other.

The mail delay did keep Australian newspapers away from the soldiers, for a while at least, so they couldn't read the stories of the growing anti-war demonstrations back home along with ludicrously odd accounts of their doings in Vietnam. The tabloid press, never keen to inconvenience a story with the truth, published accounts of alleged atrocities committed by the Australians along with the startling information that they all had malaria. The entertainer Bobby Limb, angered by this, published an open letter in the *Sunday Telegraph* to the mothers and wives of the soldiers after he returned from entertaining the troops in Vietnam. The capital letters are all his own work.

> Dear Wives and Mothers: Don't believe all those gloomy reports about your boys over in Vietnam. I've seen those chaps, talked with them, and do you know what upsets them the most? – EXAGGERATED REPORTS IN OUR AFTERNOON PAPERS... As for Australian troops slitting throats, planting the Australian flag through Viet Cong bodies – this is SHOCKINGLY UNTRUE. The soldiers were staggered by these reports... You needn't worry – the boys have NOT CHANGED INTO MONSTERS! You know, I'm not a flag-waving, noisy patriotic type, but I was 10 feet tall when, as we came into Bien Hoa for the big show there, I saw the Aussie flag waving up ahead. It was hot – incredibly hot – and dusty... I watched 400 soldiers roll up for the show, stripped to their waist, their bronzed bodies glistening with sweat. They had their guns over their shoulders and they were carrying their chairs, sun-tanned, healthy fellows. 'Down with malaria, eh?'... THEY STILL LOVE YOU – FROM THE BOTTOM OF THEIR HEARTS.

At the end of its one-year tour, 1RAR had lost 26 men killed in action and 114 wounded. It would be the last time in the war that an Australian battalion would fight and die from under an American roof. Whatever the soldiers may have thought of it all, their country clearly saw them as heroes in the digger tradition. When they returned to Australia in June 1966, almost half a million people turned out to cheer them through the streets of Sydney. Many a battalion from World War II that had never had a parade would have been thrilled to get such a reception.

> The Vietnamese hate the Americans. The Americans hate the Vietnamese. Americans hate other Americans. The local Chinese are hated by both the Vietnamese and the Americans. And the Australians hate everybody.
>
> LOCAL SAYING IN VIETNAM

Surely that's not true? . . . Well, not completely anyway. It's just this handicap we have as a nation; always trying to fight above our weight till the belief that 'we're as good as the next bloke' disintegrates into 'we're better than *all* of them'. The Australian Army brass thought so. They were convinced that our tactics and operational methods were superior to the Americans' and they wanted a chance to prove it.

Their aim was to increase our numbers in Vietnam to make up a task force of at least two, hopefully four, Australian battalions, with our own base and area of responsibility. *Then* we could show the Yanks how to win a jungle war. More and more NVA units were infiltrating the South and the Americans were on their way to half a million pairs of feet on the ground. It was time for the Aussies to kick in. You can see why it would have been attractive to both our pollies and the military – independence, a national identity as a force, and Canberra would be able to control it. The problem was numbers; there just weren't enough regular soldiers to make up the battalions. But there were enough nashos.

So they came to the ill-fated decision that would forever cement two explosive words into a controversial equation: Vietnam = Conscription. The initial two intakes of national servicemen had already been through training and were just about ready. They would be the first to go.

It was a brand-new prime minister who revealed this to the nation. Menzies had retired with a chest full of awards and the grudging thanks of his people. Harold Holt, his deputy and treasurer, was the new sheriff and he quickly let us know who was in charge. On 8 March 1966, Holt faced parliament for the first time as prime minister and there was no mucking about with domestic issues. He launched straight into a speech about Vietnam, our good friends the Americans and the announcement that the 1st Australian Task Force (1ATF) would replace 1RAR. It was a big jump.

1ATF would contain two battalions made up of approximately equal numbers of regulars and conscript soldiers, a squadron of SAS troopers, armour, artillery, engineers, signals, supply and transport, a field ambulance hospital, ordnance and shop units and an air force squadron of Iroquois helicopters. It didn't stop there. We were also sending civil aid teams of surgeons, water supply and road construction, dairy and crop assistance, millions of textbooks and hand tools, not to mention enough corrugated iron to build a few thousand shanties. Australia was emphatically going to war, with an initial force of over 4500 who would build and maintain a base and protect and fight for their very own part of Vietnam.

On the dirt road that leads to the area where the Australian base was once located, there's a decrepit windmill, leaning drunkenly, with most of its vanes missing. On the side of the tail, in faded red paint are the words 'Southern Cross' – a last, rusty marker from the five and a half years during which thousands of Australians called this place home.

It was called Phuoc Tuy Province then. The Vietnamese government has since changed its name. The Australians ended up here after they'd been offered several other possibilities that were deemed by the army and Canberra to be either too dangerous or too full of Americans. It was about the size of the ACT, most of it flat and covered by rainforest and grasslands. More than 100 000 Vietnamese lived there, though there were few men of military age as they'd been recruited, kidnapped or killed by both sides. The old men, women and children who remained were mostly farmers, living in villages and hamlets whose names are so numerous and tiny on the old maps they look like fly dirt. There were mountains to the south, cave-riddled enemy territory that would swallow more than a few Australian lives and, on the coast, the port of Vung Tau from where the highway led to Saigon. 1ATF's orders were simple – secure and dominate the province, protect and keep open the highway, and 'pacify' the countryside and villages. It was no small challenge.

Most of the Australian soldiers believed that they had come to assist and defend the people but the peasants of Phuoc Tuy watched their arrival with weary eyes. They'd been ruled by the Chinese, the French, the Vichy French, the British, the Viet Minh, the government of South Vietnam, the Americans and the Viet Cong – and their memories were long. The Australians were just the latest intruders and, wherever possible, the people ignored them. Rice mattered, a good harvest mattered, working the fields and building a house on the land of your ancestors mattered and, as long as you were allowed to do these things, then these tall soldiers with their strange voices could do as others had done before them. They too, in the end, would leave.

Other eyes were trained hard on these unwelcome guests. Communist guerrillas had been in Phuoc Tuy since 1945 and they had grown in numbers and influence till, by night at least, they controlled the province. The Australians would face about 5000 men – two regiments, a local VC battalion called D445, and guerrillas and political operatives in every village. It was a formidable military force.

The Australians would have to search for the VC in the dry season when every leaf cracked underfoot like a gunshot; and in the wet, when curtains of rain and unbearable humidity made every patrol a torture. They would have to chase them through the sludge and slime of swamps, canals and irrigation channels, through mountainous country that made the word 'rugged' seem inadequate, and they would have to find them in uninhabited jungle that held thorns, impenetrable bamboo thickets, malaria-carrying mosquitoes, leeches, scorpions, poisonous snakes and fierce green ants that descended on the unwary in a cloud of ugly bites.

They decided to locate the base on a small hill. A sausage-shaped, scrub-covered hill that still pokes up from the surrounding countryside as if sniffing the air. In Vietnamese it's called *nui dat* ('small hill') and the Australians adopted the name, though with capitals to indicate its importance – Nui Dat. The Dat. The Big Red Rat.

The defence planners wanted a location that could stand between the main enemy forces and the big areas of civilian population. It had to have space for an airfield and enough flat ground around it to defend against serious enemy attack. It had to be close enough to Vung Tau for resupply, but central enough to enable the task force to mount operations anywhere in the province. It didn't hurt that the hill was high enough to keep it above wet season floods.

Nui Dat was the obvious and prudent choice, but the decision confused the Americans. Why set up your base way out in Woop Woop when you could put it right next to the provincial capital of Ba Ria and help yourself to all the delights and services of a big town? Well, the Australian commanders had seen first-hand what that meant. Brothels, bars, food stalls, souvenir shops, laundries, and beggars and touts sprang up next to, and sometimes inside, the American bases, allowing enemy agents easy access to information and troop movements. The Australians wanted none of it. Nor did they want their men that close to temptation. Funnily enough, the Communist leaders of Ba Ria would later express their gratitude that by locating their base at Nui Dat, the Australians had prevented Ba Ria from suffering the sleaze and tawdriness that infected other Vietnamese cities.

That fate would be left for the popular, pleasure resort of Vung Tau. It was already an R&C (rest and convalescence) centre for Americans and the Australians would replace them with glee. They set up the base for the supply unit to the task force, 1ALSG (Australian Logistic Support Group), as well as 1 Field Ambulance there and, from then on, it was destined to be an Australian town. 'Vungers', the men renamed it.

Nui Dat was sealed off to the locals. In the end it was a sound, strategic decision but one which effectively prevented the soldiers from having any meaningful contact with the everyday world outside the wire. The Vietnamese way of life, indeed, the people themselves would remain an irritating mystery to most of the men from the Dat.

There were a couple of obstacles to jump though, before the Australians could settle in. In 1966, 4000 people lived in two nearby villages called Long Tan and Long Phuoc. These villages had two strikes against them – they were known to be VC friendly and they were too close to the planned Australian base. They had to go. Four kilometres in every direction free of inhabitants; that's what the Australians demanded. That would give them freedom to patrol, freedom to fire their weapons without fear of hitting civilians and effectively put the base out of enemy mortar range.

So in went the Americans and the South Vietnamese Army and out went the villagers in a long line of people and possessions down the refugee road towards 'resettlement'. It was a military necessity for the task force but it wrenched the people away from their homes, their farms and the bedrock of Vietnamese life, the burial plots of their ancestors. It created deep resentment and anger towards the Australians that never really went away.

Anyone left after the villagers were removed was, by definition, a bad guy and the Americans, the ARVN and one of the newly arrived Australian battalions, 5RAR, went out to search and destroy. The VC reacted violently and the allied forces chased them through intricate tunnel systems and bunker complexes. Patrols, artillery bombardment and air mobile operations hammered them. Long Tan village was burnt to the ground and by the time the operation ended, both sides had taken heavy casualties. Nui Dat was finally ready for occupation.

I've had me share of rubber trees
And screamin' sergeant majors
And livin' like a mongrel dog
In those stuffed-out canvas cages.
Had me share of screamin' jets
And whoopin' bloody rockets,
Beetles in me underdacks,
Bull ants in me pockets.
Had me share of mud 'n' slush
And rainin' like a bastard
And when it rains, it rains here, mate,
A fortnight once it lasted.

Had this bloody place Vietnam
And a war that ain't fair dinkum.
Had the swamps and chookhouse towns
Where everythin' is stinkin'.
Had me share of countin' days
And boots with 10-foot laces.
I've had me share, I've had it, mate
And up all them foreign places.

ANONYMOUS

When you leaf through the old battalion records of 1ATF a musty, stale smell rises up from the pages. It has nothing to do with their age. The paper is discoloured at the edges, water stained; you half expect to see a particularly toxic mould growing there. I'd smelled that odour before, when vets had taken their old webbing and water bottles out of the cupboard to show me. It's the rot that comes from too much water and humidity still clinging to the fabric. The smell of the tropics. The smell of Nui Dat. It was there from the first day they arrived.

> We left the beach in choppers and when we arrived at Nui Dat, we got out and it was all just virgin rubber, a plantation with undergrowth. Not really tended, or farmed. We did a sweep through the rubber. We were given areas and the work started, putting wire out, all that sort of thing. We were tired, everyone was cranky with the wet and the humidity; the rains had started... There was a lot of work to be done, clearing, digging machine-gun pits, setting up the guns. It was wet, red clay and then they filled up with water and you were constantly wet. You're in your gear, soaking wet, you don't wear any underwear really, you don't do that. You just wear your greens, trousers and shirt, no underpants, nothing, and your socks get wet and you have got to be careful of tinea, I mean these things happen in other wars too, it is not new, just that you have got to learn it and live with it and beat it.
>
> JOHN ROBBINS

> We came up from Vungers by truck, there was a lot of chaos, blokes were a bit disorientated. It was just bush, except it was rubber trees and I'd never seen a rubber tree in my life! And this was to become our permanent home! They started us digging the pits, the companies were laid out in their tactical areas, the battalion linked up from company to company, but it was a deadset shock. What am I doing in the middle of a

bloody rubber plantation? You were trying to find out what the enemy were, who they were, where they were and it took a while for us all to adjust. Then the first contact was, 'Holy bloody hell!' That first month was hard, it was strange. You didn't know what to think 'cos what we'd been told at home was not what was happening on the ground there.

BARRY FITTON

After two weeks sleeping on the ground, we got Second World War tents; they all had holes in them. We got some floorboards and we all dug drains to get rid of the water round the tents. We had stretchers to sleep on. We had no beer and worse, when it did come it was Millers, an American beer, probably the worst you could get...

Things start to get a bit tense with some people, living in these conditions, living out of ration packs because there is no kitchen set up. Water everywhere, red mud everywhere and it starts to test a few people; people start to do their block a bit... The first night was a bit scary 'cos we had nothing out in front of us and there was all the noises of the night. That didn't worry me too much, what worried me was dozing off. I used to doze off and make a fair bit of noise snoring and that could alert the enemy. My mates used to reckon that they were pretty safe when I was snoring, that no one would have come anywhere near us...

JOHN ROBBINS

The living conditions were shit. We made our own living conditions. We slept on the deck for a while till we finally got tents to put up. Mosquito nets up all night – Paladrin [anti-malarial medication] in the morning, Paladrin at night, the old roll-call job, 'You've got it, open your mouth, throw it in and drink it.' And the platoon sergeant would check you off against the list.

We didn't know about the snakes and the scorpions, so we became very wary when we let the air in during the day; everyone's trying to get a pair of pliers to undo the tent roll! Whatever piece of wood you could get you'd make yourself a little cupboard to put some of your stuff in. If a truck came up with those wooden pallets, you'd grab them as a floor. People flogged stuff; good quartermasters, they can always flog stuff, but that took a while for them to find. The red, stinking mud went over everything, you could have a shower in a bucket but if it rained you had mud from one end of you to the other, so it didn't really matter whether you had a shower or not...

Everything moved at night-time. It was dark, there was no moon out, I was a young kid and every noise you heard, 'That's them!' We knew nothing about their animals or different things like that, so you really didn't sleep. Your eyes were just glued, like a periscope going back and forth until you got used to things. It took a long time before you were confident in yourself and confident in the other blokes. Everyone was in the same predicament; no one knew what the shit was going to happen next.

BARRY FITTON

What happened in those first days at Nui Dat was a death. It wasn't just the loss of this one life, sad and avoidable though it may have been, that mattered. It was what that life represented. A single bullet can travel a very long way.

Private Errol Noack was 21, a rifleman in B Company of 5RAR. He'd been in Vietnam for 10 days and in Nui Dat for just one. There's a photograph of him and his dad, taken on the last day of his final leave, in which he's standing tall, just behind his father, in the garden. All six feet five inches of him is ramrod straight and he's squinting slightly in the sunlight. He's wearing a black cardigan, a thin, black tie and pointy-toed, black shoes. Very cool in 1966. He has a chiselled face and classic, blond-surfer good looks; so much so that they reckon he modelled suits for Myer in between stints as a fisherman on the bluefin tuna boats of South Australia.

After he left school he worked with his dad, Walter, at sea and in the factory; they were close because his dad was a single parent. Had been since Errol was a baby. Now, he'd surrendered him to the army. Errol was a conscript, a national serviceman. When he was called up, he did not want to go. In the end though, Errol told Walter, 'Look, Dad, a lot of people have told me how to get out of the army, but I've got a lot of terrific mates who are going. There is no way they can get out. I can't leave them.' He had too many firsts did Private Errol Noack of the 5th Australian Battalion. He was in the first group to register for national service, the first intake, the first group to undergo training and the first lot of nashos to go to Vietnam. This day was his first in combat and he was the first to die.

It was excruciatingly hot that Tuesday and bashing through the dense jungle was taking its toll on the newly arrived Australians. Several went down with heat exhaustion and the officers were forced to call a halt more and more frequently. Their men were knackered. They couldn't tell where they were on the map, except that this was nothing like Canungra. There were no obvious landmarks and one bit of bloody vegetation looked just like another so they resorted to counting paces on a compass bearing.

'A hundred, Sir.'

'Right. Turn 20 degrees north. Proceed for 50.'

And in single file, they did.

There was more than one Australian company on patrol that day and they were closer to each other than they thought, searching in a grid fashion. It wasn't standing instructions for one company to communicate with another; they had to do it through battalion headquarters. The men were tired, disorientated and edgy. This was their first patrol and they had been expecting enemy contact all day.

At 6.25 p.m., the official after-action report of B Company states, 'The next thing we knew, A Company was firing on our listening post.' Errol performed the simplest of actions. He stood up. He was hit instantly and collapsed. He had a small, neat wound to the stomach, but the bullet had ripped through his internal organs and he died three hours later in the American hospital at Vung Tau.

'Friendly fire' they call it, an oxymoronic term introduced during the Vietnam War. It added to the fuss – not only the first conscript to die, but shot by his own side! The lines of communication burned red-hot between Nui Dat, Saigon and Canberra with the ultimate result that Private Noack's death was officially announced as being the result of Viet Cong fire . . . and continues to be described that way today. The battalion and the official history believe otherwise, as will anyone who even cursorily reads the records.

The politicians squabbled over the meaning of Errol's death, both sides taking the high moral ground, and the anti-war movement claimed him as one of their own. The Cross of Remembrance in Adelaide, Errol's home town, was smeared with paint, the message reading: 'Errol Wayne Noack, aged 21. His was not to reason why.' Walter Noack was left to grieve and to blame Menzies, the architect of conscription.

> I was working at a Port Lincoln factory when a policeman, a minister of religion and an army captain came to tell me. The army captain handed me a telegram and said, 'I've got some bad news.' I read it and I couldn't believe it . . .
>
> I had a telegram from Malcolm Fraser, the Minister for the Army at the time, and a letter from General Westmoreland, the Commander of American forces in Vietnam, but I never heard a word from Mr Menzies . . . We never asked for it. It

was one of those things that happen, but there was never any future in that war. Menzies, the bloke who put us in there, never had the decency to admit it.

From its inauspicious beginnings Nui Dat grew quickly into a large military town, spreading out inside its protective 12-kilometre perimeter of wire and mines and patrols. Multiple rows of tents, sheds and workshops, roads and street signs, and flagpoles and boozers. The supply trucks kept grunting along the red dirt roads from Vung Tau. Dust or mud, it didn't matter. It was as permanent as anything could be in the funny country. For five and a half years, all nine battalions of the Australian Army would serve time here; thousands of Australian soldiers who would come, begrudgingly, to call it home.

It's all gone now of course, 40 years on. Only the brick gateposts are still standing, along with a half-filled machine-gun pit or two. The long, flat expanse of the airfield is still visible beneath the crops and houses of a village called appropriately, Nui Dat. A hundred metres away, the old VC battalion, D445, trains its raw recruits as a part of the modern Vietnamese Army. Their base stands on ground that Australians once occupied. From where I stood, on top of the hill, the drill sergeant's barked commands momentarily echoed in the still, hot air, before being lost.

It's a curious thing. I had come here because I wanted to 'walk the ground' as historians say, to understand whatever I could before confining in words the memories of the men who had lived here. I had the maps, the layout, even photos of the way it once was. I could stand there and rebuild the base in my mind's eye... but the maps stayed in my bag, the photos were neglected. The story, *this* story, does not lie in technical reconstruction or questions like, 'Where exactly was the HQ building situated?' It doesn't even lie in a careful, historical chronology, a numbing recounting of minutiae. It waits instead in the jungle on patrol . . . and in the horror of mines . . . and sex and booze in Vung Tau . . . and nashos and protest and rock 'n' roll and wives and conscription and families and loss and death and return and regret and anger and pain. It lies exactly where those men, men of my country and my time, had told me to go.

VI

SHOOT FIRST, SHOOT QUICK, SHOOT STRAIGHT

MORE OF MURPHY'S LAWS OF COMBAT

- Military Intelligence is an oxymoron.
- Try to look unimportant, as they may be low on ammo.
- Teamwork is essential; it gives them somebody else to shoot at.
- Never draw fire, it irritates everyone around you.
- Never share a weapons pit with anyone braver than you.

The Australian Task Force versus the VC and the NVA might have been a sideline operation in comparison to the American military extravaganza, but it was a gripping contest. As one unknown digger put it, 'There are only two lots of good soldiers in Vietnam – us and the Viet Cong. We should get together and do the rest over.'

The VC adopted one of Mao Zedong's sayings, 'The guerrilla must move among the people as a fish swims in the sea', and made sure they were a small, elusive target. The Australians, rightly proud of their jungle fighting skills, were determined to flush them out by constant patrolling in small groups, thereby reclaiming Phuoc Tuy Province, especially at night when the VC were on the move. They sought out enemy bases and, if the Communists refused to stand and fight, harassed them and cut off their support in the villages, starving them of food and information.

It was classic counterinsurgency – cripple the enemy and release the people from intimidation and fear. Then, they would be free to support the South Vietnamese government. Unfortunately, the corrupt, incompetent government would never be accepted in the villages, but that was outside the control of the grunts. Theirs was the art of war, not politics.

War at this level can appear to be deceptively simple – kill more of them than they do of you. But without superb weapons skills, rock-solid teamwork and tactics that have been drilled so often that they become instinctive, you don't stand a chance. When it's bullets and bombs at 20 paces, casualties *will* happen, injury and death are inevitable. To win, you can't just survive, you have to withstand loss and still be able to function as a fighting unit.

The lessons learned by their fathers in New Guinea, Borneo and Bougainville were force-fed to these 20-year-olds at Canungra and, as a result, the Australian Army had become very, very good at counter-guerrilla warfare. So good were they, and you could start an argument in any RSL with this, these young men were *better* soldiers than their fathers were. Better trained and better disciplined, they were a professional army. And, they were considerably more effective.

In war, there are always soldiers who do not fire their weapons when the heat of battle arrives. It's called 'failure to fire' and it's not hard to understand. To deliberately, consciously kill another human, no matter what the circumstances, requires an act of will that overpowers our intense resistance to taking a life. Some soldiers will die rather than do it. It's not cowardice, or even conscious disobedience.

Many will fire, but wildly, not necessarily aware that their rifles are pointing anywhere but at the enemy. Every platoon, every section in World War I, World War II and Korea, depended on the same four or five men who could aim and shoot to kill... again and again. Armies don't like to talk about this, it's a bad look for an organisation whose primary function is the delivery of death. But after World War II, they did something about it.

Firing rates, the percentage of men who actually fire their weapon at the enemy, rose from 20 per cent in World War II to around 95 per cent in Vietnam. Some say the military achieved it through training; others called it a program of conditioning that would not be out of place in a Communist re-education camp. Whatever the title, its intention was simple – the enemy are not men; they're targets.

The sneaker course at Canungra. One fresh, naïve rifleman, one instructor.

You stand facing the green wall of forest, the instructor three feet behind you. He barks.

'Fifteen rounds. Load.'

You push the magazine into the SLR held tightly in your hands. Pull up the folding sight at the back of the rifle. Set.

'Begin.'

You put one foot down and move forward, then the other. Carefully, eyes raking the tree-line. You can hear the instructor breathing behind you, shadowing your every move. Christ, he's close.

'Take it easy, son. It's not a fucken race. Search your full arc.'

What's he mean? Where's the threat coming from? Left? Right? Concentrate!

'Pick up your bloody feet! Pick 'em up! Now place 'em down gently. Weight on the front of the foot then roll smoothly onto the ball. Are you thinking, soldier? Are you thinking, where will I go when I get into trouble? Because as sure as shit you will. Look for cover. Find it, c'mon. C'mon.'

The instructor leans down, finds a wire in the undergrowth and pulls on it. Ten feet in front of the rifleman a tin target in the shape of a man crashes into view from behind a tree. Instantly the soldier half crouches and fires from the hip. He hits the target but waits a moment too long.

'Dive! Dive! Get your fucken arse down! Rifle in place. Fire again, you stupid prick! He's still there!

'Right, that's enough. On your feet. Forward.'

That was how it was done. Individually, and then in sections, platoons and companies, they drove them repetitively till any natural hesitancy to fire and to kill was driven out by relentless conditioning. See the target, shoot the target. Trust the training, trust your mates, trust the tactics. No thought, no time to consider allowed. Hesitate and you're not lost . . . you're dead. And so are others around you. It made them a formidable force, and it kept many of them alive.

The Rifleman's Song
(to the tune of 'A Groovy Kind of Love')

Any time you want to, you can switch it on to,
Semi or full auto, any time at all.
When you squeeze the trigger, I can see him quiver,
When the bullet hits him, see him fall.

Wouldn't you agree, killing two or three,
Helps make the world more free?

Any time you want to, put the bayonet on too,
Make more fun for you too, any time at all.
But when he's in my sight, there isn't any doubt,
When the bullet hits him, his guts spill out.
Wouldn't you agree, killing two or three,
Makes the world more free?
Wouldn't you agree, baby, you and me,
We've got a groovy kind of love.

ANONYMOUS

Our first contact was probably two weeks after we arrived and it was up towards Binh Ba. The platoon ran into about seven local force guerrillas. That put a shock wave right up you and they weren't far from missing us. We were parallel to a small track and they were coming along the track . . . and bang, she just hit and it was on. Our forward scout opened up and we went straight in. I had six pounds of shit in my pants and that was only in the first 10 seconds! At Canungra, we used to shout the commands but we learnt that when weapons opened up your voice is not worth a pinch of shit to you. There were a few hiccups but we did okay. On everyone's first contact, when someone's shooting at you and it's flying past your head – it's a different story to training. The few mistakes we made, we adjusted real quick. We got about three kills, and they took off.

BARRY FITTON

There were three kinds of contacts – patrol battles, where both sides basically bumped into each other, ambushes and bunker attacks. And they were all within the proverbial stone's throw. The VC were fond of dense jungle and the security of night.

Those environments reduced visibility to around three or so metres, real whites-of-the-eyes territory.

When a contact erupted and they could not easily withdraw, the VC tactic was to 'hug' the Australians, advancing as close as possible to them so that artillery and air support fire could not be called in without wounding or killing Australian soldiers. It wasn't just tight fighting; it was at astonishingly short distances. Eighty per cent of the Australian contacts were at 30 metres or less and 50 per cent were at 15 metres or less. That's about two-thirds of the way down a cricket pitch. And the action was fast and furious.

Often the Australians would not know how many VC they had killed or wounded or if, indeed, there were any. They would hear shouting in Vietnamese and fire at flashes of movement, a split second of black or green uniforms they caught sight of through the trees. Then it would be over and they would finally see the enemy when they counted the dead. Vietnamese *and* Australian. It was all so quick. There were over 4500 contacts involving Australian forces and the enemy during the war, and nearly half of them lasted five minutes or less. A very long five minutes.

> I was carrying the gun and Bert was my number two, which means he should have been here beside me to feed the belt into the machine gun. However, he was about 15 metres half-left to my rear and so I had my arm out feeding around, feeding the belt into the gun and a round came through the gun, through my arm and I immediately thought, 'Shit, I'm hit!' I know that's poetic, but it's also a fact and then Bert yells out, 'Hooky! I'm dead, I'm dead, I'm dying.'
>
> At this stage another round had come through my arm and one through my leg and I look at Bert and he is flat on his guts. He couldn't see anything because a round hit him in the head and fell out between the gun and my arm, it had slowed

right up. It fractured his skull and, of course, blood pissed all over his face. He couldn't see anything. He had a wee bit of a panicky attack and I don't think anyone would blame him for that. And he said, 'Hooky, I'm dead, I'm dead, I'm dying.'

And I looked around and he's squirming like a stuck pig.

'If you're dead, you bastard, I'll beat you by six months,' I said.

He only got hit once. I am the sucker who copped most of it. And that's putting it humorously, of course. Anyway, shot and shrapnel and shit is going everywhere. We screamed out for the medic. The medic says, 'What are you doing?' At this stage my gun was still working.

I said, 'What are *you* doing?'

He said, 'I've come out to get you.'

I said, 'Piss off. Get Bert. He's shot in the head for Christ's sake. Get him. And when you get there, yell and I'll come back.'

The medic goes over to Bert and he is trying to slap a shell-dressing on his head and the bad guys wallop a rocket in among us. Well, Bert wore none, I wore a swag of it and the medic got one bit in his bloody right wrist. Shit, he started screaming for the medic. I turned around and said, 'You *are* the frigging medic, you drongo.'

'Oh shit!'

So he dragged Bert back and then they yelled out to me and said, 'Come back!' At that stage my gun had stopped firing. I couldn't do anything about it anyway. It was just shot to shit, so I decided to leave her out there. It was no good dragging it back with me. It was a buggerance anyway and because my arm was broken I couldn't crawl. So the only thing to do was to use my left leg, and my right elbow and try and get back and the crap is probably going only a couple of inches above my head, scaring the crap out of me, as if I wasn't scared enough already. And anyway, that's human . . . and I'm looking above me and there's this tree branch and I don't know what it was, but there was something distinctive on it. It attracted the attention and this bloody thing ain't moving and I'm going 'crunch, crunch, crunch', 'Get back to that dry creek bed for God's sake!' But this bloody thing up there ain't moving, which means I'm not moving. I thought, 'What the hell?' and I felt underneath me with my good arm and there was this little root sticking up out of the ground that had caught my belt. And of course I'm digging a fire trench either side of me and I'm going nowhere. So I thought, 'Shit!' and I undid the buckle on my belt and the belt flopped off and I was back in the dry creek bed and then some prick yells out, 'They're getting around us. What will we do?'

'Getting around us?' I thought we were safe! Pig's arse. It was a good shit-fight that one. It wasn't too flash at the time.

ANTHONY 'HOOKY' HUGHES

In the end it was their training that saved and supported the Australians. They did not just match it with the VC, they were, quite simply, better. Men's lives on the battlefield are not weights and measures in a grocery store, but there is one way to quantify this – who fired the first shot? When they met each other in the jungle, when survival or victory was measured in milliseconds, who was faster?

In their encounter battles, when neither side had the advantage of surprise, the Australians got that first burst of fire out 80 per cent of the time. They saw the enemy before the enemy saw them with inevitable consequences. This was not superior Western technology; it wasn't war the American way. No 'smart' bombs or Puff the Magic Dragon raining down death; it wasn't even artillery fire from kilometres away or support from helicopter gunships. It was battle drills, field craft, marksmanship and personal and group discipline that held together and functioned under extreme pressure.

The Australians robbed the VC of their most cherished tactic – to fight only when and where they chose. In Phuoc Tuy Province, the Australians would find you, and when they could, they would kill you. And in the doing, they would, one way or another, 'pay the butcher's bill' in blood and death.

Wokka Wokka Wokka
(to the tune of 'Angels We Have Heard on High')

Wokka wokka wokka in the sky,
The dust-off's slowly coming.
As in the mud and dust I lie,
My breath is hard in coming.
Ahh, ah-ah-ah-ah – ah-ah-ah-ah
My breath is slow in coming.

Wokka wokka wokka in the sky,
The dust-off's homeward flying.
Medic kneeling by my side,
With morphine I am flying.
Ha-ha-ha-ha-ha – ha-ha-ha-ha
With morphine I am flying.

Wokka wokka wokka in the sky,
The dust-off now is landing.
Ambulance is standing by,
What is this darkness falling?
Ah – ah-ah . . .

ANONYMOUS

There is no training that can prepare a soldier for death. Until that first battle, that first crack of a bullet through the air, that first sight of maimed and mutilated bodies crashing to a welcoming earth, death must remain an intellectual abstraction. They all think they're bulletproof until the first contact. Soldiers new to the cauldron speculate and gnaw at the two crunch questions that will underpin their time in khaki – Can I shoot to kill? Will I be killed . . . or worse, horribly wounded?

> I guess most of us didn't really know whether we could really pull a trigger and shoot somebody. But when your back's against the wall, well, it's simple, it's either them or you. You do it. And it all happens so quickly when this sort of thing's happening. There's no hanging about for half a day and thinking, 'Oh, I don't know whether I should shoot him or not.' You just do. I wouldn't be sitting here if I didn't. So it happens sort of spontaneously and I guess, I suppose the training, yes, you are trained for it but you don't know if you can do it. You know you can fire your rifle and you know you can put more bullets in there, you know all that side to it, but can you really pull the trigger on somebody? . . .
>
> The first one – this is not a target anymore; a cut-out. But then when a few start whistling around you, you sort of – it's not difficult, it's not difficult. It just goes back to self-preservation; I'm going to get out of here. I've never been very religious but also you pray. I'm still not very religious, I should be but – I remember that day.
>
> NOEL GRIMES

We went to check on the bodies. It wasn't curiosity so much, it was more shock. I think that anyone who's killed someone, first off it's a bit of a shock, and anyone that *likes* killing someone is a bit of a fucking, raving ratbag.

The Beatles in Australia – fans outside the Melbourne Town Hall, 1964 (FAIRFAXPHOTOS)

Nashos training (AWM P05394.005)

Members of the AATTV training South Vietnamese soldiers (NEWSPIX)

One of the hazards of patrolling (LEON PAVICH)

A soldier from 7RAR priming a 'jumping jack' mine (AWM P01783.004)

Australian soldiers attend to a wounded Viet Cong defector (AWM CRO/68/0089/VN)

A wounded Australian helped to safety (AWM COA/66/0877/VN)

Artillerymen at work (AWM THU/67/1256/VN)

A Viet Cong mortar crew training for action (AWM P01003.024)

A welcome home tickertape parade for 1RAR, Sydney, 1966 (NEWSPIX)

Exhausted after four consecutive days of standing-to at Fire Support Base Coral (LARRY DAVENPORT)

Australian soldier and companion (ROGER HERROD)

The first, and biggest, demonstration in Australia against the Vietnam War, Melbourne, 1971 (NEWSPIX)

They were small, dressed in black; they stunk of their village, their culture. And you think, 'Shit, I've just killed a bloke.' And then, 'But that could have been me. I'm not over here to die; I'm over here to go home.' That's the first thing that gets locked straight into your head and, after that, you don't give a shit.

As soon as you had your first one, it was a relief. Not in disrespectful terms that the relief is, 'I've just killed someone.' Relief that, 'Shit, this is what's gonna happen. This is why we're here.' I felt a churning in the guts, anyone would have. We searched them, tried to find information, then buried them. The worst part was when one of your own blokes got decked and that's when you got aggro, you got sort of, 'You bastards!'

BARRY FITTON

There are very few soldiers who can state categorically that the rifle they fired or the grenade they threw actually caused the death of a particular individual. And even if they could tell you, most wouldn't. In speaking with veterans about this, I felt an inescapable comparison to teenage boys and sex – the people who really do it just don't talk about it.

Vietnam, where combat was so close, meant that more men than usual saw the face of the man whose life they took. The army has a specific, protective term for this situation. It's called having 'a sight picture', and it means that you can actually see the enemy down the barrel; the 'centre of the scene mass' (as they call it) is such that if you fire the gun, you will hit 'the target'. The soldiers depict it differently. A man who has been there and done that, who has seen the face of the man he kills; he is described as having 'seen the elephant'. Some say this refers to how big the target appears, others that it means the size of the baggage, the painful load that man will carry for the rest of his life. The life you have knowingly taken echoes in your life forever.

Language helped in the denial and softening of the immensity of what had just happened. 'We' killed the enemy, not 'I'. And we didn't kill them anyway, we 'knocked them over', or 'took them out', or 'we were mopping up'. We got the 'nogs', the 'nigels', the 'Charlies' and we fired 'rounds' not bullets. It's piss-poor mental protection and they knew it, but without it, many would have found it unendurable. The thought in the mind of every man left standing after a contact, as they looked unwillingly at the bodies, the thought that gave them guilt for years later is, 'I'm glad it wasn't me. Thank God, it wasn't me.'

> I know that this is hard to say but when you kill somebody the shock, the guilt, everything that goes with that, you've taken a life, it was either you or him, that's as simple as it comes down to. It was either you or him. Shoot first, shoot quick, shoot straight, because he's going to do the same. So you carried guilt and it played back on you, it still does but you've got to get over it because you could be now where he is... you had a lot of guilt, you had a lot of wakenings. I still have these things but anyway...
>
> You've got to come to that conclusion, what do you want? You don't ask them to surrender because they don't surrender. They never surrender. Didn't get a chance anyway, it was all ambush, quick, bang, gone, finished, over. That was it... everything was the same, nothing half-hearted, either do it right or don't do it at all. If you didn't do it at all you suffered.
>
> BRIAN WOODS

They never knew who Death was stalking and like superstitious gamblers clutched at anything that could be read as a sign. No contacts on this patrol? That meant they'd 'draw the crabs' (meet the enemy) on the next. They went round the bamboo last time and survived? Do it again this time. Their uniforms, packs and weapons carried small individual markings, words and symbols to ward off the reaper, or show their disdain for his power. It couldn't hurt, could it? It was an essential charade.

For every time they went out, every day, every time a twig snapped or a bush rustled or the very air itself seemed electrified, up would rise the certainty, the bile in the throat that gave lie to the outward display of courage – today is the day. Death is coming to visit me.

> We were in a harbour position this night and we lost six blokes. One of them, Chris, he lost half his head, poor bugger... We'd set up the platoon site, and stand-to come and Kennedy and meself are laying there and I said to him, 'Bugger this.' It's gone really quiet, the hairs on me neck stood up, the frogs, the crickets, the breeze, everything stopped. It was like being in a coffin. I said, 'Bugger this.'
>
> He said, 'What?'
>
> We were only whispering. I said, 'I'm getting down.'
>
> As I got down, Chris over the other side must've thought the same thing and as he got down he knocked his pannikin and it went 'clunk', just like that, 'clunk'. And all hell broke loose. And a rocket come up and hit the tree and it was above him and shrapnel come down and ripped half his head off. Poor bugger. And all hell broke loose. We got rocket, machine-gun fire, light arms, we got everything.
>
> BRIAN WOODS

The chopper was their hope, their saviour, their whirly-bladed knight. The machine that carried them into purgatory could also save their lives. It was rapid medical evacuation of a kind never seen before on a battlefield and it worked. Most casualties made it to a hospital within 30 minutes of battle and the blood loss and shock that had killed so many in past wars were held a little more at bay.

Frequently under fire and flying their helicopters into places they were never meant to go, the Australian and American pilots hovered above the patrols, lacerating the trees, holding their craft steady while their crewmen manoeuvred the 'jungle penetrator' through keyholes in the forest canopy to the waiting men below. They rarely missed.

> The chopper's got a winch on it. A steel cable. They drop that down, put me in a litter and winch up one at a time... As I am going up there is this big dead tree branch and I am oscillating and watching this tree branch and I am getting closer to it. 'Oh shit.' And at the same time there is 'crack, crack, crack' of rounds going past. I could see bits coming out of the chopper actually. The bad guys are trying to bring it down on us... and, sure as hell, the foot of the litter I was in hit that dead branch and tipped me up like that and I thought, 'Shit no!'
>
> Anyway, the loadmaster gave the pilot some instructions and he let the winch down a bit and the pilot moved the bird a bit and they got me up. He got me into the chopper, took me out of the litter, threw me across the bloody chopper. I was behind the pilot crunched up in the bloody corner so he could piss the winch off down to the ground for the next guy.
>
> And the door gunner was a big Negro and he looks at me and he yells, 'Is there anything I can do for you, man?'
>
> I looked at him and I said, 'Give me a frigging cigarette, will you?'
>
> 'Damn, man. We can't smoke here or the bad guys will see us.'
>
> I said, 'See us? They are shooting at us, you dickhead!'
>
> 'Oh damn!'

> He gives me a Marlboro and he puts one in his own mouth and then he is on that gun hammering away. He was just sitting there and the bloody chopper was taking hits. He hadn't noticed. He was watching what was going on, on the ground instead of what was happening up here! But oh shit, anyway they got us to hospital and patched us up. We all came good.
>
> ANTHONY HUGHES

The wounded were flown to 1 Australian Field Hospital in Vung Tau, to a helipad near the beach that went by the call sign, 'Vampire'.

> It was an appropriate name because it sometimes flowed with blood. I remember a young guy in a stretcher coming in and the ward master, these great scissors, they would cut all their clothing off, and one of his legs came off with his pants, when he pulled it. You think, 'Oh God.' I often wondered how I'd face blood, but you get used to it.
>
> FATHER BERNIE MAXWELL

An old air-raid siren would scream out across the sand dunes as the radios screeched 'Dust-off', the call sign for casualties arriving. While the pilots red-lined the choppers to well over 100 knots, the doctors, nurses and orderlies prepared for the worst. They had at their disposal a surgical ward, an ICU, triage and operating theatres, pathology and X-ray and, on some bad, bad days, it was barely enough. They were astonishingly skilful these people, and by the end of the war they had a success rate of almost 99 per cent with patients who reached them alive. The soldiers knew it for a stone-cold fact – make it to Vampire and you were okay.

> They flew us back and I remember the chopper medic saying, 'It's all right, mate, they can't get you from here.'

So I must have had a look of terror on my face. When they were patching us up, they were putting crosses on our foreheads and giving us shots of morphine. The pain was so bad that any of us that could was rubbing off our cross so we could get another shot of morphine.

While I was waiting to be wheeled in, two of the doctors came out and were drinking a glass of orange juice. As they were taking their masks and that off, there were other medics bringing out buckets with body parts in, taken to an incinerator outside, past us. And I heard one of these doctors say to the other, 'Anyway, I said to the stupid bitch . . .'

That's the way they coped, personal conversation. I remember him saying that, them drinking orange juice, probably had some vodka in it, I don't know. But they wheeled me in, and when I got inside, someone else had taken worse. They got me in, then they had to wheel me back out. They took in someone else. Eventually I went in. They told me they would take my left foot off, but when I woke up it was still on.

They cut you open from the knee down to the ankle, to the bone, to let out all the bruising. They pack it with bandages to let the ball bearings work their way to the opening. In the Second World War when people got flesh wounds, they would stitch them up, and they would find they would get gangrene because the bruising never came out. So they woke up. What they would do is open it up and leave it for seven days. Then they would trim off the flesh either side, after seven days, and stitch you up, they had to pull it tight. Then they put plaster on it. I remember one of my legs swelling up so bad they had to cut the plaster off, then it just popped open.

ROBERT EARL

Many of the wounded men still had their weapons with them – fully loaded. A medical orderly moved carefully from stretcher to stretcher, gently persuading them to let go. He had to take rifles, grenades and explosives from men who minutes before would only have surrendered them if their hands were cold and dead. The weapons went into a sandpit for collection and clearance by the engineers.

Bloodied, filthy uniforms were cut away, IV drips inserted and the long hours in theatre would begin. It's an interesting war when wounds from a high velocity, high impact rifle bullet are regarded as simple and clean. It was the dirty weapons, the mines, booby traps and mortars that left far too many fit, young men with bodies that were destroyed beyond recovery. In the ICU ward, it was not uncommon to see the upper body of a soldier not at the top of the bed, but placed halfway down it, his legs amputated. The nursing sisters positioned them there because it made caring for them more efficient, but it was a stark, confronting image. Vampire was full of those.

> We had 17 guys wounded, I think, and four killed, and the wounded were brought in. Now imagine the pandemonium, there's the helipad, like casualty, and the nurses and the medics run off their feet. But the dead were in the jungle about 48 hours before we could bring them in, we always accounted for our bodies. And they came in this late evening and 'Jungles' Jackson, the ward master rang, 'We want the chaplains to come in and pray.'
>
> I mean the guys have been dead 48 hours, you know, the best of theology . . . what can you do, but that was the army's respect for the body.
>
> That was one of the things that came through to me, this kind of rampaging, you know, the army, all their things about drinking, women, the lot, but the respect for the soldier . . . So I went down and got the other two clergymen, 'We're going down to pray.' . . . They had the body bags there, these poor devils were in the jungle for 48 hours, the bodies had turned black, the smell of putrefying flesh was incredible, and they

were covered in these great big cockroaches. So, what prayers can you say?

When we said what we thought was enough prayers, we said to them, 'Okay.' Now this Warrant Officer Jackson and about four or five regular soldiers, sergeants mainly, said to their national servicemen, 'Get off, this is not your job, this is ours. You're not here for this.'

And they were the ones that cleaned up the bodies. In new body bags, sealed them in these leaden caskets, and then they went off and got drunk. Wouldn't you?

Father Bernie Maxwell

Then, as they had in our other wars, the telegrams would arrive.

IT IS WITH DEEP REGRET THAT I HAVE LEARNED THAT YOUR SON PTE JOHN JOSEPH SMITH HAS DIED OF WOUNDS SUSTAINED IN ACTION IN PHUOC TUY PROVINCE VIETNAM ON 14TH MARCH 1968 STOP I DESIRE TO CONVEY TO YOU IN YOUR SAD BEREAVEMENT MY SINCERE PERSONAL SYMPATHY AS WELL AS THAT OF THE GOVERNMENT OF THE COMMONWEALTH OF AUSTRALIA AND OF THE MILITARY BOARD STOP

MALCOLM FRASER MINISTER FOR THE ARMY

The pain and raw grief these messages delivered into Australian homes has not lessened with the passage of time. The loss of a son, husband or brother in war is always a sadness past the telling, but one particular heartache lingers for the people who received those telegrams. Why? Why did he have to die in Vietnam? That was the question they could not answer. They did not have even the meagre consolations of the past, that their man had sacrificed his life defending the mother country against the Kaiser and Johnny Turk, or stopped the Japanese in their advance towards Australia. He had served and died simply because his government had told him to go. It was cold, sterile comfort.

The speed of medical evacuation unquestionably saved lives, but it had an unexpected and distressing side effect on the platoons. When a soldier was killed, the body disappeared into the system. There was no chance to mourn, to mark the passing of a mate.

> Having a bloke killed . . . they just take them out and you keep going on your operation. So it might be another three weeks before you get back, and when you get back there's probably another bloke there. There is nothing to suggest that that other bloke lived there, his locker's cleaned out, all his gear is gone, everything. So that's what I'm saying, they just disappeared. It's as if they were never there. It's terrible. That's why I believe . . . this grieving process . . . you know, we didn't have time. If the gear was there we could have sat around and said, 'Oh, well.' And someone could look after his gear and you would have known some of the things that he liked and you could have talked about it and, you know . . .
>
> IAN CAVANOUGH, 2RAR

When a wounded man disappeared into the bowels of the chopper and was taken up and away from his mates, they did not normally see him again either. Men who had fought and endured much together were separated in the midst of madness and mayhem, at lightning speed, and for more than a few it would be 10, sometimes 20 years and more before they encountered each other again. Back in Australia, the war over, it seemed it was too hard, or perhaps too troubling to search out the wounded one, to renew the friendship. It left a sour, bitter legacy.

> To me, years later I mentioned to someone, that was the saddest thing, that these blokes just left and you never saw them again, it didn't matter whether they were wounded or killed or whatever. And to me that's the saddest thing of the lot: there was just no consideration for the, I was going to say 'trauma', but that's not the right word, the fire-fight that you were in is over and you keep going because you might get the same thing again tomorrow so it was a continual thing. So whatever happened on the way, it was like playing football, 'Oh, he's hurt, just bring on another bloke and away we go,' whereas they should have stopped and sort of looking back on it now, we should have stopped and said, 'Okay,' and done something about our losses there, you know, so you can sort of take it in. I think that sort of aspect was really badly handled.
>
> IAN CAVANOUGH

MURPHY'S LAWS OF COMBAT CONTINUED

- A sucking chest wound is nature's way of telling you to slow down.
- If your attack is going really well, it's an ambush.
- Anything you do can get you killed, including doing nothing.
- Mines are equal opportunity weapons.
- The easy way is always mined.

Rule 1 for the use of minefields is that they are only a barrier to the enemy if they are continually under observation and always covered by fire should the enemy try to cross. If this rule is *not* observed then the enemy will easily (if carefully) find a way through and, worse, they now have a free supermarket of rather nasty weapons to use against you.

In 1967, the commander of 1ATF, Brigadier S.C. Graham, wrongly believed he could disregard this rule and Australian soldiers paid for his error with their lives. It began as an appropriate, tactical plan – to keep the VC from accessing major areas of food production by placing a minefield in their path between the coast and the inland, at a place called Dat Do. Australian engineers and soldiers from Nui Dat erected the classic layout – two parallel lines of wire obstacles about two metres high either side of a minefield 100 metres wide.

By the time they'd finished, Brigadier Graham had a minefield 11 kilometres long containing 20 000 M16 'Jumping Jack' mines. Despite some tragic deaths during its construction, it was an impressive achievement and, for a few months, it worked. The VC could not get through and were reduced to eating whatever vegetation they could scrounge, seriously damaging their capacity to fight.

But the flaw in Graham's plan was always apparent. He did not have enough troops to protect and guard the minefield at all times and was depending on South Vietnamese troops to do it for him. He had even received guarantees from the province chief that they would. However, as with so much that depended on this diseased and dysfunctional government, little or nothing was done and the minefield lay open. The VC were waiting.

An M16 mine, the 'Jumping Jack', weighs 3.6 kilograms and is about 10 centimetres in diameter and 12 centimetres tall, about the size and shape of a jam tin. It's called 'a bounding mine', meaning it fires up out of the ground and then explodes. Its workings are disgustingly simple. Essentially, it's a cast-iron fragmentation case, filled with high explosive and fitted with a pressure-activated fuse. Under the casing is another charge that hurls the body of the mine up, into the air. Three prongs protrude from the top of the mine and sit just above ground level. Once anything heavier than around three kilos applies pressure to those prongs, say by stepping or sitting on them, the following sequence begins. And once it begins, it cannot be stopped.

1. The internal firing pin is released and ignites what is called a delay train.
2. Two seconds later, the delay train ignites the charge in the base.
3. The fragmentation body is thrown into the air and simultaneously the two detonators inside the body are ignited.
4. By now, the mine is a metre off the ground and the main charge, along with booster charges, explodes.
5. Pieces of hot shrapnel, travelling at very high speeds, are forcibly propelled into whatever they meet for a radius of 10 metres.
6. Generally, any person within that distance is now either dead or dying. Even out to 20 metres, death or serious maiming will occur.

The VC understood the dangers they would meet in lifting these mines from the ground but were prepared to accept casualties. And it was often the women who risked their lives. They searched for the prongs with bare feet or their hands and, when they found them, they dug gently round the cylinder and defused the mines with hairpins. Explosions ripped through the night when they miscalculated.

Each M16 they recovered was carefully carried away, stored, and then re-positioned where it would do the most harm to Australian and other soldiers. Thousands of mines were taken this way, no one knows exactly how many, but it was probably about five to eight thousand. Dat Do was a complete, abject disaster and, a year later, the decision was made to remove it.

The final few months of its existence became a bizarre race between the Australians attempting to destroy it and the VC's nightly larceny, but the price for the original error was savage and long-lasting. Between 1968 and the early 1970s, 50 per cent of Australia's casualties in Vietnam were from the mines of Dat Do. Shrapnel knows no nationality.

We were in the Long Hai Mountains and we were going to bed around 10 o'clock at night. And I can just remember something like somebody slapping their hands over my ears, and a burning in my left shoulder. After my ears cleared, I could hear the screaming of the soldiers. I pulled out my bayonet, and went through making a safe lane. You push your bayonet into the ground on an angle and if you hit something, you stop and you put something there to make a safe lane. You put your rifles or the scarf we wore around our necks or a watch, anything you had. To make a safe lane, so you could walk in it. You go up to each wounded and clear around them, then the medic checks them out.

We called in the helicopters to get out the wounded. And when the helicopter landed at this particular spot, I could have flown out; I was hit in the shoulder. But I stopped, I was giving them a hand with the rest of them, the first lot of choppers had gone out. And I heard one of the soldiers say that the helicopter had landed in the safe lane, but it was in a semi-circle to the helicopter, so we were walking away from the helicopter and back.

He said, 'There's no more mines here.'

I can still hear him saying that. And he walked straight out into the middle, straight onto the top of another mine. I had my arms full of rifles at the time, in a semi-crouched position, and he was thrown towards me. I copped all the blast from the bottom down. The rest of the platoon, I don't know how

> many. I believe there were only five left standing out of the soldiers that were there.
>
> The choppers came in then to pick us up. They were still transporting out the wounded. It was an M16 jumping mine... they had put a snail on top of the three prongs, so all you would see was a snail. A snail... in daylight you wouldn't see it. In fact, I think it would encourage the blokes to walk on the snail anyway.
>
> ROBERT EARL

This was not 'playing by the rules'. The Australians laid their mines defensively, as a barrier or to protect bases, and their minefields were meticulously organised and recorded. After all, if you know where your mines are, you know when one has been taken and when you're ordered to clear the area, you have a map to keep you safe. They used them offensively only in an ambush, and even then they were detonated on command when the trap was sprung, and never left behind.

The VC did not believe in minefields. They saw them as a waste of both weapons and the labour required to guard them. Far better, they believed, to use mines as an instrument of terror, hiding them where the Australians were likely to tread so that the threat of 'maybe' was as powerful as the reality. Most infantrymen, understandably, would rather be shot than stand on a mine. The VC knew it was good tactics to maim or wound the Australians, rather than kill them outright, using up critical resources like medevacs and hospital care, as well as the deep psychological scars left on both the mutilated and their mates.

Any unexploded ordnance the guerrillas could scavenge was utilised – artillery shells, mortar bombs, even the giant 500-pound UXBs (unexploded bombs) that still remained, ploughed into the earth after B-52 raids. It was dangerous do-it-yourself construction – drill a hole into the bomb casing (being careful not to hit the detonator), then hacksaw a hole just large enough to fit a pair of small, Vietnamese hands inside to remove (ever so gently) the explosive core.

They would bury kilos of this just beneath the surface and it would be exploded by means of a pressure switch, or a tilt switch, using a stick or a piece of bamboo. Move or tilt the stick and it closed a circuit and detonated the bomb. It could be as simple as an artillery shell, dug into the ground, pointed upwards and detonated by a device consisting of a boot polish tin, a nail and a used battery, probably recovered from the Nui Dat rubbish dump.

As a force that was committed to going out beyond the wire, to carrying the fight to the enemy, there was no way for the Australians to avoid these weapons and there were too many days of blood and gore, of overwhelming fear and hatred of a hidden, deceitful death. For a short while, the armour of the APCs and Centurion tanks reduced the casualties, but then the VC invented combinations, weaving anti-personnel mines like the M16 and larger IEDs (improvised explosive devices) into a lethal web that could destroy the metal machines and the men who rode in and on them. A big charge would explode underneath and disable or demolish the carrier, then smaller mines would trap the defending soldiers on the ground.

A click you would never hear above the engine's roar. A spark you would never see. Detonation. The explosive compound heats up instantaneously, burning, expanding and creating a monumental blast. So intense is the heat it causes the metal casing to melt and fragment. Then the blast forces the steel outwards in white-hot shards. Anyone within 50 metres will be deaf for some time . . . if they're lucky. If not, their eardrums will be perforated and they will collapse, concussed.

Ten tonnes of APC and 17 men are hurled 15 feet in the air. A few are inside; most are catching a ride on its back. The carrier, like a discarded toy, flips on its back, twists and falls, crashing on its side and rolling. Men are crushed beneath it.

There is a gaping hole in its belly, underneath the driver's seat. The driver and the commander are dead, instantly, the driver's torso lying in two pieces. The turret and the rear door are forced backwards, over the top of the following APCs. The men who were inside the carrier have been blown out and lie in a blackened heap. The undamaged vehicles quickly adopt a herringbone formation, circling the wagons around the crippled APC, all guns pointed outwards. The soldiers riding on them dismount and move without thought into a counter-ambush drill. Patrol commanders, medics, radio ops, they all run from the carriers. The wounded. Get to the wounded. The VC depended on them doing that. M16s are buried in a scatter pattern and unwary feet find them. Courage and compassion are rewarded with violence and agony.

> We were used to blokes firing at us, not mines, we'd never come across them before. The Americans went into the Long Hai Mountains, they got taken apart, the South Vietnamese went in, they got taken apart and then in went B Company and they waited for us and they had a 500 pounder, that's what they reckoned it was 'cos it cut the track of the APC in half and they were all killed.
>
> You can't see anyone 'cos it's command detonated. They waited for us and hit us on the left flank with a 30-cal [gun], we had bodies everywhere and I went to jump off the track and the platoon sergeant grabbed me by the throat and it was lucky he did because there were mines there and the actual drill was, 'Get off the track and let's go these bastards!' And then Jumping Jack mines went off and I'd never encountered them, in all that time and yet I'd been there seven, eight months, and bingo, next minute you've got bodies and people screaming everywhere. It was a slaughterhouse and it shook the shit out of me.

The front track was cut in half, went up in the air about 40 or 50 feet. They'd buried the bomb and sat back and when it was time they let it go. And of course, they had it all mined as well, both sides, left and right, because they knew our drill – you're off the track, if the explosion was left you go right, you know . . . and someone stepped off the track, I'm not blaming no one, someone stepped on a Jumping Jack mine and there was a parallel effect and it was just carnage. Absolute, fucking carnage. We had blokes down everywhere – it's too hard to describe, I don't really want to talk about it. We got butchered. Eight dead, 26 wounded.

BARRY FITTON

I can't remember how many was wounded. Maybe 13, I can't remember offhand. There were two killed outright, then another soldier died of wounds. I remember clearing my way up to him. He was screaming in pain, and I told him to stop screaming, that he wasn't hurt that bad, that there was a lot hurt worse than him. And the medic looked at me and shook his head, because he was hit in the bowel. And I never realised that it was so bad a wound. But another one of them . . . They used to call me 'Yogi' in the army. He said, 'Yogi, give me a hand.' He said, 'I'm hit.'

I said, 'Yeah?'

. . . but I couldn't get up myself. He said, 'I've got my leg off.'

I said, 'Yeah.'

He didn't think I believed him, because I was hurt pretty bad myself. He said, 'Look, it's on my chest.'

It was on his chest, he was laying right alongside me. Yeah, it was horrific. No one understood. I was there for six months, and some say, 'Oh, you were only there for six months.' But they wouldn't let me fight from my wheelchair.

... People have asked what it felt like to be hit. It was a burning sensation, not like somebody hitting you with something. It's the actual burning. I had shoes undone at the time. I could hear my blood running, 'sssssss', from my wounds in my legs, and my boots filling up with blood. A bit of shrapnel from the casing had hit my left ankle. It sounds like something on a hot stove, something sizzling on a hot stove.

... It looks so casual in the paper when you read it. Another soldier died of wounds. They always say they were killed outright, but I saw very few soldiers killed outright. They always took some time to die, and screaming. And I did notice that when they screamed the blood from them came a lot further than when they weren't screaming. So we tried to calm them down. Some people managed to get through without seeing much... I saw more than my fair share in the time I was there.

ROBERT EARL

In the straw roofs of huts, in doorways and bags of rice, in tunnels, caves and even in that sweetest of respites from the heat, a shady clearing under the trees; they walked into more death – booby traps.

Where, exactly, was safe? Back at Canungra they kept adding to the list of 'Things to watch out for', training the next battalion to go, passing on the lessons that the in-country battalion was so painfully learning. Lessons like:

- A fishing-line trip-wire connected to a grenade inside a tin can. The pin was pulled and only the walls of the can kept the firing lever in place. Walk into the wire and the grenade pulled out of the can and detonated. They were always set at ankle height, the better to break or dismember your legs. At best, the flesh on the lower half of your body was shredded to the bone. Where was safe?

- An artillery shell strung at shoulder height in a grove of trees. Hit the wire and a bamboo trigger set with torch batteries detonated the shell. The resulting explosion removed faces and limbs, smashed elbows and left forearms dangling from butchered joints. Where was safe?
- The simplest of all. A bullet pointed upwards in a small hole in the ground. It had a nail underneath, acting as a firing pin. Step on it and the least you did was shoot yourself in the foot. Should you be so unfortunate as to wear steel-reinforced boots, then the bullet forced shrapnel into your leg. The hidden hole was just five centimetres across. Where was safe?
- You learn quickly never to take souvenirs. That North Vietnamese flag flying so alluringly from a flagpole has a grenade attached to the cord. You realise that. But what about that ever so slightly obvious trip-wire across your path? You avoid it with relief, but do not see the second one, hidden far better, three metres further on. Where was safe?

Nowhere.

> They were very clever. They would set a mine, for instance, an M16 mine; they were pulling them up from our minefield. Pulling a pin out of a grenade and sitting it down, under the ground, and sitting the mine on top, the M16, to keep the grenade loaded and fill it in. When we'd come along we'd see the mine and unscrew the mine. Make it safe at the top; unscrew the detonating device out of it. Lift the mine out and, when we did, the grenade would go off. So you were constantly under a strain with that type of thing going on . . . It only had to happen once. It spread around camp that something like that has gone on, and you were a nervous wreck. It played on your mind.
>
> ROBERT EARL

Fire-fights, constant stress, mines, booby traps – an infantryman's lot in Vietnam. Worst of all was when all these were combined in a bunker system. The bunkers were rabbit warrens of trenches, tunnels, multi-entrances and exits and firing slits. They were dug into the ground with log roofs covered with grass, matting and compressed earth. Occasionally the VC would add cement to the soil so the bunkers could resist artillery fire and even aerial bombing.

So well-camouflaged were they that the Australians would often get to within a few metres and not be aware of their presence until bullets ripped through the air. Surrounded by mines and booby traps, the bunkers had cleared fire lanes – stripped vegetation up to knee-height giving the enemy a clear view of the approaching khaki legs. Machine guns and RPGs were the welcoming committee. Only the Centurion tanks could take bunkers out, crushing the construction and the men inside. The task force lost more men to bunkers than in any other kind of battle. Every soldier at Nui Dat hated them.

> Whether you had to fight into them or whether they were unoccupied, you always went through them. You'd search the bunkers and see what was in them, if anything. Quite often you'd find maybe weapons, parts of weapons, documents, food, ammunition... by geez, they used to be able to inflict some casualties. When it comes to taking out bunker systems, they've got the advantage. They are below ground, firing basically at ground level. We are the mugs standing up, walking towards them and trying to winkle them out and sometimes you can't see the bloody things. You wait till you see a muzzle flash and then you've got an aiming point. Once you see that you are looking at a bloody black screen. I think everyone went through a bunker system.
>
> ANTHONY HUGHES

Vietnam

(to the tune of 'Summertime')

Vietnam, and the killing is easy.
Bombs are dropping and bullets fly.
Your days are numbered, there's no use in crying,
Just stay dry, my good soldier, soon you're gonna die.

ANONYMOUS

There are photographs of diggers in Vietnam taken after weeks of patrol and you can see in them the unfocused stare, the slightly slack jaw and the deeply etched lines of all combat veterans. But there's something else as well, and it's with a start you realise that they have the same appearance as refugees. They look like, and are, displaced people, afloat and lost in a dangerous world.

The war eroded them, stealing vital parts of their personalities away in incremental steps. If it wasn't the lack of sleep, it was the constant soaking that rotted their clothes and covered their heels with one, wide, liquid blister. Or the unrelenting nausea from the tension, or the weight loss from all-day, everyday exhaustion, trudging robotically, carrying your world on your back. No shelter, no privacy, shit like an animal on the ground, all the time permanently, thoroughly, buggered. No wonder some began to speak of shooting themselves in the foot – not to get out, just to get some rest. Each man had a repository of courage and endurance and he drew from it again and again until it ran dry. Then things would get bad.

> It was scary, nerve-racking and it got to the stage if we didn't have a contact nearly every day with the enemy, a fire-fight or a kill, we started to get edgy. Very edgy with each other,

very edgy, very anxious is the word. And it become so bad for a lot of people, blood-lust. I don't say a lot of people, a few of them did, it became blood-lust. And a lot of them couldn't settle after Vietnam, a lot of them stayed there...

I remember a night outside a village, we were in a harbour-cum-ambush position waiting for any enemy to come along to this village. We were just laying there and this Pollock said to me, 'This is not bloody war.'

I said, 'Course it is.'

'It's bloody not,' he said. 'It's bullshit. It's not war.'

I said, 'Shut up, of course it is!'

... And we were so edgy because we hadn't had a contact for a couple of days. Next thing here we are in an ambush position fighting, rolling around punching the shit out of each other. And that's how it used to get because you were so hyped, so trained, tense, you had no way of letting it go and this is what used to happen, yeah. Happened a few times amongst the boys, odd one here and there. Nothing was ever said. Everybody knew, just keep it quiet.

'Stop that punching each other, wait until the enemy comes and punch them if you ever get close enough!'

... It was not like the Second World War, we were on the front line every minute of the day every day we were in Vietnam. We were front line. Even in camp, you were still front line because there was no front line; it was all front line, the whole lot. Wasn't like the Second World War where they go for 14 days and then taken back for a month behind to have a rest, we couldn't do that. So you was tense all the time, you were on nerves all the time, you were expecting all the time the enemy, bombardment, mortars, sniper fire, ambush. It was just nerve-racking; it was so tense, if you didn't have a kill and release that tension, you fought amongst yourselves.

BRIAN WOODS

The frustration could erupt into the orchestrated mayhem called a 'Yippee Shoot'. Completely illegal and occasionally dangerous, these exercises in a kind of adolescent havoc were a treasured pressure release. They were fake fire-fights, dressed up to look as real as possible for the commanders.

One soldier would deliberately trip the early warning system of a harbour or an ambush, sending flares into the air. Once he was safely out of the way, usually running like an Olympic sprinter, the rest of the platoon would let rip, firing everything they had, including the M60 machine gun, into the surrounding jungle until each man's magazine was exhausted. They were all in on the joke and absolute secrecy was maintained; so much so that despite the best efforts of the NCOs to uncover the conspiracies, no one was ever charged. They were fantastic, tracer-filled fireworks displays and they left more than one platoon satisfied and smiling.

Another kind of fire though, was universally loathed. Friendly fire could come in the form of an accidental discharge of a weapon, mistaken identity on patrol, or ill-directed artillery, mortar or aerial fire. A centimetre out in your calibrations or map reading, a faulty dial on the gun that's been missed in maintenance, a wrong sighting made from a helicopter travelling at high speed through smoke and dust over an opaque carpet of jungle, and high explosive shells would land on unsuspecting soldiers from your own side. There was no way back from a friendly fire accident. Everyone lost.

Without exception, every Vietnam rifleman I spoke with acknowledged that there were times when they could easily have killed their mates or been killed by them. Only luck or a last moment realisation prevented a tragedy. Some had no luck. Tired, always expecting to be attacked, armed to the teeth and trained to respond with immediate violence, it only needed a patrol to become disoriented and turn back on itself for mate to shoot mate. Or worse.

One man, caught short and wanting a small piece of privacy, moves out beyond the security perimeter of a night harbour. Returning, he does not want to wake the others and, disobeying the rules, he skirts round their sleeping forms on the way back to his bedding. The sentry, perched over the machine gun, sees the dark shape approaching in what appears to be a threatening manner and fires. Only with the anguished cry of his dying mate does he realise that he has done the right thing to the wrong person. The army, as ever, is keen to bury 'the accident' both metaphorically and literally. Perhaps the family of the dead soldier is told the truth, perhaps not. It will depend on the need to prevent bad publicity or questions in parliament. They don't want to appear unprofessional. The other victim, the one who fired the gun, gets no comfort from the enquiry that exonerates him or the knowledge that he had simply done what he was trained so well to do. There is no counselling available. Just guilt.

Friendly fire accidents peaked during the first three months of a battalion's tour of Vietnam, fell away for a while in the middle and then rose again toward the end. It's an easy graph to understand – starting with unfamiliarity and nerves, followed by experience in the middle and finally emotional and physical exhaustion at the end. At the time, the army compared their friendly fire statistics favourably with the levels of industrial accidents in Australian factories. Which was fine, except that process workers on the auto-assembly line didn't carry an M60 machine gun.

If sometimes the Australians couldn't detect their own men, they found it even harder to distinguish between individual Vietnamese, particularly the men. To tell who was enemy and who was civilian proved baffling, especially under combat conditions. Rules of engagement, the guidelines that determine when and where military force may be used and against whom, have always caused armies problems. Try reading the guidelines issued to the Australians in Nui Dat.

(a) Fire only
  (i) When fired at.
  (ii) When a suspect is about to commit a hostile act.
  (iii) If a suspect attempts to run through a cordon and fails to halt after challenge.
(b) If in doubt, don't shoot.
(c) Don't fire into the cordon area unless the fire is controlled and the target can be clearly seen.
(d) If fired on from a house
  (i) Take cover.
  (ii) Call interpreter forward.
  (iii) Get loud hailers.
  (iv) Have interpreter advise occupants to surrender.
  (v) If no success, call for village chief and have him speak to the householder.
  (vi) If the occupants still refuse to surrender, burn the house.
(e) These are the only circumstances under which houses are to be burnt.

There were also two additional Rules of Conduct:

(a) Don't harass women and children; and
(b) Soldiers will not be used to search women.

The army needed these rules; it would have been chaos without them, but the history and culture of Vietnam bewildered many young Australian soldiers and the nature of the war alienated them further. Who were they fighting and who were they saving? The precise language of the regulations, even their well-drilled discipline didn't help when you were trying to decide whether the hand reaching under a black shirt was threatening or not.

Piece by piece their confidence and wellbeing were eroded until many of the riflemen were headed towards some kind of breakdown, physical, mental or both. So much was working against them. Patrols were rarely at full strength and often left Nui Dat shorthanded. Soldiers were left behind to defend the base or attend training courses, or were away on rostered R&R, or too ill or wounded for active duty. It doubled the tasks and responsibilities of the men who did go out.

Fewer men meant more sentry duty for each of them at night and additional risk in contacts and ambushes. Even the very training and tactics that made them such skilled jungle fighters had a downside. No one in their right mind goes repeatedly forward under fire, yet that is what they did on virtually all their contacts – when attacked, attack back. Gain the initiative by charging at them, firing. But you cannot ignore the fight or flight instinct forever and as their tours wound on, the prospect of another patrol for some men would begin a cycle of nausea, vomiting and fear before they lifted their packs and went back into harm's way.

> Someone explained to me that imagine if you're standing on the footpath and you hear this almighty noise and you look across and here's a semitrailer on its side careering out of control, sliding towards you, what would you do? Well, you'd take off.
>
> 'Okay,' they said. 'What if we could train you so when that semitrailer is careering out of control towards you, you don't only not run away, you run towards it?'
>
> So all our drills were when you were being shot at you ran forward. And that's the type of programming that happened to us. Even years later, when I was in the Army Reserves, as soon as the M60 opened up, I just used to go. It's like an old footballer, give them a football and away they go. You're just programmed to go forward, so that's a big, a big thing to overcome, that flight-fight response.
>
> IAN CAVANOUGH

Newspapers and letters from home did not help, telling them of the dwindling support for their actions and the growing protest. It isolated them and turned them in on themselves and the signs of brittleness and fragility grew stronger in every platoon.

- Rifleman Smith is avoiding his mates and has the bad temper of a cut snake. Sits in his tent when not on patrol and doesn't move. Shudders every time artillery fires. Sweats all the time.
- Rifleman Jones has a fervent wish to be anywhere except where he actually is. He has taken to making inappropriate jokes, particularly about death. Acts the goose whenever an officer is near and tries to convince his mates that the whole damn war is nothing more than an elaborate joke.
- Rifleman Williams has become a danger to himself and his section. Talks loudly to himself on patrol and wanders aimlessly away from the designated path. Cannot be used as a forward scout as he has developed a habit of stopping to look at flowers.
- Rifleman Brown has a weariness that no amount of sleep can remove; if he could sleep, that is. He suffers from nightmares, lurid imaginings and an obsessive fear that he will let his mates down. Knows he will die. Exhausted.

Every platoon commander, every sergeant and corporal watched for signs like these. If they could relieve the man concerned from duty they did it, but the shortage of soldiers meant that they nursed them as best they could, cajoling, barking, ordering, befriending – whatever it took to keep them going out. Discipline was the warp and weft of the Australian Army and the officers and NCOs did not back down from applying it.

> On our first operation a young lass was killed. She was armed and part of the party. One of the soldiers was absolutely certain

that it was him that killed her. She was in the early stage of pregnancy and he had a pregnant sister and he couldn't cope with that. He said, 'I can't go out on any more operations.'

That was okay. We got around that by giving him another task. There were other occasions when soldiers would not fire on women and children. So, in the general sense, they had that sort of respect. However, I equally have to say there were times when they didn't show respect and had to be disciplined in the sense of being spoken to.

I think the worst occasion I saw was after a particular ambush where the Claymores split apart. I arrived on the scene and there was only one person that had been killed. It was a female of indeterminate age but she could have been a teenager and could have been early twenties. She wasn't in good condition. She was scrawny and underfed and so on. And the ground was very hard and very rocky there. And they were burying her and they had dug really just a very small grave and were essentially, putting it crudely, trying to fold her body into this little hole which was quite unacceptable. I had to say something there and have that dealt with. It was under the surface, those strong emotions and those frustrations and particularly when they had lost a good mate or somebody had been wounded or whatever. And I think that wanting to hit out and inflict some damage. It's natural to take some revenge and some anger was there and it needed to be kept in check.

MURRAY BLAKE

It's an honourable and appropriate attitude. Sometimes, though, they could not be held back.

We were on an operation at company level and the forward scout got hit and he was killed. They rolled the nog that took him out, killed him, and the company actually done their temper, got aggro. They went into the drill and the aggression

> was pretty savage, anything in their road, they weren't interested. They got to the stage they would have rolled a tank, because one of their mates had just been decked. That's a natural reaction. They want revenge. It just sticks in your head and when you go out the next time you're more determined, like, 'You bastards are not gonna get us. You can go and get stuffed.'
>
> BARRY FITTON

The soldiers of the Australian Army did not commit atrocities during the Vietnam War. They did not torture prisoners or massacre entire villages. They were not drug-addled, lost souls who had mislaid their moral compass, but ordinary men who tried hard to make the right decisions, to distinguish between civilian and enemy. Generally, they managed to hold their fire in tense and confused situations, but every now and then, fear or anger, or perhaps an individual flaw in a man would win through and shots rang out. Bullets that could never be recalled.

> We had to go over this little bridge thing, culvert thing. So way up ahead of us we hear 'Boom!' Anyhow, somebody had walked on a mine or whatever . . . we still think that somebody set it off, he didn't actually walk on a mine and it went boom. Because there was a woman and a couple of kids or a child I think just quite close by. And – anyway it didn't kill him, it blew his leg off. But things like that, you didn't trust them, even the ones that were friendly saying, 'You give me this, you give me that.' So even the kids, you'd think, 'Yeah, little mongrel, you'll probably be waiting around the next corner for me.' You know, or pressing a bomb, a button somewhere – not that it was a war of technology that's for sure but you could imagine them around the corner with a plunger, the old-fashioned plunger going boom and blowing up a few *uc-da-lois*, Australians. So you got quite hardened up to a point. I used to feel sorry for the kids, they all spoke reasonably good

English because they used to teach English in the schools apparently.

The woman was shot. And it would never have hit the Australian news for obvious reasons. I mean there was an instinct to the guys – they didn't take her away and shoot her, not like a firing squad. The guys at the scene just swung around and mowed her down. First reaction. She's standing there and this bloke just got blown up, whether she was guilty or innocent, you know. So that sounds tough too but unless you're there – but that would not have been publicised. There was more of that sort of stuff happens than you will ever hear about for the obvious reasons. Imagine the uproar, I think the child was shot too of course and imagine the uproar, 'Australians mowing down innocent civilians –' blah-blah-blah.

I wasn't involved. I didn't even see that happen, but it happened, I know it happened. Because there was a lot of us this particular day. We'd been out in the bush for a long time and, oh three or four weeks, and trudging our way home. And as I said, the explosion was well up ahead of us or where I was – but that's what happened, no questions asked, they just swung around and mowed this person down.

NOEL GRIMES

There is a phrase that's used sometimes to justify this kind of incident. They call it 'the fog of war'. It's neat, pictorial, and it allows the actions that were taken to slide away from judgement into a general, forgiving haze. It's also misleading – and the men who found themselves in that place will tell you so, now, all these years on. There was no 'fog' they say; just a halfway decent bloke in a very bad place who made a decision he still cannot explain or forget. Movies and books have convinced us that the Vietnam War was riddled with this kind of behaviour, and in some hellholes where humanity had been extinguished, it was – but not in Nui Dat, not in the province of Phuoc Tuy. Were there incidents involving Australian troops that should not have taken place, that they would rather had not happened? Yes. Unequivocally, yes. Did this make them lesser soldiers, inferior men somehow when compared with their fathers and grandfathers? No.

I have sat in too many rooms with too many veterans, soldiers from the Western Front, the Middle East and New Guinea, to believe that their wars were somehow nobler or cleaner than Vietnam. I have listened as these men also wrenched guilt and pain from some dark place, memories of lives taken wrongly, bad deeds done. It is the lot of the men we send to war, the burden we demand they carry but never want to know. General Douglas MacArthur, a man for whom, like many Australians, I hold no affection, did get it right when he said, 'The soldier above all other people prays for peace, for they must suffer and bear the deepest wounds and scars of war.'

And they do have scars.

> We would bury the bastards in some instances. Sometimes they were put on armoured personnel carriers and they'd drop the trimvane on the front of it or on the tank and they'd be driven into the local village marketplace if we knew where the bastards came from. We would drop them in the village square and then the White Mice, the local Vietnam police ['White Mice' because of their white gloves and hats], or the field patrols in the village would observe the reactions of the local villagers. And they picked out the families or relations or friends or whatever. So that happened quite a few times.
>
> I don't think we ever did it that way on the first tour. The first tour it was bury the bastards. Put them in a bunker and blow the bunker in on them. It is a pain in the arse digging a frigging hole in the ground if you're not going to jump in it to protect yourself. And they're dead . . . What does it matter to us? We're away. So who cares what you do? In reality.

Everybody says we've got to give them a good Christian burial and all that crap but I am bloody sure they wouldn't do it to us. No way... It went against the grain with a lot of diggers. It's not a very nice thing to do. I'm not a very nice person, I guess. But I think I would side with the people who went against that because it very rightly helped to turn some people who might have been sitting on the fence... It may have helped to turn some people against us, which is not the aim of the game. If you are going to win the hearts and the minds, well let's win them. That ain't the way to win them. It might be the way to find some more bad people out, but some of the general populace who could potentially be in the goodies... No. You've lost them, mate. Whoever thought that one out? No, what the result of it all was, Christ knows.

ANTHONY HUGHES

When a patrol was over, the order 'return to base' was gladly given by the officers and gratefully received by the men. The unlucky walked back, the fortunate were extracted by chopper. It was like stepping through a door into a parallel world. One moment weary and earthbound, the next safe inside the bird as it rose up, banked and flew home. They sat on the floor, their minds dulled, their bodies aching as the treetops slid by a few feet below. No conversation, just grins or relief and satisfaction here and there. The crewman joking that they smelled so badly he was going to tell the pilot to drop them all into the ocean at Vung Tau and give them a much-needed bath.

Back at Nui Dat, they dragged their packs up the road to their compound, incapable of putting them on their backs again. They were a straggling, disorderly mob by now and they attracted sympathetic glances from everyone they passed. They were slow moving, for there was no cattle dog corporal anymore, hissing at them to keep up the pace. He was struggling his own way home.

In their tents at last, they fell on the iron beds, their fingers marvelling at the softness of the sheets and the scratchy, grey, army-issue blankets. The beds were only a few centimetres off the tent floor, but *they were off the ground*! There was mail waiting in a pile on most beds and some couldn't wait to devour the news from home, the family photographs, the humorous cards. They stripped off their uniforms, if such rags could be described that way, and threw them onto a pile. Later, they would be burnt. Boots were eased off painful feet, putrid socks peeled off and feet felt fresh air for the first time in weeks. Luxury. The tent flaps may have been open but the collective stench was almost visible.

No shower. Not yet. The tools of the trade were attended to first. Each man cleaned his rifle, secured his ammunition and stored grenades, the grenade launcher and the Claymore mines in the armoury. Several men pitched in to clean the M60. When it was all done and stowed, they hit the showers in relays. Luxuriating in the warm water, they wanted to stay there forever, the sheer, sensual pleasure of washing their hair for the first time in over a month making some of them almost giddy. But the line of men was getting longer and the air was blue with complaints. Step out, clean uniform, thongs on the feet. Fan-bloody-tastic.

They were excused from sentry duty for the time being. The cooks and the admin blokes would stand in for them, keeping Nui Dat protected – another luxury. Now reality paid an unwelcome visit. The empty bed in the tent, the reinforcement who was replacing Mick, or Tom, or Geoff, standing awkwardly around, unsure of what to do or say. They'd leave him there, an outsider for the moment, as they walked from company to company, checking on mates, nodding silently as they were given the toll – 'We got four nogs but Jacko's down at Vampire. Dunno how he is. Looked pretty bad.'

To other things, other, more agreeable feelings on returning. Wherever Australian soldiers have been based, whatever the war, animals became a part of camp life. There was even a kangaroo in Cairo in 1915, smuggled across as a joey on the long voyage from Western Australia. Nui Dat was no different.

> We had a pet monkey in our camp, Pogo . . . Pogo was a camp follower, never leaves camp, always stays in camp. The little mongrel, he used to take all our cigarettes, all our money, socks, hankies, pinch the bloody lot. Rotten mongrel, anyway when we were leaving there we had to take him up to the transport mob, they had a female and he was a male. And we would've been about 300 metres from it and he must've been able to smell her and we hadn't even stopped in the jeep and he was straight off the front of it, straight into the camp. All's I could see was truck wheels flying in the air and trucks being rolled over, I tell you what, he was horny. He was wanting to get in, poor bugger.
>
> We had dogs, we had a couple of old tracker dogs that they never got rid of. We had a python, a big python snake. We had an owl, a big owl. We had like a zoo at our camp. We were allowed to keep them to a certain extent, couldn't keep any tigers, elephants. They wouldn't allow us to keep elephants, can't understand, the army's just got no bloody sense of humour at all. Anyway, we tried to fill in our time. Monkeys, dogs, pythons.
>
> It was morale, having a pet. It's like having, I s'pose, photos of nude women on your cupboard doors and all this. We had pets; you'd walk past and throw them a rat or pat them or the dogs would come up and you could sit down and talk to a dog. All this sort of stuff. I think it was just that little bit of homeliness. Throw the snake a rat, the python. I didn't

ever seen anybody cuddle an ant but I mean, yeah, we had a little bit of a zoo... It was good to see them, it was soothing to see something that wasn't going to shoot back at you. It was soothing to see something that wasn't going to explode on you. I don't know how many blokes as we were going through villages would pat a water buffalo. Christ, these things roll in mud! But it was that soothing, that animal, something that wouldn't hurt you.

BRIAN WOODS

It was a tradition that every returning patrol had a BBQ prepared for them their first night back – steaks from Australia, salad and potatoes. At the time, it was dream tucker. They were also given an extra beer ration, VB or XXXX. It was all they could do to get a steak down because their stomachs had shrunk so much out in the 'J', but God, it tasted good. As the night and the beer flowed on, the Akai reel-to-reel tape decks they had bought on R&R screamed into action through brand-new, thumpingly loud, 20-watt amplifiers and the songs crashed through the humid night. It was easy to see trouble on the way.

Command cut the returned men a certain amount of slack that first night – a certain amount. Beer was their culture, their medication and their solace and it did not take much to befuddle tired, spent men. Some just puddled into happy, relieved drunks but others slid into aggression and a few plummeted lower and lower into sombre, dark places from which they were released only by unconsciousness.

The aggressive ones needed watching. The ongoing effects of long operations put a strain on relations between the men and their officers. Smouldering discontent, suppressed anger and long-nursed grievances bubbled up in them and the booze let it loose. Mostly it took the form of reasonably harmless pranks – blowing up the officers' water heater in their shower block or improvised football games that got out of hand and ended in blood and broken limbs.

But it could and did get serious. Australian soldiers have always been very keen to let their officers know when they've gone too far or when they need to lighten up a little. In Vietnam, their favoured method was to leave a grenade, pin still in, on the particular officer's bed, just as a warning. Most got the message. Every now and then, a disgruntled rifleman, pissed as a parrot and brimming with anger, loaded his SLR and headed off towards the officers' quarters, muttering threats involving revenge and justice. Fortunately, wiser and sober sergeants and corporals generally headed them off before they went too far.

Twice at Nui Dat, an attempt to 'teach an officer a lesson' tragically ended in murder. 'Fragging' it was called, after the fragmentation grenade that was often the weapon of choice. The American Army had a grave problem with it, over 330 incidents in their worst year. Both the Australians killed this way were young lieutenants, killed by men from their units. The offenders received jail sentences, though many felt they were not long enough. It's difficult even now to get the other men from those units to discuss these deaths.

Drinking was a permanent problem in Nui Dat. The supply of beer to the men was generous and rest time after patrols was regarded as a licence to overindulge. In some cases, discipline fell away so badly that soldiers at gun posts bought a steady supply of beer from Vietnamese peddlers and consumed it on duty. Hard drinking and lots of it was not just accepted but expected and many paid the price when they could not relinquish the habit at home. It was a forgivable sin among the men, one in which they took a perverse pride.

Other drugs though, such as marijuana and heroin, both in high-level use among the American troops, were definitely not acceptable. They didn't fit in with the conservative views of the diggers and the idea of 'frigging round with your mind' did not appeal to them. Instead, it frightened them with the possibility of a 'drug-crazed clown' on patrol, with a weapon in his hand and less than alert. Depending on your mates out past the wire was critical and anything that threatened that was dealt with summarily.

You'd walk into some places and you could smell the joints. It reeked. Our people . . . some did. When they were sprung, severely chastised and I don't mean necessarily formally chastised, informally. Never ever did it again after that, mate. Soldier's justice. Not the system justice. Beat the shit out of them and, 'If we get in a shit-fight, sunshine, and you are still taking that shit, you aren't coming out of the shit-fight, son. One of us is going to get you.' You don't want a half-doped fool out in the bush with you. You are relying on the bastard so . . . I don't know of any that were killed.

I had one soldier and he will remain nameless for obvious reasons. I butt-stroked him on the side of his face and bloody ripped his kisser open. He was smoking dope. No need for that crap, I'm sorry. And the medic sergeant wanted to do a report and I said, 'Let me put it to you this way. Succinctly. If one of your medics was smoking dope and one of my people came off a chopper here wounded and he was too sick to patch him up. What would you do to that medic?'

He said, 'I would do what you just did.'

I said, 'Well, no further questions, your honour.'

And he said, 'And no further report either, mate.'

End of story.

Anthony Hughes

So this was their world for a year; a universe away from the suburbs and the farms of Australia, the lecture hall and the factory floor. They were terribly young; mostly 20 and 21, and you could have fitted their understanding and experience of life into a thimble. Education was sharp and rough when you served as an infantryman in Nui Dat.

When a war is over, a nation counts the expense in treasure – how much did it cost, how many men did we lose? There is no measure for suffering, no unit of volume to add up the breakdowns. Yet that is what was fixed into these young men during the course of their tour as surely as if it had been injected into their bloodstream. What would happen to them when it ended? How would they unlearn this perverted education? It's not a question anyone asked back then, of course. What would have been the point? You were there, you did your job as best you could, and you looked for blissful forgetfulness, trying to ignore the bad moon on the rise.

VII

ME LOVE YOU LONG TIME

Fellatio
Pederasty
Sodomy
Cunnilingus
Masturbation
Orgy

When the musical *Hair* premiered at the Metro Theatre in Kings Cross in 1969, each of the words above was spoken or sung by the cast, probably the first time they had ever been heard publicly in an Australian theatre. It seemed that the Age of Free Love had finally arrived in Oz. We had nudity on stage, lascivious suggestions of orgies, and dopey slogans like, 'Do what you wanna do, be what you wanna be, as long as you don't hurt anybody.' Sadly, for lots of folks, free love was bollocks, a transient apparition, a guilty fantasy that splintered apart under the weight of history, culture and awkward refusals. The nostalgia industry extols the '60s as an age of gleeful promiscuity and uninhibited sex for everyone, but the reality was far less enticing. Don't believe your parents, you children of the baby boomers; if they tell the truth most of them would sorrowfully agree with the sentiments of Michelene Wandor's poem, *In the Sixties*.

the sixties
were full of people I didn't sleep with
joints I didn't smoke
plays I wasn't in

It wasn't that we weren't trying desperately to 'make love not war'. Pretty much every bloke I knew in the '60s was preoccupied with the possibility that he was only one small step away from entering into the dazzling world he'd heard about where women were waiting and willing to initiate the novice into excess and orgasm. Oh, if only you had the key.

On campus it appeared to be tantalisingly close, a wave of cheesecloth and nipples flowing towards you at lunchtime that made it near impossible to concentrate on your salad roll and Coke. Shiny hair, long, long legs that stretched all the way to nirvana and breasts that bounced about like two happy puppies under a blanket. There's no aphrodisiac like memory.

The principal problem was acquiring the skills required for ease and familiarity with women. The challenge for a young man in the '60s was how unapologetically masculine Australia was then. Publicly at least, testosterone ruled. To be a 'mate' was the highest of accolades and the natural order was taken to be plain, solid, male friendships. Nothing too intimate mind, best to leave a lot of that emotional stuff unspoken. Women were tolerated, sometimes venerated, but always a necessary adjunct rather than an equal. Males and females in Australia were almost as rigidly divided as blacks and whites in South Africa.

We grew up in a society of pubs and clubs that were sacred men's territory, full of important men's business. Men gathered at the bar at the end of the working day, overalled and dusty, to sink a few, shout their mates, debate and solve the nation's problems and reaffirm their rightful place in the world before going home to 'the missus', 'the wife' or 'Mum', for dinner and domesticity. The bars were noisy, animated, smoky caves leaking a soundtrack of basso belly laughs, dirty jokes and race calls from the radio out onto suburban streets. Despite the presence of barmaids and female publicans, they were a social and networking centre for men and men only.

It was not just an accepted convention that women didn't drink in these bars, in some states it was actually against the law. Mothers, on the rare occasions that they went to the pub, would take themselves to the Ladies' Lounge, where they would conduct secret business of their own. But their daughters, true descendants of the suffragettes, were never going to accept it. In 1965, Merle Thornton and Rosalie Bogner chained themselves to the foot rail of the public bar in the Regatta Hotel in Brisbane to protest the exclusion of women. The publican refused to serve them (well, he would have been fined), but a few sympathetic blokes bought them a couple of beers till the police came. It was the beginning of the end for many Australian men, and they've regretted it ever since. Ladies' Lounges went the way of the shandy, that curious drink favoured by women at the time, a mix of beer and lemonade that was supposed to be more to their taste.

It's a clichéd joke nowadays to talk about 'blokes down one end of the room and the sheilas up the other', but it *was* like that, exactly like that. If an especially brave or foolish man attempted to spend time with the women at a social gathering he would, inevitably, at some time during the night have to withstand suspicion of both his motives and his masculinity. Sometimes even the women would tease him. Outside of marriage, the opportunities for men to enjoy real friendships with women were rare, and it showed in clumsiness with women and the certain belief men had that they were past our understanding.

Women were barely represented in politics, on local councils, in the courts and the professions. If they worked, it was in shops or offices, schools or hospitals. They were defined and paraded to us as carers, wives and mothers. Which didn't leave a lot of room for sex. Not that you could speak about it openly anyway. In my Catholic–Australian world, sex was a prize most men clearly wanted, but when a woman consented to bed them, away from the sanctity of marriage, she became 'common' and they became guilty . . . and somehow 'dirty'.

What were we, as adolescent boys, to think of a society where engaging in sexual intercourse was described as 'having a naughty', during which you might, or might not, be 'in the nuddy'? Where phrases like 'they're all the same in the dark', or 'makes no difference with a bag over her head', could always produce a laugh in a group of men. Clearly, women were things to root, not converse with.

And you could forget about furthering your education in a more private fashion. We were prevented by the government from reading books like *Lady Chatterley's Lover*, *Lolita*, *Portnoy's Complaint* and the *Kama Sutra*. Police seized Aubrey Beardsley illustrations and even posters carrying the slogan – 'Save Water, Shower With A Friend'. Sex was in the dark, under the covers, behind the bushes and on the sly; and young Australian men, desperate to know and experience all they could, were handicapped on the one hand by ordinary adolescent misgivings and on the other by a hypocritical attitude that categorised women as madonna or slut, with bugger-all in between. Even officer school in the army couldn't help.

> We had to go and learn to dance, to do the waltz, the Pride of Erin. And on a Friday night, the army'd send two buses into Portsea and they'd pick up all these women, single women. And they were all shapes and sizes, you know – small, tall, fat and thin and a couple of nice ones in between. They were nicknamed 'The Dragon Squad' because most of them were dragons.

We'd have this woman dance instructor from Portsea and we'd have these women and 'step forwards and step back'. And we probably did this two weeks out of four. Then came the big night, the graduation ball, and we'd get these same girls back in or you'd line up your own girl and we were then qualified dancers so we didn't need any more instruction. Some of the women were daughters of the staff, but most of them were nurses or whatever from round the Portsea area. We weren't game to say 'boo' at that stage but as it went on you could try and get them outside and have a bit of a time with them. We'd have a little supper before they went home on the bus, we'd all sit around, scones and bikkies and a cup of tea and all this sort of rubbish. And then as they all got older and married off, a new Dragon Squad took over.

BERNIE MCGURGAN

'Scones and bikkies and a cup of tea.' What chance did they have? A large proportion of the men who served in Vietnam were young – 19 to 24. Many were either virgins when they left Australia, or at best had engaged in fumbling, stumbling exercises with the opposite sex that left both them and the girls exhausted and unsatisfied. They were, after all, no different to the rest of us. In leaving their country, they carried with them and in them the very same desires that had characterised their fathers and grandfathers in their wars, a unique mix of lust and loutishness, hunger and guilt. Vietnam would provide, as all occupied countries must, but the going rate would be high, for both sides.

Vung Tau
(to the tune of 'My Bonnie Lies Over the Ocean')

T'was in Vung Tau Vietnam that I met her,
She was 'French' and her name was Mimi.
She whispered so no one could hear her
'Would you like to come upstairs with me?'

I admit she was very attractive
I admit I was very drunk too.
So I slipped her 100 piastres,
And took my place at the end of the queue.

Forty minutes or longer I waited
To get to that room up above.
There I proceeded to indulge in
Four hundred 'p' worth of legalised love.

But when I awoke the next morning,
I was worried as worried could be,
For the sake of a few moments pleasure,
Something dreadful had happened to me.

That is the end of the story,
But the moral to you I must tell.
If you ever get leave down in Vungers,
Stay away from that old Grand Hotel.

ANONYMOUS

For the entire time the Australian Task Force occupied Nui Dat, Vung Tau, or 'Vungers', took in the tense, tired, hollow-eyed soldiers fresh from patrols and sent most of them back a few days later, hung-over and satisfied, with a smile on their faces, no money in their pockets, and, if they'd been less than careful, an unwanted visitor in their bloodstreams.

It had always attracted the wild and the wayward. Portuguese merchantmen anchored here in the 15th century and Malay pirates used its safe harbour as a base for their customary pillage and plunder. The French renamed it Cap St Jacques and turned it into a seaside resort for bored bureaucrats and ambitious plantation owners. The trucks bringing the next load of Australians to town would drive past the remnants of their mansions, on the hillside above the bay.

The soldiers were there on R&C leave and they shared the town and its delights with American troops, South Koreans, Kiwis, South Vietnamese marines and, legend has it, Viet Cong guerrillas taking in a bit of surf, sun, sand and sex themselves. For many Australians, their first trip to Vung Tau was also their first relatively safe contact with Vietnamese away from the confines of Nui Dat and the deadly environment of combat. Some men came to town simply for a rest, or to put shattered nerves back together. Others were keen to see anything other than rows of tents. But most were there for just two things – sex and booze, and nothing would stop them getting plenty of both.

They were generally taken first to the Peter Badcoe Club, the headquarters for all Australians on R&C in Vung Tau. Named after Major Peter Badcoe, a member of the AATTV who had been awarded the Victoria Cross in 1967, it had hotel-style accommodation, a big boozer with tables and beach umbrellas, and, after Prime Minister Harold Holt disappeared into the sea presumed drowned, they built an Olympic-sized pool, proudly named The Harold Holt Memorial Swimming Pool.

The club also boasted Vietnamese housemaids, a novelty for the boys from Nui Dat, but the soldiers were sternly warned to leave them alone. They stowed their rifles, changed into civvies (no uniforms or weapons were allowed in Vung Tau for Australians on leave), and were ready for the inevitable lecture before charging into town. It went something like this:

> Right, gentlemen, a bit of quiet, please. I know you're all keen to get moving but there are a few things to go over first.
>
> Number One: Remember that when you go out those gates you are ambassadors of Australia and I expect you to behave as such. Do not do anything to bring your country into disrepute.
>
> Number Two: Remain within the designated and patrolled areas and the approved establishments. If in doubt as to your location, ask your nearest friendly MP. (A pause for a full minute of whistling, boos and loud and colourful language.)
>
> Number Three: As you leave you will be issued with condoms (more whistles). Let me be frank, gentlemen. Do not dip your dick without protection. You've seen the films. The consequences of ignoring this instruction are long-lasting, painful and not something you'd want to take home to the missus or your girlfriend.
>
> One last thing: Curfew is absolute. Any man found on the streets after the allotted time will be disciplined.
>
> The padre would now like a few words...

The padres were military chaplains, representatives of the various religions practised by the soldiers. Though they were officers, they stood outside the normal chain of command. They were there to minister to the men but it could be a difficult task, like trying to encourage moral behaviour in Vung Tau. One unnamed clergyman took an unusual tack in an attempt to curb the soldiers' potential excesses. He focused on the married men and told them that having sex with the bar girls would result in them learning 'things' that would mean that sex with their wives would never be the same again. 'You will encounter sexual practices,' he told them, 'that your wives will not want to do, but you, having tasted those perverse habits, will. Trouble in your marriage will inevitably follow.' God knows what results he expected, but one can imagine already fever-bright expectations being raised even higher. Most padres, like Father Bernie Maxwell, were realists.

> You take a normal young lad away from Australia into a strange country. It's tropical. You miss your home, you have every chance of having your head blown off, you go in to Vung Tau to the bars, and the bar girl's job is to get you, you know. And they're very feminine, very attractive. I myself would, if I was in that position of a soldier, I would wonder... human nature's human nature. You miss your home, you're lonely, you've had quite a few drinks too many and this attractive girl says, 'Come and sleep with me.' For a price, of course.
>
> ...One of the jokes, the piastre was the unit of currency and one Australian dollar was worth about 1200 piastres. Now there was a kind of offshoot from the brothels called 'Hundred P. Alley', short-time, standing up. Hundred... that's all it cost, you know... I mean they're things we laughed at as chaplains, I wouldn't say laughed at, but you were quite aware of it. What do you do? Do you go down with a whip? With a gun?
>
> FATHER BERNIE MAXWELL

Like schoolkids on the last day of term, they surged into the town, a place unlike any they had seen. It was a mix of French colonial buildings with formal, tropical gardens; dull, concrete office blocks and factories; street markets, food stalls, and huts and shelters that appeared to have been constructed after a quick trip to the local tip. Some streets had a French boulevard feel about them – spacious and tree-lined – while a few steps away were side lanes not much wider than a car, their gutters clogged by refuse and human waste.

From the moment they put one foot outside the club gates they were besieged by street children, mostly boys, begging, touting for business and lugging wooden boxes crammed with cigarettes, lighters and watches for sale. If the boys couldn't tempt the soldiers with the contents of their box they'd offer to change money and failing that they'd suggest their sister who was inevitably very pretty and very cheap. In the streets, young, respectable women in Vietnamese dress, the elegant and seductive *ao dai*, floated into view like a perfect song, all melody and grace, and just as quickly, eyes averted from the awestruck men, they were gone. Bikes, pedicabs, motorcycles, carts, cars – everything was noise and clamour and pungent smells and people urinating and spitting in public. It's a long way from Puckapunyal, isn't it, Bluey?

They knew where to start though, either at The Flags or the Grand Hotel. The Flags was a 1950s-style monument, a concrete and tile monolith that had the flags of 'the free world' emblazoned on its face. Its main advantage was its location – smack in the middle of town, right next to the street of bars. The Grand was *the* Australian pub, tolerant of their rowdiness and eager for their money.

Not many of the soldiers walked around town, transportation was cheap and, for blokes used to Holden taxis, mildly exotic. They jumped aboard three-wheeled cabs based on Lambretta scooters that the diggers called 'kamikazes', bicycle rickshaws and even horse-drawn carts. You could get round the town in about 15 minutes, but very few of them were interested in the sights. Most were men on a mission, freed from the beer ration of Nui Dat and uncontrollably horny. They began a cycle of exploits – booze to sex to beach to booze to brothel – that they kept up till either their leave ended and they were poured back into the trucks bound for Nui Dat, or exhaustion and lack of funds wiped them out. Time was not to be wasted.

> The first day I went in, I don't know what time it was, it was as fast as our little legs could get us there, I know that much,

and we went into a bar. We were all drinking in the bar, about six men – me and five of me mates – and we're drinking away and then one bloke said, 'Listen, there's a massage parlour down the road, I'm going down to check it out.'

So away he goes. He don't come back and then another guy went and he don't come back. This went on down and down the row and me and the Yank – I was drinking with this Yank – and I said, 'Hey, they're not coming back, the bastards.' So I said, 'I might go down and check this out too.'

So, anyway, I went down there and I found Tony and there was this sheila spreadeagled on top of him and he was pissed. He couldn't do anything and he said, 'Get out of here, get out of here!'

And I said, 'Yeah, righto.'

And I went in there and got me rocks off, you might say, for want of a better word, because we're tense. Let's get this out of the way so we can get onto serious drinking.

TERRENCE HIPPISLEY, 1RAR

Just like Bangkok, or, for that matter, Kings Cross, Vung Tau obeyed the law of supply and demand. One side had the money and the desire, the other supplied the product. And pervasive poverty meant that many Vietnamese were neither averse to making a dollar, nor slow in seizing opportunities. The street of bars was perhaps 50 metres long, crammed with 25 bars with gloriously inappropriate names like Tex-Mex Bar, Hong Kong Bar and World Number One Bar. Each had a tiny shopfront with either a lurid sign or crackling neon above to advertise their name, a small bar immediately inside, then often a brothel or a primitive kitchen at the back. They were licensed by the military authorities and those establishments which were in the good books displayed an Australian flag or a sign. The basis for approval seems to have been a straightforward counting of unsavoury incidents or cases of VD emanating from any particular bar. A sort of three diagnoses and you're out policy.

The bars mostly catered to specialised clientele – this one for Australians, that for white Americans. There were black American only bars, South Korean bars and bars where Vietnamese marines would gather. These last were avoided by everyone else. After 10 years of fighting, the Vietnamese soldiers were definitely troppo . . . and armed. Getting your tribes mixed up could lead you into serious trouble.

> I had become good friends with some of the SAS fellas and they said, 'We know this joint. It's great. We'll go there.'
>
> We were half full of stew, of course. We went up this big flight of concrete stairs. They went up about two storeys at least. There was no railing so you had to be careful you didn't fall over the edge. We got up inside and this place was thumping like a sock full of cane toads. It was going. Anyway, Otis Redding was singing, 'Sitting on the dock of the bay . . .' It's indelibly printed on my mind. And we walked in. It was just the three of us. We got to the middle of the dance floor. It was very dark around the periphery of the dance floor and all of a sudden I realised there was no noise, except for Otis singing. It was a black bar. I thought, 'Oh no, we are dead.' Nobody spoke and it was either turn and run and be killed before you got to the door, or keep going. Anyway we got to the bar. And Speedy said, 'Give us three fucking beers.'
>
> And they heard the accent and the place gradually went back to what it was doing and I said, 'You bastards. You knew this was like this!'
>
> 'Yeah, but it's a great bar, isn't it!'
>
> ALAN ANDERSON, 1RAR

No matter who they were trying to attract, the bar girls adopted the same method for all men. They would hang by the doorway (local regulations meant they could not flaunt their goods in the street), posing and calling at any soldier walking by. After that, human nature, with a little arm-grabbing encouragement, took over.

> They had all these bars, you see, and they're really like the old cafés that we had in the '60s where they have all the cubicles and the bar there. And they'd be playing music and you're walking along and there'd be three or four girls hanging out the doorway and their object was to get you in there. And you could tell the new blokes, because they'd come out and they'd grab hold of you and they'd touch you on the bum or whatever, and the new blokes would sort of be jumping out of the way and just push them out of the way. Because you've got to understand that it's an industry . . . they'll drag you through the door and they could be anywhere from 15 to 18 or so. And you're walking down the street and, 'Hey, you boy, you come over here!'
>
> Or they'd be tormenting you, and you'd be saying, 'Oh, you're too ugly!'
>
> You always had answers for them, and you had to close the door or they grabbed you and pulled you in. Then they want you to buy them a drink and they're feeling you up. Or you might be sitting in the bar having a beer and they'd come over and they'd say, 'Oh, you like me?' And they'd be feeling you up, 'You buy me drink, you buy me drink.'
>
> And you'd say, 'No.'
>
> . . . You'd say, 'I don't like girls, I like my friend,' with your mate, and then they'd go, 'Oh, you . . .'
>
> IAN CAVANOUGH

New bars opened and old bars went out of business regularly. The military regulations covered VD and violence – the rest was left to street rules and payments to corrupt local administrators.

It didn't really matter much to the soldiers as long as the product lines remained unchanged.

In amongst the bars and inside some of the larger hotels were massage rooms or brothels called 'suck 'n ' fuck' parlours, while others masqueraded as barbershops that went by the slang term, 'steam and cream'. In these you could buy a very special haircut. The barber covered you with a large cloth and, while cutting your hair or shaving your face, he asked if you would like 'extras'. If the answer was yes, a girl slid under the cloth and presented you with a well-administered act of fellatio. A certain kind of faraway look crossed the faces of a lot of men I talked to about this. Oral sex was not a common sexual practice in Australia at the time and, not surprisingly, this pleasure became a favourite among Australian soldiers on leave. As a Vung Tau joke went:

Q: What was your worst head job like?

A: Bloody magnificent.

Some men returned to Nui Dat with astonishingly short hair.

The health plan was sensible but nobody stuck to it. Most of the men kept their issued condoms in their pockets, using them instead to keep rain out of their rifle barrels. If a girl demanded they use one, they'd either give in, find another girl, or give her an anti-malaria pill to swallow, telling her it was a contraceptive that would keep her safe.

Sex was never going to stay in a nice, neat, manageable package anyway. Men took it wherever they could find it, including a group of enterprising soldiers posted on garbage removal duty. They discovered that by gathering the most edible refuse into sparkling clean garbage tins they could trade them for sex in the poorer villages. The bins became known as 'root tins'.

The number of cases of sexually transmitted diseases like gonorrhoea, non-specific urethritis and syphilis increased and, in desperation, one anonymous padre invented a fictitious (and horrific) form of VD called 'Vietnam Rose' to frighten the men into abstinence. 'Vietnam Rose' was said to be so horrendous and incurable that if you contracted it you would be immediately sent home. The rumour went that you'd be better off either taking a gun to your head or volunteering to be a permanent forward scout. This too, failed.

Some men contracted VD so often they were charged. Others, whose RTA (Return to Australia) time was approaching, were given a PCOD by the doc, a Pussy Cut-Off Date beyond which they could no longer have sex if they were to return home uninfected. Even so, some men returned to Australia telling their wives they had 'a sort of kidney condition'.

Treatment in Vietnam was short, sharp and painful, and conducted in the VD clinic they called 'The Jack Shack'. Soldiers had to fill in a questionnaire with questions like where did you get it, was the girl a professional or an amateur, did you pay for it or was it free, and have you had it before and if so how many times. Then would come the order, 'Flop your dacks', an inspection of the infected penis, a pathology test and then the first administration of crystalline penicillin into the arse, an experience described by those who had it as similar to being injected with broken glass. So sore were you after this that sitting down was not an option for 24 hours and, consequently, it was revealed to everyone at Nui Dat that you were paying the wages of sin. Five more shots over the next few days and you were done. For now. The bar girls were also treated.

It's timely to remember that, yet again, these men were following a tradition. The first 'casualties' sent home from Egypt, before the landings at Gallipoli, were men with VD, and in World War II, Australian soldiers were issued with 'blue light' kits containing condoms and ointment. In any given conflict you could be guaranteed that around 10 per cent of Australian troops would have VD of one kind or another. It's yet another matter the army doesn't like to discuss or publicise, and in Vietnam they went to the usual lengths to pretend it didn't happen.

> We had a few cases of VD and, of course, if we were getting anybody from headquarters, or some dignitary visiting, like the prime minister or the minister for defence, or somebody like that, they used to get bundled up and put out somewhere where they wouldn't be seen. Or else they were given an ailment other than what was wrong with them ... it was taboo to get VD.
>
> And it was suggested that we give them condoms, and this sort of thing, to prevent it, but mums back home wouldn't hear of it, their little boys being given condoms. It wasn't the done thing. So everybody back home was led to believe that this didn't happen, but it was quite a problem. We had a few guys that had to have circumcisions because of infection and unhygienic conditions. And they were brought in and circumcised, and of course they were ostracised by the rest of the guys.
>
> When one of these poor individuals came in, after he'd had surgery, the guys would go in and give them a *Playboy* magazine so that it would cause them to have an erection. Or they would be lying in their beds at night-time, thinking of something that would bring on the dreadful symptom, and they would be screaming. We used to have a can of spray, which they used to put on themselves to quieten them down. It was one of those hilarious situations which broke the tension.
>
> MAUREEN JAVES, 1ST AUSTRALIAN FIELD HOSPITAL

The Australian authorities took the view that it was safer and healthier to have all the bars and brothels in the one place and nowhere near Nui Dat. The Americans, on the other hand, kept them in-house wherever they could.

> Most American bases had huge amounts of brothels in and around the adjoining town. There must have been – a conservative estimate would be about 300 000 prostitutes in Vietnam at one stage, because that was the only way to make a decent living. You couldn't make piastres working in an office. You could make a few American dollars as a house girl, housemaid, cleaning and ironing gear sort of thing. But the good money was in the prostitutes. You think of $20, and she had six blokes for the night, 120 American green for one night's work, that's two years wages or whatever. It was good money and that's why they did it...
>
> BERNIE McGURGAN

Money was one reason for a woman to sell herself, though no bar girl or prostitute was ever going to get rich that way. Survival was a stronger motive. The Vietnamese had endured foreign occupation and oppression for thousands of years and had evolved a practical approach to the collisions thrust on them by other cultures, a sort of Asian version of Nietzsche's saying, 'That which does not kill me only makes me stronger'. But this occupation was more intense and all encompassing.

Their entire country was now a war zone. Every province was bombed, occupied by one army or another, and fought on and over in fire-fights that spread to the civilian population like a deadly epidemic. Whole villages had disappeared in their hundreds and backyards had become battlefields. Even worse than the loss of home and the graves of ancestors was the collapse of a society based on family cohesion and duty. In the face of such destruction, every Vietnamese was forced to choose his or her own way through the danger. Survival was all.

> There was the occasional genuine girl trying to earn a living. But, you know, the majority of them, they saw no wrong in it, there's no use moralising to them. There was an orphanage between Nui Dat and Vung Tau, the famous Mother Augustine ran it. And I was out there one Sunday taking some stuff out to them, and I thought, 'Oh, here's a mother visiting a child, I know her face.'
>
> And it clicked, she was a bar girl from Vung Tau. So next time I went in to her, which was during the week, I said to her, 'Did I see you at the orphanage on Sunday?'
>
> 'Oh yes, Cha [Father].'
>
> I said, 'Does Mother Augustine know what you do?'
>
> 'Oh no.'
>
> I said, 'What would she say if she knew?'
>
> She said, 'She would say, you are very naughty.'
>
> That kind of acceptance of things. I thought, 'Oh God, who can judge? Who can judge really?'
>
> FATHER BERNIE MAXWELL

Soldiers and women. It's an unwavering relationship based on mutual need. Time has not weakened or altered it; only the names and locations have changed. In 1945, upright and God-fearing Australians cheered as the last of a million US servicemen who had visited our shores sailed out through Sydney Heads. They'd been classed as trouble, these men, an invasion of difference that led to the pitiful cry of complaint that they were 'overpaid, over-sexed and over here'. But while the pastors and the puritans wiped their hands and muttered good riddance, taxi drivers, publicans, brothel keepers and any number of women were weeping into their drinks. They weren't mere ships sailing away; they were treasure chests overflowing with gold and sophistication. For three years they'd enjoyed a generous waterfall of silk stockings, chewing gum, black-market food and Yankee dollars, all from polite young men from Kansas and Georgia whose impeccable manners made Australian men look like dusty oafs. One man's war was a lot of people's fortunes. Glory days indeed, sadly, gone for good.

Until 1967. There were hundreds of thousands of American boys serving in Vietnam by then and they all received regular leave – R&R, rest and recreation, rock 'n' roll holidays. They could go to Hong Kong, Bangkok, Singapore or Taipei, but the US military wanted Australia added to the list. It was close, we were allies, and it would give their boys a chance to fraternise with 'round-eyed' women for a change. The Australian government knew it couldn't refuse but a few problems had to be solved first. VD for one. We couldn't have the women of Australia subjected to that sort of moral stain. The Americans quickly agreed to give each of their soldiers a 'freedom from infection' examination before they left Vietnam. Test positive to VD and you didn't board the plane. Curiously, no one was concerned about testing them *before* they returned. The notion that GIs could contract sexual diseases in Australia and carry them back to Vietnamese women seemed of no consequence.

The other problem was race. The White Australia Policy had been abolished only the year before and, if we let Americans in, then surely we'd also have to give a warm welcome to the South Koreans and Thais who were fighting as our allies in Vietnam. Not to mention the black American soldiers. There were the same cold whispers predicting 'piccaninny babies' as there had been in World War II but politicians can paper over all kinds of unsightly cracks when it suits their purposes. The

Koreans and the Thais said 'thanks very much but we're fine as we are' and Canberra gave the Americans assurances about equality for all visitors regardless of race, creed or colour. The Australian Hotels Association even provided a written guarantee there would be no banning of coloured soldiers. American money, they knew, was always green. So to Australia they came.

Between 1967 and 1971, 300 000 Americans came here on R&R. So popular was Australia as a destination that the US Army had to institute waiting lists. And why not? We spoke English (sort of), the place looked a little like home to them and the women had familiar features. Any fallout could be contained by the simple tactic of quarantining them in one place, a place they would want to be. The buses left the airport and headed straight up South Dowling Street to the Chevron Hotel in the middle of R&R paradise – Kings Cross.

Campbell Lane
Through the window curtain rain
Long night gone, yellow day
Speed shivers melt away

Six o'clock, I'm goin' down
Coffee's hot and the toast is brown
Hey street sweeper, clear my way
Sweethearts breakfast is the best in town
Oh-oh, breakfast at Sweethearts...

There was always a buzz, a kind of crackle in the air at the Cross in the '60s. Every time our bass player's EH Holden coughed its way up William Street towards that giant Coke sign

I'd get a tingling in my arms. It would be sometime after midnight and we'd both be wound tight after whatever gig we'd played that night, the music still coursing through our bloodstreams. Kings Cross was where we *had* to be. The lights were always on and someone was always home, whether you wanted a coffee or a drink or something a little sleazier. It had always been that way, a refuge for the fringe dwellers – the musicians, the criminals, the low-life and the lost – and we loved it.

Into Brougham Street, park the car illegally and down the stairs into the El Rocco, a tiny jazz cellar that had been dug out of the ancient Sydney sandstone in the '50s. We began here, among the beret wearers and the smoke, the saxophonists and trumpet players, the artists and the film-makers. It was a place to play and listen to serious music, everything we thought cool should be. It was also a rest from the venues we were playing for money.

Don't get me wrong, we loved rock 'n' roll, but there were good gigs and there were dives, clubs like the Diamond Horseshoe in Taylor Square where our drummer had been stabbed despite the protection of the chicken-wire cage that surrounded the band. We were playing too many places where the floors were sticky with blood and booze and the punters thought of music as nothing more than a soundtrack to their piss-ups and punch-ups. Compared to those bloodhouses, the El Rocco was a beacon of sophistication.

Darlinghurst Road, the main street of the Cross, was the tollway. Nothing was for free on this drag, where even sight-seeing could land you a mouthful of obscene abuse. It was irresistibly low rent. The streetwalkers leant against grimy buildings or patrolled their territory, some waiting for a prospective buyer to speak, others in your face with temptation and price the moment you were naïve enough to make eye contact. They wore short skirts, tight jeans, stiletto heels, policewoman-red lipstick and had cleavages that defied both gravity and anatomy, pushing fantasy buttons most blokes didn't even know they had. We knew some of the girls, drank with them after their shift, and Helena, a bottle-blonde from Coffs Harbour, told me one night that red and black were the most effective colours to wear – 'More fucks than the rest put together,' she said. The spruikers outside the strip clubs, the suburban boys turned feral on bucks' nights – it was dreams and despair in equal measure.

By 1969, the Cross had become Little America. GI dollars meant that every con artist and entrepreneur worth a jail sentence was on the street, and the restaurants and nightclubs were shameless in their advertising, flagrantly displaying the Stars and Stripes in their windows. There was The Bourbon and Beefsteak Bar, The Texas Tavern, Whiskey-Au-Go-Go, The R&R Restaurant, The GI Hut and The Old San Francisco. Everything was aimed at separating the soldier from his greenbacks, and local and state authorities quietly let it happen. Prices increased on the basis of your accent and new brothels, strip joints and tacky nightclubs were opening every week.

The bastions of conservative Australia – the Australian–American Association, the Country Women's Association and the RSL – all attempted to steer soldiers away from these dens of vice. They promised instead stays in the country, family dinners, restrained parties and blind dates with 'nice' girls; but only a tiny fraction of GIs took up these enticing offers. The rest were like the Australians in Vung Tau – fresh from the battlefield and looking for sex and booze in copious enough quantities to keep away the demons.

Somehow we differentiated these soldiers from the protests against the war that were filling the streets. When the Americans first arrived, *The Sun* newspaper asked us all to remember that they 'are just soldiers who do what they are told and not the makers of policy. Do not, we beseech you, harass them about the rights and wrongs of what they have come from. Let them, instead, enjoy their leave.'

I cannot remember a single protest against the Americans while they were here. On the contrary, the protest underground even helped about 50 of them to go AWOL and escape from Australia, probably to Sweden. None were ever caught. Perhaps we were just being polite to guests, but our acceptance of them stood in sad contrast to the disapproval we were meting out to our own soldiers fighting in Vietnam at the time. Australian troops could also take R&R back home in Australia rather than Vung Tau or other Asian destinations, but few did. It was a long way to come to discover that you didn't fit in.

> It was the worst thing I ever done really, it was the hardest. Come home with a plane load of Americans, a few Australians... It was the worst thing coming home and trying to come back after four days was really, really hard. A few of the Americans never came back, I believe a couple of Australians didn't come back neither, they went AWOL... I had to get back.
>
> I couldn't stand it back here in Australia. I felt uneasy, I felt nervous, I felt uncomfortable, I felt out of place when I come back here on R&R. I just didn't feel – not at home, if you know what I mean. And when I got back to Vietnam – home. And it's a strange feeling but that's the way it was then. And coming back here was the cruellest thing on anybody. See the thing is I was out in the jungle on operations and all of a sudden word come, 'Woods!'
>
> 'Yes, Sir.'
>
> 'Helicopter will be here in 15 minutes, you're on R&R.'
>
> 'What?'
>
> And you're lifted up, taken away. There you was killing, that night you're on a plane on your way to Australia. Six hours ago you were shooting somebody. How do you handle that? And you get back to Australia, everything's, 'Where's

me weapon? Where's me grenades? Where's me bayonet?' And everything was uneasy. I didn't feel at home, I felt uncomfortable, really uncomfortable, and four days took so, so long. So long to go. I was glad to get back to Vietnam, yeah. You felt like your mates were battling and fighting and getting shot, wounded, killed and you were here having... You felt really bad, guilty.

BRIAN WOODS

That night I slept with Jim's body within arms-length of me. Well, I didn't sleep. I spent the night with Jim's body. The next morning we were reinforced with APCs and armoured tanks, Centurion tanks. It was hard to see Jim's body just rolled up in a plastic hootchie, put into the back of an APC. He was just like a bundle of rubbish.

That was the last I was to ever see of Jim's body... Late that afternoon I was lifted out of that area as I was due to go on R&R... The next morning I flew back to Nui Dat, I showered, put my polys [polyester uniform] on, ribbons, grabbed a port, was flown to Binh Hoa, then to Tan Son Nhut where I boarded an American plane which flew us back to Sydney. I had come from death to the safety of Sydney in a matter of 24 hours. I had eight days, ten days R&R – one day home, one day back, eight days in Australia.

To this day, I don't know how I got through those days. I could not speak of what had taken place. I could tell no one, least of all Glenys. I couldn't tell of the carnage that I had seen, encountered, had actually done to fellow human beings. Everything had to be fine. Everything had to be okay, portray the feelings that I was safe. I had my 21st birthday in those eight days. I had love, family and safety. It was great. It was a happy family time. I had a family ceremony, a reunion for my 21st birthday. I did not want to party. I had told that to Mum and Dad by letter. I just wanted to be at home, alive, and it was unreal to sleep in a bed after having been sleeping on the ground, not actually sleeping, lying on the ground, usually wet, usually scared. So my R&R was a tremendous relief in many ways to be back home and be in Australia, but I really don't know how I got through it.

I went back to Vietnam by Qantas. Once again, to go from Sydney, Mascot, to Tan Son Nhut, from love, safety, fun place to that horrible place again. You just can't put it into words. The transformation, you just couldn't comprehend it. I was back in Nui Dat and within four hours I was back in charge of my section, back in the jungle.

IAN LEIS, 5RAR

Turn on, tune in, drop out.

POPULAR SLOGAN OF THE '60S

Grass, dope, Mary Jane, herb, weed, pot and hash. It all got you high, stoned, out of it, whacked, and, if it was really good stuff, off yer face. All the names for marijuana were positive, a reflection of the way it was viewed then. Around musicians, it was as ubiquitous as girlfriends, though if you were serious about the band, you didn't smoke till after the gig. The Americans, progressive as always, brought in new gear – acid, speed, and worst of all, smack – sometimes called 'junk' or 'shit' or just plain heroin. The criminal gangs picked up on this new avenue of commerce and supply chased need till it was damn near everywhere. GIs carried in drugs for their own use and to sell, and the Cross quickly became a drug supermarket. Some American soldiers even mailed drugs back to Australian friends after they returned to Vietnam. It was bad times then, marked by bad deeds and bad deaths. Too many went that way, a needle in the arm, crushed and broken.

It wasn't all the Americans' fault, of course. Australia was no different to the rest of the Western world. The GIs simply helped it along. Kings Cross was on the turn and it wasn't a good look. It had always been a touch dangerous, just enough to add spice to the night; but now it was getting ugly. Drugs, especially heroin, meant junkies and violence and crime, and the dark laneways that had once felt atmospheric now belonged to the dealers and the desperate.

There were fights every night at our gigs towards the end of the '60s, men with the mark of combat still fresh in their eyes, juiced up and careless of life, ploughing into the locals and each other. We were under standing orders at the club to play 'God Save the Queen' the moment a brawl broke out. It never worked as a peacemaker, but at least it often produced an outbreak of booing that would slow things down.

Wherever you looked, the night-life was getting darker. Sex was not just advertising its wares, it was bellowing raunchily from every corner. There were topless waitresses at The Hasty Tasty Café and the strip clubs began demanding their acts go all the way. At The Pink Panther, The Pink Pussycat, The El Bongo and The Staccato Club it was all things down and dirty, and some took it further with live sex acts on stage. You knew things were bad when the Salvos arrived on Darlinghurst Road. VD cases were on the rise and the 'summer of love' had become overheated and barren.

Still, the GIs kept coming and there were inevitably girls eager to be with them. Not just the professionals but girls from the suburbs, excited by difference, good manners and generosity. We'd see them at night, holding hands with their crew-cut boys over the red-and-white checked tablecloths in the pizza place, or stumbling, a little bit tipsy, to sit together by the El Alamein fountain. When the time came for the men to go back, the girls gifted their soldier boys with a tearful farewell and then lined up again to greet the next bus in from the airport.

There were wedding bells for some, a difficult proposition because each R&R was only six days long and the legally required waiting period for marriage was seven. No matter, if the love endured, the next leave would bring about the wedding. The Wayside Chapel was the favourite venue and the Reverend Ted Noffs, a Kings Cross identity, married more than a hundred couples over the years of the R&R scheme.

War, it seemed, would bring men and women together no matter where they were, or whatever their cultural differences. But it was a simpler matter for Yankee boys in Sydney with their Anglo girls than it would ever be for the two sides in Vung Tau. Love would not run as smoothly there.

Cheap Charlie
(to the tune of 'This Old Man')

(*Uc-dai-loi* means Australian, Saigon Tea is the soft drink ordered by the girls for a high price, P is piastres, MPC means Military Payment Certificate – military money, and a mamma-san is the brothel madam.)

Uc-dai-loi, Cheap Charlie,
He no buy me Saigon Tea
Saigon Tea cost many, many P,
Uc-dai-loi he Cheap Charlie

Uc-dai-loi, Cheap Charlie,
He no give me MPC,
MPC cost many, many P,
Uc-dai-loi he Cheap Charlie,

Uc-dai-loi, Cheap Charlie,
He no go to bed with me,
For it cost him many, many P,
Uc-dai-loi he Cheap Charlie,

Uc-dai-loi, Cheap Charlie,
Make me give him one for free,
Mamma-san go crook on me,
Uc-dai-loi he Cheap Charlie,

Uc-dai-loi, Cheap Charlie,
He give baby-san to me,
Baby-san cost many, many P,
Uc-dai-loi he Cheap Charlie,

Uc-dai-loi, Cheap Charlie,
He go home across the sea,
He leave baby-san with me
Uc-dai-loi he Cheap Charlie.

ANONYMOUS

The Australian soldiers on leave in Vung Tau were, for the most part, ordinary men in search of release and relief. A few were users, exploitative and intimidating towards any Vietnamese woman who crossed their path. But they were few. Most were just out for a good time, trying to cut a good deal somewhere between market prices and their pay, which was much lower than the Americans'.

If you wanted to take the girl somewhere you had to go up to mamma-san and barter for how much, you see . . . and the ones that were beautiful would cost a lot of money . . . so you had to wait until about 9.30, quarter to 10 because then the price was starting to drop. And all night it was about $18 or

> something, you could get a girl all night for $18... We all worked out that all the good-looking girls were too expensive and more likely to have a disease because they would have had more partners, shall we call it, so we went for all the ugly ones. Isn't that a terrible thing to say?
>
> IAN CAVANOUGH

Some wanted a 'wham bam, thank you, ma'am' relationship, a commercial exchange that was quickly negotiated and consummated. Others, looking for more, found comfort and justification in the hope that a kind of intimacy was on offer.

> ...there was a bit of camaraderie, it was a bit like a friendship, or they were just as much victims of the war as you were, so you were consoling each other, I suppose...and when you went into a bar and you were sitting with another girl, if you'd been sitting with this other girl 3000 years ago they would remember and they would come up and they would have a fight over you because you belong to her, because last time when you were in here you were sitting with her, and that was the term, 'butterfly', you know, 'little butterfly', where you go from one person to another...
>
> I was a very naïve country boy, it was true. But I never thought about it that way. I didn't regard myself as that; I was just on this journey through life. And with the girls it was a friendship, it wasn't a transaction, it was because you'd go back to their place and they'd get you working, you'd be carting water for them and doing all this other stuff.
>
> IAN CAVANOUGH

Whatever their motives might have been, the sex was usually plentiful and enthusiastic.

You could get – this is good prices – there was a massage, steam bath and a nookie for $6.50. That was a lot of money in them days but all for $6.50. It was good. You'd start off with the steam bath first, then a massage and then a nookie. Sometimes different women, sometimes the same woman...

I know the second day we went to the Grand Hotel and it was where the Yanks had their R&C. They had a special hotel of their own. We had our little club and we went there. The first thing I did when I walked in there, we wanted to find someone to show us a room. You got a room and a girl for the day for $22.50. She was yours for all day and I did nothing but drink, root, drink, root, drink, root, I did that all day. I got my energy back up and she come back in her bra, every time she come back in her bra and panties I got bloody wandering hands. I felt like saying, 'Why don't you stay naked, you might be safer!'

... Don't forget I was only 19 years of age. I was bloody like a buck stallion, I think.

TERRENCE HIPPISLEY

They must have felt they'd stumbled into heaven. For young men brought up on the secretive, frustrating dance that was sexual relations in Australia, the women in the Vung Tau bars were a quick pirouette into trembling freedom. Nothing could have prepared them. Not for this.

They'd come from a land where most of the sex they knew was conducted blindly through layers of clothing in the back seats of rocking cars. You needed a master's degree in structural engineering just to get a bloody bra strap undone without looking! Now, here they were, 60 seconds into a seat in the bar and small, agile hands were finding their way past zippers for a knowing fondle, while the girl was peppering them with bullet-fast conversation that consisted mostly of encouragement to buy drinks and take matters further. That first time at least, their heads must have been spinning.

The lack of inhibitions, the unembarrassed willingness to try anything they could think of, practices and positions never dreamt of in Australian suburbs – it brought them to their knees and changed many of them forever. For a lot of the men I've talked with, that time still glows like a dull jewel in their memories. Quite a few have returned to Vietnam seeking their youth again. These women were perfect, compliant lovers and, because of the war and their culture, the men could easily abdicate responsibility and any kind of commitment or connection to the women's lives.

Some soldiers refused outright to go near the bar girls. As one said, 'I came here to fight 'em, not fuck 'em!' Others remained determinedly faithful to girlfriends, wives, or religion. Some men hated the women for their convenience and apparent lack of morals or guilt, but still took them, harshly and without care. Most sailed through, enjoying what was on offer with that singular capacity men have for 'getting it while you can'. It was only a few days and it helped to salve the pain of mates lost and the fear of more patrolling. Those who could, and were inclined to, set up relationships that lasted longer than one torrid day.

> As a young bloke you probably need a woman every so often and, I mean, when you go on operation you come so close to death so often, life tends to get very basic I suppose, so all you want to do when you go back on leave and pick your pay up is get drunk, get laid and go back to work again, that's the basic premise . . .
>
> I met a nice girl, very attractive Vietnamese in Da Nang . . . I was in this bar and she pulled up on a motorbike and she said, 'Do you want to come with me?'
>
> And I said, 'Yeah.'

She was dressed in an *ao dai*, looked very nice. So after curfew she came back and I jumped on the motorbike and went off with her... The average going price was about $5 and she was wanting $10 and $20. That's green American, good money for one night. And they'd feed you and look after you... I had my weapons, but I was probably too drunk to worry about anything.

Anyhow, she had this flat, up high on the first floor of this house and I went in there and she's got all mod cons and I said I'd like some *cua*, some mud crab, plenty of wine and we screwed for a while, then back into the booze and wine again, and then I left there the next morning and every time I went into Da Nang then, I'd go and see her. I used to give her $20 for the lot. It went on for about three months and then the next time I went to see her, there was a big, bloody Harley Davidson motorbike sitting downstairs.

I said, 'Whose is that?'

She said, 'That's my boyfriend's.'

And then she wanted to up the price from $20 to $40 and I just said, 'See you later.'

Got in the jeep and drove off. But she was extraordinarily good-looking.

And then the next girl I met, she was not so attractive but she was okay, she had a bit of French in her, French–Vietnamese. I remember her name, Ly was her name, she followed me around like a, well she followed me around full stop. I moved a couple of times and she followed me most places and set up a little house somewhere. I didn't stay there at all but I went and saw her most times... I didn't get too involved with many other women. It was the done thing.

BERNIE MCGURGAN

All of this, the bar girls, the booze and the brothels, even the shacking up by some soldiers with Vietnamese women, was quietly accepted and half-heartedly controlled by the army. It had always been so. What it couldn't control were affairs of the heart.

War brides, women who married Australian soldiers in times of conflict, had long been a muted story in the back pages of Australian military history. After World War I, 15 000 came here, perhaps 25 000 after World War II; even 650 Japanese women braved the White Australia Policy and a hostile reception to follow their men here after the Occupation of Japan and the Korean War. Australian men fell in love everywhere – from Egypt to Switzerland, from Italy to Malaya. The military couldn't ban its men from romance (how do you cage the heart?), but it could, and did, make the process as difficult and bureaucratic as possible. Even more so when the women were of a different race, no matter how attractive they were as people.

> I remember reading in *Time-Life* magazine; they were saying that the Vietnamese women were the most quiet and the most beautiful of the Asian women. And they were, they were feminine from their fingertips to their toenails. I mean my little nuns, my little Dominican sisters, had me round their little finger. They knew it, I knew it, and we got on tremendously well. They conned me, very nicely, in a very feminine way.
>
> FATHER BERNIE MAXWELL

GIs were marrying Aussie girls, everyone knew that. Newspapers featured the stories with pride, as if we should all be pleased that American men took to our women so readily. But Vietnamese partners, wives-to-be of Aussie boys, they were a delicate subject in a country divided by the war and the stories were deliberately not publicised. The army issued the forms, completed the tests, assessed the women's backgrounds and conducted the medicals, but it was left to padres like Father Bernie Maxwell to counsel both potential bride and groom as best he could.

You get a soldier in strife with a bar girl . . . I say, 'Mate, come down and we'll look at the cards. What's her name? Here she is. She's had VD the last three times she's been tested. Now do you want to marry that girl?'

It was a pretty kind of graphic thing to say . . . to the girls I'd say, 'Look, you know, if he's dumped this wife, he'll dump you also.'

In pretty graphic language sometimes.

'He's got a wife and three children, do you think you'll fare any better? You're coming to a strange country, different customs, you'll miss your home, which you will, you may not think you will. But do you think you'll fare any better? Do you think he'll love you anymore, once he's got you to Australia? Different when you were here in Vietnam, you were the only person. He's back in Australia . . .'

I don't know whether it ever worked or not, I tried it.

. . . We were very strict, our medical tests, for VD, TB also, that was the prevalent thing in Vietnam. They had to have a complete, clear, medical certificate before they could come to Australia . . . In Vung Tau, we had about half a dozen of the war brides, waiting to go to Australia. And every fortnight they'd come to the camp gate, they collect their wife's allowance. I had to go to the paymaster with them, line them up, 'Yes, this is Han, yes, she's married to so-and-so.'

Collect her allowance.

'This is Ly.'

Collect her allowance. So they lived a very good life . . . marry an Australian soldier, and he sends money back to you every fortnight.

FATHER BERNIE MAXWELL

Father Maxwell's position and authority soon became known round Vung Tau and the girls took revenge in their own unique way.

After incidents of bar girls and army welfare stuff and going to the bars, the bar girls knew me. Occasionally I'd be down at the market at Vung Tau, in uniform, crosses on, and an arm would go around you, there'd be a bar girl. They'd say, '*Cha*! When you come and see me again?'

'Get away!'

And of course the Vietnamese were looking, and they knew what they were looking at, and they'd notice you. They'd see these crosses, this bar girl with her arm around you.

'God, get away! *Didi mau, didi mau* [go away]! Out!'

Or, they'd be on their motor scooter, in their hot pants, and they're screaming out, 'Cha, we love you too much! We love you!'

'Oh, God, ground, open and swallow me!'

FATHER BERNIE MAXWELL

It was a complex, unforgiving task for Father Bernie and the other padres – they were in loco parentis and could not help but be people of their time and place. But there were, inevitably, sad, sad stories.

There'd be notes on my desk, people wanting to see me. And this particular note was, 'Padre Maxwell . . .' I thought, 'Oh-oh, the guy's not a Catholic.' Barry, he wanted to see me urgently about marrying a bar girl. 'Oh, why me? Why not take the Anglican chaplain or the PD [Protestant Denomination] chaplain, why pick on me?' Anyhow I contact Barry . . . this big guy, in his thirties, broken nose, big hands, really an awkward type of guy, he's in the construction group in Nui Dat. He told me the story, he met this bar girl in Vung Tau, she was a university student. I thought, 'Aha, that's a new approach.' And her aunt was looking after the bar but she was mamma-san temporarily, because the mamma-san was always sick, and he wanted to marry her. I thought, 'Okay, so.' 'Give me the name of the bar, name of the girl.'

Her Christian name was Françoise.

'Okay, look I'll investigate it,' thinking to myself, 'Well, you're gonna get back to Nui Dat in a few days time and Françoise will be disappeared next time you come down here, she says she's from Saigon.' So I thought no more about it, put it in the file, 'next year, whenever'.

A week later I get a call down to the main gate of the camp by this guard commander, he was a corporal and an MP. He said, 'Listen, Father, I know about your nuns et cetera,' he said. 'But there are two birds down here wanting to see you,' he said. 'And one's pretty nice.'

'I'll come down.'

So I went down and there was a woman, I suppose she was most probably in her forties, absolutely gorgeous young woman with her, and she *was* gorgeous. And she introduces herself...

'Anna, and this is my niece, Françoise.'

I thought, 'Oh my God, I can understand why Barry fell in love with you.'

I mean she was absolutely gracious...so the story was true; Françoise was a pharmacy student in Saigon. She was on holidays in Vung Tau with her aunt chaperoning her, and the mamma-san was sick so she went and looked after the bar, and 'course Françoise had to come with her, and suddenly she met Barry.

So, God, you know, this is going to be an interesting problem.

So after a few more contacts with Barry and then Françoise and her aunt were visiting once a fortnight in Nui Dat. Come up by bus all the way from Saigon, and of course they couldn't come into the camp at Nui Dat, so they walked around the perimeter, Françoise and Barry. And boy and girl can't hold hands, not done...males can hold hands, but male–female, not done. So they walked, and more than four paces behind

> them, Aunt Anna, perfectly chaperoning. Now soldiers being soldiers very quickly nicknamed them 'Beauty and the Beast'.
>
> FATHER BERNIE MAXWELL

Matters progressed until Father Maxwell had to travel to Saigon to meet with Françoise's family. They were not only reputable, but Françoise's father worked for the President of South Vietnam. After meeting the entire family, from grandmother down, Father Bernie was faced with telling it as he saw it.

> So eventually in desperation I said, 'I know this doesn't happen in your society. In our Western society we're perhaps not as religious as you are. If I was your eldest and you were asking me what was my opinion, should Françoise marry Barry, my answer would be no, and these are my reasons. Françoise is a very sophisticated young woman, she's a university student, she's very well-educated. Barry has no education; Barry comes from an area of Australia that's very primitive and all Barry knows is booze and birds most probably, and poker machines. To take your daughter from Saigon where she goes down the Street of Flowers every morning, and selects flowers for the home...' I mean, it was very elegant, 'To go to Australia, would be impossible, really impossible.'
>
> Now Françoise has sat there for the whole hour, in her lovely *ao dai*, her hands on her lap... and she looked up and she said, 'Father, you are wrong.'
>
> 'Wha...?' I looked up and said, 'In your society you don't challenge priests.'
>
> 'You are wrong.'
>
> 'Oh.'
>
> She said, 'Father, when I marry Barry and we're in Australia, I will send Barry back to school, and I will send him to university, because I will be a qualified pharmacist and I will support him.'

End of conversation. What could I say? Why? This beautiful Saigonese girl, why does she love this big oaf from back of north Queensland somewhere. It's true. I mean, I was being racist most probably. So, end of conversation.

... So about three weeks later Barry is waiting for me. 'Oh, here's the crunch.' Absolutely distraught.

'Grandmother died. Françoise's the eldest in the family, two years of mourning; she can't marry for two years.'

'Thank you, Lord.' Terrible thing, isn't it? So I thought, 'Well, there's that one solved.'

It didn't finish there ... in '75, I got a call from the PD chaplain in Townsville who said, 'I've got a soldier here, Barry.'

And I said, 'Oh no!'

'He wants to go back to Vietnam and marry his Vietnamese girl.'

I said, 'Well he can't, the two years aren't up yet.'

He said, 'He's gonna go.'

I said, 'Well, the way things are at the minute, no one'll be allowed to go to Vietnam, the place is crumbling.'

Then a letter came from her uncle ... begging me to get his niece out of Saigon. Too late. So I never felt really proud about that one because I played God. What happened to her? I don't know. Her family were a marked family.

FATHER BERNIE MAXWELL

No one knows the accurate figure, but it appears that nearly 200 Vietnamese women successfully came to Australia as wives to our soldiers.

The only problem with R&R was that it came to an end. The three-day leave in Vung Tau, the six-day whirlwind in Sydney, the sex and the temporary salvation. And afterwards they were all a little wiser, a little poorer, and definitely a whole lot worse for wear. Reality and the MPs asserted command over their lives and they trudged back onto their assigned paths, back to camp, back to patrols, back to the sharp edge of combat. Battles were waiting, waiting to claim some and elevate others. And they would be big battles indeed.

VIII

LONG TAN

> With any sort of war, I don't care a bugger what it is, it's like driving a car. If your luck's out a bus is going to come round a corner and take you right out. There's a time and a place where each one of us is going to die. I'm still alive. That place wasn't my place to die.
>
> Bob Buick, Sergeant, 11 Platoon, D Company, 6RAR

It's a small, innocuous road, only wide enough for one car. The driver knows where to stop; some fixed point that only he can see among the identical rows of rubber trees. He gets out, opens the doors and motions us down a red dirt path that leads deep into the rubber plantation. It's hot and quiet and there's no movement of air, just an oppressive weight that probably owes as much to our solemn mood as the weather.

Our guide, a chirpy Vietnamese girl who looks 13 but is probably 20, chatters away behind us as we walk and I wish she would shut up. Then, abruptly, we stop. In the middle of the path, eyes fixed, staring ahead. And, finally, she is silent. We can see it now – an image divided into squares by the lines of trees – a tall, white cross that glows dully in this green and brown place. The Long Tan memorial. It's not exactly Gallipoli, no towering cliffs or gently whispering waves here. Nor is it as dramatic as the serried ranks of headstones at Fromelles, in France. But it has its own power; that curious, other-worldly sense I've felt on other old battlegrounds; a kind of deep silence that separates the place from the surrounding landscape.

The Long Tan memorial has become the repository of memory and commemoration for Australian visitors to Vietnam, veterans and tourists alike. Yet no Australian is buried here, there are no soldiers' names carved in stone to run your fingers over, no eternal flame or heroic murals or statues. Just a white cross and an urn for incense. There is a commemorative plaque but it must be collected (for a fee) from the local police station, hung on the cross for photographs, and returned after your visit.

Neither the plaque nor the cross are the originals constructed and placed here by Australian soldiers in 1969. As with much left behind after the war, they were recycled, the cross taken and used to mark a Vietnamese grave and the brass plaque hammered into a cooking plate. The cross was recovered and resides now in a nearby military museum. The plaque has been lost.

Long Tan has become *the* battle of our Vietnam War, the name people remember (if they remember one at all), and no one seems to know quite why. It was certainly the first major battle fought by Australians and it did happen in 1966, only a few months after the task force troops arrived. But there were other battles that went on for much longer, were fiercer in their fighting and more costly in Australian casualties. The Battle of Coral and Balmoral, for example.

Coral and Balmoral were firebases, temporary locations dug into the dirt for the artillery to use, kilometres away from the safety of Nui Dat. The guns would be placed there for a limited time so infantry patrols would have artillery protection as they hunted further out in the province. In 1968 the task force fought a bloody battle for Coral and Balmoral that involved 26 days of fighting with tanks, artillery, rockets, mortars, gunships and hand-to-hand combat in muddy, blood-soaked holes. By any standards it was a hell of a fight, but it's little known outside the Australian Army, even though it ended in a definitive victory for the task force.

Long Tan rules. So much so that its anniversary day, 18 August, was designated by Prime Minister Bob Hawke in 1987 as the official Vietnam Veterans' Day, a separate commemoration to Anzac Day. Perhaps it is the nature of this battle, for it is the kind of heroism we respond to more than any other – the underdog holding out against ridiculous odds. But Long Tan has also been a source of argument, disagreement, bitterness, even bad blood between some of the men who fought here that day. Some other Vietnam veterans resent it, believing that far too much time and honour is given to just one battle when there were so many other acts of courage that have gone unrecognised.

Even the enemy caused conflict over it by lying at the time of the battle and for many years afterwards. It has taken 40 years for the Vietnamese to even admit that they were defeated, let alone the scale of their defeat. Proper recognition for remarkable acts of bravery still awaits many of the Australians.

This damn, frustrating war. Even the victories get tainted. Nothing is straightforward, nothing is simple. But it does matter, this battle. It will, in time, become the theme, the talisman of a war just as Gallipoli has, and Kokoda. So I sit among the rubber trees, perched on the white, concrete edge of the memorial, moving men and machines across the landscape in my mind, reconstructing that day. And the silence deepens, allowing the voices in.

A lot of people, before we went out, they knew that something was going to happen. It was just that no one wanted to go out that particular day and I don't know why, but a lot of the blokes that you speak to that was there on the day did not, for some reason or other, want to go out on that patrol that day.

JIM RICHMOND, PRIVATE, 11 PLATOON, D COMPANY, 6RAR

2.43 A.M. 17 AUGUST 1966

Despite the early hour, the big guns of Nui Dat were firing. They weren't aiming at anything or anyone in particular. It was a routine H&I, a harassment and interdiction mission, intended to keep any VC moving through the area on their toes and, if the artillery crews were really lucky, they might kill a few. Even though the noise was deafening, most of the sleeping soldiers in Nui Dat could ignore these occasional bursts of fire. Somehow their unconscious minds would reassure them that all was safe. Normally.

This morning though, without warning, the fire started coming the other way, back into the base. Explosion after explosion of mortar bombs and recoilless rifle rounds came fizzing over the wire and into Nui Dat. The barrage continued for 22 minutes.

That was the first time the task force had been shelled . . . every night there were shells going out and they would just fire at independent targets, every couple of minutes . . . and you sort of got used to it . . . 'Bang bang bang.' But this night we could hear 'bang bang bang' and then we heard 'thump thump thump' when they landed in and we realised that that's not going out, it's coming in . . . It was a fair way away from where we were but we worked out pretty quickly it was incoming fire. So it didn't take long for the word to come down the chain of command to us that the camp was being shelled. Then everyone was down at the forward lines and on guard.

JOHN HESLEWOOD, PRIVATE, 11 PLATOON, D COMPANY, 6RAR

They were a little more than just 'on guard'. 6RAR had been in Vietnam for only a couple of months, since June 1966, and contacts with the enemy had been hard to come by. Many of them were wondering whether they were in a war at all, so uneventful had their patrols been. Now though, everyone's blood was up, their senses racing, weapons at hand, machine guns manned, peering out into the night as their artillery fired back, searching for the VC mortar teams that had the effrontery to fire on the Australian base. Inside Nui Dat, the commanders expected a ground assault to follow the mortars and readied the men for attack.

But nothing happened. When the artillery finally stopped, there was silence. They waited a while, then stood down to check the damage. The mortars had wounded 24 Australians, two seriously. Seven vehicles and 21 tents were damaged. It was time to find out who was responsible. It was probably just a small group, trying to hit and run, a favourite VC tactic, but the Australians loved a chase and didn't mind a bit of payback.

6.31 A.M.

B Company of 6RAR, about 120 men, went out through the wire on orders from the battalion CO, Lieutenant Colonel Colin Townsend, to find the positions the enemy had fired from and determine which way they'd scarpered. They figured they'd be back by dinnertime and so carried no meal rations or sleeping gear. By 8.30 a.m. they came across the first of five mortar base plate positions and a set of tracks. Their orders were to follow the tracks, so they did. All day. They lost them and found them again half a dozen times, continually led on by the possibility of contact. Finally, it became too late to return to base so they were resupplied with rations only, no sleeping gear. It would be a rough night in harbour, resting on the ground. It seemed as if the chase had ended in frustration. Again.

---

18 AUGUST 1966

The tedium of life at Nui Dat was about to be relieved, if only for an afternoon. A concert party was arriving, featuring Col Joye and the Joy Boys, and Little Pattie; Australian entertainers who had volunteered their services to perform shows for their countrymen. Col Joye was a kind of 'mum's favourite pop singer', clean-cut and unthreatening, and Little Pattie had ridden to fame on the success of a novelty song called, 'He's My Blond Headed Stompie Wompie Real Gone Surfer Boy'. Both were celebrities in Australia so the concert, to be held later that day, was a big event for the base. The 9 Squadron helicopter crews, who were to transport the artists, were also caught up in the fuss.

> We looked up the tasking sheets for the next day and immediately one was very excited because you were down to be part of the trip taking the concert party up and Little Pattie was coming along with Col Joyc and so as a 25-year-old I was pretty excited to be able to get up close and personal with some of these famous TV stars that were coming to entertain us . . .
>
> So we all went down pretty excited and carrying on and combing our hair and all that sort of stuff so that we looked good. We lined up and chatted to them and generally enjoyed being near famous people. We climbed aboard our helicopters and headed off up to the task force area. We were able to joke and talk to them on the way up but once we got there the army moved in and away they disappeared, out of our sight. So we moved back to the helicopter pad to go through our usual boring routine, which is the hurry up and wait one,

while we wait for something else to happen, for another task to be put on. As far as we knew, in a couple of hours time the concert would be over, we would pack the band up and take them back to Vung Tau.

BOB GRANDIN, FLIGHT LIEUTENANT, 9 SQUADRON

When we got there I realised it was a huge base, you know. It was really quite exciting. And it was exciting because probably for the first time we'd have very big audiences, and, as performers, the more people that are enjoying the performance obviously the better. We'd experienced before that quite a few Australian audiences in Vietnam, and they were just the best, they were terrific. So this was a good day, and it promised to be a great day for us. And for the fellas there as well.

PATRICIA THOMPSON (LITTLE PATTIE)

One group of men would not see the concert. D Company of 6RAR. That morning Townsend decided to send them out to relieve B Company and continue the search for the VC.

They were a different kind of mob, D Company. For a start, more than half of them were national servicemen, an unusual situation that could have led to friction and unrest in the ranks, but their CO, Major Harry Smith, had welded his nashos and regulars into a united team that thought pretty highly of themselves.

Smith was a trainer of the 'keep going till it hurts and then go some more' school and drove his company hard, taking them on frequent forced marches, even in the heat of Vietnam. They were fitter and tougher than most and, as a boast, they'd adopted a Nancy Sinatra hit 'These Boots Are Made for Walkin'' as their company theme song.

We didn't walk anywhere, we fucking ran. We were the only company that went out bush specifically to learn how to make sandbag walls. Because we had to put walls around our tents in Vietnam. We were the only company that went out and specifically learnt how to make barbed-wire fences. We were the only company that did extra first aid training for battle casualties. If we were going to have an exercise we worked twice as hard as any other bastard. And this all made the company stronger and, how do you say it? Camaraderie was more cohesive, 'We're better than those turds down the road.'

I must admit, looking back now, if Harry Smith hadn't been the commander he was, and if myself and other sergeants and corporals we had in Delta Company had not been of the calibre they were, I don't think we would have survived Long Tan. I think the whole 108 would have been killed.

BOB BUICK

Right now though, there wasn't much camaraderie on display. Most of the men were seriously irritated at missing the concert, particularly as they left Nui Dat accompanied by the sounds of guitars being tuned and the endless 'test... test... test' chant of the roadies as they set up for the performance. There were three platoons in D Company – 10, 11 and 12 – along with a company headquarters group. That should have meant 125 men but, as always, they were under strength. Only 105 Australians walked out through the wire, together with three Kiwis who were forward observers for the artillery battery. One hundred and eight men... and most of them were not happy.

Of course everyone is getting excited with Col Joye and Little Pattie coming, something to look forward to and that will be good, break the rhythm of this boredom, we can go to the concert. And we were told on the Thursday morning about 7.30 or something that we would be going out to replace B

> Company. I think they found the base plates of the mortars . . . and we were going to go out and take over from them. That just pissed everyone off; they didn't like that at all. I mean, I don't think it was who was comin' – it could have been any entertainer – just the fact that it was going to be something different from what we were doing. So there was a fair bit of groans and what have you going on that morning when we were told to get our gear together, rations for a couple of days and this is what we were doing, we would be the ones to miss out and so everyone had the shits. That's how we left the base camp, everyone with the shits. Not thinking about not having had a contact, but thinking, 'Why us?'
>
> JOHN ROBBINS, LANCE CORPORAL, 11 PLATOON, D COMPANY, 6RAR

11.00 A.M.

It was hot, stale and stifling. The wet season was at its height and the air was heavy and liquid. Khaki uniforms rapidly changed to black as D Company sweated their way to the rendezvous. Five kilometres to the east of them, an RAAF helicopter was on 'psy ops', a psychological warfare mission. The chopper crew were dropping leaflets onto the newly resettled village of Long Tan, urging the enemy to desert.

> Go out and present yourself to the Vietnam Republic Force.
> Carry your gun on your shoulder with the barrel pointed to the ground.
> Place your hands behind your head.
> Don't be scared. You are welcome.

Most of these leaflets would be used to patch holes in hut walls or to light fires. Even so, both sides kept up a steady barrage of this kind of propaganda. And they were right to try because there *were* enemy troops in the village of Long Tan that day.

Reading, though, was not high on their to-do list. Preparing for an attack on the Australian base at Nui Dat was.

1.00 P.M.

D Company pushed on and met up with B Company at the edge of a rubber plantation around 1 p.m. The men had lunch together while the commanders exchanged intelligence and opinions until B Company gratefully set off for home. Harry Smith gathered his men together and D Company entered the plantation. They thought that, if they were lucky, they were closing in on perhaps 30 or 40 VC. They were horribly wrong.

3.00 P.M.

The plantation had old, played-out rubber trees at the fringes and then line after line of young saplings further in, their trunks skinny and tall. The easiest way to imagine it is to think of the pine forests you drive past in Australia. You can see a long way down the alleys between the rows of trees, but turn sideways and your vision is completely blocked. Move too quickly while staring at a fixed point and you become confused and disorientated.

Not a good place to be patrolling. Two platoons, 10 and 11, started forward, spread out in a line about 400 metres long with a space of about 10 metres between each man. It was measured, careful movement, every soldier swinging his rifle slowly through his arc of responsibility, exactly as they had been trained to do. A dirt road appeared in front of 11 Platoon and they immediately began the drill for crossing obstacles. Two sections crossed the road hurriedly while two others waited, covering them. Then, bold as brass and twice as foolish, a group of VC walked down the road, smack into the middle of the Australians.

> I looked up and all of a sudden on my right-hand side were six or eight VC dressed in greens... that didn't twig at the time. They were going along quite nonchalant. They weren't bloody interested at all and I thought, 'Hang on, these guys are walking straight into the middle of the company!'
>
> Anyway I fired a couple of rounds and knocked over a bloke and, of course, confusion reigned supreme for the next three or four minutes because we are not expecting the company to be hit in the middle, particularly in behind the forward elements. You've got two sections out the front; these guys are inside that, inside that umbrella.
>
> So it took around about two or three minutes I suppose for people to realise you know, 'What the shit's going on here!' Charlie [Victor Charlie – VC – the enemy] didn't know. He went to ground and I couldn't see him anymore because the vegetation was some half a metre to a metre high and they were down in a bit of a hollow in this road. There was a lot of yelling going on. Everyone wanted to know what was going on. We passed a message it was VC. The VC then got their act together, picked up their wounded guy and ran away to the east; they bolted out to the east.
>
> Bob Buick

The VC soldier wasn't just wounded. Buick had killed him and the body was recovered later. Something though, wasn't quite right. The enemy had dropped a weapon and the Australians picked it up. It was a rifle, an AK47, the infamous, Russian-made Kalashnikov. This was not a weapon the local guerrillas carried. Then there was the way the enemy was dressed – khaki trousers and shirts, expert camouflage and pith helmets. None of the black pyjamas the Australians were used to seeing. Just who were these blokes?

The information was dutifully reported to Harry Smith who passed it on to battalion headquarters, who passed it on to task force headquarters, and while the brass considered this conundrum, Smith, appropriately, gave permission for 11 Platoon to give chase. The platoon commander, 2nd Lieutenant Gordon Sharp, arranged his men in an extended line and they pushed on... fast. So fast, in fact, that they were soon out of sight of the other platoons. Even Smith couldn't see them through the grid of trees. This was unsafe, very unsafe. But before anything could be done, before task force headquarters could finally determine exactly who they were up against, or Smith could recall them, 11 Platoon's world changed forever.

4.08 P.M.

> We went off gung-ho in extended line, which is three sections all together in one big long line, all going the same way. We were about eight to ten metres apart and there's about 28 of us, say 20 on the front line. So we covered an area of about 200 to 250 metres across the frontage. We had no depth; it was all one thin line... As we were progressing I wasn't thinking of anything because I said, 'Oh well, these blokes have shot through again.' You know, this has been the story of every contact we've had for weeks on end and really, I suppose, I was like everyone else, you know, 'Where have these bastards gone, can't we get into a decent fight?' and all this. And all of a sudden on our left side, our left flank, all hell broke loose.
>
> BOB BUICK

John Robbins was a lance corporal in command of the section on the left.

We came under just unbelievable fire. Rifle fire, machine guns, everything. And the noise just broke open. And we went to ground . . . we all went to ground and returned fire. A lot of noise, yelling, confusion. And I mean, it is hard to describe noise, but it is pretty hard to speak when all of this is happening, and you try and return fire. And I thought this has got to be more than three or four blokes and I look up and I am taking aim, firing, and there is a line of them coming towards us. And I thought, 'God! What's happening? This is not in the book! I haven't been told about this, there looks to be hundreds of them!' And I said, 'I have got to get these blokes back in, they can't be spread out like we are.' There is a lot of room between us, there is metres between us, we were well spread out, the eight of us, so I ran and took a couple of dives and what have you and I yelled out, 'Where's Doug Salveron?' He was on the far left.

And they yelled out, 'He's dead!'

I said, 'Where's Shorty Thomas?'

And they said, 'He's killed also.' They said, 'We saw it.'

It must have been when they walked into it; they must have got shot immediately. So I said, 'Well, where's Kenny Gant?'

And they said, 'He's dead too.'

So I couldn't bring them back, it just happened like that. I crawled back to where the gun was and the gunner got killed and I saw him get killed, the bullet went bang, straight through there. And then Warren Mitchell, he is his 2IC on the gun, he takes the gun over and I am going across towards the gun and he is firing and I am going across to help keep the belt going through . . . and that's when I got hit. And Warren gets hit; he gets shot and killed at the same time. That's my best recollection. I mean, this didn't all happen within a couple of minutes, it happened over a period of time. I got hit and felt funny. Never been shot before. 'So is that what it feels like?' I look down and there is blood through the shirt.

JOHN ROBBINS

The enemy attack was brutal and explosive. Two machine guns were firing directly into one of the Australian sections, taking out most of the soldiers there. The tracer bullets were easily visible in the gloom under the canopy, but there was nowhere to hide, no cover except the miserably skinny rubber trees and the unyielding earth. The fusillade lasted for a few minutes and then it stopped. Gordon Sharp, still unsure of what they were facing, ordered another section, 10 or so men, to conduct a sweep out in front to find out what the hell was going on. It was good tactics, getting the platoon into a position where they could attack. Except the section didn't get there.

As they rose, the entire platoon was immediately under fire from several different directions simultaneously. Rocket-propelled grenades, launched from unseen enemy shoulders, hurtled through the air and all the men on the ground could hear was a terrifying whizzing sound before the trees exploded, raining debris down on them. The soldiers of 11 Platoon fired back with everything they had, fighting for their lives.

> After 10 or 15 minutes we were really starting to get in the shit. The air was absolutely thick with tracer and they were cracking the rounds and the foliage was starting to come off the trees and we were starting to take casualties all the way through. Blokes getting shot and I didn't know how many were killed. You could not move any more than three or four metres without attracting attention. As soon as you moved Charlie saw you and started to bloody open up . . . you could not talk in a normal voice. Even screaming at the top of your lungs you might only make voice communication with a guy who was say two or three metres away. Everything had to be relayed from one to another all the way down the line. Everyone was doing what they were doing in their own 10 foot square block of dirt because that's about as much dirt as you own when you've got a rifle. I was shooting the VC. How many

> did I shoot that day? Geez, I don't know, most probably 30. Who knows? All I know is that you happened to aim at some bastard and you hit him, he went down. I ended up with holes in my little bush hat, holes in my shirt, holes in my trousers, holes in my webbing.
>
> Bob Buick

4.12 P.M.

The machinations of men, their quarrels and battles are of little consequence to the greater forces of the natural world. The sky, the sea, the land, do not take into account wounded or dying men. They cannot feel the desperation or the adrenaline of the fight; they do not care about death, they obey only the immutable laws of the earth. As the battle deepened, huge, wave-like masses of air were rolling across Long Tan, coming in from the sea. Inside them was moisture and lots of it, a small ocean of water. With a devastating crack it was released over the rubber plantation and, at last, the monsoon came, the drenching, drowning rains that destroy and heal the landscape of Asia almost every year. Millions of litres of water poured down on Vietnamese and Australian combatants alike, opaque curtains of rain that eliminated visibility and turned the red soil into an ochre quagmire in seconds.

As if in response, the enemy increased their firing, attacking the Australians simultaneously on the left, the right and the front. Gordon Sharp was trying to make himself heard on the radio, calling for help in the form of artillery fire. He could not gather his men together to withdraw because they were all pinned down by enemy fire. Artillery was their only chance. This was not some small, isolated group of local guerrillas, it was something much bigger.

None of the Australians knew it at the time but they were up against the leading edge of a very large force, an enemy regiment, a well-trained, well-equipped, highly disciplined army of North Vietnamese and local battalions, around 2500 men. And their forward force, their hammer, was dropping down squarely on the men of 11 Platoon.

> So there we were, about bloody 18 of us left at this stage of the game trying to bloody survive, waiting for some bastard to come and help us. That didn't look like a real good idea because I don't think they were going to come to help us, although I kept on yelling out, 'They're coming in, the APCs, they're coming out!'
>
> You say anything for your own, to build your own strength up and you can tell people all sorts of lies when they don't know what's going on, even convince yourself at times. And there wasn't a hell of a lot we could do. We were stuck there. We were getting blokes killed. The ammunition was getting low. We didn't get any ammunition coming in. It was one of those sort of things where you had to hang in there, do what you have to do and you know when the tide turns that's when you can do something. You know, you wait until the tide either comes in or goes out before you launch the boat.
>
> So we stayed there. The VC fire was excellent. When he got closer he was starting to bloody miss us by only a matter of inches, because the closer the round passes your ear the louder the crack is. They tell me you never hear the round that hits you. I can understand that.
>
> So we were in a very, very serious fire-fight and the air is literally full of ammunition, there was tracer everywhere... the tracer was like fireflies. They were just everywhere. They were buzzing around your head all over the place. You could not move. If you moved you became a target. Once you became a target you were dead.
>
> BOB BUICK

> Sunray down. Sunray down! I repeat. Sunray is down!
>
> CODED RADIO MESSAGE TO INDICATE A COMMANDER HAS BEEN KILLED

4.26 P.M.

The first artillery shells were fired by a New Zealand unit at Nui Dat but they were off target. Gordon Sharp knew they had to be redirected and got up on his hands and knees, exposing himself to fire, so he could give a more accurate direction to the guns. Bob Buick, crouched near his CO, warned him to keep his head down and as Sharp told Buick not to worry about him, he was shot through the throat. Buick grabbed the radio and called through the message 'Sunray down!' and a shudder went through those listening. Rarely had an Australian officer been shot in the Vietnam War and the loss of a platoon commander meant this was a very different kind of battle. Gordon Sharp was 21 years old, a television cameraman from Tamworth in NSW, a national serviceman. He died on the ground in the Long Tan rubber plantation, the first nasho officer to be killed in Vietnam. Buick, the platoon sergeant, was now in command.

> That dropped me in a big bucket of shit because all of a sudden I'm looking after this group. So you have to take everything into consideration. I had been trained for this. I had been in the army for eight years as it was at this stage of the game. I was a platoon sergeant, a professional soldier, so you've got to do a job when a job comes.
>
> BOB BUICK

Alongside Harry Smith in the company headquarters group, a few hundred metres back from the battle, was Captain Morrie

Stanley, the New Zealand forward observer for the artillery. He was on one end of the radio, Bob Buick on the other. Together they began to redirect the guns. Then Buick sent Smith a desperate message – 'Almost surrounded, suffering heavy casualties, cannot withdraw, almost out of ammunition . . .' Before Smith could reply the transmission went dead. The antenna of Buick's radio had been shot away and all communication was lost.

> It is hard to explain the physical environment where it's absolutely raining, lightning and thunder, artillery around you exploding . . . rocket-propelled grenades, anti-tank guns and they were hitting the trees and just blowing the trees off about this far off the ground, some six to eight feet up. The movie people will never get it right. They will never get the actual environment right because you can never ever build something that is real. You can only build an image. And this is the most difficult thing to try and explain to people what it's like to be involved in something as big as it was for 11 Platoon.
>
> It was one of those things that every man will remember different things. Every man will see something that will stick in his mind. Another bloke will see the same thing but he'll have a different vision of it. So it's one of those very personal things that I don't think anyone can really explain in great detail.
>
> If I put you in a room and made it full of noise and sent bees in that room you'd be dodging the bees and you'd be trying to block out the sound and trying to think what you had to do next. I suppose that's most probably the closest I can come to. It is organised chaos, I suppose. There is chaos around you but you've got to be organised to control the chaos and that's what I tried to do.
>
> BOB BUICK

Harry Smith had to try to get 11 Platoon out of harm's way or, at the very least, find out *exactly* where they were. Without radio contact, he had no idea of how many of them were wounded or dead or even whether they had finally been overrun. Someone had to go and find them and 10 Platoon were ordered in. The platoon commander, 2nd Lieutenant Geoff Kendall, had his men drop their packs, fan out in an extended line and head towards the firing. The rain was still bucketing down as they moved forward and, through the mist and the mud, Kendall thought he saw a little trouble that just might hold them up for a while.

> As we went over, there's this bunch of guys in front of us, they're in line . . . and at first I thought they might be 11 Platoon, I really did because they were all wearing green uniforms, which I should've twigged straightaway, but I didn't. When we got another 10 yards on, you could see they were carrying AK47s so I just said, 'Fire!' And I just went down on my knee and started to fire and the guys did, and we just all dropped down and fired and 'woo hoo' wiped them right out. The guys further to the left, turned left and just trotted away, that's the way I would describe it anyway. Now there may have been a bugle, I don't know, their bugles blew all bloody afternoon but that probably was a bugle call that said 'cut out', but of course as soon as they cleared, we got up again and kept going towards 11 Platoon and we got maybe only 30 or 40 metres and wow, we got it. Hit from our front and from the left and the first guy hit in the platoon – and I think it had to be a sniper – was my signaller, who was hit through the chest luckily, high and right through the radio and that had to be deliberate. It could've been worse; they could've gone for the platoon commander. And there were two or three guys hit in the left-hand section but nobody badly, so I put us on the

ground again and we tried to get the radio going, which we couldn't do.

GEOFF KENDALL, 2ND LIEUTENANT, 10 PLATOON, D COMPANY, 6RAR

10 Platoon was attacked on three sides. It seemed that wherever the Australians moved, they encountered the enemy, like malevolent wasps. With 10 Platoon's radio gone, Harry Smith had now lost contact with two of his three platoons, cruelly at a time when he knew they were both under heavy fire. Only 400 metres separated Smith from his men, but for all the information he had it might as well have been kilometres. Immediately behind him 12 Platoon was waiting, impatient to get involved. In that strange isolation battle can bring to groups of men only metres apart, 2nd Lieutenant Dave Sabben, the 12 Platoon CO, did not yet know of the disasters that had befallen his fellow platoon commanders. He was just keen to get in on the fight.

When the firing broke out with 11 Platoon I really thought that Gordon Sharp had had the contact that we were out looking for. He had had the fire-fight. In military terms he had won, he had got the contact. It was his battle. We didn't expect more than a half a dozen or so for our whole tour. The radio news came back, 'Yes, I've contacted half a dozen or so.' Once his fire-fight was over, that was all. He would perhaps get a Military Cross for Christmas and the rest of the patrol was going to be ordinary for us. So I thought, 'Well, lucky, lucky, Gordon.' This is what we had trained for, for not quite a year but for a long time and it is I guess a platoon commander's dream to have 30 men in his platoon contact a small number of enemy, a small but manageable number of enemy and to obviously win at the end of the day. So my impression was, 'I wish that was me, but you know there it is, good luck to him.'

> A bit later on in the battle 10 Platoon had a similar experience and they had a fire-fight and I was still in reserve behind company HQ, 500 or 600 yards away from where all the action was and I thought to myself, 'Well, lucky Geoff Kendall, his platoon is having a nice little fight. It doesn't look too serious. He's up against about the same number of troops based on radio intercept. You know, good luck to him. What am I doing here in reserve?'
>
> DAVE SABBEN, 2ND LIEUTENANT, 12 PLATOON, D COMPANY, 6RAR

Sabben's chance would come soon enough. In the meantime, Smith badly needed to talk with his other platoons. Without communications he was struck dumb and blind, and the gunfire he could hear only made it worse. Then, through an almost surreal act of courage, he was given his voice back.

Geoff Kendall and his men were trading bullet for bullet with the enemy when an Australian voice could be heard shouting above the gunfire. Like a frantic bellboy carrying an urgent message, the voice was calling out the commander's name over and over, 'Mr Kendall! Mr Kendall!' They shouted back and an Australian soldier stumbled out of the trees into the middle of the platoon.

He was a radio operator, named William 'Yank' Akell, a private in company HQ. And he was carrying the spare company radio. No one knows quite how the 'Yank' did it, but he had run 300 metres from Smith's position through the rain and the gunfire, calling out and calling out until he found Kendall's platoon. And he'd killed two enemy soldiers along the way. Akell was awarded a Mention in Despatches for this extraordinary act. 10 Platoon was now coming under heavy mortar fire and, with communication restored, Smith ordered them back. Gathering up their wounded, they retreated. As they left they did not know that they were just 100 metres away from the beleaguered men of 11 Platoon.

4.50 P.M.

Harry Smith was facing a difficult decision. Clearly he was up against a numerically superior force and to survive he needed to get his entire company together in one place so they could fight a defensive battle. But all three platoons were separated by a lot of ground, couldn't give supporting fire to each other and getting them together would require remarkable luck. Or a miracle. The artillery was having to fire first in support of one lot of men, then another, and couldn't concentrate their shells where they would do the most good. And neither Smith nor Morrie Stanley, his artillery forward observer, had any real idea of exactly where 11 Platoon was.

Bob Buick had located a spare antenna for his radio and could finally talk with Morrie Stanley. But it was all looking hopeless. The enemy were now only 50 metres away from 11 Platoon and the artillery shells were flying harmlessly over their heads. They may have been causing death and destruction to troops further back, but the Vietnamese soldiers who had the Australians pinned down were untouched. It was asymmetric warfare again – neutralise your enemy's advantage with clever tactics. The Australians had artillery, the Vietnamese did not. So they used a method they called, 'holding the belt with one hand while punching with the other'. Stay up tight and close to your enemy in a fire-fight so that he cannot utilise artillery for fear of hitting his own men.

11 Platoon could not hope to survive much longer than another 10 minutes. They knew the rest of their company must be trying to get to them but how they could do this, or when it would happen, was unknown. Yet even then, even as death seemed imminent, they found in themselves what Australian soldiers have always seemed able to crank out – humour as black as the ace of spades and a kind of cockeyed optimism.

> You were always confident for some reason that you would get out. It was a matter of how and when. A few blokes jokingly said, 'We're in trouble here.'

And someone else would say, 'Yeah, we are, but don't worry.'

That was the kind of thing that kept happening all the way. The five of us were pinned down and we were joking. It was pouring, really pouring. It was real thick mud and a bullet would hit the mud and fly up and you'd say that if it was coming straight then it couldn't kick the mud up so there must be someone in the trees shooting down at us. So snipers in the trees. And one of the bloke's looked up and said, 'There's one up in the trees, six rows back three wide.'

And you'd say, 'It's your turn, have a go at him.'

This went on. And you might miss him and someone might say, 'You idiot, I'll get him.'

So that's what kept everyone going. There was no real panic. Everyone just fed off each other.

John Heslewood

The time ticked away, the battle continued and their ammunition was almost gone. Without a word, the few men still able to gathered hand grenades and machetes, even shovels were taken out, ready for a last stand. Bob Buick knew there was only one chance left for them – he would have to call the artillery in virtually on top of his men. He had been trained to direct artillery; all NCOs are, but only in a big-scale way. This kind of precision, within metres of your own soldiers, would normally require a specialist and even then it was not a practice to be undertaken except in the direst of circumstances. Buick called it in.

At last I said to Morrie Stanley that you better put the stuff on top of us because there was only about a dozen of us left out of 28 that were still capable of firing and, you know, if you're going to go you might as well go that way instead of getting captured or taken wounded.

Morrie being a good artillery man and a Kiwi wasn't prepared to shoot his guns onto Australians, but I was able to adjust

> the fire until it landed exactly where I wanted it . . . the artillery was coming over the top of our heads and landing about 50 metres in front of us. The whole ground was shaking. You could feel the blast on the side of the face. It was lots of flash, lots of smoke, lots of noise.
>
> Bob Buick

As the shells began to fall Buick issued instructions. 'Drop 100. Drop 100.'

Walking the fire towards his position 100 yards at a time. It was using artillery in a way these infantrymen had never attempted before. They thought of artillery as a 'big area' weapon, one that you fired at the rear of the enemy as they retreated from a fire-fight. Or you used it to pound a place where you might expect an ambush.

'I can see your fall of shot, you're amongst them. Drop 50. Move right 50. More. Another 50.'

As a soldier you aim a rifle, not a 105-millimetre artillery piece loaded with high explosive. But Buick continued to call and, with every instruction, the wall of fire crept closer. Death was raining down and the men of 11 Platoon could only pray it would not land on them.

> He yelled out that artillery was coming in and the artillery started and it just never let up. You could hear it coming through the trees and next you would see a tree just lift up and bodies. Round after round it just went on. I mean, it was hard to hear before the artillery, but now you have got machine guns rattling and tracer fire racing through the air everywhere. I thought we were deadset gone then. I thought there was no way we were going to get out of this. You don't think a lot about that but it does cross your mind, so I started to say the Lord's Prayer, I thought, 'I am buggered here.' And every time

I would get a few lines out I couldn't think of the next one and so I would have to start again. I would try and get through it and then something would interrupt me, I don't think I ever got through it. I might have started a hundred times and I never got through it. And I thought, 'Isn't it funny how when you get really in strife . . .'

So all around us was just unbelievable what's going on. I played dead for a while. I looked out and there was probably half a dozen or 10 of them. This tree had been blown up and was lying on its side and I saw them behind this tree and that's when I got the grenade out, I thought, 'I am not going to go with them.' . . . I took the pin out and I just lay with it under my stomach, put it under with this hand. And I thought, 'Well, if I get some of them to go with me it would be better, but I am not going with them. I am the only one I think in my section alive. There is no one else, there is no one here alive, they're all dead out there.'

JOHN ROBBINS

The shells were falling directly onto the Vietnamese, killing and maiming in all directions, shattering their front lines and, for the moment, halting their assault. Military historians, assessing the big picture in the desiccated air of hindsight, regard this moment as a critical one in the final outcome of the Battle of Long Tan. On the ground, it didn't feel like that.

I think most of the blokes around me were all dead and I was hit by a piece of shrapnel. Before that happened I was just talking to Shorty and I just asked Shorty, I said, 'Where's Doug?'

And he said, 'Doug's dead.'

And that's when I saw Shorty get hit by a big burst of automatic fire. I turned around; I was looking down the barrel of an enemy gun. So I had a hand grenade and I just thought, 'Oh well, I'm gone now.' So as he fired I dropped behind my webbing, which we took off when we first come under heavy fire, that's the only protection we had, so I had that in front of me when he actually fired at me and I think that's where the bullet hit. So I pulled the grenade out and I thought, 'Well, this is the only thing I've got to save meself,' because our ammunition was low and I pulled the pin out of the grenade ready, didn't know whether to throw it at him or lift me head up or what, but that's when I got hit by artillery. It was like getting hit with a 28-pound sledgehammer.

There was no pain, but it felt as if my stomach was driven into the ground and my feet and head were sort of meeting each other at the middle. I thought I was dead for the simple reason that I had no feeling from my head . . . I thought, 'Well, if I look around now I'm not going to see anybody left.' But then I thought, 'Well, if you can think this there's got to be something there.' So that's when the pain started. I still had this grenade in my hand and all I could think of was I had a piece of elastic, we used to have elastic in our trousers to hold the trousers up off the socks so I took a piece of elastic out, I wrapped it around the hand grenade and put that in front of the tree, in front of me.

JIM RICHMOND

5.15 P.M.

10 Platoon struggled back to the company HQ position and an improvised aid shelter was hurriedly set up for their wounded. Harry Smith had only one more chance if he was to get 11 Platoon out. 12 Platoon was ordered to go get them, this time from another direction. But Smith kept one section of the platoon with him, for the protection of HQ. Dave Sabben was going to get his chance at last, but instead of 30 men, he'd have only 20. It was a hell of an ask, but if Sabben or his men were troubled by it there was no sign as they headed out. They had around 400 metres of ground to get across before they would

reach the last-known position of 11 Platoon. And it would be a long time before they returned.

Back at the Nui Dat base, men were moving everywhere, like an upturned anthill. The boom of the big guns was now a constant rhythm, playing a bizarre counterpoint to the rock band up on the concert stage.

> During the second show I could sense that things were different, things were changing. I could see that officers were sort of being whisked away from the area. As you can understand, the atmosphere, when there are concerts on, is very relaxed, laid back, it's hard to believe you're in the middle of a country where there's a war taking place. It's really terrific. And suddenly things were changing, quite suddenly actually, during that second show. And I could hear more artillery in the background. And in an increasing way.
>
> So the third show began, and as it was beginning, the Joy Boys were playing, and the officer in charge of us said, 'You've got to finish – cut the show short, cut the show short. We're getting out earlier!' And it was a troubled voice that told me that. And I thought, 'No, this isn't right. Something's going on that's bigger than we know.'
>
> But the show went on, and the audience was terrific. Once again, people were whisked away from the audience, and once again, even more noise now, from artillery. For many years, Vietnam veterans who were there have told me that at one stage I jumped so many feet off the ground. I'm sure that's exaggerated, but if I did I would have known that the show

must go on, so I kept singing. But I think the fear on my face obviously showed to some people.

We did cut the show short, we were told in very clear terms, 'Get off, get off, get off!' We did. And two helicopters were waiting for us to take us back to Vung Tau. And when we got on the plane, all sorts of things happened at once. Sirens were blaring really loudly, there was lots of artillery in the background and it started to pour rain at the same time. So it was a cacophony of noise. And I knew that things were dangerous, really bad by that stage. And the speed that we were being evacuated, really, really quickly. And off we went.

And I looked back as we went over the mountains, I looked down and I could see lots of orange and red fire, and lots and lots of it. I knew that that was a big battle happening. And for the very first time then the penny dropped to me that, you know, Australians are in the middle of a war. This is fair dinkum; this isn't just doing concerts and having a good time. This is really war. I could see it.

PATRICIA THOMPSON (LITTLE PATTIE)

The big question facing Brigadier O. D. Jackson, the task force commander, was where would the next blow fall? He knew that D Company was deep in the fight and without reinforcements would likely fall. But if he sent too many resources to their aid and in the meantime the base itself was attacked . . . ? The prospect of losing Nui Dat to the enemy was unthinkable. Compromise and caution, the twin-bladed nightmare for any commander caught in the middle of a battle, were his only refuge.

A Company of 6RAR, who had just returned from a three-day patrol, were told to prepare to go to D Company's aid and an armoured personnel carrier unit, 3 Troop, were put on standby to carry them. For the moment though, nobody was going anywhere till Jackson was convinced he had no other option.

The radio in the operations centre crackled into life. It was Harry Smith, informing Nui Dat that he was now dangerously low on ammunition and requesting a resupply by chopper. He couldn't get to a cleared area and they'd have to drop it through the trees. Jackson turned immediately to Group Captain Peter Raw, the RAAF commander, and requested two helicopters to deliver the supplies. Raw refused. It was too dangerous, he said, hovering at tree-top height, foul weather conditions, inevitable heavy ground fire from the enemy; the choppers may as well have targets painted on their sides. He wouldn't risk them.

Jackson's reported reply was short and to the point. 'I'm about to lose a company, what's a few more choppers and a few more pilots!'

Raw was operating under specific instructions that he was not to allow his choppers to land anywhere enemy resistance was expected. The army and the air force had never been the best of friends, but at this time, in Vietnam, their relationship was poisonous. The army dismissed the boys in blue as precious and totally out of touch with the way a force needed to behave in wartime. The air force argued back that they were not the Americans and could not be expected to lose aircraft the way those profligate clowns did, and the army just wanted to take over their choppers. It was an utter bloody farce.

Jackson summoned the US Army aviation liaison officer and, in front of Raw, asked for his help. 'Sure,' was the reply. 'They'll be here in 20 minutes.' In the face of potentially deep humiliation, Raw wisely overturned his decision and informed Jackson his choppers would go.

> We got to the tent and immediately realised that there was something wrong because there was very intense conversation, a lot of yelling, a lot of screaming, people yelling orders and suddenly you could hear these radio calls coming in saying things were very, very bad, that they needed this, they needed

that, that there were enemy here, they had casualties here, all that type of thing was happening on the radio and it was about this time, the most vivid thing I remember was that Harry called, 'If you don't get help out to us soon we're all gone and you'll go next!'

So we asked people what's going on, what's happening, what's all this about? Those in the operations tent for the air force started to tell us that there was a very large enemy force out there and they were surrounding Delta Company and our group captain came out and said, 'They want ammunition but we can't go because it's not safe. It's terrible flying conditions. There's too many enemy out there, our aeroplanes are only support aeroplanes, they're not support helicopters, they're not designed to do this type of fighting and we're not meant to go out into an unsafe area like this in support.'

However Frank [Riley, the pilot] immediately said, 'Well I don't care, I'll go!'

My immediate reaction is, 'Hey, Frank, what are you sayin'? This is no good, I don't want to die and there are too many out there, you know this is foolish.'

And he said, 'Well, don't come.'

That was the end of it, I then said, 'Well don't be stupid, I'll come of course, but let's not get killed.'

And so we went down to the helicopter pad and moving across to the Delta Company area where they were going to provide us with ammunition to take out. At this stage you're starting to wonder, how the heck do we do this? How the heck do you go out there where there's thousands of enemy? They've got anti-aircraft rifles that they can fire at you! Any gun is going to cause you problems and how do you go out there and back again? What do you do that makes sure you come back because nobody actually wants to not come back?

Well, what gradually happened was we got caught up in the intensity of making decisions about putting things on

> board, getting loaded and getting away. People ran around trying to work out how they were going to take the ammunition out and somebody amongst them made a decision that they'd cut off the bands around the boxes so they didn't have to break those and they'd wrap them in blankets which would become beneficial to the wounded people out there and we'd just chuck them out and see what happened. It was decided they wouldn't load any magazines or belts of ammunition, they would just drop the ammunition and they could use it because that would get it to them the quickest. So, very quickly, they were loaded, people running everywhere.
>
> BOB GRANDIN

The radio squawked again. This time Harry Smith was requesting reinforcements by chopper, but they had to turn him down. The weather was against it, there was no safe landing zone and it was getting too close to dark. What they could promise was that A Company, in APCs, was on its way. Townsend, 6RAR's CO, got off the radio and ordered them to mount up and get to D Company. Help was finally coming, but no one could be sure it would arrive in time.

5.30 P.M.

12 Platoon was halfway there. They could hear the firing; they knew where 11 Platoon was. Maybe this time they could do it. Maybe the way in was clear. But they were fired on, from three directions at once. Eight Australians were wounded immediately. They'd run into groups of Vietnamese flanking 11 Platoon, trying to surround them and cut them off before the final kill. Sabben knew that if 11 Platoon was to have any chance at all he had to stop this happening; he had to force open a corridor through which his countrymen could escape.

12 Platoon stood and fought . . . and fought . . . and fought again. The rain kept on pouring, the visibility was still absurdly

low and the Vietnamese kept sending out small, probing patrols, trying desperately to find out how many Australians were out there. It only became obvious later that they never really knew. By chance, every time they sent out a group, they ran into Australians. First they bumped into 11 Platoon, then when they sent a flanking force round to wipe them out they ran into 10 Platoon, then they went the other way and there was 12! The enemy commander's battle map, the map on which his staff kept updating positions, must have shown Australians wherever he looked. If only they had known . . .

5.45 P.M.

When Lieutenant Adrian Roberts mustered 3 Troop to take them out of Nui Dat, there should have been 13 APCs. There were seven. The other six were in for repairs and maintenance. The seven he did have had worn tracks, suspension that was about to go to God, and obsolete radios. Once the soldiers of A Company were riding inside the carriers, Roberts had no way of talking with them except by shouting over the roaring diesel engines. Still, the radios let the carriers communicate with each other at least.

The good news was that he was given three more APCs from 2 Troop to bring his numbers up to 10. And, what's more, these were brand-new carriers, fresh from Australia. The bad news was that they had no gun shields to protect the crew commander from getting his head shot off, and no internal radios. That meant that the crew commander had to give directions to the driver by rigging him up like a horse. The driver had a length of rope tied to each epaulette and the commander pulled on the one he wanted. But, hey, their tracks and suspension were tiptop!

There were only a couple of holes in the perimeter wire of Nui Dat that were wide enough to let the carriers through. Roberts headed towards the nearest one, but roadworks inside the base sent him on a long detour. When he eventually arrived at the hole – it wasn't there. A new one had been opened up somewhere else by the engineers . . . and, 'Sorry, mate, but they're at dinner.' Finally, someone turned up and showed them the new exit. Then, just as Roberts was about to charge off, he was told that Lieutenant Colonel Townsend, the 6RAR CO, had decided to come with them. Roberts sent two carriers back to get Townsend and set off with the rest. His comments on this delay are not recorded.

6.00 P.M.

Now it was the RAAF's turn. Without that ammunition, it would not matter how fast Roberts tried to get there. Harry Smith and his men would go under. It would take seriously skilful flying not just to accurately deliver the ammunition, but to get the choppers out intact.

> They stopped the artillery barrage which was supporting Delta Company so we could fly out. I remember we lifted up above the trees and it was just pouring with rain and all we could see was rain in front of us . . . We couldn't put any speed on because we couldn't see where we were going. When you're flying in a helicopter, the rain's hitting the front windscreen all the time, you've got your windscreen wipers flashing but it's like driving a car in torrential rain. Your visibility just disappears and the only thing you can do is actually look out the side and down at the ground and between your feet down at the ground and you can see things that you can identify below you. So we just staggered along because we were only doing about 20-odd kilometres an hour, you know five, ten knots because we couldn't go any faster.
>
> So as we're staggering along we're saying a few things to each other. 'How are we going to find them? How are we going to see them? What's that road below us?'

And suddenly we realised, that's the road to Long Tan!

'Turn left, turn left, let's go up that way!'

So we started to go along there.

'I wonder where they are? I wonder where the enemy are? What happens if one of them shoots us? This aeroplane will blow up!'

And so you're anxious. I remember drawing myself back into my armour-plated seat thinking if I'm only small the bullet will go past and miss me and suddenly somebody yelled, 'What was that?' and perhaps that sound of the whistle of a bullet going past. Who knows, because really there was just lots of rain bashing on the windscreen, lots of noise and you really couldn't tell anything that was happening.

Within a very short time you just suddenly realise there's another road.

'Hey, that's the intersection at Long Tan. We're behind the enemy. Turn round quick, let's get back the other way!'

And so we called out, 'Throw smoke, throw smoke, we're in your area.'

And suddenly up through the trees comes this wispy little piece of smoke and I said, 'I see yellow smoke, I see yellow smoke...'

'Wrong, wrong, wrong!'

'Quick, shit let's get out of here because that must be the enemy position, they're listening to us!'

And so we did a big 360 turn. 'Throw smoke again.' And so they threw smoke again and up came some red smoke.

'I see red smoke.'

And they said, 'Right, that's us.'

So we knew and in fact it was the position... 'Roll now,' was Frank's command and he just did a 180-degree turn, rolling his helicopter onto the side and headed back and all of the ammunition just poured out through the open door down on top of the position below...

> We received a radio call, 'Spot on. Landed on top of us. Thanks.'
>
> And away we went back to the task force. We landed on the helicopter pad and the continuous noise of artillery started again.
>
> BOB GRANDIN

It was magnificent flying and Harry Smith and all his men knew it.

> I think the air force did a wonderful job and, indeed, Frank Riley was decorated for his leadership of that flight even though there were only two helicopters. They had to become involved in flying into a combat zone where they knew there was a large force of enemy firing... They had great difficulty with the rain, torrential rain coming down, and without the aid of things we have now such as GPS... They could have been fired at. They could have been shot down but they weren't... we got our ammunition and they survived.
>
> HARRY SMITH, MAJOR, D COMPANY, 6RAR

From that day on, the Australian Army and the RAAF in Vietnam began to think of each other as good blokes.

Time had run out for 11 Platoon. With his radio shot out again, Bob Buick could not keep telling his men that help was coming when they all knew it was a desperate lie. At a rough count he could only see 12 men left alive and two of them were wounded. If he was to get them out it had to be now. The artillery fire had given them a moment's respite from the Vietnamese attack and another chance was unlikely. It meant leaving behind their dead and, possibly, men who were dying. A quick glance at Jim Richmond, face down in the mud, and they knew, like the others, that he was gone. Even so, every part of the Australian infantryman's being rebels against this action – leaving your mates behind. It is against their code, their honour, the very foundations they rest their lives upon. Forty years later, the decision they had to take in that terrible moment, still troubles all of them.

> All of a sudden I could do something; at last I could do something. I had a break in the pressure of the VC attacking us. We would have to do something. I had made a decision that there is no way the company or anyone was going to come and get us and I had to make a decision – oh shit, that I've lived with all the time. You know, it's a decision I made at the time, I decided to get as many out as possible. I had no idea where anyone was. I had possibly six to eight to a dozen people who were alive. We had no ammunition. All the ammunition had been expended. Some of the guys had their grenades out in front. Some guy had a machete in his hand. He was going to take the head off if Charlie came close to him. But there was absolutely nothing we could do. We'd exhausted our ammunition. We had in fact taken as many casualties as we could. It was time to piss off. What to do? I thought, 'Do you attack?' It's one of the things that crossed my mind. 'Do I go forward straight through these bastards and keep on running?' That wasn't a real good idea. So I decided we'll go back the way we came and, if necessary, I'd go all the way back to Nui Dat. If I couldn't find any friendlies, any Australians, I'd go back and hide in the river which was about two kilometres behind me and wait until daylight and then we'd bloody make our way back.
>
> Bob Buick

The call rang out and they got up as one to run. One man was killed instantly and another two were wounded. One of them, John Robbins, was hit for the second time. They had no reference for a retreat as wild and undisciplined as this. There is no training manual with a chapter that starts: 'When running for your life from the enemy you must . . .' They simply got the hell out of there the best way they could.

> So the next thing they yell out, 'Everyone for yourself!' And I see fellows taking off, I thought Christ, there is this big heavy pack which I have lightened as much as I could . . . and I threw the grenade, threw it away and I had this backpack on and I went to ground and Alec Grant crawled over and he said, 'Do you want a hand with that, mate?'
>
> I said, 'I can't get it off!'
>
> And he was getting it off and he got shot while he was doing it. Straight through here and what do you do? But he helped me get the pack off. Blokes were running, where do you run? Which way do you go? Absolute mayhem. All of the training we had and not this, they didn't teach you everything. So you just get up and bloody run and next thing you fall down and then get up and run and then fall down. When I was running away that's when I got hit in the hand with a bit of shrapnel or something, probably from the artillery, they were using mortars too. And it actually felt worse than the elbow. So I put my hand away and I didn't want to look at that, I thought all of my fingers were gone, it just felt as though they had. They were there, but I mean I couldn't feel them, so I didn't want to look at that, I would rather look away.
>
> And then I got into this bit of a gully and there was a medic there and I said, 'Have you got something for this? Morphine, whatever?'
>
> And he said he was pretty low. He gave me a shot and while he was giving me a shot he got hit. Then he was screaming

> *he* wanted some. I said, 'You reckon you didn't have enough before and now you want it for your bloody self!'
>
> Anyway that's just how things happen, some of the humour of the day. Following that, all of the artillery is still going on, all of these shells still coming in, it hasn't slackened off at all. Don't know where anyone else is. Probably because we were together at least we were alive, we thought we were a better show now of getting out of here. And not looking back really from where we had come, but looking more to where we were going and hopeful we were going the right way.
>
> JOHN ROBBINS

It was a blind rush with no thought other than to keep going, anywhere away from the killing ground. They could have run straight into the arms of the Vietnamese, or simply been cut down by machine-gun fire, but once again luck and initiative pulled the blade away from their throats. Dave Sabben, 100 or so metres in front of the running men, made a decision that sent salvation drifting through the trees.

> I had been in my position waiting, holding the corridor open for 11 Platoon but unable to talk to them. In the time that I had got there 11 Platoon's radio had been shot out and there was no way of us advising them that we were there. I could only hope that the longer I stayed there the longer he realised that there were no VC behind him, and that that must be because there are Australians behind him so that he would then move back towards us. We knew that they were still alive, or that some were still alive, because every now and then we'd hear a round of firing and the fact that the VC were still firing into the position told us that there was still someone there, it was still worth waiting...
>
> I was running low on ammunition, and I'm sure they must have been, and it occurred to me that if I had one of my

soldiers throw a yellow smoke grenade in the direction of 11 Platoon, that in the dim of the plantation, in the darkness, and it was beginning to get dark now, that they would see the yellow smoke and they would realise that typically the VC wouldn't carry that so they must be Australians, so that they would come to the smoke.

DAVE SABBEN

6.10 P.M.

Sabben's inspired plan succeeded and the 11 Platoon men saw his smoke. They forced themselves up and on they ran again, dodging through the trees for another 75 metres, calling out to identify themselves till they crashed into the middle of 12 Platoon. Mate welcomed mate, but only for a moment. They still had to get back to company HQ. They were too small a force to withstand a frontal attack and Sabben had been ordered to withdraw as soon as possible.

The wounded were sent first, those who were still reasonably mobile helping those who weren't, while Sabben, Buick and the soldiers who had not been hit, protected their withdrawal and slowly followed behind. As they crept back, Sabben noticed about 70 enemy soldiers forming up to make an assault on the very place to which they were heading. Fortunately, they had not yet seen him. He placed his men and three M60 machine guns quietly in position and waited.

We had three working machine guns at that stage, I put a machine gun down each avenue of rubber plantation trees and we just quietly waited for them to come, knowing that the wounded had already left our position . . . they passed directly in front of us and they formed up as we would have done, with the same spacing as we would have done and they moved off at the same rate as we would have done and at that time I thought, 'These are regular soldiers. These are my opposite number. They're not some little village outfit that's dressed in black pyjamas and so on, these are professional soldiers and they're bloody good!'

They were well-equipped, and they were obviously well-trained and well-disciplined, and this group moved off and up they came. And they did exactly as I thought they would. They came in three ranks and we let the first rank through and, as the second and third rank entered into the lanes where I had the machine guns, I gave the order to fire. Well, you have to see the decimation that a machine gun can make at 40 yards on a line of infantry soldiers. It was almost total. They almost all went down. The front rank took fright, turned around and ran through the fire of the other two machine guns. So out of that group which was probably 60 or 70, not many of them would have ever walked again...

DAVE SABBEN

As the Vietnamese fell to the ground, the wounded Australians, including John Robbins, finally made it to company HQ.

I felt as though I was secure then. I had that immense feeling of, 'We have made it. We are out of that bloody terrible thing we have been through and we're there!' And really the dangers were all still there, it wasn't over, but when there is more of you it makes you feel safe, I think.

We were wandering around in a daze pretty happy to be back in here and Kirby came over and knocked me arse over head, big Jack Kirby [the company sergeant major], more or less lay on me and said, 'Get down, you stupid bugger!'

I said, 'Get off me, if they don't kill me you will!'

The weight of him. And he was running around organising things, he got all of the wounded up on this one bit of a knoll in the rubber, all of the wounded were assembled there and they re-inforced the perimeter as much as they could.

> I didn't know we were out of ammo, I didn't know all of that, you don't know what's going on. You don't know what's going on in the base, you have got no idea what's going on elsewhere. I didn't really know what went on in other areas until I read a book on it, years later, in the 1980s. I mean we didn't talk about it much afterwards, that's another story I guess, when you come home and go different ways. In fact I came home early, the other fellows didn't come home until the end of the 365 days or whatever, so when they got home they were discharged the next day and we didn't get a chance and we didn't really get together for 20-odd years, so there was a lot we didn't know. Often used to think about it, what did they do? Where were they? What happened?
>
> JOHN ROBBINS

Sabben, Buick and the rest of the men arrived. At last Harry Smith had his company in one place . . . except for the missing. A great many thoughts were with those men, out there somewhere. It had been over two hours since 11 Platoon had been attacked and only their courage, their training and their tenacity had kept them alive. From 2nd Lieutenant Gordon Sharp to Sergeant Bob Buick to Lance Corporal John Robbins, down to every private in the platoon, they had kept their heads, stayed in control and kept a force many times larger than them at bay. Now the entire company would need to find those same reserves. The last stand of Long Tan was about to play out.

Withdrawal was not possible for Harry Smith and D Company. There were too many wounded for them to travel at speed, and leaving them behind was never an option. They would fight where they were. By good chance they were squeezed into a small dip in the ground, giving them a tiny advantage over an attacking force, but there was no time to dig firing pits or erect any sort of defences. They would have to battle with what they had.

Smith arranged his men around the perimeter, they had no idea from which direction the attack might come, and he moved among them, talking, encouraging, checking on the wounded. For a few moments there was a potent, roaring silence, enough time for every man to contemplate what might come at them out of the dark.

> Harry put us into a defensive position and the thought occurred, 'Well, there's nowhere to go now. We're all here. We're on the best piece of ground that there is around. We can't pick up 20 or 30 wounded guys and make a tactical movement. We're here. We're here.' And where are the APCs? Because that's the only thing that's going to save us now. The APCs, and possibly dark, but we knew that the VC operated in the dark so at that point I suppose I was starting to get clouded, 'Wait a minute, we're not out of it, there is still something to be feared here.'
>
> DAVE SABBEN

6.20 P.M.

Without warning, two enemy machine guns clattered in the dark, their fire moving across the company like a killing cloud. It was a preparatory tactic, to force them to keep their heads down. The Australians had no idea of how many Vietnamese there were out there, or how many they might have killed. It was completely possible, even likely, that they would be overwhelmed, yet their spirits were high. D Company was together again and that meant a great deal to them. So far they'd given as good as they'd got and they had real confidence in themselves and each other.

Then a voice was heard calling in a broad Australian accent, 'Don't shoot! Don't shoot!' It was Sabben's platoon sergeant, J. 'Paddy' Todd. He'd been shot through both ankles during the rescue of 11 Platoon and had crawled back 70 painful and bloody metres to the company. There he was, waving his hat in the air and just a tad pleased to see them. It put steel into every man.

6.35 P.M.

And so it began. Bugles blew, whistles shrieked and the first wave came towards them. They could see the enemy through the trees, shadowy figures in the mist and rain.

> They started to take us on in a big way and they just used the human wave assault and they would line up and then roll into us. We would mow them down – and I have to say that. Our machine guns and fire from our rifles just mowed them down in their front echelons, in their front lines, and their bodies just fell on top of each other and almost mounds of bodies. They would then get up and form up again and come on again over the top of the bodies and keep on pushing on . . .
>
> There was a continuous volume of machine-gun and rifle fire and coming at us like millions of fireflies. Red ones, green ones and white ones as these tracers just came towards us, over our heads in most cases, although I remember looking in front of me and Jack Thompson, my mortar fire controller, was lying behind a rubber tree. It wasn't great cover because the rubber trees are that long and his head was that wide so it really wasn't of much use but it was psychological protection and . . . I remember looking at Jack and looking over him towards the enemy and seeing the tree just above his head being peppered by tracer rounds just going straight through it.
>
> You know it's all very well to look back on it now and think about it, but at the time there was an awful lot of noise,

> rain, smoke, machine guns, you name it. But I don't think anybody really was frightened. Somebody said to me once was I frightened and I said no, I was too busy to become frightened. All I was doing, in fact, was doing what I had been trained to do.
>
> HARRY SMITH

Human wave attacks are relentless, unnerving, and hideously wasteful of men. They had last been seen in Korea, when Mao Zedong threw millions of his peasant soldiers headlong into the hellfire of modern cannon. The death toll was horrific and no one expected the tactic to be seen again. But when a sheer mass of men is your primary weapon, as it was for Hanoi, any misgivings about the cost in lives are conveniently buried under the lust for victory.

The tactic was not exactly military genius, but it was often effective. A first line of assault attacked at speed and many of them would be hit. All would go to ground, wounded, dead or untouched. A second wave of men would be running behind and, as they reached their position, the survivors of the first line would leap up, join up with the second line, clamber over their own dead and continue on. The line progressed further with every charge, rolling on with what appeared to be an inexhaustible and invincible force, till they rolled right over their adversary. It was as if the wave was self-perpetuating and no matter how many times you shot a man, he kept getting up again. Bullets through ghosts. The defending soldiers had to deal not only with the hole in their guts that said defeat was coming, but the clear, unimpeded 'sight picture' of every man they killed – there was no hiding behind the comfort of distance now. There he is, *see him* . . . kill him. Ten and 12 Platoons took the brunt of the attack and Private Noel Grimes remembers how even the distance of 50 metres helped him to do his job that day.

> Once the bullets start flying the limbs are falling down and the little twigs and big twigs off the rubber – they were falling everywhere and it was dreadful. But all you can sort of see is – I mean, possibly it's a lot harder to – oh, I don't know, I was going to say perhaps if I was as close as I am to you and someone was threatening my life, it might be harder to be sort of point-blank and pull a trigger on somebody, maybe. But on the other hand, if you knew they were going to do it to you, it probably wouldn't make a whole lot of difference, I don't know. But they were distant enough and in the appalling weather – I mean you couldn't see a face, put it that way. You could see a body, a person, so that probably helped the cause a bit, but there were so many of them and, of course, they were darting and diving and, as you can imagine, they weren't just standing there, they were on the move and they were on the move towards us. So you'd see them disappear so you assume you've hit somebody. That's what it really amounts to when they're not terribly, terribly close to you. I mean you just pull the trigger and he's there and then he isn't. You think well...
>
> NOEL GRIMES, PRIVATE, 12 PLATOON, D COMPANY, 6RAR

Even with the resupply the Australians only had a limited amount of ammunition and a dwindling number of men to fire it. Without help they would unquestionably go under. It was time for the artillery. Command at Nui Dat had asked for more assistance and Morrie Stanley now had three batteries to call on – Australian, Kiwi and American, and he called on them loud and long. Just as Bob Buick had done, he walked the artillery fire closer and closer to his position until the gun commanders told him it was too dangerous to continue. Harry Smith's reply to them over the radio was precise: 'If you don't bloody well fire the guns you can write us off!'

It was an unenviable task for these commanders and their gun crews. They were five and six kilometres away from their targets, near the limits of their range, and they had to deliver their shells with no margin for error. They had to manhandle the heavy ammunition from its boxes, load it and fire the guns in all-encompassing darkness, and under wave after wave of torrential rain, knowing the whole time that every round they sent screaming into the night was potentially lethal to their comrades. The steady hands they needed were weakened further by the fumes. Every time a shell is fired it releases toxic, cordite fumes. Normally the gases are dispersed, but under the weight of the rain there was no wind and the poisonous gases were causing gunners to faint and vomit. Every gunner affected would reel out of the line, recover and rejoin his crew. They were, quite simply, magnificent. In total, the gun crews fired 3500 rounds that day and there can be no question that without them and their miraculous accuracy, D Company would have been wiped out.

A 105-millimetre artillery shell fired from five kilometres away pursues a long, graceful arc through the air on its way to the target. As it approaches, it sounds to the men underneath its fall like a train entering a tunnel, but the whistle brings death and destruction. If you are inside its deadly circle when it lands, there is no escape. The best you can hope for is instantaneous death. Its value as either an offensive or defensive weapon is the number of men it can kill or maim and the fear it can instil. And that is exactly how Morrie Stanley and Harry Smith were using it. They trusted the men of D Company to stop the front lines of assault – they were aiming at the reserve lines, the ones behind, waiting to attack. Dave Sabben, controlling the fire of his platoon, watched the results in fascinated horror.

> The typical idea of artillery firing is a flash and bodies hurtling and so on, and that's what you get from the films, but reality isn't like that. There's a sudden impact where you see the

whole environment just shudder, just vibrate, and then everything is just steam and smoke and you don't see anything and anything that might have been shattered has gone and as the smoke and the steam dissipates you see the leaves just falling down or whatever else was there just falling down...

All guns would fire at once which means that all the shells would come over at once, all the impacts would happen at once and there would be a string of that... Several times we saw the reserve lines simply wiped out, just simply eradicated. They're just there and then there was steam and smoke and then they weren't there. Looking at it remotely it was fascinating, certainly not for those people. Some units didn't fire all their artillery at once. They fired each gun in a series and in those cases you wouldn't just see the whole ridge line or the whole avenue light up, there would be a 'Bang! Bang! Bang! Bang! Bang!' in a series and that was more spectacular because once you knew that there was going to be a bang there, you knew to look ahead to where the next bangs were and, awful as it is to say it, you could see the troops and you could see the impact and you could see them disappear and you could see that next thing they weren't there. It probably took five seconds or so for the blast to clear... After the first couple you adjusted to it and it's amazing how we just did adjust to it.

Again, it comes back to the training. This is the circumstance I'm in, this is the environment I find myself in. This is what I need to know. I need to know where my troops are. I need to know where the enemy is. I don't need to know how scared I am. I don't need to know that I need a drink of water or something. I'm totally focused on what I need here. I've got my map. I've got my radio. I've got my weapon if I need to fire it. Your environment closes around you and in my experience nothing else matters.

DAVE SABBEN

More assaults were launched and, again, Stanley called the artillery in, shredding the Vietnamese reserve lines. D Company soldiers saw pieces of bodies, arms and legs of enemy soldiers flying through the air, and one particular sniper who suffered a direct hit from an artillery shell in a tree – one half of his body remained lodged there, the rest fell to the ground. So close were the shells now that Australians were also taking hits from shrapnel. And all the while, the tracer ripped through the gloom and the machine guns raked their position with near-continuous fire.

A Vietnamese machine gun crew rushed forward with their weapon and frantically set it up only 50 metres away from the Australian front line of defence. The company sergeant major, Warrant Officer Jack Kirby, seeing them, hurtled out from the perimeter through rifle fire and killed the crew, silencing the gun permanently. It was typical of Kirby. Bullets didn't seem to bother him. He was constantly moving around the company area, standing, talking with his soldiers, measuring out their ammunition, joking with them one minute, assisting the wounded the next. Every one of them remembers 'Big' Jack. Already a veteran of Korea and Malaya when he went to Vietnam, Kirby was a bit of a hero to the men though he would have rejected that nonsense outright. Gruff in manner and as straight as a cricket pitch, he was the man you wanted beside you when things got grim, the archetypal digger.

They kept coming, the VC and the NVA. No one could have doubted their courage as they stumbled and clawed their way over the bodies of their dead, desperate to broach the Australian defences. It seemed as if there was no end to it all, no end to the men willing to die, no end to the bullets, the tracer fire, the explosions. The air was almost liquid with the rain and the heat, and a heavy mist had risen from the ground, about 30 centimetres high. The Australian riflemen would rise up from the earth to fire and, as they did so, their heads and shoulders appeared briefly above this fog, strangely disembodied figures. They aimed, fired, and sank back down into the mist. Most of the wounds they suffered were head and chest shots. Here and there a lone enemy soldier would struggle right up to their lines or even manage to get a few feet inside the circle. He would be shot instantly. Four Australians had been killed in the attacks so far and another seven wounded. D Company had seen little action since they arrived at Nui Dat but now death was alongside each of them, unwanted and unnerving, but as immoveable as stone.

> When a soldier is killed or wounded – it's an unbelievable thing. You don't believe that it's happening. You can see a soldier lying there and there's a flinch and they go slack... it's not an hysterical flinging of the arms in the air and a double somersault backwards, it's not like that at all. If he's standing up it's like his legs are just cut out from under him. He just collapses. He just collapses and he lies still. If he's lying on the ground there's just a flinch... All of us, all of us soldiers had never, I would suggest, seen a dead body before, a corpse. We'd certainly never seen someone killed or wounded. We had had very light contact so far in Vietnam. I don't think that we had ever seen artillery fall and I don't think for the company, for the 100 or so soldiers that were on that battle-ground at the time, that we had ever touched or seen at close quarters a body, and to see what's happening and to know what's happening and to understand what's happening is just a chill... You hardly see any sign normally. I'm not talking about someone who gets blown up and there's a leg missing or something very obvious, I'm talking about a person that's taken a bullet in the chest or a bullet through the head and there's nothing. There's no indication. There's no heroics. The implication in your head goes along the line of, 'Oh no, oh no, that just can't be, tell me it's not!' and it doesn't matter whether you knew him or not. In that split second of witnessing that you have an image in your head – that guy he will never

> hold his kids on his lap. He'll never have a Sunday lunch with Mum and Dad again. You just sense the loss and that's indescribable. I'm probably not making a good go of it now, but that's the way it is. It's just an indescribable loss that you feel on that person's behalf and you see it once and it doesn't get better the second time and it doesn't get better the third time... you feel the loss for that person, the person that's just existed before and doesn't exist anymore.
>
> DAVE SABBEN

The Vietnamese, despite their mounting casualties, were gaining the initiative the longer the battle lasted. Artillery fire was only just keeping them out, and how much longer the men in the company area could hold out was questionable. If the enemy launched wave attacks from several directions simultaneously the artillery power would be diluted trying to stop them and some, if not hundreds, would break through the Australian lines.

6.45 P.M.

The infantrymen had a nickname for the APCs: 'Khaki cabs'. Good for taking you from A to B, but not much else. Their official name was the M113 Armoured Personnel Carrier, not exactly Thundercloud Mark IV or Rising Storm, even though they were made by the Americans. Aluminium in construction, they were about 12 tonnes in weight and could reach speeds of 55 kilometres an hour on land... and 5.3 km/h in water. They carried two crewmen and could transport 10 riflemen but were not really designed to get involved in a direct-fire battle. They were better off carrying troops to the battlefield while protecting them from shrapnel, small arms fire and ambush. Or at least, that's all everyone assumed they could do.

The eight carriers commanded by Lieutenant Adrian Roberts were now poised on the bank of the Suoi Da Bang creek. They had to get over it to get to Long Tan. Roberts knew there was a crossing point here, used by the local bullock drivers, but it was drowned now under a rushing torrent, the creek swollen by the rain into a dangerous, swirling mass of water. To add to his problems, the APCs were handicapped by worn steering systems that meant they couldn't control the big metal beasts in water. But he ordered them in anyway.

Banged and bashed by the current, they went round in circles, more like a stick thrown in by a child than an amphibious military vehicle, till finally they huffed and puffed their way up the opposite bank. Before they could set off again, a call came in on the radio ordering Roberts to halt while Townsend, the 6RAR commander, caught up.

Adrian Roberts had only just been promoted to lieutenant, had no previous experience in armoured personnel carriers and was doing a job normally done by a captain. But he could hear the desperate calls from D Company on his radio and decided at once. It was no contest. He ignored the order and pushed on, leaving one carrier behind to show the CO how a raging creek should be crossed. He now had seven APCs, the infantrymen of A Company on board, mostly national servicemen in his crews and virtually no experience of working with infantry in battle. As the tracks banged and clanked down the road to Long Tan, Adrian Roberts would have had every right to take a long, steadying breath.

They reached the road where 11 Platoon had had their first contact with the VC around three short hours before. Roberts positioned three carriers in a straight line on either side of his, about 40 metres apart and prepared to advance on a front 300 metres wide. Again the radio blared. Again the order came. 'Wait for Townsend!' Having disregarded it once, it wasn't all that difficult for him to do it again. Besides, sunset was almost on them and the light was nearly gone. He gave the order, 'Advance in formation.'

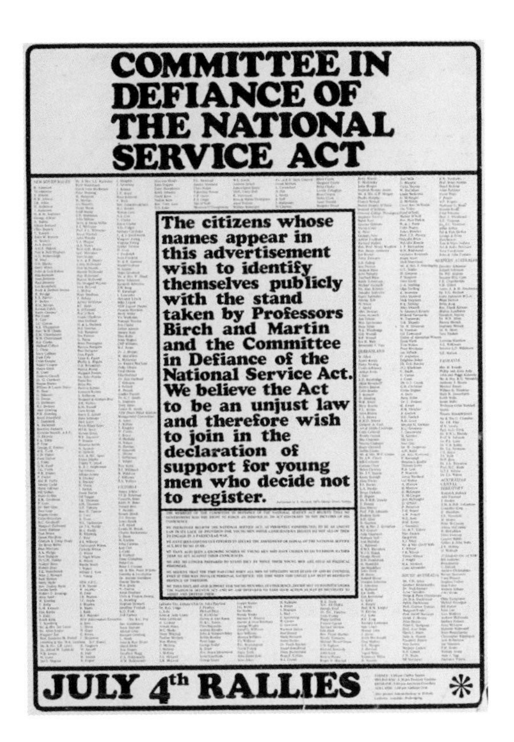

Anti-conscription advertisement (AWM ARTV03044)

Entertainment in the field – the Dustbowl at Nui Dat (JOHN STRANGE)

Geordie Richardson *(left)* and Bob Buick tending Jim Richmond after Long Tan (NEWSPIX)

Searching for further mines after an APC was damaged (BUD COSTELLO/PHIL KADOW)

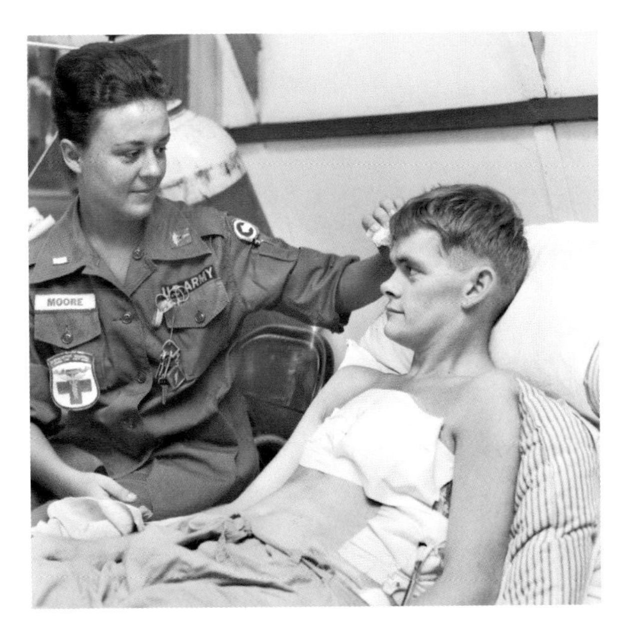

Jim Richmond in hospital after Long Tan (AWM CUN/66/0717/VN)

Dustoff (MICK KING)

A Huey helicopter re-supplying (GEOFF BURT)

A normal load when on operations (AWM WAR/70/0026/VN)

An APC after hitting a mine (DAVID WEIGALL)

Celebrating Christmas in South Vietnam (RON HEDGES)

A bar in Vung Tau (MICK KING)

Typical Vietnamese street scene (NORM COOPER)

The normal routine continues (JOHN JANSEN)

A Vietnamese refugee boat on the way to Australia, 1977 (NEWSPIX)

The APCs trundled forward into the rubber plantation. Where they entered, the trees were young, only a few metres high, and the foliage on their crowns was at exactly the right height to smash into the faces of the commanders on top. The monsoon had started up again as well so between wayward branches, the advancing dark and the curtains of water, visibility was appalling. They didn't know D Company's exact location, but they could hear the sounds of battle and headed towards it, the noise from their own diesel engines and metal tracks muffled by the heavy rain. Without warning a large force of soldiers appeared through the trees, moving determinedly in an arrowhead formation. They had not yet seen the carriers. The question for Adrian Roberts was . . . who exactly were they?

> The ground seemed to stand up . . . across our entire front is this great group of infantry moving from east to west in pretty determined fashion and in formation. And they all had green bush hats on, although they had rounded crowns when you looked closer and they had camouflage on their backs, but just for a split second I thought, you know, 'It's D Company!' There was just this momentary pause. Then the carrier on my far right, Richard Gross, said, 'It's the enemy!' and I opened fire and then we opened up right across.
>
> ADRIAN ROBERTS, LIEUTENANT, 3 TROOP

Caught by surprise the VC took the full force of the Australian fire but recovered quickly and returned it in kind. The infantrymen inside the carriers joined in, firing through the hatches and out the back of the vehicles. One platoon couldn't resist the temptation and leapt out of their carrier to wade into the enemy. They killed perhaps 40 men before Roberts could restore order, get them back inside and continue the advance. With their 50-calibre machine guns at full roar, the APCs ploughed through the

Vietnamese, killing some and crushing others beneath their metal tracks. It was gruesome and disturbing.

> We got them back into the carriers and then we started to edge forward is the only way I can describe it, it's a matter of firing and in some cases actually running over the people and we kept going...they were actually falling back to the east in good order. They were going back firing at us, covering the others as they were pulling out. They were dragging their wounded actually. They seemed to have loops around their ankles and they were dragging their wounded out and they were going across our front and out to the northeast. It's a pretty grim business.
>
> ADRIAN ROBERTS

The APCs burst through the Vietnamese lines into a clearing and then drove into another part of the plantation where the trees were taller and less of a hindrance, so Roberts had them all pick up speed. D Company was straight ahead now. But as the APCs cleared the trees again, they ran headlong into another large force of VC just 20 metres in front. This time there was no hesitation and both sides let loose with every piece of weaponry they had.

> The fire was just enormous. What I remember were these sorts of explosions, little white explosions all around you in the trees, and if you looked left and right there was tracer fire. Ours is yellow and the VC fire was green... I mean you got to the point where you thought, 'Where are the holes?'...it was pretty ferocious...they didn't just run out of it, they fought back and fought back hard...
>
> You can't stop. You can't do all the things you've been taught. You can't do reconnaissance round to the left and right of the enemy that's in front of you. You can't find out

> how big he is because at the back of him somewhere is D Company and they're being overrun . . . then on the right-hand side there was a hell of an explosion and a rubber tree fell down in front of the carrier that was 20 or 30 yards away from me, across the sunken road. It was Corporal Carter's carrier.
>
> Adrian Roberts

The explosion was a round from a recoilless rifle, an anti-tank gun. This meant real trouble for the APCs. John Carter's machine gun jammed and he scrambled up, out of the hatch, and stood on top of his carrier. As the Vietnamese rifle crew hastily reloaded for another crack at them, Carter's driver threw his Owen gun up to him and both he and the Vietnamese fired at each other. Carter's shots killed the gun crew and fortunately for him their round smashed into the fallen tree in front of his carrier, exploding it into thousands of fragments. The driver threw up more magazines to Carter and he kept firing, killing three more VC before ducking back down into the relative safety of his vehicle. Roberts, watching on, said later that it was like viewing a film in slow motion.

The recoilless rifle was trouble even without a crew. Roberts ordered his troop to halt, obeying the first law of armour – where there's one anti-tank weapon, there's bound to be another so you go no further till you've found it. This was particularly so for the APCs; one round from behind and both the carrier and all the men inside would be annihilated. Roberts had to stop.

But what makes sense to armoured corps blokes is just unnecessary caution to an infantryman. Captain Charles Mollison, the commander of A Company, was in Roberts' vehicle and he yelled at him to get going. Roberts ignored him, concentrating on the search for the gun and the welfare of his troop. That was too much for Mollison. An epic argument broke out between the two commanders, growing in intensity and volume till their shouting voices could be heard even above the battle. For five long minutes they were at a standstill until Roberts was satisfied and they pushed on.

The whole time this argument had been raging, the battle was too. Carriers were being raked by machine-gun fire and crews were going down, one dead, others wounded. Roberts was frantically calling on the radio, urging his men over and over to control and aim their fire.

> I had to keep constantly issuing orders to them to, 'Fire low, fire low!' I remember saying that over and over again because a 50-calibre round can go almost 4000 metres if it's fired straight out and somewhere up in front of us was D Company. We had to fire down because I had this tremendous fear of actually hitting someone from our own forces . . . I remember also, 'Keep the line straight!' Saying that over and over again, 'Keep the line straight!' . . .
>
> Artillery was falling and I don't know whose artillery, whether it was ours or theirs or somebody's and I reached down and got my steel helmet and jammed it down over my beret. I did that kind of instinctively. It was pretty futile. If something had hit you it wouldn't have made a hell of a lot of difference . . . What crossed my mind all the time was I had to know where the carriers were, and I had to get up there. I had to get to D Company . . . You haven't got time to be frightened and you haven't got time to be reflective. When it's over it's like coming in on a wave, the bloody wave comes back on you and then you remember. Then you remember what it's like to shoot at someone and hit them. Then you remember all the bad bits and then you have to deal with that.
>
> ADRIAN ROBERTS

Another carrier's machine gun jammed when a round became stuck in the barrel. The APCs carried spares, but nothing could be done, not here where bullets were whizzing around like vengeful flies. Somebody, however, forgot to tell the crew that. Both the driver and the commander of this carrier were national servicemen and perhaps they had forgotten their lessons... or maybe they'd learned them too well. The driver stood up, got out of the hatch and, in full view of the Vietnamese, began to replace the barrel, calmly going through the procedure exactly as he had been taught to do all those months ago in training. The crew commander was at his side, helping him. They pulled the jammed barrel off, stored it inside (well, you had to explain it to the quartermaster!), fitted the new one, took up their respective places inside the carrier... and resumed firing. Roberts asked the driver later what the hell he was thinking and received the reply, 'It was all right. If I didn't look at them, they wouldn't bother me.'

The fortunes of war. Both men survived. Another 45 enemy were killed.

7.00 P.M.

The Vietnamese were retreating from the APCs as Lieutenant Colonel Townsend arrived with the other three carriers and they all lined up for the final advance. Artillery fire from Nui Dat was still crashing down and the men in the APCs had to brave that shellfire as they surged up and past D Company, firing at will and launching into the force that had been hurling human wave attacks at the Australians. They pushed on for 500 metres and finally came to a halt. And everywhere, in front of them and around them, khaki-clad Vietnamese rose up from the ground, fired a few last despondent shots, and disappeared into the rubber trees. They had been preparing to deliver the final blow to the trapped Australians of D Company and now they had been cheated of their prey.

The artillery was redirected to chase after the retreating Vietnamese and all rifle firing stopped. Life and possibility began to seep back into the men and some noticed for the first time that it was now dark. They gingerly got up from the ground or climbed out of the back of the carriers or stood slowly on top of their hatches, and for a moment each one considered his fate, or his luck, or the fact that his legs could barely hold him up and that he wanted a smoke, or a beer, or just to go to sleep for a very long time.

It was over.

> I recall looking across to my right, which was to the south, at about seven o'clock and all of a sudden amongst the noise of the machine guns and artillery there appeared the noise of diesel engines and here were these armoured personnel carriers coming through the gloom, guns firing, and some of my forward soldiers got up, because the enemy, as soon as these tanks arrived the enemy just turned and left. Now there was not another shot fired and I think a lot of my soldiers thought that they were never going to arrive and that we would never get out of it and a lot of them stood up and went over and gave the carriers a gentle pat on the side and certainly shook the hand of the armoured corps guys and probably some of the A Company guys that came out in the carriers. We were certainly very pleased to see them to say the least.
>
> HARRY SMITH

> Without the artillery and the APCs that day, there was no way in the world we would have got out of there. I mean, you get a bit of luck now and then . . . but nothing as much as what I had that day getting out of there, should never have got out. Luck, fate . . . the rifle fire had ceased and so you have got a feeling of relief that you're there and disbelief at what's just happened.
>
> JOHN ROBBINS

What I remember was this silvery blue of the cordite from the artillery that had been dropped. It was floating like a mist and you could hear the groans of the wounded and what have you out to the front and you were sort of straining, looking into the mist, and then the darkness came on and you couldn't see anything after that.

ADRIAN ROBERTS

By the time that the APCs actually stopped and the troops on board got out and got into positions and there was no firing, it was just absolute silence, total silence between artillery rounds. So silent that you could hear the engines on the APCs as they cooled down, clicking and ticking away and there was just an absolute hush. Some people say that they could hear the wounded moaning and so on. I couldn't. I couldn't hear that. All I could hear was the tick, tick, tick of the engines as they cooled down and the total silence every now and then punctured by artillery . . . It was an amazing feeling. It was a fabulous feeling because at that stage your mind is able to go back and say, 'What have I just been through?' . . . And you look around and you see who's still there and you wonder, 'What are they thinking?' I was probably in a better position from the rest of my platoon because I knew who had been wounded, but for the digger on the front line, unless it was the soldier next to him that was shot, he didn't know whether his mate, the machine gunner from the other section, had been hit or killed and so they were all beginning to look around in the dark, in the deep dim, I suppose looking around to check, 'I wonder if Harry's okay, I wonder if Bob's okay, where's John?' and you could see that they were still in control but that they were, you know, 'We're saved, we're okay.'

DAVE SABBEN

The battle had ended as sharply as it had begun and it was difficult for a while for the men to get their bearings. They stood in small groups, mostly quiet, smoking and drinking from their canteens. Some soldiers tore into their C-rations, gobbling food as if they hadn't eaten for days. A count was made – four dead, 16 wounded and 16 missing. Enemy casualties were unknown at this stage, but they were confident they'd caused considerable damage. The trouble was no one knew how much and, without enemy bodies to show, it looked on the numbers as if they had received a bad beating – 11 Platoon near wiped out, D Company ineffective for the moment and 16 Australian soldiers missing. Certainly back at the task force it was initially viewed as a disaster.

It had been many long hours since the first men had been wounded and they were in critical need of medical attention. A landing zone was cut out of the bush and they were carefully carried or helped out there to await the choppers. It was still pouring with rain and pitch black and as he lay there, John Robbins could finally let go.

> Time meant nothing to me, I don't know how long it took, I think I had a nap; I was probably asleep for a while. I know that someone told us that they were chopping an area and they were going to bring the choppers in. They were out chopping timber; I don't think they wanted to move us too far from where we were; night and security reasons with the enemy... all I can remember is the choppers coming in.
>
> John Robbins

The helicopters were ordered not to use lights because of the possibility that they would alert the enemy to the landing zone, but Adrian Roberts helped them down by using a method he'd tried once before. He had the APCs form up in a square around the landing zone, open up their hatches and turn on the inner lights of the carriers. It was enough. One after another, American and Australian choppers dropped out of the blackness and gathered up the wounded till only the dead remained. Bob Grandin and Frank Riley flew in for the final pickup.

> When we arrived it turned out that all the wounded people in fact had been taken and so somebody said, 'We'll put the bodies on board.'
>
> So they ran over and suddenly started throwing into the back of the helicopter these rolled-up ponchos, which were just a ground sheet in which the body had been wrapped, and instantly of course you get the smell of dead bodies. They start to smell quite dramatically in the tropics very quickly. There's still lots of juices and blood dribbling out and so you're very aware that you're suddenly in a very unpleasant environment.
>
> We lifted off to take them back to the hospital and you're very aware then of what's happened. I mean we've just arrived in country about six weeks. You haven't come, as a pilot, face to face with people being killed and suddenly you are, and so it's a dramatic turning point in the reality of the war . . .
>
> When we got back to the hospital the bodies were taken and we flew across to the area where we parked our aeroplanes, got into our jeeps, went back to our villa where we lived and our cooks had all stayed up. It was about two o'clock in the morning by this time. The cooks had stayed up. They had big steaks cooking for us, plenty of beer for us to drink and everybody sat around talking about the events finding it very difficult now to go to sleep or to come down off the high and the intensity of what had happened during the day.
>
> BOB GRANDIN

Big Jack Kirby, the company sergeant major who had kept everyone's spirits up, survived Long Tan and the lasting image some of his men have of him at the end of the battle was his massive frame striding towards the evacuation area, carrying two Australian casualties, one over each shoulder. He was awarded the Distinguished Conduct Medal for his actions.

What is it we say about the best of us . . . that we lose them all too often and too early? Six months later, in February 1967, Jack Kirby was hit in the chest by 'friendly' artillery fire and died before he could be choppered out. The battery that fired the shells was the same one that had saved him and his men at Long Tan.

Once the wounded had been evacuated there was little else to do till morning. The distant boom of the artillery continued as the guns searched for the enemy, firing more in hope than knowledge. No one knew where the VC were and they were certainly not going to go looking for them in the dark and the rain. Each man was turned in on himself now, and the devils and the demons and the endless replays began. What was a solid, efficient unit of men only a few hours before was splintered into small, isolated islands, and they did not, could not, talk with each other. Some, like Dave Sabben, felt strangely useless.

> I was suddenly a minister without portfolio. My sergeant had been wounded in the fire-fight before we had withdrawn back to the company and so one of my corporals automatically took over his role. He organised the remaining platoon soldiers. There was someone organising the wounded soldiers. There was someone organising with the company commander what was going to happen next. I had nothing to do. I sought out one of the other platoon commanders and we just sat with our backs up against an APC looking into the darkness. There was nothing to discuss. What could I say? I was just deflated, I suppose, a drained feeling. I remember drinking a lot of water.
>
> DAVE SABBEN

A few metres from Dave Sabben, his fellow officer, 10 Platoon's Geoff Kendall was playing out the possible scenarios. What nagged at the edge of all of their minds was the fate of the 16 missing soldiers. These were men used to solving problems with quick, decisive actions and the waiting was cruel, giving them time to imagine the worst.

> We were really afraid that night – waiting to go back in or do what we were going to do the next day – that they'd get our guys . . . we don't know if they're all dead or if any are alive or what. We're terrified they're going to get captured or they're going to get mutilated or something like that, all the silly things you think of. We were also pretty worried that we were going to go in the next morning and find it's all been swept clean, there's nothing there and no matter what we say for the rest of our lives nobody'll ever believe us. They'll say, 'Well, they had a bit of a scrap, lost 18 guys and went home with their tail between their legs.'
>
> GEOFF KENDALL

Some could not think of anything but survival and relief. John Robbins, section leader of 11 Platoon, was spirited away with the astonishing speed that characterised medical evacuation in this war. He would never command his men again.

> They took the worst first and I went on a chopper, I don't know who went to Vung Tau with me. But it was a pretty good trip. One of the best rides of the war. I guess you're thinking about how lucky you are. So I get down to 36 Evac [evacuation hospital], by this time it is probably midnight. We get out of the chopper and each person had a team and they more or less put you on a stretcher and whisked you into a room just inside the doorway of this hospital and all of these tables and things and they put you in there and big

scissors this long and she just got up, this nurse, and cut all of the clothing off you and cut down your boots and brought around a trolley and threw the clothes and everything into there and then they started to clean you up, get the mud and stuff off you. That's about as much as I can remember. I can remember them giving me a needle and half dozey you go into the operating theatre and it is like *M*A*S*H*, here they are all of these doctors and things hanging out everywhere, operating on any number of people at one time, teams of doctors working and fixing people up, all American doctors. Young fellows, our age and whatever. And so you're there and next thing you're out to it and wake up the next day and here you are in plaster or whatever and you really only know what you have done or where you have been and you don't know much else.

And then it starts to sink in, you start to talk to others about how did so and so get on? You don't know about his section or whatever, who did you lose? And he doesn't necessarily know so there is a lot of anxiety about who made it and who didn't. What's happened since? Did they come back the next morning? You just don't know. Well I knew that I was going home. And that was a relief. Here we were, wanting to bump into them and have a bit of a crack at them, but I didn't want to have another go, I thought, that's enough.

JOHN ROBBINS

One man was particularly isolated, unable to have even the simple comfort of the presence of his mates. Two hundred metres from the silent, exhausted men and the APCs, he was lying on the reeking, blasted battlefield.

I thought then, well, I'll have to try and survive the night and the only thing to do with me wound was to lay in the mud and try and pack the wound with mud to try and stop the bleeding. I knew that I had a bad wound because before we went overseas they take you through with the doctors and that to give you a lecture on all types of wounds you could have, and I remembered this one was a sucking chest wound because I could feel the air being sucked in through me back. So I knew what sort of a wound I had because that's what he told us it would be like. So I just packed it full of mud and rolled on my side and just tried to survive the night, which was fairly long. I yelled out a couple of times in the night for a medic but I just got fired upon so I just kept quiet and tried to survive the night and the artillery kept pounding me all night. I did hear movement around me but none of it was friendly so I just tried to keep as quiet as I could.

JIM RICHMOND

19 AUGUST 1966

Nui Dat was almost emptied of troops by the next morning as they had all been sent out to Long Tan. By the time the Australians were ready to re-enter the plantation almost an entire battalion was present. Artillery was firing and even air strikes were called in to attack suspected enemy positions. They were not taking any chances. It was decided that the first companies would go in aboard the APCs until they reached the battlefield and then continue the search on foot. D Company was to be one of those first units and they would head straight for the 11 Platoon position and the missing men. Some saw it as perverse that they should be sent back there so quickly, but Harry Smith was adamant that this was the way it would be.

I was terribly worried because I still had 15 of 11 Platoon missing and I didn't know whether they were alive, dead or had been captured, and we'd heard all these terrible stories from the Americans up in the northern provinces, what atrocities were committed to American soldiers that had been captured

> on a battlefield and I must say that I was troubled all night. Indeed, I didn't want to leave the battlefield. I argued with my commander that we should have stayed on the battlefield all night but I didn't win the argument and we were forced to withdraw back to a safer area to get the casualties out. I was also very keen to get back there first thing the next morning because they were my soldiers that were missing and my company, but the matter was taken out of my hands and it escalated into, not a company's return, it became a battalion, and then really a task force order where we had more VIPs around us than there were soldiers before we were allowed to go back in there! But when we did get back in I went in with Adrian Roberts and his section of tracks first. I insisted on doing that although somebody suggested we should have been sent back to base and sent on leave. I refused to do that. They were my soldiers and I wanted to see my own soldiers whether they be wounded or unfortunately killed in action.
>
> HARRY SMITH

The rain had cleared and the day was bright and mockingly sunny. The carriers started their engines and clanked into the plantation. They were slow and careful, watching every point of the compass. There was no other sound, no sign of people, no shots fired. Inside the carriers, the men of D Company had mixed feelings about their return.

> We were trained to kill people and, let's face it, it's one of those sort of things that's extremely difficult, to kill another human, but you are trained psychologically and everything to do it. What they don't train you for is when you've got to go back into a battlefield. They don't train you for the carnage. They don't train you for what you witness when you go in there. Long Tan, I had no idea just what happened at Long Tan. I knew what happened in my little bloody paddock but

> I had no idea what happened 30 or 40 metres away behind me, 100 metres behind me and so on...
>
> As we went back in the next morning, we had amassed a battalion of soldiers, we had three or four companies there, three or four hundred Australians, armoured personnel carriers, clear skies, we had aircraft on call, we had helicopters available – but I really didn't want to go back in again because I did not want to go in there where all these kids had been killed or missing, but I had to go in. I had to go in because they were my soldiers... the heat was starting to build up and the stench that comes off rotting human flesh is worse than the stench off any dead kangaroo or any beast. The human flesh has got a totally different smell about it and the whole place was like a perfumed garden... odours.
>
> BOB BUICK

The APC reached the location of the company HQ and the soldiers dismounted and took up an attack formation. They advanced, prepared to fight all the way if necessary. But there was no resistance. Instead, they entered a desolate, bizarre world of devastation and horror. Everywhere trees were either blown apart or missing all their vegetation. The ground was thickly covered with leaves and branches as if it had been diligently mulched. White latex, squeezed out of the trees by shells and bullets, bled in long lines down the trunks. In a great circle around the HQ it was a dead land, blasted into nothingness by the power of the artillery. Weapons, ammunition and pieces of equipment belonging to the Vietnamese lay around in piles. And then they saw their first bodies. Enemy casualties. Some were whole, some in shreds and pieces. They could not tell who had been torn apart by the shells and who had been killed by rifle fire. In some places, where the human wave attacks had taken place, they lay in grisly heaps. The smell of death fouled the morning air.

> It was like a Hieronymus Bosch painting. There were bodies and bits of bodies and legs and all the other pieces of humans scattered everywhere. It was terrible. I mean our artillery had really got amongst the VC and it was like a charnel-house, absolutely frightful. At that stage the only good thing is you're so numb and so drained that you can't take it on board... The first group of enemy, well the first group of people we came on, were three bodies lying side by side. They had no boots on. In fact you could almost feel the anger on the carriers because our presumption was that these were our blokes, but as we got closer they weren't, they were Vietnamese. It was a 60-millimetre mortar crew. I remember it vividly because the top of one of their heads was off and his brain was on the ground. A little bit further on lo and behold there's an Australian leaning against a tree, very clearly Australian, and he had been part of this missing section. I don't know his name but he'd walked out. He'd followed us out and he was absolutely stuffed and he leaned against the tree. I remember he sort of was angry because it had taken us so long to come back in and I don't blame him.
>
> ADRIAN ROBERTS

The Australian soldier was Private Barry Meller of 11 Platoon. He'd been shot through the mouth in the first battle and then hit again in the leg as they withdrew. He couldn't keep up and hid among the trees during the night. Meller gave his mates the benefit of his temper at being left behind but, in truth, they simply had not noticed him go down during the mad rush towards 12 Platoon. He was hurriedly evacuated for treatment.

From all across the battlefield reports began to come in of the discovery of enemy bodies. So quickly did the numbers climb that a request was made for a bulldozer to be sent out to help bury the dead. As the initial total mounted to 113 it became clear to everyone that D Company had not suffered a crushing defeat. They had instead won a startling and unexpected victory. As they took this in, the inevitable discoveries were made of wounded VC, still alive on the battleground. The trauma of Long Tan was not yet over.

> We saw lots and lots of dead VC. All they were was meat. They were people before, the day before, they were not now. There were limbs here, limbs there. I came across one VC who was twitching with half a head and his intestines out; digested rice from his intestines was spilling out on the ground. He was put out of his misery, the poor bastard.
>
> Bob Buick

The man could not survive. He was shot through the heart, giving him 'the peace he deserved'. Elsewhere another mercy killing took place and then two wounded but armed VC were killed when they refused to surrender. The Australians were tired, strung out and very, very jumpy. Even dead VC were fired on if they looked in any way suspicious.

> Certainly there were people that were shot. In every case that I saw and I know there were a couple in my platoon... our soldiers were under orders, they said, 'If anybody's in a fire position and you don't know if he's alive or dead, shoot him.'
>
> And there were just literally dozens of people like that, dozens of people who were lying in positions where they could've been lying behind a tree ready to shoot you and so people, just as soon as they saw them, they shot them. Almost invariably they were shooting dead people, but that happened, yes, it did happen and I don't excuse it and I would do it again... The Viet Cong are notorious for having live guys among the dead guys and shooting people, so if you are in any doubt, put a round into them and make sure. If he puts his hand up and wants to give up, good, we'll take him

prisoner. If you can see he's alive and he's helpless, okay, fine, we'll help, but don't take any chances. If you think the guy could be alive – shoot him. And I would do it again tomorrow if I had to do it again, 'cause that's just the way it was. But some people could say it was a war where they were shooting wounded – not true.

GEOFF KENDALL

Some people said exactly that. In 1968 a journalist stated that any wounded VC found at Long Tan were shot, implying that they were unarmed and therefore the action constituted a war crime. It was picked up by Australian newspapers, twisted into not just wounded, but wounded *civilians* being shot and immediately blew out into a huge controversy. A subsequent investigation cleared the soldiers without reservation. It had been a tawdry distortion of the truth and came from a blind belief that as the Americans had been involved in atrocities, so must we. It did the men of D Company a gross disservice.

Anyone who could be taken as a prisoner on that day was – three of them, in fact. Bob Buick found one.

We came across this poor little 16 or 17-year-old North Vietnamese and he was absolutely terrified. He had been told that us white bastards eat them and he was shit scared we were going to eat him alive. Anyway Detto [Private P. Dettman] rested the barrel of the M60 on his forehead and I called for a medic. Now this young fellow had been shot in the groin and flyblown and he was lying there and I can imagine, 16 years old, absolutely dead scared. Detto was about six three or four and built like a brick shithouse. And I am six foot and I wasn't any weakling in those days. And they came up and the medic got a bottle of iodine and just poured it straight into the wound and this kid didn't even flinch, he just looked and then he picked out all of the maggots. And we put a dressing on him.

We found out later that he had come down from North Vietnam only a month and a half before, he had walked down the Ho Chi Minh Trail for three months, walked in, he had carried a couple of mortar bombs, they went in the tube, bang, bang. So what he had carried for two months gone in two seconds. He didn't know what he was up against, he was just told to go. Sometimes I wonder if he is still alive, I might buy him a beer.

Bob Buick

They pushed on to the 11 Platoon position and there, at last, they found their missing soldiers. The searchers stood for a while, staring in disbelief at the tableau laid out before them. The men were still in their fighting positions, in a straight line, facing the enemy, their rifles loaded and aimed. They were all dead, but the rain had given them grace, washing them clean of blood and, for a moment, they seemed to be alive. Helplessly, with a desperate conviction, one searcher futilely called out to them, but they were long past hearing. No man who stood there that day has ever forgotten that sight and they will not speak of it for long.

As they moved closer a terrible depression settled on them, the finality of the loss now all too real. Then a voice called out Bob Buick's name. It was weak, but unmistakeable. Jim Richmond was, astonishingly, alive.

I did hear the APCs, the armoured personnel carriers, come in, and I heard a few blokes' voices which I didn't recognise at the time. Then I heard them come closer so I yelled out. I heard Sergeant Buick's voice so I just put me hand up and yelled out to him and that's when they found me and I reminded them then that there was a live grenade, I thought, still in

> front of the tree in front of me... I heard Sergeant Buick's voice and I thought well now that they're here I reckoned I would be okay. So I put me hand up and he's not a good-looking bloke Bob, but I nearly could have kissed him that day!... I knew I could survive then once I seen them come in and get me again... They patched me up on the field there then and then they called in the armoured personnel carrier. They put me in the back of the armoured personnel carrier and then they got me out to a landing zone so that the American helicopter would take me back to 36 Evac Hospital in Vung Tau there.
>
> JIM RICHMOND

As the size of D Company's victory became clearer, visitors began arriving at Long Tan – staff officers, members of the task force command, intelligence officers, and journalists. It seemed as if every man and his dog wanted to take a look at what was rapidly becoming a famous piece of real estate. The curiosity, the voyeurism, was understandable, but their timing was badly askew. They were intruding on the raw emotions of exhausted, traumatised men and they quickly discovered their insensitivity was not welcome.

> All the generals and the photographers and a lot of them were getting around the area. They were getting around in their nice starched greens and pointing a rifle at a dead body and their mates were taking photos for them. They would come up and talk to you and a few of the boys told them to get out. They didn't want to talk to them. Didn't want to talk about what happened. That upset the blokes more than anything else. All these people from Saigon and Vung Tau coming out. They came out to the battle scene so they could report to their superiors and that sort of stuff... to be part of it. The brigadier came to have a look around to say he had been there. But

they brought a lot of hangers-on with them. There were hundreds of weapons and other equipment and at that stage we had it all bundled up in this big area and they were all coming up and picking up weapons, cocking them and playing with them and this sort of stuff. We were sitting around having a smoke at this stage and saying, 'Have a look at these posers.'

JOHN HESLEWOOD

I couldn't come at the act of wrapping up my blokes. I couldn't do that. I don't think anyone in D Company handled their own guys. I think someone else did it. I didn't really notice. I just walked round in a daze. Very angry, extremely angry, because once we had secured the battle area in came the helicopters with officers, the task force commander, majors and captains, all these bastards who had cold beer every night and never walked the weeds. All the staff officers all of a sudden came out to have a look around. One major said something that bloody pissed me right off and I dropped him. In fact he's lucky I didn't shoot him with my Armalite. The RSM bloody grabbed me and bloody hunted me off.

And this newspaper bloke came up and wanted the story . . . They were living in Saigon, they would hear about something, jump in a chopper, come down, get their story, fly back to Saigon and send it away in a cablegram and then get on the piss again by four o'clock in the afternoon. Bugger that; I wasn't going to talk to these turds. Anyway I threatened to shoot this Pommy bloke and Jack Kirby came over and grabbed him and hung him off the branch of a tree. And he was only a small fellow, five four or five, and he looked so funny hung up by the scruff of his neck on the branch.

I was totally emotionally drained. I was not prepared to see what I saw. I was not prepared to handle bodies late in the day. They were flyblown. You grab hold of an arm and you pull them into a hole and their arm would come off and

> his whole body would be full of maggots. These type of things... We got rid of our guys. We wrapped them up in ponchos and we put them in APCs and we sent them back to Nui Dat... For days after you can't get the stench – if you handle someone who's dead, you can't get the stench off your hands. If you're a smoker like I was in those days every time you lit up a cigarette you could smell death. It's another one of those things you can't explain. If you've witnessed it and been there and done it you'll remember it, but then you try not to remember it and this is the whole thing. I have been trying not to remember and I think we all do that.
>
> Bob Buick

The clean-up continued for the next two days. The Australians were very particular about burying enemy dead, unlike both the Vietnamese and the Americans who often left enemy corpses where they fell. The intelligence unit also regarded the bodies as a treasure-trove of potential information and the soldiers collected all personal belongings as a matter of course.

But it was a disgusting, gruesome task. Besides the stench and the flies, rigor mortis meant that many bodies could not be buried without the Australians having to cut and break the tendons so they could straighten out the limbs. Rapid decay caused the corpses to fall apart as they were carried and sometimes, after often necessarily shallow burial, arms, legs and entire torsos would resurface during the night. Others were dug up and interfered with by wild pigs and the remains had to be re-buried. The soldiers moved through disgust to numbness and, in some, a kind of bleak, morbid joking sprang up.

Members of B Company came across a decapitated enemy corpse. They located the head and smuggled it back to Nui Dat. After allowing ants to clean it of all flesh, they hung the skull over the door of their boozer. B Company was known as 'The Phantom Company' and their bar now went by the name of

'The Skull Cave'. A lot of photographs were taken of that boozer. It was the same grim humour that had been on display in the trenches of Gallipoli and the swamps of New Guinea.

Dave Sabben, like so many, was deeply affected by this terrible time. The heat of battle, hard training, adrenaline, the survival instinct, anger and revenge can all assist a man to function well as a soldier; calculating, disciplined, driven to succeed. But to have to deal so intimately with your fallen enemy causes undisciplined, emotional humanity to intrude into the frame.

> When we had to clean up the battlefield the worst thing for me was the fact that myself and my troops had to go around, and it wasn't just a matter of picking up a piece of body and moving it to a communal ditch, we had to search everything. We had to search the packs, the equipment. We had to search their pockets. We had to retrieve wallets. There were photographs of families. They had families. They had Mum and Dad and the kids and there were photographs there wrapped in plastic against the humidity. There were little letters, books, dried flowers pressed in the pages of a book. We had to retrieve all of this along with the documents and the equipment and the metal, and we had to take them into a central point so that the intelligence people could start piecing together what unit were they from, what rank they were, where they came from, where they had been operating...
>
> And 10 per cent of our emotions were the thrill of the victory and you could see the devastation. You could say we won, we won, but 90 per cent was this letdown, this awful dread that what we were witnessing, not that we had caused it, because most of it we weren't witnessing people that we had actually shot, we knew that artillery had fallen or someone else in the company had shot them or something, it wasn't a personal guilt but it was just an overwhelming dread of just loss. I mean, yes, they were enemy soldiers but by that stage

we knew that they were like us. They were trained like us. They were serving their country like us. We didn't have to agree with their politics but they were just doing what we were doing and there but for the grace of God were us...

It took us two days to clean up the battlefield, burying what we could of the bodies, collecting all the weapons and so on, collecting all the intelligence and the most difficult thing for me to see was the growing pile of personal effects which we had to accumulate. The weapons, yes, the photographers were taking photos of the weapons and they're in the War Memorial now. There's pictures of lines of machine guns and AK47s and Claymore mines that were never set and mortar bombs and so on, recoilless rifles. There's pictures of those but no one turned around and took a picture of a pile of notebooks, diaries, wallets, plastic envelopes of family photographs. No one took that photograph and no one will ever know how pathetic it was to see them sitting there just under a rubber tree, collected lives sitting there waiting to be disposed of. It was terrible.

DAVE SABBEN

The Battle of Long Tan made headline news in Australia. Little that was reported from Vietnam was as clear and as victorious as this and it was exploited to the hilt. For a day or two anyway. Then, as was always the way with the Vietnam War, divisions and questioning began. It centred on the unusually high numbers of national servicemen involved, 11 killed in action and 14 wounded. 'Nashos used as cannon fodder!' bellowed the press, and when that began to lose its fizz, they suggested that the enemy had concentrated on 'young, inexperienced national servicemen' at Long Tan. Exactly how the VC told the difference between nashos and regulars was not revealed. The soldiers at Nui Dat dealt with this nonsense in their own way, wearing cardboard signs round their necks with the words, 'Don't shoot me – I'm a regular!' Meanwhile the captains and the chaplains in their khaki cars began their sad journeys. One was to Beryl Gant, the mother of Kenny, a private in 11 Platoon.

> I was sitting at the window playing 'Somewhere My Love' I think it was, I was listening to that on the radio and trying to read a book at the same time, and I happened to look out the window and I seen this green army car coming down the road. I didn't put much to it, you know. I thought, 'Oh no, he's only been away a little while.' But the next thing a knock come to the door and my husband went out and it was one of the army men and the army chaplain. I didn't go out. I just sat waiting. And he come in and he said somebody wants to see you out the front. So I went out, straightaway I knew that something was wrong and they told me Kenny had been killed. I couldn't get it into my head though. I couldn't believe it. I just said, 'No,' I said. 'It can't be him!' and we didn't get the news until the Saturday morning. He was killed on the Thursday.
>
> BERYL GANT

It would be three weeks before Beryl and the other families would receive their sons' bodies for burial.

The D Company officers were assembled by task force command, debriefed on the battle and then briefed on what they should say before being taken to Saigon and presented to the world's media. The soldiers were given a week's leave in Vung Tau, effective immediately, and the bars and the brothels got a hammering. Down the road, at the American 36th Evac Hospital, Little Pattie and Col Joye responded to an army request that they visit the wounded.

I think performers are pretty used to putting on a smile and putting on a brave front. But I thought that was pretty hard. And I remember standing outside – Col had his guitar and we were ready to go into a particular entrance of the hospital and we were saying to each other, 'How do you feel?'

'I'm all right, how are you?'

And I said, 'Oh yeah, I'm all right.'

But we weren't. We were feeling pretty teary and sad and propping each other up. Eventually the door opened and we went inside and, of course, we didn't cry. But much later I did. Just seeing the many wounded and the young faces, you know. They all looked like my brother. They all looked so young. They were 19 some of them. And they were just baby-faced, brave, terrific Australians. Really something that day, for me. I suppose if there's a turning point – we all have turning points in our lives, you realise later on, where you grew up and I grew up that day. I really did. Big time.

PATRICIA THOMPSON (LITTLE PATTIE)

6RAR was awash with congratulatory messages, from the South Vietnamese and American military commands and the Australian Prime Minister, Harold Holt. But in Vietnam, it wasn't military victories that ultimately counted, but who won the propaganda battle that inevitably followed. Within 24 hours of Long Tan, Communist cadres were at work in the province, telling every villager of the great and glorious victory that had been won at the expense of the enemy Australians, hundreds of whom had been killed by 'our country's liberation forces'. A few days later Radio Hanoi announced in part:

The Australian mercenaries, who are no less husky and beefy than their allies, the US aggressors, have proved as good fresh targets for the South Vietnam Liberation Fighters . . . according to the first reports, in this battle the LAF [Liberation Armed

> Forces] put out of action 400 Australian mercenaries, thus annihilating two full-sized companies, heavily decimated another, set afire three M113 armoured cars, downed one US jet fighter, and captured a great quantity of arms and munitions.

The North Vietnamese units involved were awarded medals and the propaganda was passed on to all Communist troops and the villages of Phuoc Tuy Province.

At the time, the Australian soldiers dismissed all this as the usual Communist claptrap they listened to every day. Even when a local village erected a banner congratulating the Australians on their victory, the soldiers joked among themselves that the village had an alternative one that praised the VC, hidden away for when the guerrillas came to town. But as the years passed and service in Vietnam became something you did not admit or discuss at home, recognition by the Vietnamese of what *really* happened became very important to Long Tan veterans in Australia. If they couldn't get respect from their countrymen, surely they could have it from fellow men at arms? But the official Vietnamese histories perpetuated the lies. They still do. Only recently has a lone VC commander, himself a Long Tan veteran, admitted to Bob Buick and Dave Sabben that, yes, they were beaten by the Australians.

Some recognition did come from their own side, though it was marked by military incompetence and small-minded, churlish behaviour by the Australian Army and government. The Americans were open-hearted and generous, President Lyndon B. Johnson awarding D Company the prestigious Presidential Unit Citation 'for extraordinary heroism'.

The South Vietnamese too were determined to honour the men of D Company, but their gesture was turned into a joke. The Commander of the Vietnam Armed Forces and Chief of State, General Nguyen Van Thieu, arrived at Nui Dat to award the men the South Vietnam Cross of Gallantry only to be told by the Australian command that government policy would not allow them to accept it. The parade was delayed for an hour while Thieu's aides scurried to a nearby town to find some kind of replacement gift he could give the men.

In a surreal ceremony President Thieu then presented D Company officers with lacquered, wooden cigar boxes, the NCOs with cigarette boxes and the privates received dolls dressed in national costume.

You might have expected that, after all that, Australian civilian and military authorities would have been at pains to ensure that at least they would get it right, but your expectation would have crashed and burned. Military decorations were awarded under a quota system – so many per battalion. Harry Smith was recommended for a Distinguished Service Order, but a superior downgraded that to a Military Cross. Smith in turn had recommended Dave Sabben and Geoff Kendall for the Military Cross but, alas, the quota had already been dispensed to other officers for excellence in non-combat duties so they both received a Mention in Despatches instead. Gordon Sharp was recommended for a Mention in Despatches but received nothing. Bob Buick was awarded the Military Medal.

In all, 15 Commonwealth decorations were awarded to individuals, but the use of the quota system in the face of the soldierly qualities and the military achievements displayed that day in August 1966 was, and is, deeply insulting. It didn't help that officers not on the battlefield at Long Tan received awards for the action. Some of the veterans of Long Tan continue to feel cheated and disrespected by their service and their government. They continue to campaign for justice.

In the months after the battle none of this occupied them. They were dealing with stress and 'battle fatigue', empty bunks and vacant places in the mess, and the inevitable arrival of reinforcements. For the rest of their tour, D Company would be looking over their collective shoulder, wondering when the next blow would fall.

> The sense that we had gone through something that was so terrible that a third of us, one out of three of us, had either died or was wounded and most of the wounded were repatriated to Australia, never left the company. The company was always aware. It was like the ghosts were still in the company area. We were always aware that we weren't the company that we were, partly because you lose so many original troops and then other people come in and your reinforcements change the flavour of the company because they haven't shared the training experiences. They haven't shared the 70 or so days that we were before the battle and then, of course, they hadn't shared the battle, and they felt it too. They felt like they were outsiders because we were part of a club that they didn't belong to and it was just there for the rest of the tour.
>
> DAVE SABBEN

I've heard it said and seen it written that Long Tan does not compare with Gallipoli, or the Kokoda Track. Well, it doesn't. But why would you even want to make the comparison? They were all bloody dreadful places to be and anyone who survived them is to be respected and, in some acutely personal way, is separated from the rest of us forever. But, just so you know, here are some facts and conclusions from the Battle of Long Tan.

- The total number of men in D Company on 18 August was 108.
- They were up against VC 275 Main Force Regiment, VC D445 Battalion and 45 Regiment from the North Vietnamese Army – around 2500 men.

- That means they were outnumbered about 24 to 1.
- By every reckoning, except the Vietnamese, the NVA and the VC had up to 800 men killed in action and perhaps 1000 wounded. NVA Hospital records admit over 800 killed
- The Australians suffered 18 killed (17 from D Company and one from 3 Troop) and 21 wounded.
- It was an 'encounter' battle. Both sides simply bumped into each other. Wrong place, wrong time. But because D Company held out, the planned attack on the Nui Dat base was frustrated and the potential disaster and loss of life that attack would have entailed did not take place.
- For the rest of the time the Australians were in Nui Dat, the enemy did not launch a major attack on them again.

D Company were well-trained and disciplined Australian soldiers who were superbly led by their NCOs and their officers, and when they were pushed to the limits of their skills, their fortitude and their toughness, they responded as they had always hoped they would. And they paid for it.

> After Long Tan I said, 'No, I'm not going to get close.' Then when a mate of mine was killed later in the year, we had a mine incident in 11 Platoon that took out another 13, and a mate of mine was killed in February and by this stage of the game I decided, bugger this right, mark the roll, so and so marched in right, if he was killed or wounded, so and so marched out . . . they actually to me became a number. It got so bad that even years later blokes said to me, 'Do you remember me?'
>
> 'No, who are you?' And he'd mention a name.
>
> 'Oh yeah, how are you going?'

And that bastard turned around and said, 'You know you're nothing but a bloody arsehole, mate. I was in your platoon and you don't remember me!'

But I consciously made the decision that I wasn't going to get too close to anyone after Long Tan. People say that that's the wrong thing to do. You're the platoon sergeant, you're their mother, you're their father, the big brother and all that. Sit in my shoes, mate, and you don't get too friendly with any bastard because you never know how long they're going to be with you. I got two reinforcements on the 17th August at around about five o'clock in the afternoon, the next day both those kids were killed, so why would you want to get close to anyone? I still don't get too close to people, but that's the way I controlled my life, that's the way I do my things. Other people do it their way. I don't criticise them, they shouldn't criticise me.

BOB BUICK

The first day, the day I woke up in bed at the hospital, I had a dream the night after that and all the blokes in the dream were all me friends, all me mates that were killed and I just said to them, 'It's only a dream and when I wake up you'll wake up in the morning with me.'

Well, that dream has kept with me from Long Tan till now... I don't know why but the one that stays with me all the time is the young blokes, their faces are like they're still young... I see their faces, Doug, Shorty, Mitch, Glen... and I still tell them that when I wake up that next morning, that they'd all wake up with me. But they never do.

JIM RICHMOND

IX

WINNING HEARTS AND MINDS

When Australian soldiers, matey, open-hearted and unsubtle, went to Vietnam, it's unlikely that they thought much about the Vietnamese people or their history, or the reasons behind the war – soldiers rarely do that because they can't afford to let politics get in the way of soldiering. Most of the soldiers generally accepted that they were on a mission of salvation of sorts, keeping the South free from Commie invaders. While they would not have expected thanks from the South Vietnamese, they were certainly not prepared to be ignored or rejected as the latest in a long line of invaders by those very same people. But it was inevitable.

Wind the view backwards for a moment and try a comparison between us and them. Between the years 1788 and 1966, when Nui Dat opened for business, Australia had 177 years of European history. Despite a rugged start we flourished, living in the face of an often hostile land, instinctively disdainful of the original owners and permanently nervous about the presence of all those people of colour to the north. Australia formed us as a people – hard times and the land itself taught us interdependence. We turned to each other in need and found trust and safety; we developed self-reliance, a mocking sense of humour and a strong, national self-belief that could turn quickly into unpleasant and aggressive insularity.

On the other hand, behind the Vietnamese lay 3000 years of history. A chronicle of centuries peppered with invasions, oppression, wars, massacres, famine and unlikely victories against impossible odds. The Vietnamese had learned that life was a constant struggle, and enemies were to be expected everywhere. To survive they had to be careful, to be circumspect, to keep their most secret thoughts and hearts to themselves. In the face of shifting alliances and deadly power struggles, silence, secrecy and trusting no one except family can help to keep you safe. Above all, they learned to endure. To outlast their enemies.

Australian soldiers carried our culture to Vietnam, that place so completely unknown to them, and neither they nor the Americans were mindful of Vietnamese ways, let alone Vietnamese hearts. It would not have occurred to most of them to consider them, for that is not what they were there for. Nor would they have been inclined to investigate the lives of people who were mostly invisible to them except as symbols, just as they were to opponents of the war. The protesters back in Australia thought of the Vietnamese as either innocent victims or revolutionary heroes, struggling against oppression and imperialism. In Vietnam, many Australian soldiers saw their enemies, the VC and the NVA, as faceless fanatics, 'mad Commie bastards' who had been conned by propaganda and brainwashed into mindless sacrifice. Their allies, the South Vietnamese, they did not consider to be much better, though for different reasons.

> It was pretty primitive for them . . . a lot of them came from the southern end of South Vietnam and some of them hadn't seen their families for ages, so it was all pretty grim. They had two uniforms, one that they wore until it fell off their back almost and some of them were walking around in rags, the other uniform was kept for best, they weren't to wear it.

But if they had a big parade or guard of honour they'd put on their good uniform, have the guard of honour or the parade, take it off and put the rags back on again. They were all underfed; suffering from rickets. There was an assault course so I said, 'We'll give them some assault training.'

But that was a waste of time too, they just weren't athletic, they can't sprint, they can't pick up their knees, though they can jog for miles at a time. And they weren't good at throwing themselves over walls or climbing ropes and you didn't expect this to happen anyhow frankly. So I sort of suggested we remove that from their training.

But I'll never forget this sergeant, he was a PT instructor, he said, 'Oh we'd better give them some warming up exercises before we put them over the obstacle course.'

He knew what to do, anyway they all touched their toes and there was 'Crack! Crack!' and I said, 'What's that?'

And it was all their bones just cracking, and it's the most uncanny sound so I said, 'We'd better stop that.'

And we put them over a few obstacles but their heart wasn't in it, they weren't strong enough, didn't have enough energy. Later on I spoke to the American Army doctor in Hue and I told him about this cracking, he said, 'Oh yes, because they've all got rickets, vitamin deficiency.'

Not enough protein, not enough vitamins. So actually I did find out that they were supposed to be getting a package of vitamins in their big rice cauldron . . . they were supposed to put this package of orange crystals, which was supposed to be a sort of vitamin supplement, don't know what it was, that was obviously being siphoned off by somebody and being sold on the black market. So I was able to track that down and get it dumped into the rice, but I don't think it did any damn good at all. Their diet seemed to be fish heads, the rest of the fish went into cans which was sold at export, but there seemed to always be a head and a tail; I never saw a body of the fish anywhere in any of their soup. Pretty miserable vegetables, oh maybe once a week they got a bit of meat, which I could recognise as meat. So their diet was pretty rough... not enough protein, not enough goods were in the vegetables, no fruit, even though Vietnam, of course, was a very fertile country, it just wasn't available, the war effort had slowed down a lot of the rural production.

ROBERT HAGERTY, AATTV

Isolated inside Nui Dat, most of the infantry soldiers were prevented from close, daily contact with the Vietnamese. They encountered them only on patrol, or when they were searching villages, or on R&R in Vung Tau. It did not make for a deeper understanding. The most positive sentiment expressed was from a compassionate few who considered them to be 'poor bloody bastards'.

It was the Australian Civil Affairs Unit (1ACAU) and the AATTV who had the closest encounters and, for them, time with the people brought them face to face with a few home truths.

You quickly realised the Vietnamese that you were dealing with – most of whom were civilians – their goal in life was to have a family, have kids, educate those kids, and get their own house. And you start to think, well hey, that's nothing special, that's universal, that's basically what most people strive for in life. We had the advantage of being in villages; we were always eating in homes and getting to know people, so we knew the Vietnamese probably better than the other Australian soldiers.

If you think of an infanteer, his working life, his working day, is being out on patrol, out on ambush. He's trying to kill someone who's trying to kill him. He goes on leave, he goes down to Vung Tau, he goes out with a wallet full of money,

> he comes back with no money, he's got a hangover and there's a very good chance he's got a good dose of venereal disease. For 12 months that guy is conditioned negatively with every interaction he has with Vietnamese. They're trying to kill him, or they take his money, they give him VD or something like that. It's of absolutely no surprise that most of the Australians who went to Vietnam don't like Vietnamese, or came back disliking Vietnamese and a lot still do. On the other hand, we saw differently. We saw enough to know. There were Vietnamese I did trust, there were Vietnamese that I didn't. And some I liked, some I didn't like. It was just a society, as a society is in any town that you're in, in Australia.
>
> BARRY SMITH, 1ACAU

Civil affairs, or working with the locals, had been a critical part of Australian operations in Vietnam from the beginning. The tactic came directly from the army's counter-revolutionary warfare textbook, a sort of warrior welfare for civilians caught up in a war. The basic idea was that if the army helped improve the local people's living conditions they'd be less inclined to help the insurgents and, because they had a nice new house, or a well, or a road, they'd feel positively towards both the local government and the foreign soldiers. Though, of course, the army expressed it in far grander terms. After constructing a new marketplace in a village called Hoa Long, the Australian commander marked the ceremony by presenting the province chief with a scroll that read:

> The Australia Government in cooperation with Free World forces and your National Government in Saigon, respectfully presents this market place to you, the citizens of Hoa Long, with the belief and hope that in a free and open market place, truth will prevail and where truth prevails, men will know themselves and their neighbours.

Unfortunately less than a year later that same marketplace had become notorious as the location where Australian and South Vietnamese forces dumped the bodies of local VC they'd killed. They hoped that people in the crowd would react to the sight of the corpses and so give themselves away as VC supporters. The practice was quickly stopped, but it was the perfect illustration of the riddle at the heart of civil affairs action in a war zone – as an army, a fighting force, do you help or hinder; build or destroy?

> We thought we were doing a pretty good job in civil affairs. We were dicking around the province winning the hearts and minds of the villagers while handing out volleyballs and chickens, while other people in the task force were killing their kids. I know which would have had more effect on me.
>
> BERT JORDAN, 1ACAU

Malcolm Fraser was responsible for the creation of the Australian Civil Affairs Unit in 1967. He was the Minister for the Army then and believed passionately in the worth of civil aid. The Australian Army had completed a few modest civil projects in the early years, but they had had to take time and money away from their real job, so Fraser set up the unit solely to give aid to the South Vietnamese. 1ACAU was an army unit, staffed by officers and men from the Australian Army, and, as such, it came under the operational control of the task force commander. The unit arrived in Nui Dat in 1967 with one section deployed to Nui Dat and the other to Vung Tau. 1ACAU was given a clear mission statement that it was to 'win the support of the local population for the Government of South Vietnam with the subsidiary aim of obtaining goodwill towards Australian forces and Australians generally'. Nothing like blatant propaganda to help to bring about victory.

A project would come to fruition and the locals would say, 'Oh, thank you, Australia, for doing that for us.'

And we would say, 'Oh no, don't thank us, your government in Saigon cares about your welfare and they know that we've got the capacity to help you, so they asked us to, so really you should be thanking your government in Saigon.'

Now, I might have put that to sound a little bit facetious, a little bit cynical, but it's not meant to be. The whole idea was to win over the support of the local people for the government in Saigon. In retrospect, we all know it didn't work. But at the time that was the idea. It was not altruism in any form; it had a very, very strong military and political motive.

BARRY SMITH

The ACAU stayed in Vietnam till the end of the war and they weren't exactly lazy. They built schools and kitchens, houses and orphanages, sewerage systems and roads and wells and bridges. They improved rice harvests, chook breeding, sorghum growing and even the birthrate of the local pigs through artificial insemination. They pulled teeth, gave injections, cut and stitched, and saved more than a few lives from malaria and tuberculosis. They trained Vietnamese kids to be brickies and carpenters, welders and electricians, even Boy Scouts and soccer players.

WHAM, the Americans called it, 'Winning Hearts and Minds', a phrase still in use today and which was countered at the time by the mad-as-a-cut-snake American General Curtis LeMay when he said, 'If you grab 'em by the balls, their hearts and minds will follow.'

We were the first people and we had to stick our foot in the water and test it all out and we got a bit of criticism, I believe, from various people, who thought it was a lot of codswallop. There was the odd article in the newspapers, in the time that I was in Vietnam, which were not terribly complimentary,

> saying, 'Do we really have to do this sort of thing? Is it losing sight of the main aim of the exercise with the military force?' There were one or two people in the task force who were not terribly imbued with the thought of this 'civil affairs' business. 'Let's get on with the soldiering bit. Give me more bloody ammunition, give me more guns. Let's get stuck into this.'
>
> JOHN McDONAGH, COMMANDER, 1ACAU

Combat soldiers and officers had little sympathy for the work of the Civil Affairs Unit. Round Nui Dat they were called 'noggie lovers' and 'the bleeding heart brigade' by men who believed in bayonets not buildings. Task force command expected them to gather military intelligence as they moved around the province and were taken aback when the men resisted, saying that spying would compromise their relationships with the Vietnamese. It didn't help that 1ACAU often had their photographs in the newspapers – smiling village kids in their new schoolhouse was a far more attractive news story to editors than endless patrols and low body counts.

Soldiers train and fight under rigid army rules and regulations, and quickly learn to accept what they have long described as SNAFU – 'situation normal, all fucked up'. It's the same on the battlefield; all armies know the rules. But when the front line is someone's backyard it can get very messy, very quickly. In Vietnam the army operated under an American system called Solatium, a compensation scheme for damage to civilian property caused by military activities. It was a sliding scale of payment that worked well when it was, for example, a hut that was smashed up. But what about a life?

> There'd been an incident... basically a 29-year-old woman who had seven kids and a husband... They would have been a very, very poor family and the Australian engineers were building the road between her village and Dat Do and it was

wet and the road was closed – roadblock signs were up, but she went around them – I don't know exactly what happened, but she collided with a bulldozer and she was killed. I knew nothing about this . . . but I was told, 'Okay, this has happened, now under the system we've got, two chests of clothes that have been sent up from Australia and here's $30 and here's the words that you use. Now go down, give the clothes to the father who's been left with seven kids and give them all the clothes.'

. . . I took one look at these clothes and realised that – I mean no one wears jumpers in Vietnam, I mean no one, it never ever gets cold enough and most of it was useless and what might've been useful was certainly not in good condition. It was a bit of an insult to be given pretty rubbishy stuff. And I said to the 2IC in the unit, 'You can't go down and pay a bloke $30!'

'Mr Smith, you'll go down, you know what your orders are so . . .'

And I went down into the village and went round to the house and, of course, with everything that'd gone on, people came from everywhere so there was probably, I don't know, 100 people, 200 maybe, standing around. And I gave this fellow two chests full of rubbish clothes and $30 and I always maintain that if the guy had had a weapon in his hand he would've shot me. The look of contempt in his eyes was something I'll never forget.

That actually affected me quite emotionally that experience, because you just realise the enormity of what it was for him and then to me the insult of coming out and giving him $30 and a whole heap of useless clothes. So I went into the refugee service in Ba Ria and the woman who ran it that I knew quite well and I said, 'Look, this is what happened.' I said, 'But it didn't work. Why didn't it work?'

'You had the right words,' she said. 'But if I'd gone around I would've taken a candle or a flower.'

And I thought, 'Yes, we take a sympathy card in our culture, we'd give something that indicated grief but we wouldn't put a price on it.'

How offended would you be if I said, 'Look, sorry we killed your wife, but here's $30 to get you over it.' Now that's probably three months salary for him, on the one hand it's a lot of money. But to me the Solatium system was totally flawed. You just don't buy your way out of some problems, maybe a broken ox cart you do – but you certainly don't with a human life.

BARRY SMITH

The Australians who worked with Vietnamese were on a hiding to nothing, no matter how hard they tried. Everything they did was based on there being a viable government in South Vietnam which their work would support. But at every level, both in Saigon and the villages, the bureaucracy was uncaring, inefficient and corrupt. Then there was their own task force, which was necessarily hell-bent on kill, capture or control of the enemy. Military operations inevitably disrupted local life and when the commanders decided to destroy or remove an entire village, they also destroyed the personal histories of family after family. It was 1ACAU which was left to clean up and resettle the people. And even if they managed to generate good feelings between the soldiers and the villagers, every man, woman and child 1ACAU encountered knew that the Australians, like others before them, would not, could not, stay. Why trust in them?

Nobody could doubt the good intentions of the unit and others in the Australian force; some of the men could even have been described as idealistic. But the failures were sadly predictable and the idealism soured into dismay and disillusion. They found it hard sometimes not to see the Vietnamese as ungrateful. As well, just below the surface, there was a permanent undercurrent of condescension towards the Vietnamese that could sometimes tip over into outright racism.

Even the physical differences worked against any kind of meaningful cooperation. By comparison with the tall, loud and often crude Australians, the average Vietnamese was a small man with a high-pitched voice, cheeks that rarely needed a razor and a face that seemed cryptic and remote to Westerners. Vietnamese ate food the soldiers found incomprehensible (like dog meat) and would have come second in any test of physical strength with their Australian allies. The average Australian infantryman's pack would have toppled a Vietnamese soldier onto his back like a stranded turtle.

Then there was that habit native to many Asian cultures, men holding hands in public. The sight left Australian soldiers gasping with disbelief. Despite all this, one-on-one, Australians generally managed to treat a Vietnamese as they found him, making no judgements based on colour or culture. As a group, though, they were unremittingly prejudiced. Even those who worked with the Vietnamese every day were ultimately led into disparaging comparisons.

> You have got to appreciate that the Vietnamese are a different race altogether and they're a bit of a dirty race at times. I mean, you can be anywhere in Vietnam and a woman or a man, if they want to go to the toilet, just squat down in the street and do it, all over the place... And, you know, I laughed the other day, I saw someone recommend that you could eat the vegetables from the delta, which is south of Saigon. I wouldn't eat them because they're grown in human excreta and lots of germs and diseases go through that way. And you'd probably end up with anything, even the water; the frozen water they get is full of bacteria.

I'll never forget one other time, I was down south, one of the jobs I was doing and they had these little toilets above the little dams, and they had a little jetty going out and a toilet on the end and you go and sit down over the hole there and do your business and you'd be sitting there and you'd hear this 'snap, snap'. And it's these fish jumping up to grab the remains, you see, and these same fish, they use them to make what's called *nuoc mam* sauce, which is Vietnamese sauce. They get these fish, crush them in these vats and run percolated water through them and that makes this bitter Vietnamese sauce which is used on all meals, so, it's really smelly stuff, but it's really strong, so it takes the taste of everything away. You don't know what you're eating; you could be eating snails, dog, eel, snake, meat, meat from anywhere.

BERNIE MCGURGAN

Like their grandfathers before them mocking Arabs in a Cairo street during World War I, the diggers of Nui Dat insensitively saw humour where others saw insult.

I tell this with reddened face and head hanging, but if Buddhist monks were seen from time to time – of course the head being the most sacred place, you don't touch a Buddhist on the head. You'd see a monk with a shaven head and an Australian slightly 'oiled' would wander over and rub this guy on the head and say, 'G'day, Curly.' And that usually led to a bit of a chase, with the Australian suddenly discovering he'd gone a little too far. It wasn't pretty.

AUDIE MOLDRE

At times it all resembled a cross-cultural train wreck that everyone could see coming but no one could halt. In one operation the task force destroyed a series of small hamlets and villages to prevent the Viet Cong from using them as a safe harbour and so more than 1000 people had to be resettled. 1ACAU built them a brand-spanking new village elsewhere, clearing the land and constructing roads, housing, pens for their stock and water tanks. The only trouble was that they designed and built it in brutally straight lines and right angles, just like an artificial suburb on the outskirts of an Australian city. The higgledy-piggledy nature of a Vietnamese village, the crazy quilt of laneways and yards, gravestones and gardens that develops and changes over time was completely ignored. There was no history here, no past that these people could recognise. So blinkered was the Australian command that they even boasted once other villagers saw this wonderful place, they'd want one just like it!

For a while, windmills were seen as an answer to the perennial village water supply problem and they did indeed work – no electricity required, water on tap for everyone. But again, good intentions were fouled by misunderstanding.

> We put some new windmills in and the colonel of our unit, he was very proud of this. There was a well dug and a Southern Cross windmill put up and the next day there was a big opening, and back he came. There was a bit of wind blowing and they released the hold on the windmill, and around went the wheel and up and down went the rods and out came the water. He put his mug under and drank a mug full of water to show them how great it was. That afternoon he was in hospital with the worst stomach bug you've ever seen. They found out that somebody overnight had emptied the toilet bucket down the well.
>
> EDWARD SCHUNEMANN, 1ACAU

In the end, all the windmills fell into disrepair. The Australians had erected them properly in well-chosen locations but they neglected to teach the Vietnamese how to maintain them. Sometimes it seemed that Australian decision-makers operated on the basis of the three wise monkeys – or else they saw Vietnam as they believed it should be rather than the way it was.

> The Australian government donated millions of dollars to start up a dairy farm in Vietnam. 'Cause milk is a scarcity in that country. So they exported a herd of Jersey cows into Vietnam and they set up this you beaut dairy farm with people running around in white smocks and so forth. We flattened rice fields to grow grass . . . and I was asked to escort our ambassador because he was going to do the official opening, on behalf of the Australian government.
>
> Well, we arrived there, went down by chopper and there was a South Vietnamese band there and all the dignitaries and the ribbon was cut and the speeches were made and – have you ever seen unhappy cows? There was this whole herd, they looked very forlorn and unhappy standing in these rice paddies. Anyway it would've been about nine months and it all disappeared, you could smell barbecued cows all over South Vietnam. The Viet Cong got in there and helped themselves and I think some of the locals did too. It was just a sheer waste of money.
>
> JOSEPH VEZGOFF, AATTV

And even when the unit had a win – when they made water flow where there had been none, or built a school for children who had never attended a class, or created friendship and trust where there had been only suspicion and fear – they were punished in the worst possible way.

The Viet Cong and the National Front for the Liberation of South Vietnam would bring down brutal reprisals on the people who had accepted Australian help. Village chiefs, administrators and police had their arms or legs chopped off as a warning, or were left bound with wire and assassinated in the main street. Mines were detonated in schools, children blown apart, buildings destroyed. The VC rarely destroyed the Australian-built wells or the windmills, the marketplaces or the medical centres. Just their own people. It was ruthless, inhuman . . . and successful.

South Vietnam might have worked; as a government, as an idea. Maybe even should have worked. There were well-educated, intelligent and honourable people scattered liberally throughout the military and the bureaucracy, at every level. There was goodwill on both the Vietnamese and our side, at least at the beginning. And there was a desperate need to succeed. So what went wrong?

> We needed outside support. We could not manufacture weapons or ammunition. We needed war machinery in order to conduct the war. But a lot of foreigners, American and other allied forces, some of them acted like they were our 'big boss' – I didn't like it. And I would tell our American advisers, 'We need you, but before you come to this country, you should at least have a basic knowledge, at least the history, the culture of our people. We do not need that kind of attitude. We need friends, not a boss. We have had too many bosses before you.'
>
> I never thought that the war could be won, because we lacked the proper ideology. The American people, I appreciate what they did for us, I am grateful, not only to them, but to the Australians. But because of the war, people suffer too much, so when people have something to wrap around themselves, like a good job working for the Americans, open a big bar and the girls come in as bar girls; make a lot, easy money. So the whole society changes. My wife, a schoolteacher, she could earn only about 500 a month, for example, but a bar girl could make 10 times that. She goes shopping, she just

> throws the money down like that so that everybody sees it – the society has been changed, completely. A new class had come up and we looked at that class as the servant of the Americans. We became worse than we were under the French. Everybody rushed to learn English in order to work for the Americans. Officers who spoke English tried to connect with American advisers so they could have influence, get a promotion.
>
> COLONEL VO DAI TON

In a word, it was money. Soldiers in the ARVN were paid $20 a month; even their generals received less pay than an Australian infantryman. A general, a commanding officer responsible for the security of the country, was paid less than a bar girl, or a taxi driver, less than an interpreter or a housemaid, or any one of the hundreds of jobs created to service the huge American presence. But these same soldiers were all expected to fight and die in the service of a country that valued them so little.

Dollars seeped like a poisonous, black tide into every crevice of a culture based on village traditions and family obligations. And every Vietnamese knew where their true loyalties lay – to their family. Is it any wonder that obtaining money by whatever means was far more attractive than blindly following a corrupt government and a fake nation? Bribery, misuse of funds, theft, fraud, robbery, smuggling, nepotism and a spiderweb-like black market became all but institutionalised. The cargo ships docked at Saigon in an endless stream and, between the wharves and the goods reaching their final destination, everyone pushed their snouts in the trough – Vietnamese *and* American.

Cars, radios, TVs, airconditioners, cigarettes, beer, whisky, sides of beef, caviar, butter, machinery, tools, guns, rockets, grenades and laundry detergent; anything and everything you might want or could dream of or could trade, anything you could sell, market or flog was available in a vast, underground economy that was the true, beating heart of South Vietnam.

You could even trade in people; girls, boys, how about fresh virgins from the country sent to the city to get them away from the war? Met at the bus stops by gangsters and mamma-sans, they were auctioned off to the highest bidder. And every loss of face, every humiliation, every act of begging or stealing, pimping or whoring forged another potential recruit for the Communists.

> From small things, the Communists could make big things. There would be a girl, she was very poor, she could not afford to go to school; so she goes to work in a bar. She marries an American GI, but she had a boyfriend, a Vietnamese boyfriend. He sees her go with the GI, because the GI has money, so what does he do? He joins the NVA to fight against that American. It was that kind of war – starting with small things and becoming a big movement.
>
> COLONEL VO DAI TON

We were small beer in all this, of course, 8000 Australians as opposed to half a million and more Americans. And our self-imposed isolation behind the wire fences of Nui Dat prevented us from causing too much damage. But we contributed in our own modest way to the inexorable dismantling of a culture, of a people. For that is exactly what was happening.

> By the time I'd come home and really had time to soak in the experience, and come to some sort of a sense of what it was that we were trying to do and what we might achieve, I really felt that if the war was going to be won, it was going to be won by the Vietnamese themselves, with minimal outside assistance. I felt that we certainly didn't need a commitment of half a million ground troops . . . the tooth to tail ratio was such that there were only 100 000 of those out in the field doing the fighting. The rest were in the cities doing, I'm sure

in a lot of cases, very important work and valuable work and doing it with good consciences. But you also had an increasing black market; you had private soldiers that had the purchasing power of the Vietnamese colonels, you had an army's allies who had the capacity to destroy a culture, and economy, to drive the Vietnamese people into something that they weren't. Drive their daughters into prostitution. The money spoke and the money spoke in the cities.

And so the people who were recruiting for the Viet Cong didn't really have to raise the subject of Communism, just on the basis of being a good, nationalist Vietnamese, you could win enough of them over . . . huge numbers of people were destroying the underlying basis of everything that was good about the Vietnamese culture, were not helping our cause. They were helping the Viet Cong recruiters, to the point where I would quite happily say to you that if I were a Vietnamese in 1968, I would have been out in the bush, fighting people like me. Simply because, as a nationalist, I couldn't have stood watching the things that were happening.

I'm not saying that the Vietnamese are squeaky clean and that they were wonderful and that it was the rotten imperialists, the allied powers that destroyed the whole thing, far from it. But I do think that we were just supporting the wrong people for the wrong reasons. And we needed less of that, we just needed people who were prepared to fight alongside the Vietnamese, die alongside them if need be, but be there to fight with them.

AUDIE MOLDRE

Perhaps the saddest part of all was that the Vietnamese themselves could not understand why America was there, why Australia was there. They understood invasion, for it was their history; they understood the Chinese wanting to subjugate them, to add them to their empire. They even understood the motives of the

French when they remorselessly exploited Vietnam's resources and drove the people into slave labour. But through all those terrible years Vietnamese culture, society and family life had been allowed to exist, even to flourish. Yet these latest intruders, who had come, they said, for the sake of freedom, for the benefit of all Vietnamese, were bringing about the destruction of the country, body and soul. Everything they did seemed designed to rob the Vietnamese of dignity, of integrity, of any kind of capacity to determine their destiny.

Many Americans and Australians had come with the best of intentions, and with the best of intentions they robbed from the very people they had sworn to aid. They robbed them of their ability to act for themselves; they robbed them of their future. In 1969, an unknown South Vietnamese officer anonymously published a poem called *Letter to the People of the United States*. This is part of that poem:

Though you, my friends, have molested the young girls of
my homeland
Though you, my friends, have acted with a lack of
politeness, with a deficiency of civilization
Have acted in a way that is not human
We are ready to be understanding
We are ready to forgive
You are soldiers far from home
Soldiers not fighting for your own nation
Soldiers gone off to defend a freedom of no
commercial value
We have had to think of this
To understand this for a long time now
We want to find some words of praise for you
We want to find a gesture with which to express
our gratitude

Don't be suspicious, my friends, don't jump to any
false conclusions
We are people with hearts that are still hearts
We are people who know pain, who know shame
We are not puppets under the lenses of your cameras
We are not a troop of entertainers
Under your teasing eyes
You, my friends, have come to Vietnam
You, my friends, have drunk the water of this tiny nation
But you have not yet understood the soul of this people.

A false world had been created in South Vietnam – a bizarre concoction of ideology and money, ambition and greed – and it could not last; its own weight would drag it down. Everyone knew it. It was just a matter of time.

X

IT BECAME NECESSARY TO DESTROY THE TOWN IN ORDER TO SAVE IT

Vietnam was what we had instead of happy childhoods.

MICHAEL HERR, 1977

Memory does strange things to the truth, particularly when it's personal. When we look back on our lives, most of us are susceptible to giving ourselves more importance in any given scenario than we truthfully had at the time. We write ourselves better dialogue, are convinced we acted more honourably than we did, even pretend we were somewhere we weren't. We can even revise history as a nation. Once an event has been absorbed into our collective consciousness, especially if we've all viewed television footage of it, somehow it becomes part of our individual histories, as if we were actually there. A seductive alchemy transforms that moment from simply being an event that happened at the time to being something that happened to *us*.

Vietnam was like that. Talk to people over the age of 50 in Australia and it's astonishing how many of them apparently attended the moratorium marches or protested outside the American Consulate, or were arrested by the police and thrown into paddy wagons. It makes Australia appear to have been a hotbed of protest, a kind of antipodean Russian Revolution. The truth is rather different.

Vietnam was certainly the one name, the one subject you could get a response to from just about anyone in Australia in the late 1960s. It couldn't be contained; everyone had an opinion. Newspapers were full of it, TV news programs nurtured it, politicians mouthed platitudes about it, parents were bewildered by it and the young took to the streets and protested over it.

As a concept, as an icon, Vietnam was central to the lives of most young Australians at the time, especially those at universities. The Vietnam War and conscription became the catch-all container for every act of rebellion, dissent, disobedience and just about anything we didn't like about the universe our parents inhabited. It was a war started by their generation after all and to be against it was to show integrity in the face of established power – schools, teachers, police and governments. It helped to define the 'them' versus 'us' struggle and acted as a convenient moral umbrella, a hiding place from the responsibilities that the older generation were saying should be our lot.

The Australian government may well have wanted to maintain and cultivate our relationship with America and 'halt the Communist onslaught', but the politicians weren't the ones who were being told to go to Vietnam. The war affected young men more than anyone else. They were the ones who could be chosen in a farcical birthday ballot of stupendous unfairness. They were the ones who would be sent to a war that was increasingly unwanted and despised. They were the ones who could not even vote against these decisions. There was a lot to oppose if you wanted to.

Nonetheless, the rumblings of dissent were slow to begin. By the end of 1966, after Prime Minister Harold Holt had ordered the task force to Nui Dat and the first nashos had died in battle, protest in Australia gathered in frequency and intensity, but it was still a vocal minority pulling on the pants leg of a quiescent, sluggish majority. There was no mass movement, just groups of like-minded people speaking out. The general opinion of the populace was that protesters were all 'ratbags and Commie lovers' and were best ignored. Save Our Sons, the women's organisation fervently opposed to conscription, was probably the nearest thing to an acceptable face of dissent and even they sometimes felt like the proverbial voice in the wilderness.

> One of the Save Our Sons' actions that I liked least, I think, was this – we used to roll up at the Swan Street barracks in Melbourne every time there was an intake of national servicemen and this would be early in the morning, which was troubling enough, to get there at the crack of dawn, usually cold and bleak. And we'd be there with our banner, which used to get caught up in the branches of the trees inevitably because there were loads of them in that particular area; but worse was that we used to get abused by a lot of the parents or family members who were there to celebrate the departure of their young, the young man of their family and that was very off-putting. They'd be there with their bottles of champagne and I felt that was an obscenity, but we did cop quite a lot of abuse and I just hated the atmosphere there. It was very, very unpleasant.
>
> JOAN COXSEDGE

It was in 1966 that the first real fault lines began to appear in the landscape. American B-52s were dropping bombs on Hanoi and the world was outraged. President Johnson needed friends badly, so when Harold Holt came to Washington to support him, Johnson gave him the full White House treatment – a 19-gun salute, a formal dinner and a marine band playing the Australian national anthem. Perhaps the flattery affected Holt's judgement, but his first speech in Washington became the one for which he is most remembered.

> And so, Sir, in the lonelier and perhaps even more disheartening moments which come to any national leader, I hope there will be a corner of your heart and mind which takes cheer from the fact that you have an admiring friend, a staunch friend that will be 'all the way with LBJ'.

Holt had incorporated LBJ's recent campaign slogan into his speech and probably thought it a rather clever thing to do. But to a lot of Australians, particularly the young, it was abjectly submissive and deeply embarrassing. Holt didn't speak for them. It was even worse when LBJ returned the favour and toured Australia just before Holt faced the 1966 election. The crowds, and the welcome, were rapturous. There was an almost childish gratitude displayed by many Australians that, for the first time, an American president had deigned to visit us. Despite newspaper editorials requesting that all naughty children behave themselves and 'show good manners', protests did occur. In Sydney they threw eggs and tomatoes then lay down in front of the motorcade, and in Canberra they practised their chanting – 'Hey, hey, LBJ, how many kids did you kill today?' It was protest on training wheels but organisational lessons were being learned and the excitement of civil disobedience was infectious.

> LBJ was staying in the Canberra Rex Hotel on Northbourne Avenue and a friend of mine took me to the demonstration. It was the first time I'd been in a crowd where people were all of like mind and there was something about the atmosphere, whether it was all the spotlights of the television cameras or the cameras on tripods or the police all in their white hats and blue tunics, it meant the occasion had a kind of a tension and an excitement that I certainly hadn't experienced before. I was 17 and still at school.
>
> The upshot of the demonstration was an anticlimax because President Johnson came in through the back door and we

> didn't actually see him. I saw the girl who had emblazoned upon her T-shirt 'Make Love Not War', which became quite famous in the ethos of the time . . . So that was my first experience of a demonstration. I would say that I was not a committed anti-war protester at the time that I went to it. I went partly out of curiosity, partly because I was being cajoled into it by a very good friend of mine who was very anti-war but I stood there and by the end of the evening I was shouting out the odd slogan but terribly self-conscious about hearing myself do so.
>
> ALAN GOULD, AUTHOR

Vietnam is always called 'the television war', because of the pictures it brought to the small screen every night at six o'clock and their supposed effect on opposition to the war. But other images from that time remain fixed in Australia's collective memory even more firmly. In Melbourne, where hundreds of thousands of people turned out to cheer for the president, two students plastered his car with paint and were attacked by the crowd for their accurate aim. The American press corps, hungry for any sign of dissent, sent footage and photographs around the world of the presidential limousine spattered with red and green paint while Johnson steadfastly waved from inside the car. No one mentioned the enormous crowd of welcoming Australians. Even more importantly, no one nowadays remembers them; the photographs are the memory.

Myth struggles with reality in shaping the popular history of those years. Images overwhelm the facts, particularly the frozen frames, the photographs that appear to capture not just a moment in time, but to be the reality of that time; and with time, they have become the remembered truth.

There was a girl, Nadine Jensen was her name. She was 21, a typist from Campbelltown in Sydney's southwest. She went into the city one day in June 1966, carrying a large bag. The streets were crowded with people, half a million of them, standing 10 and 12 deep behind barricades lining George Street. They were there for the parade, a welcome home for the men of 1RAR, back from their year's service in Vietnam. The band struck up, the Governor-General, Lord Casey, straightened up to take the salute, and the march began.

It was a tumultuous welcome. Ticker tape rained down on the soldiers from every building, children waved Australian flags, paper roses were thrown into the air by women and you could barely hear above the applause of the crowd. There were a few isolated protesters holding placards but the crowd saw to them quickly. An elderly man hit one with his crutch and a woman took to two others, beating them about the head with her umbrella.

Then, as the first soldiers reached the Town Hall, Nadine poured a mixture of red paint, kerosene and turpentine over herself and ran headlong into the marching troops. She smeared paint over the 1RAR Commander, Lieutenant Colonel A. V. Preece, and the next few soldiers in the ranks, then stood, red paint streaming down her body, her arms raised in the air as the remaining ranks marched carefully around her.

She was arrested and pleaded guilty to 'offensive behaviour' the next day in court. She said that she was not a member of any organisation but had wanted to show her own opposition to the war. The magistrate fined her $6 and placed her on a good behaviour bond, then suggested she should be remanded for psychiatric examination. Nadine replied that she had already been examined by two psychiatrists and found to be 'normal'. She left the courtroom and disappeared into Australian folklore.

A half a million people went to the trouble of attending that day. They came to welcome home Australian soldiers from a war in Vietnam; to honour their service to their country. In 1966, four years into our involvement in the war. But no one remembers that. They remember Nadine. They remember the photograph of a lone woman standing in the middle of the street, her clothes drenched in paint, surrounded by marching soldiers, row upon row of saluting arms, eyes fixed on the governor-general. Every Vietnam veteran I have talked with remembers the woman and the red paint, the perceived insult to their uniform, to their service. But not one of them spoke of the half a million people, or the enthusiasm of the reception. One single action, one potent photograph has become the accepted truth.

Exaggerated actions like Nadine's allowed the general public to condemn most demonstrators as not 'real' Australians. Those early protesters were committed and passionate, but they were not getting through to the rest of the country. Most Australians still supported our involvement in the war, as well as conscription; in fact three out of every five people said they did. In November 1966, in an election fought on exactly those issues, Holt romped home, squashing a quarrelsome, divided Labor opposition and shocking the anti-war movement to its boots. It was a great victory for Holt, bigger than Menzies had ever achieved, and it appeared that Australia was now firmly involved in the war till its end, conscripts and all.

It seemed as if everyone got a little lost after that big election win of 1966. The re-elected conservative government meandered on, smug in the knowledge that not only did they enjoy a huge margin but according to the latest poll, 50 per cent of the people wanted them to keep fighting in Vietnam – Australia believed in the war. The Labor opposition was a hopeless rabble and Harold Holt didn't have to raise a sweat in defence of his policies, which was just as well because his government was lacklustre and uninspired.

But pride as they say, will always tip you arse over apex when you least expect it. In December 1967, Prime Minister Harold Holt, a keen spearfisherman and diver, did what he'd done a thousand times before – he went swimming alone in the surf.

Whether it was the rough seas, or whether he was foolishly showing off to the attractive young women on the beach or whether he was just another Australian who underestimated the ocean, Harold Holt went missing. His body was never recovered and the conspiracy theories ran the full hysteria from stress-related suicide to a foreign submarine parked off the beach to collect him because he was really a spy for the Chinese. Perhaps the most appropriate moment of his disappearance came when a young television reporter faced the camera live at the beach and solemnly informed viewers that for the moment at least the search had stopped and, 'Things here have come to a dead halt.'

John Gorton became prime minister. An ex-RAAF pilot, Gorton's features resembled an unmade bed, some say the result of a crash-landing during World War II that threw him face-first into the instrument panel. He was a cigarette-smoking, nonchalant larrikin who was completely unsuitable for the task of reinvigorating the government due to a worrying habit of permanent indecision.

Across the chamber he was faced by the new leader of the opposition, Gough Whitlam. Another ex-RAAF man, Whitlam was the new breed of Labor politician, smart and hungry. But he faced a marathon assignment in reforming his antique party and bringing it kicking and whingeing into the modern age. Opposition to the war and conscription, previously a front-of-house Labor policy, was quietly sidelined until the opinion polls indicated it should return. Whitlam would go on to become one of the true icons of Australian political life, the memory of his leadership still able to generate reverence and scorn in equal measure among those who lived through it.

The anti-war movement, like the politicians it despised, was also aimless or fragmented, each group critical of the others. There were the people who believed in Communism and wanted Vietnam to join the Soviet–Chinese team, the people who had no idea of what should or could happen in Vietnam but believed we shouldn't be there, the people who didn't want to be conscripted and the people who just liked to protest about society in general. Even a short list of some of the organisations from that time gives a sense of the chaos:

- Students for a Democratic Society
- Students for a Democratic Nation
- The Vietnam Solidarity Committee
- The Association for International Co-Operation and Disarmament
- The Congress for International Co-Operation and Disarmament
- The Revolutionary Socialist Students' Alliance
- The Workers and Student Alliance
- The Acid Liberation Marxists
- The Strawberry Collective
- The Spectre of the Left Opposition
- The Socialist Cynics

And that's not to mention the Maoists, the Trotskyists, the Leninists, the anarchists, the libertarians, the democratic socialists and the socialist democrats.

Then there was the language. Attending meetings or planning committees, even just engaging in pub conversation with any of these folks meant you had to be familiar with the vocabulary. There was activism, imperialism, anarchism, capitalism, existentialism and racism. Or you might discuss pacification, alienation or dehumanisation. And you couldn't leave out revolution, alternative lifestyle, counter-culture, bourgeoisie, sexual liberation, women's liberation, national liberation and black power. It was a liquorice allsorts bag of causes – and unity, or even a temporary coalition, eluded them. For a time. The mood was changing, if slowly. Devastating images were to come, perceptions were to change, and more myths were waiting for their true believers.

Three American military police are frozen in a photograph. They are crouched behind a wall next to the US Embassy in Saigon. It is January 1968 – the Festival of Tet. The men have their guns at the ready and their faces are strained and wary. On the ground next to them are the bodies of two other American servicemen who had been shot and killed moments before. The dead men lie carelessly sprawled, face down in the dirt, their fingers curled. Blood is pooling beneath them. On the other side of the wall, the American Embassy, symbol of power in South Vietnam, is under siege . . . by Americans. They are attempting to wrest back control of their own building from the enemy.

Sounds bad . . . looks bad . . . was bad. But it was another illusion. Not that it didn't happen – it did. It was more that this small-scale action, in which 24 combatants were killed, came to mean far, far more than all the pitched battles of the war in which thousands died. It was an upside-down victory.

Tet is the lunar New Year, the most sacred holiday on the Vietnamese calendar, when the country stops work and families gather together for three days. It is a time to forgive, to cancel debts, honour ancestors, forget the problems of the year just gone and set a course for the one ahead. In 1968 it was also a time of peace, an agreed seven-day cease-fire from the war. Which is why it was so shocking that on that day more than 80 000 Viet Cong and NVA troops launched a massive and well-coordinated surprise attack on cities, towns, airfields, military bases and government installations all across South Vietnam. It was unprecedented in size and style. The enemy were out in the open, in numbers, for the first time, risking annihilation. And for three weeks the blood flowed as never before.

In Saigon they had infiltrated the city in small groups of two and three, disguised as peasants, refugees and ARVN soldiers on leave for Tet. By the night before the festival there were five enemy battalions scattered throughout Saigon. For weeks weapons had been smuggled in under truckloads of vegetables and rice, hidden in flower carts and coffins. The attack began in the early morning.

Nineteen VC commandos blew a hole in the outer wall of the American Embassy and entered the compound. They overwhelmed the five MPs on duty, killing three. The others rushed inside the building and locked the doors. The VC had all the explosives they needed to blast their way into the embassy, but, with their commanders killed in the initial onslaught, the remaining attackers lost their way and, within six hours, all were dead. The embassy itself was never breached.

A failed mission for the VC. Complete destruction. It was typical of what happened everywhere in what became known as 'the Tet Offensive'. Hanoi had begun the attack knowing they would not be victorious. What they wanted instead was to regain the initiative from the Americans. And they wanted the Americans to understand once and for all that if they wanted victory they would have to up the ante to obscene levels. It was a terrible, cynical sacrifice of lives. In those three weeks the Communists lost over half their attacking force, over 45 000 men; nearly as many deaths as the US suffered throughout the entire war. The casualties on the other side – US, ARVN, Australian and South Korean forces – totalled just over 4000. The North Vietnamese Army was completely defeated, the Viet Cong all but destroyed. They did not achieve even one of their tactical goals. But they had their victory nonetheless. It just didn't come in the way they expected it to.

American reporters in Saigon lived in the embassy neighbourhood. They watched the battle; filmed it, photographed it. When it ended they kept recording, capturing images of embassy employees covered in blood, dead bodies in heaps on the bright green lawns, clerks used to carrying pens now wielding guns. Pieces of concrete lay strewn about where explosions had hurled them; immaculate white walls were pockmarked with bullet holes. Death lay among the flowerpots and palms and into the midst of it all strode General William Westmoreland, the US commander, to hold a press conference.

He stood among the destruction and told the press that a great victory had been won across the country. The enemy had been comprehensively defeated. And as for the embassy, 'It's a relatively small incident . . . don't be deceived.' No one believed him then. And no one would later.

In the months before Tet, the public in America and Australia had been assured that the war was being won. But they now knew over 40 cities and towns in South Vietnam had been simultaneously hit by the Communists. They had been told that victory in Vietnam was just around the corner. But they saw the embassy, the *American* Embassy in Saigon attacked. They saw it all, the bodies and the blood, and they decided they were being lied to. Then came another indelible image.

On the second day of Tet the streets of Saigon were still in a state of war. Fighting continued to erupt as South Vietnamese units ferreted out Viet Cong from the buildings they had captured. Eddie Adams, a photographer from Associated Press, and an NBC cameraman were chasing a report of a battle that had broken out near a Buddhist pagoda. They heard shots and rounded a corner towards the noise.

Two South Vietnamese soldiers appeared down the street, roughly pulling a man through a doorway. He was VC, dressed in a checked shirt and black pants. His hands were tied behind him and he had obviously been beaten. The soldiers walked the man towards Adams and then, for no apparent reason, backed away.

Adams had his camera to his eye, taking shots of the prisoner. Without warning, another man entered the frame, took his pistol from its holster and extended his arm, holding the gun to the side of the prisoner's head. Adams, like all reporters in Vietnam, had seen this many times before – the threat of the gun held there while an interrogation was conducted. This time would be different. As Adams pressed his camera shutter the man holding the pistol fired once, shooting the prisoner through the temple. He slumped to the ground, life gone, as Adams clicked again and again.

The shooter was the police chief of South Vietnam, Nguyen Ngoc Loan. He walked away from the body directly to Adams and said, 'They killed many Americans and many of my men. Buddha will understand. Do you?' Then, surrounded by his men, he left.

The film footage and Adams' photographs were sent round the world that night and, though the footage was screened, it was the still photographs that had the greatest impact. The frozen moment of death it captured overwhelmed viewers with voyeuristic revulsion. It seemed to be a gratuitous murder, an emblem of a war that had left behind all pretence at Geneva Convention niceties or displays of mercy for the defeated. Despite it later surfacing that the man was the commander of a Viet Cong 'revenge squad' that had executed unarmed civilians earlier that day, including Loan's young godson, all that remained in people's minds was the image of his distorted face as the bullet struck. Few people could believe that they had witnessed an apparently casual murder. Images burned into their memories.

Loan was severely wounded a few months later, his leg almost severed by an enemy machine gun during another battle. In a curious twist, he was rescued that day by an Australian war correspondent, Pat Burgess, a reporter for Fairfax newspapers.

The police chief was flown to Australia for treatment but once his identity became known the outcry to remove him was so great that he was taken to America and hospitalised there.

Loan escaped from Vietnam at the end of the war but the photograph would never leave him. He was reviled and persecuted for the rest of his life, settling finally in the USA, in Virginia, where he opened a pizza restaurant and, for a time, prospered. Once again though, his identity was revealed and the business went into a decline. He died of cancer in 1998, aged 67.

Adams would always hate what his photograph had achieved. He said at the time of Loan's death, 'Still photographs are the most powerful weapon in the world. People believe them; but photographs do lie, even without manipulation. They are only half-truths. What the photograph didn't say was, "What would you do if you were the general at that time and place on that hot day, and you caught the so-called bad guy after he blew away one, two or three American people?"'

Adams wanted people to understand the complexity of war, of that moment, but it couldn't happen. The perception, that this was an inhuman act in an inhuman conflict, was stronger than the truth. It was the only way his picture made sense to us.

The public perception of the Tet Offensive in Australia and America overwhelmed the facts. It didn't matter that the enemy had been decimated. It didn't matter that more than 14 000 Vietnamese civilians were killed by retaliatory US air strikes. It didn't matter that countless homes had been destroyed. What they heard instead was the bizarre logic of the American major who said in defence of the bombing of the town of Ben Tre: 'It became necessary to destroy the town in order to save it.' And they decided that no one in charge knew what they were doing.

It didn't even matter that during the offensive in the city of Hue, the Viet Cong systematically hunted down, tortured, murdered and in some cases buried alive over 3000 civilians whom they described as 'enemies of the people'. What mattered finally were the pictures and the footage that made the conclusion seem so obvious – we are not being told the truth. It wasn't the reporters; it wasn't 'media bias' for all that veterans like to believe it was. It was what the public decided to believe. In America, LBJ's approval rating plummeted and he stopped the bombing, replaced Westmoreland and announced he would not run for president again. In South Vietnam the people gave up on their government and desertions from their army doubled. In Australia the government announced that there would be no increase in our commitment to Vietnam. It was unthinkable to many but the belief was growing stronger – we might be losing the war.

The Tet Offensive reinvigorated the anti-war movement and brought alliances into being for long enough so that demonstrations and protests grew bigger and louder, and attracted more attention. Conscription became the rallying flag as more young men resisted the call-up and went public with their defiance. The government had already imprisoned a few resisters after their trials but had made the mistake of placing them in military prisons. The treatment they received at the hands of their soldier guards was deliberately rough and the outcry immediate. To lessen the damage the government amended the legislation so that those who refused national service and were found guilty by the courts would now be locked up in civilian jails. No one was fooled.

The very notion of jailing a young man for two years in Pentridge or Long Bay just because he acted according to his conscience angered many, and more ordinary citizens joined the anti-conscription ranks. The churches and even members of the

RSL weighed into the debate on the side of the resisters and polite but insistent civil disobedience multiplied.

The whole world seemed to have contracted a fever of protest and upheaval. French students almost brought down their government rioting in the streets of Paris. The Soviet Union crushed a rebellion in Czechoslovakia and there were riots in Britain, Japan and Mexico. Martin Luther King Jr, the black American leader, was assassinated and two months later so was presidential candidate, Robert Kennedy. All in one year, 1968.

The World War II generation was at a loss to either explain or understand the rapid-fire changes. Everywhere they looked their kids were questioning or ridiculing their values and choosing their own – communal living, long hair, sex before marriage, drugs and disobedience. The world our parents knew had clearly lost its senses and all their touchstones of stability and order had been savagely cut adrift. Who *were* these people? These distressing, disorderly, disreputable young people who were once their adored children?

Of course, not every young person was like that, and for some who were it was more a fashion statement than a sincere belief. The most flamboyant, the loudest and proudest, were generally at university and not a few were radical frauds. They sought 'lifestyle' rather than labour, wanted to 'express themselves' rather than conform, were more likely to follow Ché or Buddha than Jesus, and approved only of their music, fashion and drugs of choice.

Most of them didn't really protest but talked a lot about it and waved a desultory hand of agreement in the general direction of dissent. When questioned about their views they gave the expected replies of disillusioned, disaffected youth. Their hypocrisy was that their revolutionary ways were 'more honoured in the breach than the observance'. They were having too good a time just at the moment, thanks.

But the ones who did take it seriously, who wrote the leaflets and organised the meetings, distributed the pamphlets and led the demonstrations, were seeing a rise in their profile as the war now began to sputter and cough. The newly elected President Nixon had announced the first withdrawals of American troops by the end of 1969 and the Australian government had indicated they would do likewise when the time came. For the first time, the gallup poll in '69 indicated that more Australians wanted the troops to come home than wanted them to stay and the anti-war movement had a renewal of energy. But they also had new problems. Violence was an unwelcome gatecrasher at more and more protests as the radicals fought for control with the moderates. Windows were smashed, buildings trashed, marbles and firecrackers were hurled dangerously under the hooves of police horses, and placards, rocks, fists, bottles and batons were all weapons of choice.

The Australian government portrayed the protesters as unpatriotic and dangerous, and sent the grey men of the intelligence services out into the streets to spy on their citizens.

> The surveillance of protesters was very blatant. Nobody made any secret about it, back then before high tech took over. We used to have the Special Branch plods sitting at the back of every meeting hall that we were at and they would have their notebook and their camera and they'd be taking down the names of people who were there and what was said and car numbers outside and all the rest of it and they made no secret of it... And they went even further than that. They would actually come up to you. They would make a point of this. They'd come up and say, 'Now how's Uncle Fred getting on at his job?'...or 'How's Auntie Freda getting on? She's had problems, hasn't she, with some of the kids?' and they'd run through all the details. The idea being of course that they

> knew everything about you and the idea was to intimidate you and to make you fearful so that you wouldn't take part in these meetings and rallies. But it didn't really work. People got used to their presence.
>
> But I would have to say this, that there was a more worrying aspect to it and particularly I think people should bear in mind that Special Branch do the legwork for ASIO so all the information that they did take down ended up in ASIO files. Now that could be used against people, and was used against people, and certainly they had great and very tight connections with personnel officers in many business houses, big business places and they would just ring up, or the personnel officer would ring ASIO up and say, 'Have you got anything on John?' and they'd look up and they'd say, 'Yes, he takes part in anti-war stuff.' And so on and so forth and the bloke wouldn't get the job and he wouldn't know that he didn't get the job or why he didn't get the job.
>
> JOAN COXSEDGE

Australian news coverage of protest at home and the war in Vietnam began to change in tone around 1968 as well. Before that, Australian newspapers and television had not been particularly biased against the war or government policy and had rarely deviated from the official handouts. At best, they had been communicators of basic information.

> The Australian media as a group had really no influence on the war at all. The media as a whole, of course, but the American media, television; television dominated. Our first war on television in our living rooms every night, but American television. Not Australian television. The role of the Australian media was zilch, absolutely. Nobody gave a bugger about it.
>
> ALAN RAMSEY, JOURNALIST

They hadn't had much to write about. Unlike their American colleagues, the Australian media were kept on a short leash by their own army in Nui Dat. Australian soldiers were forbidden to talk with them without authorisation and, when they did, it was always either the party line from officers or banal, mumbled sentences from suspicious diggers. How the Australian media must have envied the American reporters and their easy access to the talkative GIs who inevitably had a story and could tell it well. The Australian reporters thought the Phuoc Tuy effort was boring and safe and that the 'real war' was everywhere else.

Then, in 1968–69, American journalists began to reveal the existence of atrocities committed by their troops and Australian reporters followed in their wake. Newspapers and television in Australia increasingly criticised the war and the government and told the Australian public, in full and bloody detail, of the horrific acts. By extension, they implied, we were sharing in the sins and the shame. And the sins were grievous indeed.

On 17 March 1968, *The New York Times* reported in a page-one story: 'American troops caught a North Vietnamese force in a pincer movement on the central coastal plain yesterday, killing 128 enemy soldiers in day-long fighting.'

A standard story for the Vietnam War, of no great importance in the sum of things. What *The Times* didn't know was that it was a deliberate lie, manufactured by elements of the US Army to stop the truth from shining on the foulest of deeds.

The day before the article appeared, the men of Charlie Company, 11th Brigade, Americal Division, entered a small village called My Lai in south-central Vietnam. They were not fired upon as they walked in, nor were there any other signs of hostile activity.

Charlie Company, around 120 men, had lost a third of their unit killed or wounded in the preceding two weeks, mostly from booby traps and snipers. They had not seen the enemy who had dealt them out death and they had not had the chance to fire back. They were primed for revenge. The night before, their superiors had given them a clear instruction to destroy the village and everyone in it. They were told that they could assume that anyone still remaining was either Viet Cong or a sympathiser. The next morning, led by a Lieutenant William Calley, they followed those orders.

They herded the villagers into a ditch and executed them with automatic fire; they bayoneted old men, shot praying women and children in the back of their heads, and raped, sodomised and mutilated. They shot people crouching on their knees, in their backs, even when their hands were in the air. Not everyone in the company took part, but enough did, and Calley not only led them, but forced some of them through it. They took the lives of perhaps 500 civilians in that village – old men, women and children. They took so long to kill them all that they had to stop for a break to eat their rations and smoke a cigarette or two. Their average age was 20.

We know what they did because, despite cover-ups by the army at every level, the sickening facts leaked out. We know what they did because a few courageous men spoke out. And we know what they did because there was a camera there, in the hands of a military photographer named Ron Haeberle.

The photographs were not published until a year later, in *Life Magazine* and a Melbourne tabloid newspaper – *The Sunday Observer*. The fact they were in colour made them all the more abhorrent – a trench full of corpses laying crumpled on each other where they were shot; a baby, the blood from its wounds smeared in wide ribbons across its body; a group of terrified women and children huddled together in panic, seconds before they too were murdered. *The Sunday Observer* was prosecuted for obscenity for publishing the photographs, but the charges were later dropped.

Though it took a year for them to surface, the facts of the murders at My Lai burst upon a disbelieving world. It did not seem possible that this atrocity had taken place, even less so that it was committed by American troops. For a while many Americans clung to the desperate belief that it was a disgusting hoax perpetrated by the Communists and that the photographs were fabricated. But slowly, painfully, the truth emerged and then even more incidents were revealed. American veterans lined up to give evidence of the war crimes in which they'd been involved – free fire zones where anyone was a legitimate target regardless of innocence or guilt; the CIA's Phoenix Program of ruthless assassination of suspected VC, a program that had gone off the rails and committed savageries like collecting trophies of ears and other body parts cut from enemy corpses; electric torture using field radios; the poisoning of village wells and rice crops; rape, assault . . . and on and on until innocence and pride in country and service were trampled in the dust. Even Australian soldiers, who were not accused of any incidents, were tainted by association.

Investigators recommended 30 prosecutions for the atrocities at My Lai and 30 more for the cover-up that followed. But the US Army would not accept it. Ultimately only 25 men were charged and all but Calley were acquitted at trial or had the charges dismissed beforehand. Calley was convicted of killing 22 civilians and sentenced to life imprisonment. After sentence was pronounced, he rose to his feet and said, 'Nobody in the military system ever described them as anything other than Communism. They didn't give it a race, they didn't give it a sex, they didn't give it an age. They never let me believe it was just a philosophy in a man's mind. That was my enemy out there. And when it came between me and that enemy, I had to value the lives of my troops, and I feel that was the only crime I have committed.'

The reaction to the verdict in America was astonishing. To many, Calley was a scapegoat, a man who was only doing his duty. They were angered by the army's failure to convict anyone further up the line. They believed the army sent Calley to Vietnam to kill and should not punish him for doing what he was told. Then there was the distorted and confused view of 'it never happened and besides they deserved it', and some even attempted to portray Calley as a hero. A song, 'The Battle Hymn of Lieutenant Calley' sold over 200 000 copies in three days.

> My name is William Calley, I'm a soldier of this land,
> I've vowed to do my duty and to gain the upper hand,
> But they've made me out a villain, they have stamped me with a brand,
> As we go marching on . . .

President Nixon, responding to the opinion polls, commuted Calley's imprisonment to house arrest. He was set free just three and a half years later and now lives in the state of Georgia, managing a jewellery store. He refuses to talk publicly about Vietnam.

My Lai was a powerful and undeniable image of a war that was sliding into unthinkable inhumanity and it became the trigger for the next waves of protest. American troops may have begun to leave Vietnam, but the anti-war movement in both Australia and the US wanted all the troops out now. The Australian government was boxed in. It did not want to be seen to be responding to the protesters, 'the law of the street', but clearly if the Yanks were going home, then so would we.

The basis on which we had originally entered the war was now looking like yesterday's strategy. The South-East Asian states the government had been so concerned about, the 'dominoes', had not fallen to Communism and were increasingly stable and prosperous. Malaysia, Indonesia, Singapore and Thailand no longer needed the paternal eye of the West upon them and it wasn't as critical now to keep America involved in the neighbourhood. Australia had entered the Vietnam War to gain credit with America and to maintain the protective presence of our big brother. Now they were departing, we could not possibly stay. Gorton and his cabinet were sidelined by Washington in these decisions and it left them confused, indecisive and probably a little hurt. The bewilderment they felt was obvious in a line from the Defence Minister, Alan Fairhall, when he said, 'The war is inevitably moving towards an unpredictable end at an indefinite date.'

There was also trouble at home as anti-conscription feeling spread. The Committee in Defiance of the National Service Act was formed in 1969 and confronted the government head-on. This group of academics, resisters, politicians, clergymen, students, businessmen and unionists placed an ad in *The Australian* (other papers refused to print it) with 853 signatories from all over Australia encouraging eligible young men to resist conscription. Everyone who signed was in breach of the Crimes Act but the government played ostrich and refused to act. So the members of the committee did the government's job and prosecuted each other. They were found guilty in court and fined. They refused to pay and became liable for time in jail and the government dug its head further down into the sand. Now it was clear. The protesters had the authority; the government was morally empty.

Something approaching panic spread in Canberra. The cabinet secretly discussed a new law that would allow them to jail offenders for up to a year if they were part of an assembly that disturbed the peace. As a piece of repressive legislation it would have been admired by the Communists, but cabinet wisely backed away. The wind was gathering speed.

Moratorium is an odd word with a long history. Originally it meant a delay in the payment of a debt, usually authorised by a government when it wanted some breathing space from its creditors. The American peace movement adopted the word and changed it to mean a halt to all work, a refusal to allow business as usual to proceed. It certainly sounded more impressive than 'strike'. The response across America to a moratorium march was astonishing as several million people took to the streets in the largest gatherings ever seen in the US.

As they had done before, the peace groups in Australia decided to adopt the tactic and put aside their differences to discuss it. At first they kept the students and the radicals out but, eventually, in an unexpected display of unity, virtually all the anti-war and anti-conscription organisations joined forces. An Australian moratorium march was set for 8 May 1970, to take place in all the capital cities. It would be easier said than done.

> A lot of people see the huge rally that came in 1970, but they forget all the hard work that created that moratorium and the one that followed it. We used to meet every couple of weeks in the Railways Institute Building in the city and we were made up of all sorts of people – some with great passions, ideological commitment – in a way we were again

> very representative of the community because there were full-blown socialists, there were communists, there were anarchists, there were Christians, there were Jews. There were women, there were professionals and, of course, the fights were just unbelievable and we sometimes would drive each other crazy by arguing over one point in a slogan, but of course out of all of that passion came an agreement around a common cause if you like, and that was to do what we could to stop that war and to oppose conscription. In a way the arguments were also, I think, representative of our strengths because it also meant that the people who represented this wide spectrum of society went out to their various constituencies and were able to argue the anti-war message and I think that helped in the development of the movement.
>
> JOAN COXSEDGE

Working together was giving them a bit of fire in the belly and they were beginning to understand their collective power. Then they were given real ignition. Just as troops were leaving Vietnam, President Nixon began another war in neutral Cambodia, sending in a force to destroy the Viet Cong bases located there. American anti-war groups erupted with protests that blew up into violence and destruction. The National Guard was called out to restore order but they blundered in tragic fashion. On 4 May 1970, at a university in Ohio called Kent State, national guardsmen opened fire on the assembled students – without warning, without orders. Four students were gunned down. The unwarranted killing of their own children produced the most traumatic time of the war in America and, for a while, the country hovered between grief and rage. It was four days before the planned moratorium march in Australia.

Everyone's foot went to the floor. Some predicted blood on the streets if the march went ahead, while others like Dr Jim Cairns, the Labor politician who had been elected Chairman of the Moratorium Committee, pleaded for peaceful civil disobedience. A few went completely over the top. Billy Snedden, a federal minister, described the organisers of the march as 'political bikies who pack-rape democracy'. Militant groups warned that if the police turned it on, they'd get it back in spades. It was like two edgy boxers before a prize fight, vying to out-shout each other with threats.

The pressure kept building, and it was all about size. The march was obviously gathering momentum. The peace groups, the militants, the uni students, the unions, they were all expected to participate. What stunned everyone was when schools got involved. Thousands of schoolchildren were coming and sympathetic teachers were helping them. Posters and badges appeared everywhere and the debate accelerated. You couldn't ignore it. One side saw the march as the death of democracy and the other believed it was democracy at work. The churches split and signs, badges, placards and posters were banned from schools, shopping centres and church grounds. All police leave was cancelled, reinforcements came into the cities from the country and everyone waited for what they feared would be a violent, divisive day. The first march, a rehearsal of sorts, took place in Canberra.

> The Canberra demonstration was held two days before the main one around Australia and it was a very cold, wet, blustery day and we marched from Civic over to Parliament House ... It was a feeling of marching along with people all of like mind, a sense that finally opinion was starting to flow our way ... On the day itself one was gladdened by the sight of secretaries from departments, young secretaries from departments, public servants, some people from blue-collar sections of the community, all marching together.
>
> ALAN GOULD

The biggest march was in Melbourne and it produced three shocks. One was the size of the crowd, around 100 000 people. The second was who marched – people from every part of society. And the third was the good-natured, optimistic mood of the marchers. Jim Cairns began it by hitting exactly the right note in a speech before they began, at the assembly point in Treasury Gardens.

'When you leave here today,' he told them, 'realise a sacred trust. You have the trust to stand for peace and for the qualities of the human spirit to which we must dedicate ourselves. Our spirit is the spirit of peace and understanding. Our spirit is opposed to violence, opposed to hate, opposed to every motive that has produced this terrible war... We *can* overcome, ladies and gentlemen, and I have never seen a more convincing sight than I can see here now to give me confidence that we *shall* overcome.'

And on that day, for that day, they did. They marched 60 abreast, taking up the whole street and their chanting filled the air. 'Stop the war! Stop the war!' They were a multicoloured ocean, a tide of people who understood their power and miraculously used it well. They filled five city blocks as they sat down and took control of their city, waiting for Cairns to speak again. Jim Cairns never shone again as he did that day, a man whose principles and essential decency surrounded him with light, and they praised him, honoured him and listened to him. When he finished, the crowd stood up and, in a wonderful moment of incongruity, gave three cheers to the amused police. It was done. The following day, an editorial in *The Age* expressed the stunned delight and relief everyone was feeling.

> It was, without doubt, the most impressive demonstration seen in Melbourne. The sheer weight of numbers alone was staggering... more significantly, the demonstration was non-violent; there were neither broken heads nor broken windows

> to mar the pleas of the marchers for peace in Vietnam. It was an admirable achievement...

The marches in the other capital cities were smaller – the largest in Sydney with 20 000 people. But they too were peaceful and impressive. Only in Adelaide did things get a touch sticky. A thousand marchers ran into a group of soldiers from 3RAR who had just returned from Vietnam and a nasty battle broke out between the two sides. It took police hours to get it under control. And that was the other, unseen side that happy, peaceful day. One part of us, the one that was helplessly caught between the government and the people, gained little from the march except confusion and bitterness.

> I was awarded a Military Medal for my actions [in Vietnam]... and we got the invitation to be presented by the Governor-General, who was Sir Roden Cutler at the time, at Government House in Sydney. My mother and father came down with me and my fiancée. After the medals were presented – and it happened to be on the same day that the large moratorium march was in Sydney... we were told not to wear the medal that we were presented with outside the gates of Government House for fear of reprisals. So having been recognised by your government we were then told by the government to take it off and that hurt deeply. They recognised you on one part and then within the space of 60 minutes didn't want it to be known to anyone. And, apart from Anzac Days, that's the only time I've worn the medal. I don't use the initials after the name, except in one or two cases where I've written letters about the war to various newspapers. But I think that, more than anything, drove home to me the feelings that were there against the people that served in Vietnam. That you'd done your duty, but no one really wanted to recognise you for it. And not to acknowledge it.

I then went back into the heart of town to where the march was, because my fiancée was working in the Woolworths building at that time. You know, she was proud, but you couldn't go into the building with it on because of all the crowds that were out on the footpath. You had to take it in, in your pocket. And then when you get inside to show her friends, to pull it out of your pocket, you know. That's not a true way to treat anyone that's been presented with any form of medal, any decoration. That hurt. You know, it still does...

PHIL BAXTER, NATIONAL SERVICEMAN, 6RAR

The march was a triumph for many, but the pain wasn't over yet.

Most people old enough to remember the Vietnam War will remember the photograph – and the sharp intake of breath it caused the first time they saw it. A naked Vietnamese girl, screaming with pain from the hideous burns to her body, running down a road directly towards the camera. Behind her, the sky is dark with oily smoke. More than any other photograph, it became the defining image of the war.

It was June 1972. The fighting between the Communists and the forces of South Vietnam had reached new levels of intensity. Forty kilometres from Saigon, the village of Trang Bang had been captured by the NVA, and the ARVN was trying to get it back. The battle was in stalemate when the ARVN commander called in air support from the South Vietnamese Air Force. His soldiers, and the war correspondents and photographers tagging along with them, settled down to await the planes. The NVA had probably already gone, withdrawing as they always did, and it was more than likely that there were still villagers in the houses, but the air strikes were called in anyway. That was the way of this war.

Two Skyraider aircraft, leftovers from the Korean War, flew in at low altitude and began their runs. Explosive bombs first, then the incendiaries – a lethal mix of explosives, white phosphorus and napalm. Then they pulled up and away. There was no returning fire from the village. Just a wall of fire and the pungent petrol smell from the curtain of napalm that rose into the air.

Then they saw them. Terrified, wounded and burned villagers – running from the devastation towards the soldiers and press standing in the road. There was a woman clutching a baby who was clearly already dead and another small child with his skin peeling away. Then a young girl ran screaming; ripping off her burning clothes and screaming. Nick Ut, a Vietnamese photographer for Associated Press, turned his camera in her direction. '*Nong qua!*' she screamed. '*Nong qua!*' Too hot! Too hot! She reached him, moved on a few metres, and stopped. Ut and another reporter poured water from their canteens on her burns and Ut carried her to a minibus, rushing her to the hospital at Cu Chi. She lapsed into unconsciousness.

Her name was Phan Thi Kim Phuc and she was nine years old. At the hospital, wounded soldiers filled the wards and the corridors. No one had time for a small girl who was so obviously beyond hope. Nick Ut pleaded her case. He told the doctors he was a reporter, told them of his photograph, begged them to try – and they did.

Publication of Ut's photograph was delayed when an AP editor in New York rejected it. Nudity, particularly full-frontal nudity, was simply unacceptable in newspapers then. But other editors understood its value and the decision was overturned. The next day, every major news outlet in the world featured Kim Phuc.

In the hospital at Cu Chi, Kim remained close to death. Her chin was fused to her chest and her left arm almost destroyed completely. She stayed in hospital for 14 months and endured

17 operations. Finally, she was allowed to return home, just before the war ended.

Nick Ut was awarded the Pulitzer Prize for his photograph, but he did not see Kim again for many years. The Communist regime in Vietnam continued to use an unwilling Kim Phuc as a propaganda symbol until, on a return flight from Moscow to Saigon in 1992, she and her husband defected to Canada where they now live.

The photograph of nine-year-old Kim had an extraordinary impact. It seemed to affect people at some intuitive level, causing profound, almost primitive responses. It was a symbol somehow not just of this war but of all unnecessary suffering. It made debate about Communism or democracy, about rights or wrongs, irrelevant, and in some unmeasurable way added to the certainty that our part in this war had to end... and soon.

XI

WHY DON'T THEY JUST BLOODY LEAVE US ALONE?

I had a sense of, 'Whoops, we've lost it,' from the minute I arrived. The military machine that was operating there in '68, when I arrived again, it was in tatters. You can see when armies are no longer in a state of high morale, you look at weapons that are rusting and people that are running around smoking dope and people that are doing this and that. And just thinking, 'God, this is a gone goose.'... the conclusion that I'd come to, that we had been backing the wrong cause and we were doing it the wrong way, just seemed to be verified in my mind. You've only got to look at the way armies deploy, what state they wear their uniforms in, how they construct their bunkers, how their defences are set. There's ways of picking people, by the time all the sandbags are leaking and things are being left in disarray and rust, and nobody really seems to care very much...

To go to a large American base and find, for example, ghettos inside those bases with guys with a red bandana and the pink glasses and the long hair and smoking dope and basically a no-go zone, if you wanted to keep out of trouble. And that's getting pretty bad, that's getting pretty bad. You

> know when an army's got to that stage of disrepair. Just about everything was wrong with Vietnam...
>
> AUDIE MOLDRE

There is a type of so-called 'Asian' behaviour that we have been convinced of by movies and popular culture, the one they call 'face', as in – 'he did it to save face'. It's all about ruthlessly preserving self-respect and ego, such as being in a conflict and knowing you're wrong, but not being able to admit it because that would mean revealing that you've made a mistake. So, you do almost anything to avoid the inevitable embarrassment. In particular, you lie.

The image fits easily with our fantasy of 'the inscrutable East', the unknowable enigma. But it was never peculiar to Asian culture. We're all susceptible to wanting to maintain face. President Richard Nixon, like John Kennedy and LBJ before him, tried to save face over Vietnam long past any sustainable point. For a while he delivered clichés at every press conference – 'the end is in sight', 'there's light at the end of the tunnel'. After his critics began saying that the only light was coming from an onrushing train, Nixon changed his language from 'victory' to the watered-down, 'peace with honour'. But he was not willing to withdraw without some kind of win, even if all that could be salvaged was a secure non-Communist state in South Vietnam. Another strategy was devised.

It was as awkward in its language as it was doomed in its intention. 'Vietnamisation' was the name they concocted and it still looks ugly on the page. It was a fraud; a cover-up by which they could lower US casualties by progressively withdrawing their troops while continuing the war using South Vietnamese forces, supported by American bombers. It was time for the South Vietnamese to carry the burden of their own freedom, they said. There was no apology for the grievous insult it contained, the extraordinary gall with which it was presented.

Hundreds of thousands of South Vietnamese had already died in this war, their country lay in ruins and their culture was despoiled, but *now* they were to bear the brunt of the sacrifice? It was breathtakingly cynical.

Some military men, often those who had become closest to the South Vietnamese, believed it was possible, but only if they were given the right kind of support, from the right kind of people.

> The thing that has not often been spoken about is their stoicism. These were an enormously courageous people. When they went into battle they weren't uniformly good, nor were they uniformly bad. In some cases they fought magnificently. I think we had a view at the time: 'Don't you worry about this; we're here to do it for you.' It put to one side the fact that they'd been fighting a lot longer than the short time we were there... I sat with one chap who told me that in his lifetime, he was probably in his late fifties, he had seen *nine* occupying armies! Was he war-weary? My God, yes.
>
> You can't say that the North Vietnamese were a tremendously powerful, well-motivated, well-drilled force and that they had something which the southerners did not have. That's not true – not in the man-on-man sense. You didn't have a northern force that was brave and true and a southern force that was ready to cut and run at any point. If the southerners were well led, they would fight just as well. The best of their Special Forces had seen things that we could only imagine – regiment on regiment battles.
>
> ... I witnessed the virtual mutiny of one American group. Nixon announced the decision that the Green Berets would be taken out of Vietnam. The order given to them was, 'Remove your green berets and revert to Ranger patches and berets.' And I was sitting with a group of them... and they were ready to tell Nixon to stuff it, because they were prepared to fight and die with their Vietnamese brothers... and that's what the

> Vietnamese needed. If you were prepared to go and do things with them, live the same life, eat the same dust, those were the little ways you could make a difference. You can't make it with numerical strength.
>
> AUDIE MOLDRE

But no one was prepared to go that far. Or at least, no politician. The South Vietnamese were encouraged to wage war virtually on their own. In February 1971, 15 000 of them went into Laos on a mission to remove the Viet Cong bases located there. They walked into a trap sprung by five NVA divisions and, despite US air support, they were massacred. Nine thousand of them were killed or wounded, and men fell from the sky as they desperately tried to grab onto the skids of the evacuation helicopters. Nixon appeared on American television shortly afterwards to announce that, 'Vietnamisation has succeeded.'

Everybody was war-weary, everybody was demoralised. North Vietnamese troops were defecting to the South at the rate of 20 000 a year. South Vietnamese troops were deserting in huge numbers – 120 000 a year from an army of one million. And the Americans – well, General Creighton Abrams, the US commander, said at the time:

> I've got white shirts all over the place – psychologists, drug counsellors, detox specialists, rehab people... Is this a goddamned army or a mental hospital? Officers are afraid to lead their men into battle and the men won't follow. Jesus Christ! What happened?

Vietnamisation meant desertion by us and the Americans and the South Vietnamese knew it.

> I was asked to accompany an Australian captain from the Team as an interpreter, to check on the students we had

trained at the Jungle Warfare Training Centre ... there was a Vietnamese colonel, a regimental commander. There he was, surrounded by his five American counterparts, two full colonels and three half colonels, and three out of five of the Americans have got cigars in their mouths, and the Vietnamese colonel could speak more than adequate English but, because I was there, he was using me. My captain began by saying, 'Colonel, is there any way we can improve our training or further assist your particular unit?'

And this colonel just looked at me, because I'd given it to him in reasonably good Vietnamese, he just looked at me and said, 'You know the best thing you can do for us? See those blokes behind me?' He said, 'Get rid of every one of them!'

I turned and I said, 'The colonel feels that ... ah ... um ... the commitment of advisers to his unit is ... ah ... exceeds his requirements.'

Well, I could see this Vietnamese colonel, he's sitting there and he's got this smile on his face saying, 'This is going to be fun.'

And of course, five Americans lean over, cigars are being puffed furiously, and the question was, 'Why?'

And he said, 'Look. This mob are going to be gone, very soon. My son is a battalion commander. The only thing he knows at the moment is to advance to contact and when he encounters resistance, he calls in an air strike, or he withdraws and calls in artillery. When these blokes are gone ...' he said, 'My son is going to die, because he has no idea of how to move forward and engage.'

And I thought, 'That's it. That says it all.' You take away that technical support and what have you got? Even if they had left them all the fighter aircraft, even if they had left all the artillery pieces with them, it wouldn't have done the job. Infantry in the end must seize and hold ground.

AUDIE MOLDRE

I sat with them in the dining room of an RSL in Queensland. We'd gone there to get away from their menfolk for a while, to have a chat. Four women, all wives of Vietnam veterans. Actually no, more than that. All first and only wives. It's important to mention that fact because, apart from it being a badge of honour they wore proudly, it also meant that they were there when their boy-lover turned into a man and they were there when that man came home, a different person to the one who left. And they were still there, all these years later.

They were frank, unafraid and funny, their humour undercutting the occasional emotional outpouring. And they were mates, all of them, with the ease that comes from troubles shared and pretension scoured away. As I watched them tease and mock each other, remembering stories from the past with gales of laughter, I realised that I was actually talking with a group of Vietnam War veterans. They had not gone to Vietnam, they had not served in Nui Dat, or Vung Tau, or Saigon; they had not walked the weeds on patrol. Yet they were surely veterans of Vietnam and all its baggage, just as much as their husbands were. So, as the sky outside darkened and the cups of tea progressed to beers and a gin or two, they remembered that time.

They knew from their mothers what it was to wait for your man to come home from a war. They'd heard the stories and seen the faded Box Brownie photographs of the smiling face under the slouch hat that was their father. But their war, they maintained, was different to that of their parents. They had no sense of being part of something that was worthwhile, but rather, shame and sometimes fear dominated their lives. And they still resent it.

You weren't game to acknowledge that your husband was in the service. You never told anyone until you got to know them really, really well, because they'd look down on you, or cut you dead.

CAROLYN FITTON

The posties weren't delivering the mail to them, the ships weren't taking stuff over, a lot of things were going on. And my eldest son had just started school and the other kids were telling him that his father was going to be killed, that he wasn't coming home. And my lawnmower broke down, and it was the last straw, and I took it to this Italian that did lawnmower repairs. And I think because he was so isolated from all this and he said, 'What's the matter?'

And I just broke down. I said, 'My lawnmower won't start, one of the boys has just got over the measles, the other one's in trouble at school and my husband's in Vietnam!'

And when I got home that night I thought, 'My God, why did I go like that? And to the lawnmower man!'

But I just felt that he was away from it all – I mean, Australians were all doing it, my husband was spat on in uniform when we were in Adelaide. And then the army brought in that if they had to travel, they weren't to do it in uniform.

MARJORIE STEVENS

The army had a Father's Day luncheon, at the Wentworth Hotel, for the wives whose husbands were in Vietnam and when we arrived there, there was nothing on the noticeboard, it didn't say who we really were and we were told, 'Don't tell anybody that you're army wives and don't tell them where your husband is.'

MAUREEN PRICE

The wives and girlfriends suffered an almost complete lack of information. Not everyone had television sets and many of the women refused to watch them anyway, reasoning that if you didn't see the battle footage, you'd worry less. Newspaper reports were frustrating because of the paucity of information they carried. The women had no real sense of the world in which their men lived or the dangers they faced. Vietnam was to them, as it was to most Australians, a mystery of a country, far, far, away. Some faced the possibility of their husband's death head-on.

> Ross and I decided that if he was killed over in Vietnam, his body wasn't to come back. He would have been buried at Terendak Garrison in Malaysia or been cremated. Because you'd get notified that your husband had died and then it would be roughly about six weeks before the body came back to be buried so that grief was relived again. We lived at Ingleburn Camp and you'd go to the Infantry Centre to post your letters and there'd be a funeral and the word would get around that so-and-so was coming back. And to see the wives there, it was horrendous. And at home that night, you'd lie in bed and think about it.
>
> MARJORIE STEVENS

The regular army wives tended to live in the married quarters of the various bases. It threw them together and, in that, they found comfort.

> You stuck with the other wives. Your sanity, your wellbeing was with these other women. And all the wives worked in together and you looked after one another's kids and you were there to cry on one another's shoulders. If you had a bad day, you supported each other.
>
> MAUREEN PRICE

But the army was not known for its sensitivity towards the institution of marriage. Even more so when one of their men was lost.

> You only had six weeks to get out of the married quarters if your husband was killed. You had to be out. Six weeks and he's just been killed! They could have made it six months but, oh no, six weeks and you were out.
>
> CAROLYN FITTON

Living on the base and deliberately ignoring the TV kept them cocooned, but it couldn't completely protect them from the vindictiveness of some people. Cowardly attacks were made on the women by anonymous letter writers. Unable to get at the soldiers, they attempted to undermine the wives. It was a loathsome tactic and, inevitably, no one has ever admitted responsibility for it.

> I lived in a semi-circle in the married quarters where all the husbands were away in Vietnam and there were about six wives, and one of them, only a young lass, she got a poison-pen letter. She had a little boy and she hadn't heard from her husband for two or three weeks. And she received this letter that had his rank, his number, everything – a typewritten letter.
>
> 'While you're worrying about him, he's over here shacked up with a Vietnamese girl.'
>
> And she burst into tears, tore the letter up and came down to see me and I said to her, 'I know it's hard, Robyn, but we know it's not true.'
>
> 'Cos we'd had an officer come round and tell us, 'Your first impulse will be to destroy the letter, but keep them.'
>
> They reckoned it was the wharfies that were doing it and they wanted to keep all the letters as evidence. Eventually it just stopped, we didn't know why.
>
> MARJORIE STEVENS

Doubts, loneliness and misunderstandings all contributed to the difficulties they faced. All long-distance marriages are problematic, even more so in wartime, and as ever, some went searching for solace elsewhere.

> I had my youngest boy in '67 at Liverpool Hospital and it was amazing how many babies were born there and left there for adoption. There was this beautiful baby girl, older than a newborn, in the nursery and I said to the sister, 'What's the matter with her?'
>
> And she said, 'Her mother came in, in labour, and we had to take the baby in. We think she's an army wife from Holsworthy. We get quite a few.'
>
> MARJORIE STEVENS

Army bases are not exactly hotbeds of illicit sex and bed-hopping escapades, but like the society of which they are a part, they have their share. One of the more apocryphal tales is best described as 'the laundry detergent system'.

An army wife is alone and lonely. Perhaps her husband is serving in Vietnam, perhaps he's away on a course, perhaps he's training in Canungra. She would like some company, but discreetly.

So on the window shelf of her laundry, visible from the street, she places a box of the laundry detergent OMO. Her signal is thus run up the flagpole – OMO, meaning On My Own.

Then, one day, the husband returns, perhaps unexpectedly. Wishing to warn her lover that he should not come to the house, she hastens to the laundry and replaces the box of OMO with one of FAB.

And so the whole base now knows that the Fucking Arsehole's Back.

The moratorium march in May 1970 had left everyone involved in a bit of a daze. It had been so successful that it was hard to stop the elation. No one suspected then that that was as good as it would get. There was a conviction among the protesters that at last they had fully expressed their power and that from now on the government would be forced to listen to what the people *really* wanted.

But the caravan had moved on. The announcement in April 1970 of the first withdrawal of Australian troops produced a feeling among the general public that the war was all done and dusted. For a brief moment it was exciting, even fashionable, to march against the war but now other matters were claiming people's attention. Protest and dissension were heady weapons and the focus of complaint shifted to other concerns like women's liberation, pollution, abortion, censorship and the treatment of Aboriginal Australians.

The uneasy truce that had held together the various anti-war and anti-conscription groups was also fraying. Everyone wanted to hold another moratorium but how it should be conducted became a matter for increasingly bitter argument in the months after the first march. Some wanted to repeat the style and feeling of the first, but the more radical elements were determined to increase the level of provocation and cause a deliberate collision with the authorities. And, in a move that would be deeply resented by veterans for years afterwards, there was a campaign to openly support Hanoi and the National Front for the Liberation of South Vietnam. University students claimed to have gone as far as to raise money for medical supplies for the Viet Cong.

Arguments broke out at all the meetings held to plan the second march. The Maoists fought with the Trotskyists who were brawling with the Communists who could not agree with the anarchists . . . and so on forever. The gatherings became so confusing for anyone not familiar with the various ideologies that many left the peace movement and did not return.

By now the government had woken up to the publicity powers of the marches, but chose not to defend its policies on the war. Instead, it deflected attention by beginning a campaign of 'law and order', characterising the protesters as a threatening, lawless minority whose only wish was to destroy Australian society. Gorton accused them of 'challenging the verdict of the ballot box'. Conservative state governments took up the cause with enthusiasm, promising that their respective police forces would not allow the streets to be taken over by 'this unruly mob'. They were encouraged when there was a bad bout of violence between Victorian Police and demonstrators from La Trobe University. The batons came out and broken limbs were the result.

In the face of this, the various protest groups reached agreement and the second moratorium march went ahead in September 1970 and, while not as well attended as the first, it was still impressive – 100 000 marched across Australia. But this time it got ugly, particularly in Sydney, where I was marching.

It started when they wouldn't let us march on the roadway. We'd done it before, at the first moratorium but, for some reason, this time it wasn't on. No one seemed to know what was going on, not the march marshals or the police. It was a mess. We were moving like a wild river, without rhyme or reason, just flowing down whichever street we could, wherever there was no resistance from the police.

The noise was incredible: 'One . . . two . . . three . . . four . . . we don't want the Vietnam War! . . . Two . . . four . . . six . . . eight . . . stop it now, negotiate!' Office workers were hanging out their windows, watching the entertainment below. We gave it to them too. 'Out of the office and into the streets! Out of the office and into the streets!' Most stayed where they were.

In Wynyard Park we gathered to listen to the speeches, but you couldn't hear much. Then we moved outside the railway station. The police kept pushing people off the roadway and onto the footpaths, but there were too many bodies to fit. Something was going to happen, you could feel it.

I still don't know where they came from. The first I saw was a flying wedge of coppers, like a giant rugby scrum with a few at the front and the rest behind, stretched out like a triangle. They ran at us and somebody screamed and then we split into two groups, like a school of fish that's sighted a shark. The coppers broke apart and began viciously grabbing people – by the arm, the neck, the throat, anywhere they could get a hold. Behind them we could see a line of paddy wagons, back doors open, motors running. You had to hand it to them, they were well-organised.

A whistle blew and voices were yelling, 'To Town Hall! Sit down in the street! Now!' we turned and ran. Some dropped their banners, a couple of people fell over and friends helped them up. The people in front of us stopped suddenly and spread across the road. And then the rest of us saw them – a wall of police, two or three deep, stretched across the street.

It went quiet for a moment and then the police simply swept forwards. A plain-clothes copper in a hat kept indicating to the uniforms who they should grab, and scuffles and fights broke out as we fought back. People were getting hurt now. Two girls crouched protectively over a boy lying face down on the footpath, blood pooling under his hair. They were screaming abuse at the police and one of them had tears flowing unnoticed down her face. Another girl was grabbed and dragged towards the vans. Her friends went for her, pulling at the police who had hold of her, striking at their arms. More police joined in and threw them back into the crowd. A baton was raised and suddenly blood spattered across clothes. There was a murmur through the crowd, almost like a sigh, then everyone went for it, me included. I remember being kicked and throwing a punch and then not much else.

We were in court the next day, nearly 200 of us. Charges of obstruction, resisting arrest, abusive language, and a couple of malicious damage to property. Fines all round and we went to the pub for a drink. That was Sydney, September 1970.

Two months after the second moratorium, in November 1970, 8RAR returned to Australia, the first battalion to be withdrawn from Vietnam without being replaced. They marched through the streets of Brisbane and tens of thousands of people welcomed them home with ticker tape and applause. There were no protesters.

Prime Minister John Gorton, who always seemed to be warming the seat for someone else, finally self-destructed and voted himself out of office in March 1971, the only prime minister to ever do so. It was clear to him that he no longer had the support of his party. The conservatives were dazed and confused, but worse was to come.

The man who replaced Gorton had wanted the job so badly, and for so long, that his ambition came close to being embarrassing. Sadly, his greed for the power of the PM's office was matched only by his unsuitability. William 'Billy' McMahon was as unprepossessing a man as had ever led a country. Balding, he had feeble wisps of hair on either side of his head that gave him the permanent expression of a befuddled koala. He had ears like the open doors of a Volkswagen and a fluttering, high-pitched voice. The cartoonists loved him and the satire flowed, but that was all that did. Gough Whitlam, the leader of the opposition, must have been delighted.

At least McMahon kept the soldiers rolling out of Vietnam, announcing a second withdrawal, but it was like watching someone slowly bleeding to death and even the newspapers that had long supported the Australian presence in Vietnam began criticising the government for prolonging the pain. Bring them home, they told McMahon, all at once and do it soon.

Compared to America, events in Australia felt like a small sideshow. Huge demonstrations took place across the USA in April 1971, culminating in 500 000 people marching on the capital, Washington. Then a batch of secret documents concerning the conduct of the war was published by the *New York Times*. The documents became known as the Pentagon Papers and they sent America into public turmoil and angst, not only because of the information they revealed, but over the question of whether publication of secrets like these was a traitorous act during a war.

In Australia the focus was all on one tiny paragraph of the material. It disclosed that the South Vietnamese had not asked Australia for help, as Menzies had told us in 1965, but that Menzies had manufactured the offer. The media jumped on it, whipping up a frenzied froth of indignation, but the Australian public sighed, shook their heads over the perfidy of politicians and turned back to their own lives.

There was a tiredness in the public mind over Vietnam now, a weariness with the war and the increasing deceit and corruption that clung to it. Australians wanted it to end, as soon as possible. But, as has always been our way in this country, we left it to others to bring it about.

A third moratorium march was held in June 1971, and even though the numbers were respectable (50 000 in Melbourne), it felt like old history. The marchers were peaceful, the police almost benevolent and it petered out into the nostalgia of, 'You should have been at the first one. Now *that* was a demo!' The protesters were different too. Students dominated the numbers, allowing the government to dismiss them as irrelevant.

What action there was came from the anti-conscription movement. Anger over the unfairness of the system and the very nature of compulsory service had not abated, and the government helped it along in 1971 by confirming that conscription would continue after the war had ended. Then they amused everybody with farcical chase and capture escapades.

First, there was a publicity disaster when the Victorian government jailed 'the mothers'. In April 1971, five women from Save Our Sons were sent to Fairlea Women's Prison for 14 days. Their crime was to hand out anti-conscription leaflets to young men registering for national service. They were charged with wilful trespass and hauled off to jail – over the Easter holidays. The press loved it, describing them as 'married women with 25 children between them who will be without their mothers this Easter!'

> When I went to jail for daring to tell young men what their options were as far as conscription, in other words don't register or be a conscientious objector, and we were doing that during the registration period which meant you were breaching the law. Sent to jail with four other women, the 'Fairlea Five', bunged in just before Good Friday 1971. Terribly worried about the kids, particularly my youngest one, Christopher, who was at primary school. I shouldn't have worried. When I finally came out of jail after two weeks he came out to me very proud and he said, 'Oh, the kids said is that your old woman who was on the news!'
>
> And he was as happy as Larry. So there you go.
>
> JOAN COXSEDGE

They served 11 days with three days off for good behaviour.

Then law enforcement agencies and the draft resisters on the run from them began having fun playing complicated games of 'hide-and-seek'. The escapees from the draft would boldly announce where they would be and at what time, and right on the button the police would burst through the front doors only to see their prey disappearing out the back. The Attorney-General, Senator Ivor Greenwood, consented to appear on the ABC current affairs program *This Day Tonight* to debate the issue, only to be confronted with one of the more famous draft evaders, Michael Matteson. Greenwood was in the ABC's Canberra studios, Matteson in Sydney. The moment they were off air, Greenwood ordered the Commonwealth Police to nab Matteson but by then he'd already scarpered.

Matteson became a bit of a legend in the anti-conscription world. After the ABC debacle, the Commonwealth Police had another crack at him when two of them jumped into a car carrying Matteson and handcuffed themselves to the young man. Gotcha! The driver, thinking fast, drove the car into the grounds of Sydney University, jumped out and called for help. Students came running and surrounded the police while someone fetched a pair of bolt cutters. A few moments work and Matteson was free to escape again while the two abashed officers were summarily booed off the campus. It was seriously funny entertainment but the government could not see the joke, even though occasionally the police had a laugh.

> Eventually they put a warrant out for my arrest in order to appear before the court and one lived underground as it was called. It was all quite exciting and there were cars to spirit us away from demonstrations if the Special Branch looked as if they were moving on us and this was happening all over the country... I remember hitchhiking back from Sydney on a rainy day... and I got picked up by a young fellow not much older than me and we got talking and we got on well and I

started blabbing about all the safe houses there were and the network of succour that we draft resisters could depend on and then conversation lapsed and after a while to renew it I said, 'Oh, and what did you say it was you did again?'

And he said, 'Ah, I didn't say.'

I said, 'Well, what is it you do?'

And he said, 'I'm a Commonwealth Policeman, Alan.'

And I said, 'Ah.'

We drove on in silence for a bit and he could have taken me straight to the Canberra Watch House, it would have been his duty to do so but he didn't. He dropped me at the Queanbeyan turn-off and he said, 'Don't let us get you.'

And drove off into the night and I was rather grateful for that.

ALAN GOULD

The Past lies upon the Present like a giant's dead body.

NATHANIEL HAWTHORNE

The Vietnam years left their mark on a lot of people – bright flames for some, deep scars for others. And many of the feelings are as pervasive and strong today as they ever were. It's difficult to find other occurrences in Australian life where personal and social histories have combined to leave behind monumental grudges like those held by some veterans towards the protest movement during the war.

The worst thing I ever saw in my life, I saw Jim Cairns standing on the steps of Sydney Town Hall with his arm around a North Vietnamese delegation, in the middle of '71 it was.

There is Jim Cairns, the future deputy prime minister, with his arms around this North Vietnamese delegation at a time when we are still fighting them! They were killing us and we were killing them and here he is in Sydney town with his arms around the bastards, you know?

BERNIE MCGURGAN

The memories of many who participated in the protests over those years are that there was never any bad blood shown towards the men serving in Vietnam.

I think it's terribly important to understand that the anti-war people that I mixed with, and certainly the members of Save Our Sons, were never, ever opposed to the young men who went to the war. We felt that they were victims of the system and they weren't to blame at all, and that showed up later on because they were treated with absolute contempt by successive governments when they came back ill and they needed help and they didn't get it... I think they had a rotten deal during the war and afterwards and possibly they still are getting a rotten deal.

JOAN COXSEDGE

There were never any organised, formal protests against soldiers in Australia. On the contrary, welcome home parades were held for a number of battalions throughout the duration of Australia's presence in Vietnam. The parades attracted large, affectionate crowds and only an occasional, often lone, dissenter. But it seems that it was the personal that hurt; it only needed one person to attack their service for some veterans to get the sense that everyone thought like that, everyone looked at you like that.

I was spat at, called a 'baby-killer'... to treat us like that, with so much vengeance and hatred... it was just disgusting.

And to this day, I still don't like those people. They can go to buggery as far as I'm concerned. Purely because they treated a fellow Australian in that manner, which I would never do. We were going through our own problems, let alone the crap that they were throwing at us.

So no, I've never forgiven them, never forgotten them, and never will. They say now that we have apologised and we have given you welcome home marches and all that sort of stuff. No, so what? It's too hard... I shouldn't be like that, but I can't help it. That's the way I am, that's the way I feel.

ROBERT BELL, 1 AUSTRALIAN ARMY FIELD HOSPITAL

And occasionally, there has been a moment of clarity.

I know that in some places, and some instances, animosity and personal abuse and attacks were directed against military families, and I had an experience of that when I was talking on this subject in 1987 and an ex-nasho fellow had a yarn with me. My sense of it was that we always directed it against the politicians, in particular the Liberal Party, and to some extent against the personnel in the Department of Labour and National Service. When it got to demonstrations there was some conflict and sometimes it was provoked by us and sometimes it was provoked by the police... but it certainly happened as a way of transferring your animosity against the government to an enemy who was at least present and you could see.

[This] ex-nasho came up to me and he said,'Oh look, I respect your stand, Mr Gould, but I was a nasho and I went to Vietnam and when I came back my girlfriend took me to a party and as I was coming through the door they tipped offal on my head. What do you think about that?'

And I said, 'I'm disgusted and dismayed by it.'

He said, 'Yeah, but you can see my point, can't you?'

And I said yes, not quite seeing what his point was. It transpired that he had been under some kind of therapy for 15 years ... and I was dismayed by it, partly because when I looked back at the kind of person that I had been in that period, I couldn't be certain that I wouldn't have laughed along with everyone else to see this fellow spattered with blood and offal. So what I'm saying is that the times made us histrionic and they made us histrionic because of the nature of the war itself, the cruelty of it, the massive extension of it, and the increasingly vitriolic nature of the opposition to it and the kinds of things that we were called. So, in some sense, it was an ugly time because it made people on both sides of the fence more ugly people than they needed to have been.

ALAN GOULD

Perhaps the most illustrative example of the distance between the protesters and the veterans is an anonymous poem given to *The Sun* newspaper in Melbourne in 1970 at the height of the moratoriums. Apparently written as a group effort by a company of soldiers on an Australian base, it's sarcastically titled, *There Is No War in Vietnam.*

Take a man and put him alone,
Put him thousands of miles from home,
Empty his heart of all but blood,
Make him live in sweat and mud.

There is the life I have to live,
And why my soul to the devil I give;
You, please, boys, swing in your easy chair,
But you don't know what it is like over there.

You all have a ball without near trying,
While over there your boys are dying.
You burn your draft cards, march at dawn,

Plant your signs on the Parliament lawn.
You all want to burn the bomb,
There is no war in Vietnam.

Use your drugs and have your fun,
And then refuse to carry a gun.
There is nothing else for you to do,
And I'm supposed to die for you?

I'll hate you till the day I die,
You made me hear my best mate cry,
I saw his arm in a bloody shred,
I heard them say, 'This one's dead.'

There is no war in Vietnam.

The carnival was nearly over. Slowly, methodically, Australian troops were withdrawing from Vietnam. McMahon and his cabinet were conscious of army concerns about the speed of their departure (there was the same amount of work to secure the province but fewer soldiers to do it) and of keeping faith with the Americans. But the decision was taken out of their hands.

The old bogeyman of Communist China had become troublesome again. In 1971, it seemed likely that the United Nations would admit China as a member and it was clear that, as a state, it would soon become respectable. Even the Americans were making tentative gestures towards the Chinese on matters of trade. The Australian government dithered about, not wanting to seem to be too accepting of the old ideological enemy, but equally concerned not to lose lucrative wheat sales to the very same Red China.

Gough Whitlam moved quickly while McMahon vacillated. In July 1971, after announcing that any future Labor government would recognise the People's Republic, he led a delegation to Beijing. It was an extraordinarily brave decision for a leader of the opposition from uninfluential Australia at a time when no other Western leader had gone to China, and it made news around the world.

McMahon thought Whitlam had made a serious mistake and delivered a speech in which he said, 'I find it incredible that at a time when Australian soldiers are still engaged in Vietnam, the leader of the Labor Party is becoming a spokesman for those against whom we are fighting.'

Poor Billy. Not only had he not caught up with what everyone else already knew – that the Chinese were *not* behind the Vietnam War, but he was allowed to make a fool of himself by the Americans.

McMahon had told the American Embassy in Canberra he would be making the speech and they had given him no reason not to do so. What they neglected to tell him was that at the same time Whitlam was in Beijing, so was Henry Kissinger, the American Secretary of State, preparing the way for President Nixon to make a formal, historic visit. Four days after McMahon's speech Nixon announced that he would go to China with great fanfare. If the Americans had decided that China was now perfectly acceptable, then McMahon could hardly continue to complain about Whitlam doing the same thing. As happened so often during his prime ministership, McMahon appeared to be behind the main game, desperately playing catch-up to the big boys.

His cabinet now forced the issue of the Vietnam withdrawal. With China America's new best friend, they were clearly going to pull out of Vietnam sooner than anyone expected. Nervous about Australia remaining any longer than they had to, the cabinet convinced McMahon to act. In August 1971, he announced that all remaining Australian combat troops would be withdrawn from Vietnam by Christmas. Also, the time required for national service would be reduced from two years to 18 months. It would soon be over.

Australia sighed with relief and the anti-war movement was quick to claim credit for the decision. Even now, they still do. But while displays of domestic dissent like the moratoriums and the public opinion polls had made life uncomfortable for the government, the decision to finally withdraw was based on other political realities. We were leaving South Vietnam because the Americans were and all the long-held reasons for staying, like dominoes, Communist expansion and the need to support democracy in South Vietnam, were as nothing against that hard fact.

It was fortunate for McMahon's decision that the Australian force in Phuoc Tuy Province had succeeded in their task. He could claim they were leaving the province in good shape. The intent of the last two years of operations called 'pacification' and 'Vietnamisation' meant that they had brought guerrilla activity in the villages under control, maintained security for the local population, kept the VC from using the villages for refuge and food supplies, and were progressively handing over the responsibility for all this to local forces.

The two remaining battalions in 1ATF were good at their craft and had endlessly hunted the local guerrillas. The VC could barely operate and they moved around at great risk. The Australians owned the day and the night, and any attempt at operations by the enemy was likely to result in an Australian ambush or worse. Prevented from obtaining food from the village harvests, the VC were constantly hungry and their morale and physical condition were worsening. Provincial roads were opened to traffic, all the markets were busy and the VC were neither assassinating local officials nor extorting tax payments. It was so quiet that many in the Australian command thought it was a waste of time keeping 1ATF there.

The Australians were spending more and more time training the local soldiers in their tactical methods, taking them on combined operations, encouraging them to patrol as often as they did and, as a result, casualties dropped. During 1971, only eight Australian soldiers died in Vietnam.

But it was a transitory security, a veneer of peace. Certainly the VC were quieter, but their organisation was still intact and capable of regeneration the moment that circumstances improved. The Australian-trained local forces were, as always, underpaid, ill-equipped and lacking in any motivation to risk their lives for a government they so completely distrusted. 1ACAU projects continued but no hearts and minds would be won in Phuoc Tuy Province. Everyone knew the Australians were pulling out. Everyone knew what it would mean the moment that Nui Dat was surrendered back to the jungle. They would be back where they started and anyone thought to be sympathetic to the departed occupiers would be punished when the Communists inevitably returned.

> We knew the day that we were due to be pulled out. That was known ahead of time, or a rough date, but what really surprised us was that we weren't being replaced and we were all very, very disappointed about that because we knew the job wasn't done and we knew that when we left. We felt in a way that we were running away, that we were deserting the Vietnamese. We all felt that and we still talk about that today, that we walked away and left them and we didn't think that was right. Some political decision. The politicians had put us

> there and all of a sudden the politicians were chopping our legs from underneath us and pulling us out when the job wasn't done. We felt very, very bad about that.
>
> TONY EY

The Australians could do little about it. They couldn't even fight effectively any longer. As they approached their departure date, operations were scaled back – the thought of useless casualties occupied many a mind. But war is not an activity that can be carefully measured and apportioned, and men were placed in danger through unwillingness by their superiors to prosecute field actions fully. They were, in turn, answering to their political masters.

> In the final stages, in the command post at the task force, they were monitoring a battalion attack on a bunker complex and they had a direct line to Canberra and Canberra was saying, 'How many casualties have we taken?' And once the casualties got over a certain number they'd say, 'Call the action off.' Now you try telling that to a battalion commander in the middle of a bloody attack! You're going to do more damage than you are good. You scratch your head and you're thinking, 'Why don't they just bloody leave us alone!'
>
> ALAN CUNNINGHAM

It added to the frustration and anger that the soldiers were feeling. There was a job to complete they believed, a job they were good at and wanted to do, and now they were being prevented from doing it.

> I'll give you one example that will always haunt me. It was right towards the end when it was decided that operations would be scaled down, that we didn't want any more Australian casualties. Nine Battalion was up in the northwest of the

province on a feature that I think was called Slope 27. And they suffered quite heavy casualties... of course, the battalion was quite demoralised...

It's my understanding that it was a couple of days later that the forward company of 9 Battalion was still advancing along Slope 27 when, to the utter amazement and disbelief of the forward scout, there was a group of about 15 Viet Cong gathered, as a class, in front of a guy who was giving them a lecture on something or another. Here was this group, bunched together and this guy just said, 'Oh... yes!' And he called his machine gunner around to a position and even as he was talking to his platoon commander, 'Boss, you're not gonna believe this!'

The platoon commander said, 'Wait. Fifteen is too many by Australian standards for a platoon.'

Even though, these people, their weapons were down by their sides and they were grouped, they were bunched. He said, 'Wait.' And he spoke to the company commander, who must have been directed to report any large numbers to his battalion commander. So the whole thing went through and it came back down with the order to withdraw.

Now I just can't conceive – and this is so un-Australian to me. You've lost mates, you're there as a military force, you're there to kill the enemy, you have this cakewalk of an opportunity in your front and ultimately, for what I believe were political reasons, just in case one Australian was wounded in the subsequent attack, you leave it alone, you walk away from it. Why? Why bother even sending the battalion out on the operation if that is going to be the result?... The job wasn't back in Australia, the job was in Vietnam.

AUDIE MOLDRE

The countdown to the end occupied their last months. In the past, RTA – Return to Australia – had been a momentous day in a soldier's life. From the first day he arrived in Vietnam the count began – '365 and a wakey', meaning you had 365 days and one morning to go before you could go back home. Some men had calendars on which they crossed off each day; others made elaborate constructions that involved a *Playboy* centrefold divided up like a jigsaw puzzle. Each day another section of the naked body was revealed until in the last few days you reached 'home'. Now, though, everyone was leaving together.

In the end, the Australian Task Force left Vietnam in December 1971, with considerably less fanfare than when they had arrived. A large convoy of trucks carrying soldiers and materials roared out of Nui Dat headed for Vung Tau and the waiting HMAS *Sydney*. The town of Ba Ria was on their route and in a final undignified, insensitive moment, MPs took over the intersections in the town, physically manhandled Vietnamese out of the way and generally behaved like boorish occupiers. There was a lot of disappointment in the air that day. At Vung Tau Harbour, unwanted materials and vehicles were simply tipped into the water and no one really cared. It was done, it was over and, in exultation for some and shame for others, they were going home. Nui Dat was empty.

> It was eerie. I had been there back in 1966 when it was crowded with thousands of young soldiers with a purpose. Now there was no one. Just the empty husks of corrugated iron buildings, often half-stripped by local scavengers ratting for timber and iron. The weeds were coming back everywhere. It was a military ghost town.
>
> BRIGADIER IAN GEDDES, COMMANDER,
> AUSTRALIAN RESIDUAL FORCES, 1972

They left behind inevitable defeat for the forces they had trained and went home to a country that wanted to forget the war. For some of these men, that would mean years of restlessness and uncertainty, a future of disorientation and displacement from their own people. In a fictitious document, allegedly from the Department of Defence, some Australian soldiers produced 'a solemn warning' to friends and relatives of the behaviour they should expect from their returning soldier. It was typically grim, military humour.

> Show no alarm if he prefers to squat on his haunches rather than to sit on a chair, pad around the house in thongs and a towel; or if he slyly offers the postman cigarettes to buy, and picks at his food suspiciously as if you were trying to poison him. Don't be surprised if he answers all questions with, 'I hate this f... place!'... Be tolerant when he tries to buy everything at half the marked price, accuses the grocer of being a thief and refuses to enter an establishment that doesn't have steel mesh over the windows and bar girls.
>
> ... For the first few months (until he is housebroken), be especially watchful when he is in the company of women, particularly young and beautiful specimens... He will gaze in awe and fascination at blonde hair, blue eyes, clean sheets, hotels and tight sweaters. Remember that his only contact with white women has been via the centre pages of *Playboy* magazines and he probably thinks that all girls have staples in their stomachs. If you wish to disillusion him, do so gently.
>
> ... He will constantly look at the trees, not because he is particularly fond of trees, but because he suspects snipers.
>
> ... He should be a rational human being again in about a year. Try to make him feel important and occasionally boost his morale by whispering, '*Uc-dai-loi* number one'. Explain to him that miniskirts are respectable and that rain is sometimes necessary... Keep in mind that beneath this sunburnt and rugged exterior there beats a heart of pure gold. Treasure this,

> for it is the only thing of value left . . . Above all, humour him. The Viet Cong could not shatter his composure, but civilisation just might.

There was more truth there than perhaps they knew.

XII

IT WAS LIKE TURNING YOUR BACK ON YOUR BEST MATE AND WALKING AWAY

Kill 'em all and let God sort 'em out.

POPULAR US SERVICEMEN'S PHRASE

In February 1972, after the last Australian support troops had left Vietnam, there were around 70 members of the AATTV still remaining along with a protective platoon at the Australian Embassy. What had once been a force of over 8000 was now a token presence. Vietnam slipped off the front pages of our newspapers and was no longer a feature of the six o'clock news. It was like the end of a bad marriage – don't want to see you, don't even want to hear about you. But young Australian men continued to be conscripted and, from time to time, demonstrators took to city streets again, though it was more in hope than promise. No one was interested.

As the Americans continued to withdraw their soldiers, Hanoi tested their resolve. The peace talks between America and North Vietnam that had begun in Paris three years before had broken down yet again. Now it was the dry season in Vietnam; good timing for an offensive. The North Vietnamese Army crashed across the DMZ, probing the strength of South Vietnamese forces and the dwindling US support. The charade that the war had always been caused by a popular guerrilla uprising in the South was finally discarded. This was a full-on invasion by the NVA to conquer and capture the entire country. And for a while they succeeded, taking control of a sizeable amount of territory till the ARVN and US air support pushed them back.

Nixon ordered the US Navy to mine harbours in the North so supplies from the Russians couldn't get through, and the tactic worked. Most of the captured territory was regained. The troop withdrawals continued until all US combat soldiers had gone. Only air force personnel and support staff remained. It's a measure of just how overwhelming the US presence was that even this token force totalled 43 500 Americans, still in Vietnam.

A conservative Australian government had taken us into Vietnam and a conservative government pulled us out. Over the 10 years of our involvement in Vietnam, Australia had been governed by four of them – led by Menzies, Holt, Gorton and McMahon – and it had been downhill all the way. Now our participation in this divisive war was about to end, and it would definitely be with a whimper, not a bang. McMahon announced an election, to be held on 2 December 1972, and Whitlam responded with the first of the slogan-driven, commercial-heavy, froth, fizz and spin election campaigns that have bedevilled us ever since.

'It's Time' was the Labor Party campaign slogan and it seemed that most of us agreed with it. McMahon looked old-school, a part of the generation that was rapidly being left behind, while Whitlam gave every appearance of someone who actually lived in the second half of the 20th century. There was such a strong sense of inevitability about the coming conservative defeat that Whitlam began behaving like a PM-in-waiting.

Even so, the power and the passion surrounding the Labor Party victory in 1972 seems so strong in memory that it's a shock to look at the figures and realise that they only just won with 49.59 per cent of the vote. Clearly, a lot of Australians were still suspicious of them, even after 23 years of Liberal Party rule. But nothing could dampen the jubilation surrounding Whitlam's victory. Many Australians had a sense of finally winning the struggle, of at last being on the path to change, and that all of their work and long, hard hours on the outer had all been worth it.

> Reflecting back it was a period of incredible change politically and every other way. It sort of was a watershed time, I think. It was like an unleashing of a huge amount of energy that had been held back during the Cold War period of the '50s and the early '60s and, all of a sudden, this huge energy came out and it manifested itself in the anti-war movement. But it didn't even stop there, really, because all of that channelled Whitlam into becoming elected in 1972 and that encouraged him to produce policies that in a way supported more independence... And it was the forerunner, or, if you like, the mother of feminism. That came out of it. The anti-nuclear movement, the environmental movement. All of these movements were directly born, I think, from that huge channelling of energy during that period and some of us kept going and are still going. Some didn't, some dropped off and went back and still talk nostalgically about that period as if it was the best time in their lives. But others just kept plugging away...
>
> JOAN COXSEDGE

The feelings of optimism and confidence after that election were so strong and seductive that they laid impossible expectations on Whitlam's government, expectations it could never have fulfilled, no matter what talents it contained.

They did though start as they would finish – in a blaze of activity and publicity. When it became clear that he had won, Whitlam, intoxicated with reaching the summit and impatient to begin after all those years in the foothills, instituted a two-man ministry of himself and his deputy, Lance Barnard, while he waited for the final election results. Within their first few days of taking office they put into play their list of promises:

- An immediate end to conscription and any planned action against evaders.
- National servicemen could leave the army or the Citizen Military Forces immediately should they choose to do so.
- All prosecution actions for evasion of the draft were dropped and the seven men in prison for evasion were immediately released. (Interestingly, the freedom for the government to re-introduce conscription was not removed from the legislative books and is still there today.)
- All members of the AATTV were to leave Vietnam immediately and only the embassy guard would be left in Saigon.

This was the style of the Whitlam government, the one that came to be known as 'crash through or crash'. Like the child who's waited all week for their birthday party, they ate all the cake and unwrapped all the presents . . . then paid for it the next day as they lay groaning. Those first dramatic decisions divided the country. The anti-war movement and the opponents of conscription were elated and they were joined in spirit by all those who considered the changes to be long past time. But many of the fifty-odd thousand who had served in Vietnam, and others who believed that we had deserted our responsibilities, felt it was a time of dishonour and disgrace.

On the other side of the world, Richard Nixon had gone to the American people trumpeting that 'peace was at hand' in Vietnam and that he was the man to deliver the nation from the pain of the war. But the Paris peace talks had collapsed in a messy heap. The President of South Vietnam, Nguyen Van Thieu, believing he had been betrayed, refused to accept the agreement worked out by the US and North Vietnam and the Hanoi delegation took their ball and went home. President Nixon decided to bomb them back to the table.

Operation Linebacker, it was called. An ironic name given that it means a defensive player in American football and there was nothing defensive about this onslaught. Over 12 days there were 729 B-52 sorties over Vietnam and about a 1000 by fighter bombers; 20 370 tons of bombs hurtled down, more than they'd dropped in the last three years; 26 planes were lost and 93 airmen killed, captured or missing. Over 2000 Vietnamese were killed. And it all took place while much of the world celebrated Christmas.

Despite the intent of the bombing raids to strike military and industrial targets, and despite the fact that, for the most part, that is exactly what the bombers hit, the outrage and condemnation around the world was loud, long and immediate. Whitlam joined in, sending a personal letter of protest to Nixon. This was quite a departure from 'all the way' with the USA and Nixon was furious. Some of Whitlam's ministers, especially Jim Cairns, let rip with a few unguarded lines, calling the bombing 'the most brutal, undiscriminating slaughter of defenceless men, women and children in living memory'.

Diplomatic relations between Australia and the US went into a cold snap and for a while both sides were frosty with each other. It was all 'full of sound and fury, signifying nothing' really, except for Whitlam wanting to show that he was a different proposition to his predecessors. When the bombing stopped, so did the chest-beating.

In January 1973, the Governor-General of Australia, Sir Paul Hasluck, formally declared the cessation of hostilities between Australia and Vietnam. The Communists had returned to the negotiating table and, at last, the Paris Peace Accords were announced, bringing to an end the longest peace talks in history, from 1968 to 1973. Virtually the entire agreement was exactly as it had been before the Christmas bombing. The USA got their POWs back, President Thieu remained President of South Vietnam (for the moment at least), and the NVA were allowed to leave some of their troops in the South as part of the cease-fire. This produced a strange situation in which there were bases dotted throughout South Vietnam flying the VC flag. The strangest one of all was a small group of NVA soldiers stationed at Tan Son Nhut Airport in the heart of Saigon.

Now the agreement was in place, Whitlam wanted to open diplomatic relations with North Vietnam. But he had a problem. Both Saigon and Hanoi claimed to be the legitimate government of all Vietnam and Whitlam had to be careful not to apparently choose one over the other. In the end he recognised the Democratic Republic of Vietnam in respect of the North, and the Republic of Vietnam with respect to the South. It was no more than weasel words in diplomatic language; a bandaid stuck over a wound that everyone knew could not heal.

In March 1973, the last American troops left Vietnam, and only a few advisers and protective companies of marines remained. The South Vietnamese faced off against the North, alone. Nixon attempted to reassure Thieu that support would always be available, writing, 'we will respond with full force should the settlement be violated by North Vietnam', but that was to prove as durable a promise as Nixon's hold on office.

Watergate was the name of the scandal that brought Richard Nixon down. A screw-up of a burglary at the Watergate Hotel in Washington DC by members of the Nixon administration opened up a cesspool of lies, criminal acts and cover-ups that eventually seeped under the door of the Oval Office and forced Nixon to resign in August 1974. The entire grubby episode intensified the growing public and media cynicism about politics and politicians, casting the conduct of the Vietnam War into an even more unfavourable light.

Congress, war-weary and distrustful of Nixon's motives, had already begun to reduce aid to South Vietnam as the Watergate disaster gathered momentum. What had been billions was reduced to millions, and when Nixon waved a hearty goodbye and climbed into his helicopter and permanent disgrace, Vietnam lost its last defender.

America had turned South Vietnam into an aid junkie and the withdrawal of money caused a short, sharp spiral into chaos. The economy whirled out of control, inflation skyrocketed and, in the cities, mass unemployment reduced millions of Vietnamese to a meagre existence. In the street of bars, the girls were left to offer their charms to empty chairs.

The South Vietnamese military felt the loss of aid like a hammer blow. They were short of equipment, short of ammunition, and short of faith in their one-time protector. They'd been force-fed a diet of the latest military technology and unlimited air support, but the fleets of helicopters, the fighter planes and the B-52s were gone. Even the machinery and weaponry they did have were rapidly rendered useless by an inept, Kafka-like bureaucracy that lost critical spare parts or kept them hidden behind mounds of red tape; an almost non-existent training program that meant nobody knew how to maintain the equipment, assuming they could get the parts; and a lack of discipline and planning that literally left the tools of war rusting in the rain.

Much of the leadership of the combat units was either inadequate or corrupt. Even in the face of imminent destruction, the same old games of nepotism and influence were being played and generals kept on installing dangerously inexperienced officers into command positions, leaving their soldiers vulnerable, rudderless and dismayed. Some ARVN officers even sold food and war matériel to the enemy, and it was common knowledge in the coffee shops and bars that every part of the military and the government had been infiltrated by VC agents. Military planning and operations were conducted under a constant air of suspicion, disgust and apathy.

The soldiers of South Vietnam saw no reason to die; they had nothing to die for. It had been stolen from them by a criminal line-up of crooked, self-serving leaders and an American protector who was ultimately unprepared to make the sacrifice it was now demanding of the Vietnamese. Most of the soldiers of the ARVN were without a purpose, without a reason to fight, except for self-preservation.

Both sides ignored the cease-fire demand of the Peace Accords and broke it almost immediately, but Hanoi needed to rebuild their army. The Chinese and the Russians were both keen to help – more than a billion dollars a year in military aid poured in until, for the first time in the war, the NVA had military superiority. The first few divisions were sent over the DMZ in a probing action to see whether the US would re-enter the war. But the new president, Gerald Ford, the Congress and the American people had had enough. There were no bombing raids, no retaliation of any kind. South Vietnam lay there passive, ready for the taking.

In January 1975, North Vietnam began the last, major offensive of the war. This was not a people's revolutionary war, as Ho Chi Minh had always prophesied and desired. This was an onslaught by a powerful army using heavy, conventional weapons; a disciplined infantry force against a weak, ill-equipped opponent. There was only ever one possible end.

It was an ignominious rout. By the end of March, almost all South Vietnamese resistance had collapsed. A third of its soldiers were either dead or missing and half its weaponry had gone.

The NVA had control of more than eight million people and 12 provinces and, while the rest of the world waited in dull resignation, the country that had been South Vietnam contracted into the city that was Saigon and waited for the last act in their 40-year long tragedy.

A million stories of death, oppression and escape were about to unfold.

We knew one day we would be overrun – but we did not know what day. Many felt that it would happen in 1973, after the signing of the Paris Peace Accords, so we had some luck that it lasted till 1975.

We were in heavy fighting at Duc Duc and I was medical officer for the regiment. I was in a hospital about three kilometres from the battle. We would get about 30 or so wounded every day, some very bad, some with malaria. There was shelling everywhere. There was a small hill and we got a bulldozer and dug so we could work inside the hill but we had to leave the ambulances outside and the shells hit the ambulances. We treated North Vietnamese soldiers too; we kept them alive because the Second Bureau [intelligence] wanted them. But we treated everyone equally. We had a motto on our insignia and it said, 'Forget yourself, save people'.

Just before the end, the rumours started. That if a girl had gone with the Americans she would have her nails pulled out and her fingers cut off. They were so scared, so scared. We all said we don't know what our future will be with the Communists.

VAN NHUNG TRAN

At the end of the war, only five generals suicided, because they lost the country. But the rest just ran, like rats. And went to enjoy a new life, forget everything. If they had stayed home, even with our lack of ammo and American aid money, we could have survived at least for three or four years and motivated the people to stand up. Before, when we did not have any American money, we could fight against the Chinese, we could fight against the Japanese, we could fight against the French. Why now did we have to run?

President Thieu gave the order to withdraw all the troops and everybody was just exhausted and didn't know what to do or where to go, the whole country was in boiling water, so people just tried to escape, you see.

It was carnage, no laws, no regulations, no order, nothing. And everybody trying to run. Discipline had begun to break down a few months before the fall. You saw officers trying to grab the backs of Americans, trying to flee the country. They sent their wives and kids – they were already gone. The spirit of the fighting was very low. But only the low-ranking officers were to die – the top ranks fled.

COLONEL VO DAI TON

We knew it was the end after Pleiku. We just did not have any petrol. The soldiers had no grenades, no bullets. I had my wife and four boys return to Saigon in a C-130 and, if I had not been shot down, we would have escaped then. I was shot down a week later on 27 March 1975. Da Nang. My last flight.

The general arrived at Da Nang air base and said that everybody had to leave and not fight the enemy. I thought it was crazy, Da Nang could be held. But we had no petrol, no weapons. I thought that if Da Nang was lost, we would lose the whole South. I was in my squadron's quarters and the enemy shells started to fall on the air base. We were ordered to fly the helicopters to the beach . . . the marine corps who were there wanted to keep us so they could use us to escape out to the American ships. But eventually they released us and we intended to fly to Saigon step by step, looking for fuel on the way.

There was storm and rain all the way and at Chu Lai the NVA shot at my chopper and the other pilot was wounded. I was carrying officers and their families. There were about 28 men, women and children in my aircraft. The weather was getting worse so I had to land and wait till about five o'clock, till it improved.

We took off, but the NVA saw us and shot us again, shot us down. They shot the tail rotor away, it was very dangerous, we had to land. Then an officer, the squadron's chief of operations, shot himself inside my helicopter, suicided. I am a Catholic, I could never do this, but in the province he came from, it was terrible, they had killed all his people and he believed he would die anyway.

The women, all the people behind me, they were screaming. At the time I did not know what he had done, I was concentrating on flying the chopper. There was a rice field and I managed to get it down. Everybody was screaming and trying to get out. The NVA began firing at us and we all started to run. I didn't see the others; they had gone in a different direction.

I ran about 500 metres away and jumped into a bomb crater, water up to my neck. I waited about 10 minutes and couldn't hear anyone following me so I climbed out and went into the woods. I had dog tags, I had $10 000 inside my uniform, photos of my wife and children and a knife. I buried them all except the knife and I hung the dog tags in a tree above them because I thought one day I will return there and collect them. I guess they're still there. That was my last flight. It was horrible.

I stayed in the jungle until nearly sunset and then I went out and stopped a villager. She was very scared and wouldn't talk to me, 'You are military. The VC are coming!'

And she ran away but the next one, a man on a bicycle, he stopped.

'Okay, I have a son like you. I don't know where he is. I see you and I miss my son. Here, have a drink.'

But while I was talking to him, the NVA grabbed me from behind, AK in the back. They said, 'Are you the pilot of that aircraft?'

And I said, 'No. I'm just a foot soldier. I just followed it when it crashed.'

But the cadre, he kept the rifle at my head and said, 'You are the pilot. You are very cunning. You want to continue to fight us!'

I thought he would shoot me but I was calm and peaceful, I don't know why. He kept on at me but I had no weapons except the knife and he took that away.

They took me to a village but everything was confused and I managed to escape. I tried to get to the beach to get a boat but the beach was already occupied and I was arrested again. Many, many people were now captured and I knew it was all right now; they were not going to shoot me.

VO MINH CUONG

The South Vietnamese Army did resist for a time and many battalions fought bravely and well. But any chance of real opposition to the invasion from the North was destroyed when, in March 1975, President Thieu inexplicably ordered his best divisions to desert the front line and return to protect Saigon.

Their withdrawal degenerated into an out of control panic and the last knot of defiance was untied. By early April, 17 NVA divisions had closed in, choking off all land routes into and out of Saigon.

Now the true madness began. Anyone with enough money got themselves or their families out through a clandestine operation they called 'the black line'. They could be seen at any airport that was still functioning – long lines of well-dressed Vietnamese scurrying aboard waiting aircraft as their furniture and treasures were loaded in the hold. Strangely, the two most common possessions they could not bear to leave behind were electric fans and caged songbirds. Those without the necessary cash, and that was most people, became refugees on the road to Saigon.

An entire country was falling but somehow the world's attention became focused on the plight of a couple of thousand orphaned babies. Perhaps they tweaked the slumbering conscience of the West, or perhaps they were an easier target for assistance than adult refugees; whatever the reason, their story was taken up by media everywhere and pressure mounted on governments to help them.

Whitlam thrashed about in indecision for a while then gave the order on 2 April for the RAAF to render assistance in what became known as Operation Babylift. It began tragically on 4 April when an American C-5A Galaxy jet, the biggest transport plane in the world at the time, took off from Saigon with 243 orphans on board. The older children lay in cargo nets and the babies were in rows, nestled into cardboard boxes along the floor of the plane, watched over by volunteer carers and servicemen and women. Thirty minutes into the flight the plane encountered serious mechanical failure and turned back to Tan Son Nhut Airport and safety. As it approached the runway, the crew lost the last control they had and the plane plunged down, skimmed off the Saigon River and ploughed into the rice paddies that bordered the airport. Two hundred souls perished that day, 143 of them children.

The flights continued. Around 2000 children were evacuated to America and about 1600 to Europe, Canada and Australia. Once it became known in Australia that the babies were coming, there was an astonishing rush to adopt them. In New South Wales alone, where just 14 babies would be settled, the government received 4000 requests for adoption applications. Some people protested what they saw as a wrong decision to rip the children from their own culture and consign them to an uncertain future in an alien land; others considered them to be the lucky ones.

Saigon was now virtually surrounded and what had been a reasonably ordered exodus of people became an insane scramble for a place on a plane. The Americans were flying Vietnamese out in their thousands, mostly those to whom they owed refuge or who had bought their ticket through suspect means, like CIA collaborators and senior members of the South Vietnamese Secret Police. As they were hurried by armed marines onto the planes at Tan Son Nhut, they passed the government memorial that was dedicated, 'To Our Noble Allies... Their Sacrifice Will Never Be Forgotten'.

Some departures were embarrassingly public. On 21 April 1975, President Thieu appeared on television in Saigon to say his goodbyes to South Vietnam. He denounced President Ford, Henry Kissinger, Congress, and basically anyone who was American for their failure to support him and his country. Openly crying, he ended without a hint of irony, with these words: 'I depart today. I ask my countrymen, the armed forces and religious groups to forgive my past mistakes I made while in power. The country and I will be grateful to you. I am undeserving. I am resigning, but I am not deserting.'

Under the protection of the CIA, he flew to Taiwan, then settled in London and eventually died in America in 2001. The legend persists that his plane to freedom was weighed down with gold.

If Thieu lived up to the shoddy tradition of departing despots, the American Ambassador to South Vietnam, Graham Martin, travelled a different road. Until circumstances forced him to, he refused to even contemplate evacuation and emphatically gave his word to the Vietnamese people that he would not 'run away in the middle of the night'. He was a strange figure in those last desperate days, grey with exhaustion, arguing with Kissinger in Washington that he should stay in Saigon, chain-smoking and ill with pneumonia, still in grief over the loss of his soldier son in the war. But in the end, he too, would have to go.

Saigon was a doomed city teetering on the edge and Westerners were now at risk from marauding gangs of retreating ARVN soldiers wandering the streets, armed and angry. It was time for the last Australians to leave. Geoffrey Price, our ambassador, had requested that all his Vietnamese staff and their immediate relatives, along with other Vietnamese who could be included legally, be flown to safety in Australia. But Whitlam agreed to give 'temporary residence' only to the immediate families of 'non-official' Australians, Vietnamese students currently in Australia and Vietnamese who had worked for the embassy and could prove their lives to be in danger when the North Vietnamese took over. He told parliament just 600 people would qualify. Price fought hard against the decision but Whitlam overruled him.

The Australian government's decision appeared to many people to be insensitive and cruel, owing more to their sympathy for Hanoi than any real concern for the trapped Vietnamese. Malcolm Fraser, the new leader of the opposition, attacked Whitlam's response as 'inadequate and inhumane'. But the flights began and, even though over 3500 adult Vietnamese applied to come, only 342 were approved and a pitiful 76 of them ultimately escaped. It was a shameful end. Hundreds of Vietnamese who had given their loyalty and trust to Australia were abandoned as peremptorily as the furniture in the embassy waiting room. As Fraser said, 'One can only hope that the North Vietnamese troops who are now overrunning the country show more compassion than the Whitlam government.'

Whitlam dropped his government further in the muck when two diplomatic cables were leaked, one of which he'd sent to Saigon and the other to Hanoi, in early April 1975. The cables showed a clear partiality and favour towards the Communists and implied a cavalier disregard for the plight of those in the South. The subsequent public outrage added to the electorate's growing unhappiness with the government and by the end of the year, like Saigon, it too, would fall.

And so, on Anzac Day 1975, the last official Australian presence in South Vietnam was removed. We left pretty much as we'd arrived, in disarray and public division, keeping true to the end to the miserably deceitful nature of the Vietnam War. It was entirely appropriate that a Labor politician should tell a newspaper columnist at the time, 'Australia lied its way into Vietnam and was now lying its way out.'

FLASH

DE WTE #2378 1190107

Z 290101Z APR 75

FM THE WHITE HOUSE

TO AMEMBASSY SAIGON

SENSITIVE VIA MARTIN CHANNELS WH50782

TO: AMBASSADOR GRAHAM MARTIN

FROM: HENRY A. KISSINGER

1. THE PRESIDENT HAS MET WITH THE NATIONAL SECURITY COUNCIL AND HAS MADE THE FOLLOWING DECISIONS:

A. IF THE AIRPORT IS OPEN FOR FIXED-WING OPERATIONS TODAY, YOU ARE TO CONTINUE THE EVACUATION OF HIGH RISK VIETNAMESE BY FIXED-WING AIRCRAFT. YOU ARE ALSO TO EVACUATE BY THE END OF THE DAY ALL AMERICAN PERSONNEL AT TAN SON NHUT AS WELL AS ALL BUT BARE MINIMUM PERSONNEL FROM THE EMBASSY.

B. WHILE YOU SHOULD NOT SAY SO, THIS WILL BE THE LAST REPEAT LAST DAY OF FIXED-WING EVACUATION FROM TAN SON NHUT.

C. IF THE AIRPORT IF UNUSABLE FOR FIXED-WING AIRCRAFT OR BECOMES SO DURING THE DAY AS A RESULT OF ENEMY FIRE, YOU ARE IMMEDIATELY TO RESORT TO HELICOPTER EVACUATION OF ALL REPEAT ALL AMERICANS, BOTH FROM THE DAO COMPOUND AND FROM THE EMBASSY COMPOUND. FIGHTER CAP AND SUPPRESSIVE FIRE WILL BE USED AS NECESSARY IN THE EVENT OF HELICOPTER EVACUATION.

WARM REGARDS
0200

They'd been planning it for months, the final evacuation from Saigon. With that dubious talent the American military have for making everything sound like a movie, they dubbed it Operation Frequent Wind and the trigger that would set it off was the announcement on Armed Forces Radio that 'the temperature in Saigon is 105 degrees and rising', followed by Bing Crosby singing 'I'm Dreaming of a White Christmas'. That would set them running.

As it turned out, the evacuation was hurried on them a little quicker than they had anticipated. The NVA struck without warning on 29 April 1975, shelling Tan Son Nhut Airport and killing two marines on guard, the last American soldiers to die in Vietnam, so the evacuation was immediately shifted to the defence attaché's compound and the embassy. They would have to get out by chopper.

Those last two days of the Vietnam War forced many Americans (and others) to experience the bitter taste of their failure at a personal level. There were the Vietnamese faces pressed hard into the bars of the locked US Embassy gates, waving the worthless paper promises given to them by American employers and friends, begging someone . . . anyone, to recognise them, to rescue them. There were the babies thrown over the barbed wire of the embassy, in the hope that mercy and compassion would save them, there were suicides and murders, there was looting and the insane euphoria that can strike when despair passes into resignation. And over it all hung the stench of betrayal, real and imaginary.

Inside the embassy they were burning money, four million dollars worth. They were shredding reams of paper, lists of names, secret files, records of spies, collaborators and assassins; they were trashing their offices in a last futile gesture of defiance and destruction. And all the while the tanks got closer.

Seven and a half thousand people were evacuated that day, an astonishing figure. They were taken out on overloaded choppers flown with consummate skill by young marine pilots, and as each helicopter lifted up from the island rooftops they sucked up the charred dollar bills and the shredded paper into sad little ticker-tape whirlwinds of loss and regret. They flew directly to the US Navy ships waiting out to sea and as each one disgorged its load, it rose wearily back up and returned to the dying city.

The ships were a magnet for anyone attempting to escape. South Vietnamese Air Force pilots commandeered their own helicopters and flew them out to sea, dropping the aircraft like wounded dragonflies onto the steel decks. But they took up too much space, endangering the incoming embassy flights, so over the side they went, millions of dollars of Iroquois helicopters pushed into the welcoming embrace of the South China Sea. The fleeing pilots became desperate and deliberately ditched their craft into the ocean next to the ships, some jumping from their helicopters at the last moment, narrowly escaping decapitation as the blades sliced into the waves. And all through the night, it continued.

APR.29.75.162+
XXKK.ONE
S E C R E T
523–119-FYI (OT25) FREQUENT WIND ©
REPORTS ARE THAT THERE ARE 200 AMERICANS LEFT TO EVAC. GUNNER SIX TO GSF COMMANDER BRING UP PERSONNEL UP THRU THE BUILDING DO NOT LET THEM (THE SOUTH VIETS) FOLLOW TOO CLOSELY. USE MACE IF NECESSARY BUT DO NOT FIRE ON THEM.

At 2.30 a.m. on 30 April 1975, Henry Kissinger phoned Graham Martin and told him to end the evacuation. The ambassador took a last walk up the stairs to the roof carrying an attaché case, a suit bag and the neatly folded Stars and Stripes. As he flew out to an aircraft carrier, below him lay the twinkling diamonds of the headlights of the NVA trucks, waiting patiently to enter Saigon. Twelve marines were the last to leave the embassy building, throwing cans of tear gas down the stairwell to hold back the remaining, desperate crowd.

Along the wide boulevard of Tu Do Street, the NVA tanks clattered past groups of South Vietnamese, quietly watching and waiting. They drove over pile after pile of discarded ARVN uniforms, boots and all, thrown away by deserting soldiers anxious to avoid detection. Two tanks approached the ornate gates of the Presidential Palace, locked against them. They paused for a moment, perhaps aiming their vehicles, then Tank 843 crashed through, coming to rest on the front lawn.

Finally, it was done.

In Australia, we watched it happen on our new colour television sets and for most of us it was another day of bad news from somewhere else. If we felt anything at all it was relief that the damn thing was over at last and we probably said something just like that in conversation the next day. But there were other Australians sitting in their lounge rooms who had other memories.

> I felt bloody shitty actually. For the simple reason it very simply wasn't finished the way it should have been. I'm not saying we should have won. That would have been preferable of course to losing, but the way it was done was a heap of shit because we left many, many good South Vietnamese people in the lurch and it was like turning your back on your best mate and walking away. It shouldn't have happened. That is politics though. That's rough shit. Nothing to do with us, but it left a very nasty, dirty taste in a lot of people's mouths. It still does.
>
> ANTHONY HUGHES

> I felt I was there. Part of me wished to actually see it – but that would have been stupid. It was disappointment, but the end of a chapter – 'It's all over, red rover'... I was thinking of the Vietnamese, all the ones who gave us true and loyal service, who reciprocated, with whom we were engaged in a common cause. All of those people who perhaps we might have been able to get out of the province and eventually back to Australia. The ones that stayed behind – I mean it still hurts to hear how long some of them were put into the reform labour camps – 10 years. No one stayed in the Hanoi Hilton that long. Certainly a lot of them would have suffered mightily.
>
> AUDIE MOLDRE

The world waited for the bloodshed that had been threatened, the taking of vengeance by the North Vietnamese, the inevitable executions. But the new Vietnam was to punish some perceived wrongdoers in a far more insidious fashion than by using a merciful bullet.

Eventually I was taken away with 70 other men. We walked for one week into the jungle, tied with Claymore mine cable. There were three or four others from my unit, they were very scared. I don't know why, but I wasn't. They were walking us up towards the Ho Chi Minh Trail. I spent the next four months there. A thousand of us were there and many died, 40 from the 70 I came with. They did not give us rice, nothing, only cassava. They beat us one by one. They took away all our clothes and shackled our feet, chained us to each other and we had to stay that way for 35 days. The toilet was where you lay.

Finally, they took us to the jungle, to grow cassava, some call it manioc. It was all we had to eat, it was terrible. I was four months there and then they transferred me to a bigger camp on the plateau, no mosquitoes. We cleared the jungle and grew rice until 1979, the war with China. Because we were near to the border, they moved us then to Pleiku.

Eventually I was allowed to see my wife once a month, for 15 minutes. She would bring me some food, some medicine. I had to make at least 60 confessions, day after day. They kept saying, 'No! These are lies!'

I told them some things. I said that I went to America. But I never told them the whole truth, my whole life. I was there until 1981. Six years. They sent me to learn how to become a carpenter. And at least, when you went out of the camp, you could find some fruit and eat it. Inside there was nothing.

Gradually I became the leader of that carpentry shop, the head carpenter of 80 other detainees.

VO MINH CUONG

We got a message that all ARVN officers had to go to the schoolhouse with enough food for 10 days. At the time my wife was pregnant, she cried. She did not think that I would come back. I tried to tell her that I would stay alive, that I would come back. I thought I would come back, I didn't shoot any people, I just worked as a doctor.

They kept us at the school for three days and then they said, 'Tonight, everybody should be ready.'

And we were worried, we didn't know. And the whole school was very quiet, only the wind and the sound of the leaf falling, because no one could talk. And we saw 20 trucks come in, very well-covered. Each one had a driver and a guard with an AK ready. And they said, 'Go in. Go in.' And they drove round and round from 10 o'clock at night till four in the morning and we didn't know where we went. We couldn't see outside.

In the morning, we came to a former camp of the South Vietnamese Army, the engineers. And we entered the gate and some of us recognised it. We were told to clean it up and build our houses, our toilets. We had to cut the trees, the bamboo, and we made something like a barracks. There were about 200 of us, all captains. We were given a little rice, a few vegetables, a very small piece of fish. Never enough food. One of my friends, he counted the grains of rice in his bowl – 948 grains!

They said, 'Tomorrow, we will give you your first lesson.'

And the lecturer came in. His first lesson was, 'The imperialist Americans invaded our country. They are the number one enemy!'

We had this for about three hours every morning and every night we had to discuss about each lecture. And we had to confess our mistakes from the past. My friend said, 'I made a mistake. I burnt one acre of sugar cane.'

The lecturer said, 'Not enough. You did not make a simple mistake like that. You killed people! You should confess that you killed people!'

At the end of each week, we would go to meet the leader, he was a card member of the Communist Party and, like a father in the church, he would accept the confessions of all the prisoners. I did not think I had made a mistake because I did not kill people, I treated people, but he said, 'That is wrong, very wrong. For example, in one day you treat perhaps five people. In one week you treat 35 people, in one year 1500 and in five years you treat 7500 people! You create one division to fight against the revolution. You made a big mistake. You should be shot!'

I nearly collapsed. That they could condemn like that. He asked us all, 'Wrong or right?'

We all said, 'Right.'

And we had to clap our hands. So I had to confess.

After confession they did nothing, they just wrote a report about you. You also had to write your biography. Where were you born? Who was your father? Is he a landlord or not? How many oxen did he have? How many acres of land did he have? How many shops? Where is his money? Where has he gone? Where is he hiding? And after that, you listed all your activities against the revolution.

The lessons went on for a couple of months, brainwashing. They tried to get rid of all the things in your head. At night, some of my friends would get depressed and cut the arteries in their wrists. Suicide. Another friend, he heard the news that all his land was confiscated and his wife had miscarried and died. He hanged himself. Some tried to escape; they shot them in front of us. I was in that camp for three years.

A couple of weeks before I was released they told me I could relax and they gave me more food. And after that they gave me some cloth to make new clothes. Then they said, 'We have release papers for you.'

I was in heaven. I walked out in just my clothes, back to the city, back to my parents' home. They cried. They did not know where I was for three years.

VAN NHUNG TRAN

XIII

IF WE LOOK LIKE HAVING ANOTHER WAR, SEND THE FRIGGING POLITICIANS

YOU ARE NOT PERMITTED TO TAKE INTO AUSTRALIA ANY OF THE FOLLOWING ITEMS:
a. Drugs
b. Pornographic literature or articles
c. Weapons
d. Ammunition and/or explosives
e. Foodstuffs
f. Unprocessed timber or plants
g. Boots and shoes with mud or soil on them
Note: A 100% baggage search is carried out by customs on arrival at Mascot Airport whilst some members on each flight are subjected to a body search.

ARMY BRIEFING NOTES, QANTAS CHARTER SAIGON–SYDNEY

There is a piece of archival film that's instantly recognisable to many Australians. It lasts only 20 seconds or so and it was shot on black-and-white 35 millimetre. It shows a man in a suit dancing along a street in the city of Sydney. His hat is clutched in one hand, his coat-tails are whirling about and his feet are skipping and dipping as he sashays along behind the vehicle carrying the camera. All around him is pandemonium – oceans of ticker tape, couples locked in passionate embraces, walls of streamers falling through the air. And every face is scrunched up in uninhibited joy. It was the end of World War II.

That footage became an iconic piece of Australiana, just as much as Bradman at the crease or Whitlam in full fury on the steps of Parliament House on the day of his dismissal. It represented an entire nation united in relief, in hope, in loss. It meant an end to hostilities, a victory in which all Australians could share; it meant coming home and beginning, all in one, captured moment.

It would never be like that with the Vietnam War. It couldn't be. Apart from the fact that the entire country had not been involved as they were in World War II, there had been too much division, too much anger and distress for too many people. Especially for those who were no longer called 'returned servicemen' as their fathers had been, with all the worth those words implied. They were now described as 'veterans', people who had been through a long experience. They had much in common these vets – the shock of arrival in Vietnam, the tension of patrolling, the tent lines of Nui Dat, the bars and girls of Vung Tau. Now they shared something else – coming home.

The more fortunate ones had travelled by ship, passing time on the decks of HMAS *Sydney*, enjoying a beer or three, sharing their stories, taking a breath before re-entry. The others came back by plane and were hurtled into life in Australia with ferocious and disturbing speed. A soldier could literally have been on patrol in the jungle at seven in the morning and standing on the tarmac at Kingsford Smith Airport in Sydney that night. No matter how they came back, none of them ever forgot their return.

It wasn't until you were home that you realised what was happening. When the government brought you back in late at night like they were sneaking you in. That's what we felt like. We were sneaking in at night so no one can see. It was clear they were embarrassed by us. That wasn't a very pleasant feeling.

... My family was outside waiting and all of a sudden I was back in reality and that took a bit to acclimatise. You wake up in the morning and you shake your head a bit and think, 'Where am I?' Life goes on around you. You have never been to Vietnam. Nothing's different. Nothing's changed but in your head you are still in Vietnam, so a pretty weird feeling. I think every bloke has it.

... You are home and it's not real and, of course, you feel the animosity around you. You pick up a newspaper or switch on the TV. We were bad people. Nobody wanted to know you. In fact I know blokes that denied it when they were confronted, 'You been to Vietnam?'

'No, no, no.'

It was too much hassle. There was too much flak... I went home on leave and, of course, they are glad to see you but it wasn't something you talked about. I mean you didn't volunteer the information that you had been to Vietnam to anybody. You sort of closed the door. I'm home, shut that door...

I'll never forget my early feelings; 'Is this for real?' – you're sitting there and people are behaving as if nothing's happened! Talking about the footy. And you're sort of shaking your head – you haven't come down yet. Vietnam was a seven-hour flight and you're back and, Christ, you can't believe it. 'What's wrong with these people?'

The first time someone asks you, 'What was it like?'

You think, 'Oh, they're interested.'

But it's too big a thing to explain, it's impossible to explain so you just say, 'Oh yeah, it was this and this and this.'

But you soon find out and you don't say anything. You avoid the question if you can, get around it. How the hell could you explain to someone who hadn't been there? So it's better that nothing's said. The human mind gets indoctrinated or programmed or whatever you want to call it and you can't just switch it off like that, you can't just transition immediately and be back where you were. And that's why any young fella that goes to war is never the same human being ever again, he's lost something big from inside and you can never change that.

TONY EY

Tony Ey had some luck. He was a regular and returned to the comforting embrace of the family that is the defence force. All those who continued on in the army, the navy or the air force, were all kept safe, at least for the time being, behind a protective shield of acceptance and respect for their service. It was not like that for the national servicemen. They were cut adrift by the army and the Australian people, left to deal with whatever demons they might face without any concern for their welfare, without even the common courtesy of a thank you. It was a careless, shameful act then . . . and it remains so today.

We had been travelling I suppose 10 days straight at this stage, on the aircraft carrier and then two days on the train. It was about four o'clock in the afternoon when we arrived and I remember seeing my mother, but I could only see her for a few seconds because then they threw us on the truck and out to Watson's Bay. So we're herded on this truck and a bloke says, 'Well, what are you blokes doing out here?'

We said, 'Well, we're going to be discharged.'

'No, can't do that here. You've got to go to Ingleburn.'

So back in the truck out to Ingleburn . . . and I got discharged from the army. But before I left I had to pay for a piece of webbing, on our book where they record what you've been issued and what's been returned, it was left off, it wasn't ticked. And he said, 'Where's your webbing?'

I said, 'Well, it's back at Nui Dat, we left it there for the blokes who are coming after us to have spares.'

He said, 'Oh, well, you'll have to pay for that.'

. . . They had to give us a medical before we left and I remember a fellow gave me a hearing test and I couldn't hear a couple of the tones and I said to him, 'Oh, what about those couple of tones I can't hear?'

He said, 'Oh, it's nothing to worry about.'

Then I had to go down to the dental unit and he looked at my mouth and he said, 'Oh, yes, you need three fillings.'

I said, 'Oh.' And I'm thinking, 'Well, is he going to do them now?'

He said, 'Yeah, we can do that for you, we can fit you in, in three weeks time.'

I said, 'Three weeks time, you've got to be joking.'

He said, 'Or you can sign this form and we can let you go now.'

'Give me the form.'

So I signed the form, so no dental work.

And we were just discharged, no ceremony, no nothing, just gone.

IAN CAVANOUGH

Australia, through the agency of its elected government, had chosen as a nation to enter the war in Vietnam. As a people we had agreed with our government's decision to support and maintain our alliance with America and to fight where they fought. We had agreed enthusiastically with the belief that our national security was threatened by the spread of Communism in South-East Asia and had shared in the fear that demanded it must be stopped. We had sent our soldiers to Vietnam, regular and conscripted, without any real idea of what they faced. We had asked them, as we had asked Australian men before them, to defend our country against its perceived enemies, to wage war on our behalf.

And now the war was seen as a mistake by the majority of the nation. But it wasn't the politicians who felt the consequences of that; it wasn't the bureaucrats or the military strategists, or even we, the people. It was the soldiers. They had only been dimly aware of the protests while serving in Vietnam; they'd seen the odd newspaper report or letter but shrugged it off as a noisy minority of 'long-haired ratbags'. It was their wives and girlfriends who had felt the brunt of the disfavour. But now the soldiers were home they were unprotected targets and many were bewildered and frustrated by their reception.

> They didn't have to focus their hatred on the soldiers. We were doing our job. We were professional soldiers sent there by our government, the government that they had elected largely, and the national servicemen who'd had their marbles come up in the lottery of life and had been sent to Vietnam. They had done their best. They had seen their mates die. They'd seen people wounded and screaming beside them, and to come back to Australia and see that, it was just terrible and that's had a dramatic effect on my life and every other soldier that's ever been there. I hope that in our future wars we don't do that again.
>
> And it was with great concern that I went out into public places after that experience of our march back through Sydney. After a very short time I went down to Melbourne and my father took me to his Returned Services Club and I'd been asked to tell them about my experiences and I did that and the old diggers said that wasn't a war, that I didn't know what a war was. I was just devastated. I never joined the RSL after that. I came away and just couldn't cope with it. It was bad enough with the civilians but to have the old diggers say that, it was terrible.
>
> BILL HINDSON, 1RAR, SAS

I was doing a guard on the cenotaph in Martin Place, the army mounted a guard there every Thursday and I was on that guard when someone out of the crowd, as I'm in the middle of a 'rest-on-arms-reverse', which is probably the crucial memorial stage of the job that we were doing there, and someone walked out and spat in my face.

I was tempted to pick up the rifle butt and hit the person. I didn't and I stood there and I just didn't feel like a soldier. I didn't feel that I had done my duty for my country like everybody else had, you know like my grandfather and my father before me. It was the greatest insult that could have occurred. I was later told that had I struck him with the rifle butt that I would have been charged with assault within the army system. That was the ultimate insult to me as a veteran.

RAY PAYNE, 1RAR

They were back in the world too quickly and they were naturally slow to adjust. As with all soldiers returning from the parallel universe of a war, they struggled at first with the sheer ordinariness of the behaviour that was expected of them. Other, older soldiers could have told them that this would happen, but in the deafening silence that followed Vietnam no one was talking about the war.

I used to swear a lot. Terrible. I didn't know I was bloody saying it. I used the 'fuck' word like an adjective practically... over there that's all we used. 'How are things?' 'Fucking good,' or, 'Fucking bad,' or whatever it was... My sister said later that for dinner sometimes I'd say, 'Pass the fucking butter,' and I didn't even know I'd said it and Mum, she must have got so used to it for that period when I was going through that stage, she didn't blink an eyelid. Just head down and kept eating.

PETER KERCHER, 1RAR, 7RAR

I was real edgy. We got a bit of shit put on us. I was good for about two weeks because we were pissed all the time and we were picking up bloody sheilas and Christ knows what else. We were reckless little bums, I suppose. And then you'd sorta slow down a bit and then you'd go back to your old places and someone's only gotta say a slight word or a car backfires – I remember doing it in George Street in Sydney, I hit the deck at the lights. Me sister's standing beside me and she said, 'What are you doing on the bloody ground!'

BARRY FITTON

In some parts of Australia, the old ways died hard – fortunately. Many a small country town, either untouched by the social division surrounding the war or refusing to acknowledge it, welcomed their sons and brothers home as they had always done. The war memorial in the main street meant more to them than just memory. After national service and enduring the Battle of Long Tan, Noel Grimes went home to the central west region of New South Wales. It was a wise decision.

Stuart Town gave me a big public reception. I'd been home a little while and out of the army a little while. I didn't especially want it but they insisted. And in a small village everybody goes and it was quite a big do, nice. It was just a welcome home thing that was in my home town. And so I've never – you know, I've heard reports of some guys saying, oh they were in a pub in Sydney having a drink, and as soon as they know you've been to Vietnam or whatever they don't want to know you and all this, but I've never ever found that with people . . .

But I've basically tried to get on with life... If people know I've been, fine; if they don't know, I don't tell them, it's as simple as that. I had to go, I did it. I keep saying, 'Home in one piece' for which I'm eternally thankful. And now, well I'm a bit older now, I've got a few knee problems and aches and pains but I'm here, aren't I? I've got a lovely wife and two lovely children and two lovely grandchildren. You can't ask for much more, Vietnam or not. Despite Vietnam, put it that way.

NOEL GRIMES

In that first year or so after their return, many of the Vietnam veterans suffered the same dislocations, nightmares and anxieties that all soldiers who have been through combat endure. Where is it safe? Whom do you trust? How do you sleep? Without warning their hearts would beat faster. For no apparent reason their palms would grow sweaty, their stomachs turn over, and always the unwanted images would return.

As it had been in 1919 and 1946, it was their women who saw this and dealt with it – in their kitchens and lounge rooms, out in public and in the once-upon-a-time refuge of their bedrooms. They never knew if it was just their man or all of them that were like this, they never knew what it was that would light the fuse. When I talked with the wives about this time in their lives, they spoke as if with one voice.

When he came home he was as pleased as punch to see us, but I knew there was something, a barrier. And to be perfectly honest I didn't know how to handle it. I was just so pleased he was home.

MARJORIE STEVENS

There was always something there.

CAROLYN FITTON

We laugh about it now. He hadn't been home for very long and I rolled over in bed and I cuddled up into his back. Well, I ended up on the floor and he whisked my arm right up and he said, 'How many times have I told you not to cuddle up when we're on night patrol!'

And I thought, 'Hullo! What's this all about?'

MARJORIE STEVENS

About three months after he came home, we're in bed and all of a sudden here's Allan, fit as a mallee bull, I'm 90 pounds sopping wet and he's choking me and he's yellin', 'You didn't have the piquets out! You didn't have the piquets out!'

I don't know how I got the strength to get him off me!

MAUREEN PRICE

Well, I was told, 'Get up that hill! Go on!'

And I said, 'Well, if you let go of me neck I will, 'cos maybe I could breathe then!'

CAROLYN FITTON

Yeah, I've gotten into trouble a few times because I've gone to sleep and I'm supposed to be on watch. They don't know they're doing it.

MARJORIE STEVENS

You know what I found hard? For all that time I'd been in control of the home, the kids, the money and everything and he comes home and wants to take over! Well, I've been doing this job, this is my job. And that caused uproar like you wouldn't believe and him storming out. He was also upset that he couldn't be a father. Every now and then, being the child of a Vietnam vet can cause hassles because they can't remember the man that went away, they can only remember the man that came home.

MAUREEN PRICE

Barry would never hit the three girls – but his anger! His anger was shocking, at the slightest thing. And you'd go around on eggshells and you'd think, 'Oh, God!'

CAROLYN FITTON

You could never pick it. It was like an explosion. Ninety-nine per cent of the time he'd be fine, but then he'd go off for no reason.

MARJORIE STEVENS

And you think that you're the only wife going through this.

MAUREEN PRICE

Eventually the sheer kinetic forces of daily life and the insistent, public silence about the war won out. The nightmares were fewer, the swearing was brought under control and they learned to live among women again. It was, if not peaceful, then at least quieter. For now. War never ends for those who fought it.

The Communist Party of Vietnam, the vanguard of the Vietnamese working class, the faithful representative of the rights and interests of the working class, the toiling people, and the whole nation, acting upon the Marxist-Leninist doctrine and Ho Chi Minh's thought, is the force leading the State and society.

ARTICLE 4, CONSTITUTION OF THE SOCIALIST REPUBLIC OF VIETNAM

Ho Chi Minh had died in 1969, well short of his goal of a unified Vietnam. But the people of the North, enthusiastically encouraged by their Communist leaders, had elevated their adoration for him from great leader to near god. When news of the fall of Saigon reached Hanoi, there was a spontaneous outpouring of emotion. Thousands of people rushed to the centre of Hanoi and danced and cheered under a huge portrait of Ho that bore the reverential slogan, 'You Are Always Marching With Us, Uncle Ho!' They chanted, 'Long live Uncle Ho!' and praised his foresight and courage. Saigon was immediately renamed Ho Chi Minh City and they began referring to him as Him. In death, Ho had become an even more powerful and necessary figurehead. Now, at last, with victory achieved, his words could come true: 'Once the American invaders have been defeated, we will rebuild our land many times more beautiful.'

How wrong he was.

The government in Hanoi had promised that when peace came, there would be no reprisals against their former enemies in the South. But there were, just not on the scale the West had threatened. Nonetheless, over 10 000 people were officially executed in those first two years of Communist control. They had promised representative government for the South, but that too was dispensed with as soon as they took over. Believing the South to be a corrupt, lazy society they moved quickly to 'cut out the badness', closing the bars, brothels, shops, restaurants and nightclubs, shutting down the newspapers, locking up the writers and opinion makers. There was to be no reconciliation, no room for 'filthy imperialist ways'. The colourless, passive pall of Communist thought and action dropped like a cloak over the South and beneath its cover the real work of 'reform' began. Those that could, ran.

The NVA confiscated my house, confiscated everything. I said to them, 'Please let me go out to buy some cigarettes.'

I wore only my shorts, no shirt.

'Okay.' They said, 'You have only five minutes, go to that shop over there.'

And I said to my wife, 'Meet me there.'

And we ran. We ran to the bus station. No money. And my wife had to sell her ring and we bought some tickets and went to Vung Tau. We stayed in a church with a lot of other people, we were all Catholics. And I disguised myself as a fisherman by changing my clothes and cutting my hair. I asked my wife to dye her clothes black.

But the priest looked at me and said, 'Jesus Christ! You don't look like a fisherman!' He said, 'You have to go.' And he gave us the money to go in a boat.

The NVA were too busy occupying the land to worry too much about the sea so two weeks after we arrived in Vung Tau we tried to escape. But the motor broke down and we were arrested by local police before we passed the last bit of land. They detained us for one month in order to make an investigation. No one knew who I was. And in the boat were three officers, they had brought along their albums, their photos, so they were identified and sent back to Saigon, but me, they didn't know anything. So after one month I asked them to release us so we could go back home and they did.

We organised another escape and we said, 'We'd rather die in the ocean than live under the Communists.'

We went to Malaysia. I steered the boat.

I came to Australia because I wanted to be near my country. When I came here [in 1976], *The Sydney Morning Herald* interviewed me and I said to them, 'We came here not to enjoy a new life. We have come here to get another chance to go back and fight against the Communists.'

They made a big article about that. I did know that Australia was a peaceful country, very friendly. Also, I did not go to America because I did not want to be near those Vietnamese officers who had fled from the country so they could enjoy their new life.

COLONEL VO DAI TON

More than a million people in the South were ordered to report for what was euphemistically called 're-education', though the only education available in the camps where they were taken was the primitive art of survival. Soldiers, bureaucrats, intellectuals, politicians, religious leaders, anyone who had worked for the Americans, in fact anyone of whom they were suspicious, was rounded up, locked up and, for the most part, forgotten. There were no charges, no courts and no trials and the people they imprisoned endured years of backbreaking, degrading manual labour, near starvation, and political and personal brainwashing on an enormous scale. Many died. Even more wished they could. No one was released without being broken in either body or soul.

The countryside was a devastated ruin. Almost two-thirds of the villages in the South were wrecked and 12 million acres of forest were destroyed – bombed out of existence or defoliated. The land held millions of unexploded bombs and landmines and there were over two million widows, orphans and disabled people on both sides of the DMZ.

The economy was at marketplace levels. Nixon had promised $4.75 billion as reconstruction aid at the time of the Paris Peace Accords, but not only was that now refused, in 1975 all of Vietnam was placed under a full economic embargo by the USA. It would last for 20 years.

There was no money. Millions of South Vietnamese were relocated by the government to the 'new economic zones' – unproductive farmland where crops failed and famine followed. The indigenous tribes, like the Montagnard and the Hmong, were forced down from the highlands onto the plains in an attempt to either turn them into 'Vietnamese' or wipe them out.

And everywhere people snuck back illegally into the cities. Schemes and plots to escape were rife, and the trickle of refugees that began at the end of the war became an unstoppable flood over the next few years. Australia was about to receive an unexpected end to its war.

> I went to Saigon when I was released from the camp and began looking for the organisers of the escapes. I paid for new, forged identity cards; I paid off the Public Security men. For one year I looked for a way to escape. The first attempt failed. My wife and four children were arrested by Public Security. But it's easier in Saigon than elsewhere to influence them and they were released.
>
> We tried again. I needed my freedom, our freedom. As a last test, my wife and I put two pieces of paper in a cup, one with 'go' on it, the other blank. If it was 'go' then we would, if it was blank, we would stay. I tried to choose the paper but she said, 'No! With your age now, the years ... you're unlucky. You're not going to take it.'
>
> My wife took it. It was 'go'. I go. It wasn't superstition, just a last test.
>
> We saw many ships but none came to rescue us. The fourth night we saw a big light on the sea. I couldn't see a horizon so I could not understand this light. I didn't realise it was an oil rig. Eventually we came very near it and we realised that it was American. But they would not let anyone climb up. We had no water and the children were becoming unconscious in the sun. We were circling the oil rig and the pilot of our boat asked if anyone could swim. I said that okay, I could and he gave me a life vest but I declined because I wasn't used to it. I jumped out of the boat and swam about 200 metres to the rig. It was a very rough sea and the boat could not approach.

When I got to the first step on the rig, everyone on the boat was cheering, they were very happy. I climbed up to the rig floor and an American came over and said, 'Right. You go. You cannot stay here. I will give you water.'

I said, 'No, I will not go. Whatever you do.' I argued with him, 'Your President Reagan talks about human rights!'

There was a second American, the deputy director, a very good man. He came to me quietly. 'You don't go. If you go, you know, your boat is leaking – don't go. I have a Vietnamese wife and I'm telling you – don't go.'

Okay, so I stay there. Eventually we tied the boat to the rig using two ropes and then I went back. Then they came and said all right. A Netherlands ship came to pick us up and I said, 'I don't want to go to America. Any other free land, but not America.'

They took us to Malaysia, to an island called Pulau Bidong, a place where thousands of Vietnamese ended up before they left for other countries.

When they interned me they discovered I could speak English and I became an interpreter for a while, for the CIA, for the UN. For a man named Richard from ASIO. He was looking for Viet Cong intruders. He would say to me, 'Special interview. You are not allowed to tell anyone else in the camp.'

He told me that many sons of the cadres had escaped and were trying to get to America, to Australia. I did not take any money from him but I said I wanted my family to go to Australia. We stayed in the camp for three months and then they said we could go to Australia, to Sydney. They were very kind to me.

I love Vietnam as the country of my birth but I do not want to be a Vietnamese citizen as long as the Communists still rule. I love Australia as the country that saved my life and my family's.

VO MINH CUONG

Perhaps two million Vietnamese escaped this way, but thousands of them died in the attempt. Storms took them without trace, their boats leaked and sank, and thirst and starvation overwhelmed them. They were robbed, raped and often murdered by pirates, and even if they did reach a refugee camp, long years of waiting for acceptance by another country would follow. Yet still they came. Every boatload was a remarkable cross-section of Vietnamese society – teachers, doctors, ex-soldiers, shopkeepers, students, single mothers with mixed-blood children, fishermen and farmers. There was even the occasional Viet Cong, disenchanted with life in the new Vietnam.

The first boat to reach Australia tied up at the Darwin dock in 1976; a fishing boat carrying three Vietnamese men. Over the next 10 years, 94 000 refugees from Vietnam, Laos and Cambodia would settle in Australia, only 2000 of them coming by boat. The rest were processed and accepted from the camps, or came as part of the family reunion program.

Australia quivered with division and tension about the Vietnamese. Gough Whitlam and the Labor Party actively resisted any large-scale refugee program from Indochina while Malcolm Fraser and his Coalition government legislated to permit 15 000 a year to arrive, many more than even the refugee advocate groups had hoped for.

The Australian Labor Party, which had removed the White Australia Policy from their platform only 10 years before, appeared heartless and insensitive to the plight of the Vietnamese. Bob Hawke, the then Federal President of the Labor Party, said in 1977, 'Of course we should have compassion, but people who are coming in this way are not the only people in the world who have rights to our compassion. Any sovereign country has the right to determine how it will exercise its compassion and how it will increase its population.'

Yet still they came. In Vietnam, no one heard the bitter arguments, the pompous justifications or the sensible-sounding rationales for restriction of refugee numbers. They were too busy saving their lives.

> It was time to escape. I had two five-year-old children. My wife and I made the decision. I couldn't live there like that, with my conscience. They pushed me. If you didn't do what they wanted, they called you a 'reactor' and sent you back to the camps. The whole country seemed to be escaping. They used to say that, 'If an electricity pole could walk, it would escape too.'
>
> I organised a room at night and opened a small surgery. I treated people there and some people had money. I treated about 40 people each night and gathered a reasonable amount of money.
>
> In 1984 we escaped. We had to pay for four places on the boat. The owner gave me a cheap price because he said if anything went wrong with the people on the boat, I could treat them. So we paid US$1500. We did not know where we would go; we would just go to the sea. I taught myself sea navigation, by the stars, at night, and learned all the flags of the countries, because some East German ships, Russian ships, the boats would ask them for help and they would take them back to Ho Chi Minh City. I learned this by heart and kept it in my mind. I got a map of South-East Asia, a Russian map, and at night I took my candle and I measured to each place – Borneo, Sumatra – and I organised five possible places to go. I did this by memory, not written down, because if the writing was found I would be sent back to the camp.
>
> My boat was about 60 metres long and there were about 102 people on it. We went straight out from the coast, from Vung Tau. I navigated us about 400 kilometres, about three days. Then I saw an antenna, a big one. It was an Indonesian Navy station. They gave us food and water and directions and we landed in Indonesia.

We went to Pulau Galang, to the refugee camp, but because I worked in obstetrics they had me working every night. Because the people here now were free, the girls would go with the Indonesians and get pregnant. And the refugee law was that if you wanted to settle in a third country you could not be pregnant, so everyone tried to make an abortion and they would be bleeding. Every night the loudspeaker would call my name – babies being born or bleeding.

Australia was paradise to me.

VAN NHUNG TRAN

The last ebbing of the refugee wave brought to an end our Vietnam years – or at least, it seemed that way. The '80s were upon us, the 'me' decade, when dubious individual rights forced their way to centre stage. Perhaps it was the self-absorption, but that time also produced the first reassessments of the Vietnam War and the news wasn't good. The wounds the war had inflicted on politics and society were clearly still fresh and new wounds were being uncovered on a regular basis.

As it had been during the war, so it was afterwards in the wash-up – America led the way. Stung by its defeat, the US temporarily retreated from its role as the world's policeman, and no president wanted to be the leader to commit ground troops again. The Communist bloc in Eastern Europe was cracking at the edges and the main game morphed from being a struggle between the two superpowers to an eruption of regional conflicts. In South-East Asia, the Americans reduced their involvement to cursory levels, and Menzies' original goal of keeping them engaged in our neighbourhood, the reason for sending our troops to Vietnam, became just another piece of discarded political history.

In Australia, Vietnam veterans behaved for a time as all men returning from a war do. They drank a little too much, got into a few fights, stayed unsettled for a year or two and then knuckled down to living life again. Their personal stories varied of course. Any army is simply a reflection of the society from which it originates and its soldiers the same diverse collection of personalities as the rest of us. Some vets came back having undergone bad experiences in Vietnam and, though they had a hard time for a while, they worked through their difficulties and moved on. Others had significant, ongoing problems, but mostly managed to keep a lid on them. A few returned severely damaged and stayed that way, unable to prevent their lives from spiralling downwards. They were no different in this than their fathers and grandfathers had been.

But always there was this other matter that nagged at them, this strongly felt separation from Australia's military traditions, from respect and honour. Their war was neither worse nor easier than any other before them; in fact comparisons of that kind are not only odious but useless. How does one ultimately differentiate between this horror and that? Is it worse somehow to be shelled into madness at Pozières or starved to the point of near death in Changi? To watch mates die slowly on the Kokoda Track or to have your legs blown off by a mine in the Long Hai Mountains of Phuoc Tuy Province? There is no answer because the question itself is fatuous and offensive.

Yet it was asked and answered for the Vietnam soldiers, whether they wanted it to be or not. Sadly, it was an insult mostly delivered by World War II men, members of RSLs; and they were often returned soldiers who had not seen combat themselves. Whether every individual who returned from Vietnam encountered this, or the abuse, or the rejections, or the spitting, or any of the long list of offences finally didn't matter. They all believed they did. For to do it to some was to do it to all. And the strain began to show.

> I was drinking too much and smoking too much and fighting too much. And then she decided to leave me. I don't know what the problem was. I never beat her up or anything like that. But I was carrying on a bit, I suppose, I was drinking to excess. That was just an after curse of the war for most people who participated.
>
> BERNIE McGURGAN

> You didn't know who was going to have a shot at you; you didn't know who was going to have a jibe at you. RSLs wouldn't have anything to do with us, you couldn't join RSLs, they didn't like us, they didn't want us. People didn't want, you didn't dare tell anybody. 'Was you in the army?' 'No, not me.' 'You go to Viet . . . ?' 'No, no, no.' And this is what happened for years, you wasn't game to tell anybody. You kept it quiet, your medals, you threw in the bottom drawer under all your underwear, you never pulled them out again. Things like that. It happened for years and years. It went on, some blokes are still doing it, it was that bad, it affected them that bad. So it was a thing that, even though you wasn't guilty, people made you feel guilty. And you didn't want to be, you know, you've done the right thing. I know I've done the right thing and I don't care what they say.
>
> BRIAN WOODS

Fed by a surge of American movies like the *Rambo* series, *Taxi Driver*, *Apocalypse Now* and *The Deer Hunter*, the image of the Vietnam veteran became lodged inside the public's consciousness as a particular kind of social misfit; a dangerous, slightly loopy, besieged yet lethal victim. Yet again, the American experience bled across into Australian sensibilities and our veterans were painted the same disturbing colour. There was little they could do to prevent it. Many had chosen to keep their involvement in the war to themselves, while those who were going public at the time were agitating for what they considered to be long overdue recognition. They were particularly keen to gain compensation for illnesses they maintained had been visited upon them and their families through their exposure to defoliants and herbicides, notably Agent Orange.

A number of discontented vets set up an organisation to lobby for their specific causes – the Vietnam Veterans' Association of Australia (VVAA), itself an indication of their separation from other returned servicemen. Veterans of previous wars had depended on the RSL to promote the campaign for veterans' rights, but a lot of the Vietnam men now neither trusted nor respected that establishment. Inevitably their loud and public calls for 'special' treatment combined with the popular perception of Vietnam vets as mentally unstable gave them the unfortunate air of being whingeing victims.

There were other complications. In middle age, many of the veterans began to display symptoms of a debilitating anxiety condition called Post Traumatic Stress Disorder. Once called 'soldier's heart' or 'battle fatigue' it had been dismissed in the past as a temporary state of mind that would eventually recede, leaving many an ex-soldier to fight a long, lonely battle against depression and breakdown. But the medical profession gave it a formal title and diagnostic recognition in 1980. Its effects could easily disable a sufferer without them ever understanding why. Many of the vets saw even an admission that it might exist as weakness. It brought them hard up against the example of manly behaviour set for them by their fathers.

The men of the 2nd AIF may well have endured utter horror during World War II at Tobruk or Rabaul, Bougainville or Greece, but when they came home they were expected to 'get on with it' and most of them did. They took the view that bad things happened in this world and there was bugger-all you could do about it. You couldn't make sense of it because there was no sense to make, and thinking about it too much would drive you mad so it was better not to. They locked off that part of themselves, never speaking of it, never being asked about it. Only now, in the last stages of their lives, are many of them encountering the nightmares again and the resurgence of what they thought was buried.

Their sons, on the other hand, live in a society that no longer believes in merely 'getting on with it'. It is no longer acceptable to just 'get over' a traumatic experience and the Vietnam veterans were encouraged to examine and display their feelings. It was a hard ask for some.

> 'What the hell is PTSD?' I'd never heard of it and I'm not going to talk to a complete stranger about how I feel! What sort of a man does that? No way in the world. So I refused to do it.
>
> I've since done it and it was very good. It did me a lot of good. In fact I went and did it, what they call a PTSD course – and it was fantastic because I sat down with other veterans and we just sat there and listened and talked and the doctors and psychiatrists say, 'Well, how do you feel about this?' and then they would try and explain perhaps why you feel that way or what contributed to it and, once I started to discover what the so-called symptoms are and causes, it made me stop and look at my father. All my life I thought my father was just my father and that was the way he was, but now I can see what he went through in World War II. He's probably got the worst case of PTSD that I've ever seen. The most anti-social, in some respects, man I've ever met, but there's a lot of them about.
>
> TONY EY

In 1984, the Vietnam Veterans' Memorial, 'the wall', was dedicated as a national monument in Washington, DC. A few months later, on the 10th anniversary of the Fall of Saigon, thousands of middle-aged men, Vietnam veterans, marched through cities across America, taking part in what was dubbed, 'The Welcome Home Parade'. It was the beginning of reconciliation between American soldiers and their country, the start of forgive-and-try-to-forget. Two years later, in 1987, Welcome Home Parades were held in Australia. In Sydney, 25 000 veterans marched.

> I went to the Sydney one; I went to the Canberra one as well. Just because I wanted to be back amongst those blokes. It was exploitative sure, but I knew fellas were going to go there and I wanted to be there with them again. I wanted to catch up with them. It was very exciting, to be back with these fellas in a group, together, and that's what it was for me. I did get the feeling from the people that they were just pouring out their hearts, 'we're sorry', on the day I felt that coming from people, they were apologising to us. And I accepted that. You don't go down looking for it but it happened . . . and to this day on Anzac Day, you can see the younger generation, turning around, people are actually – they sort of look at you as if to say, 'Thanks', you know, 'You did your bit.' And also a bit of sorry. They know what happened. And it makes you feel better.
>
> TONY EY

It's easy to be cynical about the Welcome Home Parade because some of the action surrounding it was shameless. Yet again an American idea was fitted uncomfortably onto an Australian experience, and it was outrageously exploited by the media and every politician that could get near it, not to mention some members of the veteran community. It was a temporary solution for a complex and enduring set of problems that nevertheless allowed people to glibly assume that, after this, all the difficulties were sorted. Still, the majority of the vets who attended didn't feel that way. Some took consolation from it; others, justification. And all of them seemed to get back the one thing that mattered most, the treasure that all ex-soldiers value so highly – their mates.

> I remember when there was going to be a Welcome Home Parade in Melbourne, after Sydney, and we had to seek information or register or something in Melbourne. And I went to this place and obviously the room was absolutely full of Vietnam veterans, from all walks of life. I didn't know one of them, but for some reason I had a sense or feeling of... calm... and safety... It was almost like being home again. I remembered that sensation particularly and I liked it, and it was good. It surprised me, it really did. I know that Vietnam veterans all over Australia, they're there for me, if I ever need them.
>
> ROBERT BELL

> There's a huge comfort zone when you're round those fellows... I could try and explain it to you and you might understand, most people wouldn't. It's funny; you don't really want to know anyone else, no one else matters. If you've been through a war zone with fellows, they become part of you, they're mates for life. You've shared something that no one else can understand – they can understand. And you don't want new relationships.
>
> TONY EY

Reunions, something that had never really caught on with the Vietnam vets, began to blossom. Even the women had to make room.

You'll never really know what they went through and I've come to accept that. You'll go to the reunions and all you'll hear is the laughter, you'll never really know. We just support them in every way we can.

MARGARET DAY

I was very jealous of Allan's mates for a very long time until I realised that his life and my wellbeing depended on those mates. And once I accepted that I was as right as rain.

MAUREEN PRICE

You're pushed into the background a bit, at reunions. It's basically the boys are over there, the women are here. You hear them, they laugh and carry on and you do get jealous and you think, 'Well, hang on a minute, why can't we be over there amongst you lot?' So we go over now but it's, 'Oh, what do you want? Do you want a drink?' They just clam up.

MARGARET DAY

Yeah and then it just naturally fans out and they collect somewhere else so you go over and you get into that little group. If you can't beat 'em . . .

CAROLYN FITTON

Everything was for the soldier in our day. I had an officer say to me one day, 'You know, Mrs Price, the army comes first. The wife's just an afterthought.'

And I turned round and I said, 'Without these wives, you wouldn't have a lot of soldiers.'

It's funny, we never signed up but we did – for life.

MAUREEN PRICE

In August 2006, the 40th anniversary of the Battle of Long Tan occurred. In previous years this day had passed quietly, generally observed only by groups of veterans. Now though it was granted an importance, a symbol of the new position the Vietnam War was taking in Australian memory. Services were held across Australia while a media event took place in Vietnam, at the original battle site. Significantly, it was attended by the Prime Minister, John Howard.

The day before that service, the Australian veterans who had travelled to Vietnam to take part had a stand-up row with their government, represented by the Australian Ambassador, Bill Tweddell. It seemed the official service was scheduled to start at 3.40 p.m, the time the battle began. But the veterans were determined that *they* were the only ones who had the right to hold a service at that time. Anger mounted and one veteran, David Limpus, buttonholed the ambassador, saying, 'The line is drawn in the mud here at Long Tan, and we are going to conduct our service at 1540 hours. If the government is so righteous in caring for Vietnam veterans, it is time they showed us today. Put all the politics and pollywaffle bullshit to the background.'

The dispute was resolved peacefully and the veterans won their timeslot.

The legacy of any war is complicated and long-lingering, hopefully diminishing as the years pass by. But the scars of the Vietnam years can still flare up into an angry redness, making it clear that for some of the protagonists the divisions remain, defying time and distance.

> I was a professional soldier. I had a job to do. I reckon we did it bloody well. We all did it well. You know the Australians, I think, did better than all of them; but I tell you what, if we look like having another war, send the frigging politicians. Send them first then put the army in charge because once you

put politicians in charge of armies and war they screw it up every time, and I mean that, deadly serious. So they can make all the decisions and take no blame. Even all these years on they still take no blame.

BOB BUICK

It's been said probably by someone much wiser than me that the soldiers win the battles but the politicians win the wars or lose the wars, and Vietnam was no different. The politicians sent the soldiers in. We were not very well-equipped. We were not very well supported. We won the battles. We lost the war. The soldiers did wonderful work and, whether it was the senior military commanders or the politicians, their work was brought to nothing. We won the battles and we lost the war. A hell of a shame. A hell of a waste.

DAVE SABBEN

A lot of guys have suffered since the conflict. A lot of them are suffering at our age, which I find very depressing, but having said that, I often wonder whether if we took a cross-section of the community, another 57 000 people, and looked at them, what would the proportion be of people who aren't travelling too well at our age anyway? You know, we've got natural debilitation going on and we've got hair loss and weight gain and prostate problems and people are being made redundant at work and their families are leaving and wives leave and they have drinking problems. That's pretty widespread. That's not unique to Vietnam veterans; and I look at the people who've made a success of their lives since Vietnam. People like Tim Fischer. People like Peter Cosgrove. The Governor of Queensland. The Governor-General. These people have experienced exactly the same things that I did and all my mates did and they got on with their lives. I think, sadly, for a lot of the guys that was the best thing that ever happened to them and because nothing that good has ever happened since, it's destroying their lives but we've all, you know, we've all got the opportunity to make something of our lives.

STEPHEN LEWIS, 12 FIELD REGIMENT

I joined the RSL for a little while... and a lot of the 80-plus guys were saying, 'Yeah, well now it's time to hand over to you young blokes.'

And I thought, 'Hmm. You were probably 25 or 26 or 30 when you got home. You made another life and a career, you might have gone on to study the law or become a doctor or whatever; you've had a life. You actually had unit reunions; you marched proudly through Sydney and Melbourne and now that you're disbanded and you're brought together by age and saying, "What did you do?" "Oh I served on the such and such..."'

Now, in our late fifties, we're seen as 'the young'uns'. Of course we would be, but what – we're supposed to suddenly take over when we were given such a backhander from them?

'You guys didn't go to a real war. What did you ever see?'

As a young 20-year-old what are you supposed to say to that? If they went over the top at Bardia, sure, I take my hat off to them. But if they never got outside New South Wales! It's only coming out now, 'Oh I never saw much at all, you know. I was actually a pay clerk...'

Or something like that. I don't disparage that, but why did you make the immediate assumption that I had seen nothing? I just don't understand it.

Everyone who served in that task force to me was there for a common purpose and was a comrade in arms, didn't matter what their contribution was. And I guess I feel that it's a little bit unhealthy that instead of being able to move into the mainstream of vets, you're kind of marginalised and you start your own little Vietnam veterans' associations and you get together and have a whinge about things. I mean there's a lot of positives I know but... I don't feel inclined to join these organisations.

AUDIE MOLDRE

I wouldn't have missed it for anything. I feel very fortunate that I've experienced what I have in my life; I wouldn't change it, not for the world. It's the mates but it's also that I look out there at neighbours and friends and their life seems to be just a plateau you know, it cruises along and they go to golf and there's nothing exciting in their lives and I think of what I've done and I've reached these highs and lows and these massive adrenaline rushes... I was sent to Vietnam, I was 23 years old, at the absolute peak of my physical fitness, I considered myself to be a professional in my job, in my attitude.

You get to Vietnam. You're in the middle of a war zone. This absolute rush the whole time. The absolute pinnacle of life. When you come off that peak, everything's downhill, you'll never get back there. It's there, you've done it, but for the rest of your life you're trying to find it again. And I was told that the reason I first went back to Vietnam was that I was going back to try and rediscover what I'd lost there. I believe that. Now. I left part of me in Vietnam, I left my youth, I left my innocence.

TONY EY

In some ways and for some people, the Vietnam War is still being fought and cyberspace has become the battleground of choice. There are websites out there devoted solely to interminable justifications of the American–Australian position at the time and others that proudly put forward long and convoluted explanations as to why *we* didn't actually lose the war – the South Vietnamese did. Defeat is too bitter a pill for some, even 40 years on.

Strangest of all is the phenomenon that sprang up in Australia and America after the Welcome Home Parades – the fake veteran. 'Wannabes' they're called, men who for a variety of distorted motives purchase medals and uniforms, research and construct their false military histories and then attempt to pass themselves off as Vietnam veterans at RSLs, veterans' organisations and even at Anzac Day marches. Some have never served while the majority appear to have once been members of the army reserve or in non-combat units. Many have been outed and a group once calling itself the Coalition of Patriots for Military Honour Australia, run a website detailing case histories and warnings. They maintain that over 200 impostors have been revealed so far in Australia and New Zealand. How curious it is that a title that once earned its owners public scorn should now be the subject of such desperate desire.

Vietnam lives on in all kinds of way.

People don't ask you about Vietnam. As far as how did you get on? Or how did you cope? Or how are you going now? They tell you. They tell you what we did, what we shouldn't have done. And after a while it gets to you, to a point where I lived in a fantasy world, where I didn't want to know that I had been over there. And when I went for treatment, actually, I seen a psychiatrist, eventually, when I finally cracked. And he asked me if I was a vet, and I thought he meant a veterinary surgeon. Because I had isolated myself. I hadn't drunk with a Vietnam vet or anything, I just kept to myself. When I sleep during the day, I have my wife sit in a chair in the room. It's the only way I feel safe. I've got two security cameras. The majority of my fencing is barbed wire around the top of the fencing. I feel very insecure. I've got four guards. Two German shepherds and two Belgian shepherds in different sections of the yard. I feel I'm getting better, I'm coping better. I leave the security cameras on all night, so I can see who comes and who goes, or what's happening. The dogs let me know as well.

ROBERT EARL

I still know vets who say, 'How the hell could you go back to Vietnam?'

And I say, 'Well, you want to go, mate, it'll clear some of the skeletons out of your closet. You need to go back, and you don't avoid it, you've gotta confront it. Go to Anzac Day, catch up with your mates, you'll feel better for it. Life's too short to hold grudges, you've gotta forget it, it was a long time ago.'

I've been back to Vietnam 26 times, people can't understand it. I love the place. Half the population of today weren't even alive when I was there, I don't hold any grudges against the Vietnamese. What happened then was another world; it's nothing to do with now.

I ran into a bloke the other day, he was SAS and I knew him, and he was talking about rice, we got onto rice, and he's never been back to Vietnam, has no interest and I said, 'Oh, I love rice.'

And he said, 'Oh, if you saw what I saw in the rice paddies . . . !'

I said, 'What the hell has that got to do with rice for Christ's sake! This is all grown in Australia!'

And he's got this fixation about everything Vietnamese is as it was 40 years ago and he holds all the same grudges and I said, 'Mate, you're a dickhead.' I said, 'You've got to get this shit out of your head, you're going to carry this to your grave. That was another life, it's not now.'

TONY EY

All things are easy when looking backwards through the prism. We get to rewrite our actions, correct our errors and flaws, make it all work out properly. Vietnam was a righteous war, say some these days, it prevented the collapse of other Asian nations into Communism and was simply a small battle we lost in the larger war we won – the Cold War. Others reply that it was a moral tragedy, a bloody and unnecessary error that ended in a justifiable defeat we should be very slow to forget.

Somewhere along the way in writing this book I lost all care for the political pluses or minuses that are a legacy of the Vietnam War; the historical summations, the considered conclusions. I couldn't keep Charlie, my rollie-smoking vet who loved a black joke, out of my mind, and I didn't want to. The simple truth I am left with is that we failed him, as we failed all those soldiers. They did not enjoy the same welcoming embrace that had been given to returning soldiers from our other wars; they were not rewarded with the same dignity and respect that would have helped in some way to overcome the wounding experiences they had undergone. We did not say to them, as we had said to their fathers and grandfathers, 'Yes, you have done regrettable things. You have been shot at and shot back, you killed and saw mates killed in return; you lived amongst the worst that man can do but you did it in our name; you did it because we asked you to. You deserve now to return to your family, to regain your life.'

We did not say that. Instead we presented them with rejection and hostility, and, even worse, with silence. We kept from them for too long the forgiving grace of acceptance and, in doing so, marked them, and us, forever.

STATISTICS

Over 61 000 Australians served in the Vietnam operational area.
42 700 Army
12 858 RAN
4706 RAAF
1118 Civilians
51 staff from philanthropic organisations

520 servicemen died.
2398 were wounded.

804 000 Australian men registered for National Service.
63 375 were called up.
19 450 served in Vietnam.
200 died.
1479 were wounded.

It is estimated that the overall casualties of the war totalled almost six million and its cost was $176 billion USD.

NOTES

These notes contain references to sources of information where these are not obvious in the text, and sincere thanks are given, and acknowledgments made, for the help provided. Information that has not been referenced here or in the text has been drawn from the author's interviews and correspondence.

Many of the quotes throughout the text are taken from the Australians at War Film Archive collection of interviews. The Archive was commissioned by the Department of Veterans' Affairs for the Australian Government and full transcripts of the interviews can be found at:

http://www.australiansatwarfilmarchive.gov.au

The intent of the Archive is to record Australians' experiences of war and its enduring impact on their lives and on Australian society.

All quotes from the following people are from their AAWFA interviews, as numbered below.

Alan Anderson	#1886
Phil Baxter	#2580
Robert Bell	#436
Barry Benson	#734
Bob Buick	#2181

Ian Cavanough	#2152
Ian Clarke	#630
Adrian Clunies-Ross	#795
Joan Coxsedge	#2564
Matthew D'Arcy	#709
Robert Earl	#639
Maurice Fairhead	#1104
Beryl Gant	#2578
Alan Gould	#2559
Bob Grandin	#2572
Noel Grimes	#1939
Robert Hagerty	#1732
John Heslewood	#1749
Bill Hindson	#2557
Terrence Hippisley	#800
Keith Houley	#2183
Anthony Hughes	#2093
Peter Jarratt	#1351
Maureen Javes	#1048
Bert Jordan	#2154
Geoff Kendall	#2139
Peter Kercher	#1640
Stephen Laverty	#1134
Ian Leis	#794
Stephen Lewis	#1154
Father Bernie Maxwell	#2424
John McDonagh	#2172
Geoffrey Morgan	#948
Ray Payne	#2575
Ronald Perkins	#1271
Alan Ramsey	#2568
Jim Richmond	#2576
Adrian Roberts	#2558
Michael Rodger	#1416

Dave Sabben	#2585
Edward Schunemann	#1399
Harry Smith	#2571
Barry Smith	#2144
Wallace Thompson	#907
Patricia Thompson	#2582
Anthony Thorp	#2209
Darcy Tilbrook	#2354
Joseph Vezgoff	#671
Brian Woods	#2014

THE VIETNAMESE ARE DESCENDED FROM DRAGONS AND FAIRIES

p.37 *A Tale of Two Soldiers* words and music by Pham Duy. From *Understanding Vietnam*, Neil Jamieson, University of California Press, 1993, pp. 321–322.

p.54 ibid, *Follow in the Steps of the Vanguard*, p. 223.

p.58 *The Age* May 13th, 1954.

p.59 ibid.

HISTORIANS WILL RECALL THIS DAY WITH TEARS

p.65 *Harvest of Fear*, John Murphy, Allen & Unwin, 1993, p. 110.

p.78 *To Long Tan: The Australian Army and the Vietnam War*, 1950–1966, Ian McNeill, Allen & Unwin, Sydney, 1993, p. 54.

p.86 Brigadier O.D. Jackson, Interview 9 March 1972, pp. 27, AHQ file 707/R2/39, AWM 107.

p.87 *The Age*, 30 April, 1965.

p.88 *The Australian* 30 April, 1965.

p.88 Commonwealth Parliamentary Debates, H of R, 46, 4 May 1965.

WHAT THE HELL AM I DOING HERE?

p.101 Department of Labour and National Service Files, National Archives of Australia, Canberra.

p.108 ibid.

p.109 ibid.

p.109 *A Decade of Dissent* Greg Langley, Allen & Unwin, 1992, p. 18.

p.120 *A Decade of Dissent* Greg Langley, Allen & Unwin, 1992, pp. 103–4.

WELCOME TO THE FUNNY COUNTRY

p.149 *To Long Tan: The Australian Army and the Vietnam War, 1950–1966*, Ian McNeil, Allen & Unwin, 1993, p. 168.
p.151 *Sunday Telegraph*, 3 January 1966.
p.152 *Men, Stress, and Vietnam* Peter G. Bourne, Boston: Little Brown, 1970, p. 170.
p.161 *A Decade of Dissent* Greg Langley, Allen & Unwin, 1992, p. 211.
p.163 ibid, p. 49, p. 211.

SHOOT FIRST, SHOOT QUICK, SHOOT STRAIGHT

p.170 The statistical information in this and the preceding paragraph were sourced from the studies of Dr. Bob Hall and Dr. Andrew Ross, University of New South Wales Defence Studies Forum, UNSW at the Australian Defence Force Academy.
p.172 Sourced from the studies of Dr. Bob Hall and Dr. Andrew Ross, University of New South Wales Defence Studies Forum, UNSW at the Australian Defence Force Academy.
p.198 Australian Army Operational Research Group. Report 1/71 Accidental Casualty Study–South Vietnam, Major J.H. Adams, p. 21.
p.198 *To Long Tan. The Australian Army and the Vietnam War 1950–1966* Ian McNeill, Allen & Unwin, 1993, p. 270.

ME LOVE YOU LONG TIME

p.213 *In The Sixties* Michelene Wandor, Maitland (ed.), *Very Heaven* pp. 129–33.
p.226 Sourced from *No Need for Heroes* Sandy MacGregor as told to Jimmy Thomson, Calm Pty Ltd, 1993.
p.231 Material regarding R&R in Sydney principally sourced from *Six Days to Live*, a thesis by Lila Oldmeadow, University of Sydney, 2003.
p.234 *The Sun* 4 October 1967, p. 3, sourced from *Six Days to Live*, a thesis by Lila Oldmeadow, University of Sydney, 2003.

WINNING HEARTS AND MINDS

p.352 Anonymous, *Understanding Vietnam* Neil Jamieson, University of California Press, 1993, pp. 349–352.

WHY DON'T THEY JUST BLOODY LEAVE US ALONE?

p.388 *Patriots: The Vietnam War Remembered From All Sides*, Christian G. Appy, Viking, Penguin, New York, 2003, p. 395.
p.414 The website of the Veterans Support and Advocacy Service Australia Inc, http://www.ausvets.com.au

IT WAS LIKE TURNING YOUR BACK ON YOUR BEST MATE AND WALKING AWAY

p.430 *A Nation at War: Australian Politics, Society and Diplomacy during the Vietnam War 1965–1975*, Peter Edwards, Allen & Unwin, 1997, p. 336.

p.430 General R. Ford Presidential Library.

p.433 ibid.

IF WE LOOK LIKE HAVING ANOTHER WAR, SEND THE FRIGGING POLITICIANS

p.456 *The Sydney Institute Quarterly* Issue 19, Vol 7, No. 1, March, 2003, p. 16.

p.465 *Sydney Morning Herald*, August 19–20, 2006.

BIBLIOGRAPHY

Appy, Christian G. *Patriots: The Vietnam War Remembered From All Sides*, Viking, Penguin, New York, 2003.

Beaumont, Joan *Australian Defence: Sources and Statistics*, Oxford University Press, Melbourne, 2001.

Blair, Anne *Ted Serong: The Life of an Australian Counter-insurgency Expert*, Oxford University Press, Melbourne, 2002.

Breen, Bob *First to Fight: Australian Diggers, NZ Kiwis and US Paratroopers in Vietnam 1965–66*, Allen & Unwin, Sydney, 1988.

Burchett, Wilfred *Catapult to Freedom*, Quartet Books, London, 1978.

Buttinger, Joseph *Vietnam: A Political History*, Frederick A Prager, New York, 1968.

Chanoff, David & Toai, *Doan Van Portrait of the Enemy: The Other Side of the War in Vietnam*, Random House, New York, 1986

Cockington, James *Mondo Weirdo: Australia in the Sixties*, Mandarin, Melbourne, 1992.

Coulthard-Clark, Chris *The RAAF in Vietnam: Australian Air Involvement in the Vietnam War 1962–1975*, Allen & Unwin, Sydney, 1995.

Davidson, Lt Gen Phillip B. *Vietnam at War: The History 1946–1975*, Sidgwick & Jackson, London, 1988.

Edwards, Peter *A Nation at War: Australian Politics, Society and Diplomacy during the Vietnam War 1965–1975*, Allen & Unwin, Sydney, 1997.

Gerster, Robin & Bassett, Jan *Seizures of Youth: The 'Sixties' and Australia*, Hyland House, Melbourne, 1991.

Grey, Jeffrey *Up Top: The Royal Australian Navy and Southeast Asian Conflicts 1955–1972*, Allen & Unwin, Sydney, 1998.

——*The Australian Army*, Oxford University Press, Melbourne, 2001.

Hackworth, Colonel David H. and Sherman, Julie *About Face: The Odyssey of an American Warrior*, Macmillan, Sydney, 1989.

Haran, Peter & Kearney, Robert *Flashback: Echoes from a Hard War*, New Holland, Sydney, 2003.

Hayslip, Le Ly *When Heaven and Earth Changed Places: A Vietnamese Woman's Journey from War to Peace*, Doubleday, New York, 1989.

Jamieson, Neil L. *Understanding Vietnam*, University of California Press, London, 1995.

King, Peter *Australia's Vietnam*, Allen & Unwin, Sydney, 1983.

Langley, Greg *A Decade of Dissent: Vietnam and the conflict on the Australian home front*, Allen & Unwin, Sydney, 1992.

MacGregor, Sandy & Thomson, Jimmy *No Need for Heroes*, Calm Pty Ltd, Sydney, 1993.

McKay, Gary *Bullets Beans & Bandages*, Allen & Unwin, Sydney, 1999

——*Australia's Battlefields in Viet Nam: A traveller's guide*, Allen & Unwin, Sydney, 2003.

McKay, Gary & Nicholas, Graeme *Jungle Tracks: Australian Armour in Viet Nam*, Allen & Unwin, Sydney, 2001.

McGregor, Craig *Profile of Australia*, Hodder & Stoughton, Sydney, 1966.

McNeill, Ian *To Long Tan: The Australian Army and the Vietnam War, 1950–1966*, Allen & Unwin, Sydney, 1993.

——*The Team: Australian Army Advisers in Vietnam 1962–1972*, University of Queensland Press, Queensland, 1984.

McNeill, Ian & Ekins, Ashley *On the Offensive: The Australian Army in the Vietnam War 1967–1968*, Allen & Unwin, Sydney, 2003.

Murphy, John *Harvest of Fear: A History of Australia's Vietnam War*, Allen & Unwin, Sydney, 1993.

Ninh, Bao *The Sorrow of War*, Martin Secker & Warburg Limited, London, 1994.

O'Brien, Michael *Conscripts and Regulars: With the Seventh Battalion in Vietnam*, Allen & Unwin, Sydney, 1995.

Pierce, Peter, Grey, Jeffrey & Doyle, Jeff *Vietnam Days: Australia and the impact of Vietnam*, Penguin, Melbourne, 1991.

Pollard, Rhys *The Cream Machine*, Angus & Robertson, Sydney, 1972.

ACKNOWLEDGMENTS

In a lifetime of making documentary films I've learned that one always stands on the shoulders of historians, and it was the same with this book. I remain indebted to all the eminent works written in Australia about our Vietnam War and the clarity and direction they gave me. In particular, I would refer any reader wishing to know more to the various volumes of the official history published by Allen & Unwin in association with the Australian War Memorial. They are comprehensive, clear and immensely informative.

I owe a great debt also to my researcher, Lieutenant Colonel Brett Barlow, who provided me with a constant flow of background knowledge and guidance, all the while commanding the Lancer Barracks in Sydney and then returning to a full-time army posting. He gave me an understanding and respect for Australia's armed forces, both past and present, which I could not have found anywhere else.

The people I interviewed provided the indispensable flesh and blood to clothe the facts and figures. Nothing can substitute for the words and perceptions of those who were there and I remain humbly grateful for their trust and generosity. As well, I wish to record my gratitude to the Department of Veterans' Affairs for permission to use material from interviews contained in the Australians at War Film Archive. The Archive is a federally funded project of remarkable breadth and diversity and a resource whose value will only increase over the coming years.

A number of photographs have also appeared in *My Vietnam* (published by the My Vietnam Trust/Stephen Lewis), and thanks are due to Stephen Lewis and the individuals credited.

Matthew Kelly, a non-fiction publisher at Hachette Livre Australia, was the instigator and shepherd of this book. His enthusiasm, endurance and clear-headed guidance went well beyond the bounds of duty and my dependence upon him was always well-placed. I thank him unreservedly, along with others in the Hachette office, notably, Deonie Fiford.

Professor Jeffrey Grey of the Australian Defence Force Academy kindly reviewed the manuscript for me at a critical stage, correcting mistakes and suggesting changes that helped considerably. My thanks go to him; though, it should be noted, any and all errors and omissions are mine and mine alone.

I must also thank my wife, Lizzie Butler. To put up with my obsession was one thing, but to provide endless encouragement and perceptive editing along the way was an achievement of Herculean proportions. The book is the better for her gentle touch.

Finally, to all the Vietnam veterans with whom I have shared a drink or a laugh or a tear, may this book, in some small way, provide your countrymen and women with a greater understanding of what you did – and what was done to you.

INDEX